HANDBOOK
FOR
CHRISTIAN LIVING

HANDBOOK
FOR
CHRISTIAN LIVING

Thomas Nelson Publishers
Nashville

DEDICATION

This book is dedicated
to
LAURIE MICHELLE KAUSRUD
my fourth grandchild
whose bright eyes and quick wit
are a joy to her
grandfather's heart

Published in Nashville, Tennessee by Thomas Nelson, Inc., Publishers, and distributed in Canada by Lawson Falle, Ltd., Cambridge, Ontario.

Unless otherwise noted, the Bible version used in this publication is THE NEW KING JAMES VERSION. © 1979, 1980, 1982, Thomas Nelson, Inc., Publishers.

Printed in the United States of America.

Library of Congress Cataloging-in-Publication Data

Handbook for Christian living / [edited by] Paul A. Kienel.
    p.   cm.
Includes bibliographical references.
ISBN 0-8407-7661-6
    1. Christian life—Handbooks, manuals, etc. I. Kienel, Paul A.
BV4510.2.H35 1991
248.4—dc20
                                        91-3874
                                          CIP

CONTENTS

FOREWORD

Recent surveys by the Barna Research Group indicate that though ninety-three percent of all Americans own a Bible, half have never read it. Only eighteen percent of those who call themselves "born-again Christians" say they read the Bible daily. A 1990 Gallup poll revealed that many Christians could not name the first five books of the New Testament.

Yet this nation enjoys a history of solid commitment to God's Word. George Washington claimed that "It is impossible to rightly govern the world without God and the Bible." As recently as the middle of this century, Dwight Eisenhower spoke of the living value of the Scriptures: "To read the Bible is to take a trip to a fair land where the spirit is strengthened and faith renewed."

During pioneer days, the American West kept in touch with the established portion of the country through the Pony Express, a 1900-mile trail from St. Joseph, Missouri, to Sacramento, California. Forty men, each riding fifty miles a day, utilized 500 of the best horses in the west to make the journey in ten days. Their clothing was light—their saddles thin. The horses wore small shoes or none at all. Yet each man carried a full-sized Bible, presented to him when he joined the Pony Express team.

Today our problem in the evangelical community has little to do with availability of the Scriptures or opportunity to accumulate knowledge. Pastors, Sunday school teachers, youth directors, Christian schoolteachers all work to plant God's truth in young lives, to sow the seed of Scripture with hopes of reaping a harvest of righteousness.

In some lives, thank God, that harvest comes forth. Seminaries and Christian colleges provide a finishing touch for lives influenced by the Bible in earlier years. The unprecedented attendance at the most recent Urbana Missions Conference reflects the biblical awareness of thousands of college students, most from secular institutions.

Meanwhile, drugs and crime thrive in our streets and many urban centers have become killing fields where even the youngest children must fear for their lives day after day. Where is the breakdown? Why does a church which can spend millions on lavish buildings and television programming seem to have so little impact on the barbarian culture around it? Where is the "light of the world" Jesus told His followers they would be?

Surely part of our battle is being lost in the trenches of application. Children and teenagers hear Bible stories and even memorize Bible verses, but never make the connection between learning and life. They may know something about what the Scriptures say, but do not follow through to activate that truth in the turmoil of daily existence. Church historian John D. Woodbridge stated the problem succinctly in a most helpful book entitled *Renewing Your Mind in a Secular World.*

> Though evangelical Christians affirm that the Bible is an infallible rule for faith and practice, many of them compartmentalize their faith in such a manner that biblical teachings do not much affect the way they live on a daily basis. They profess sound evangelical doctrine but betray those confessions by their deeds. They do not consciously seek each day to live under the direction of biblical ethics. (Chicago: Moody, 1985, p. ix)

The *Handbook for Christian Living* represents an attempt to close that gap a bit. Its entries treat the many kinds of issues young people face in the late twentieth century. Each issue features appropriate biblical texts and a specific application to life prepared by experienced Christian leaders who live by God's truth as their map and compass. Articles have been written with teenagers and college-age students in view, emphasizing an objective and didactic approach to plugging Scripture into society.

The multiple uses of this volume seem immediately obvious. Like any handbook it should sit on the desk or nearby shelf, ready to grab when pressing questions arise. It can help with research, provide answers for discussions with unbelievers, help prepare devotional talks, and even serve as a daily guide for worship readings.

Parents will want to give this book to teens (and older children). Christian schoolteachers will see a resource to augment their integration of faith-in-life for both classroom and extracurricular activities. Every church library should house several copies, making them conspicuously available to the targeted readership.

But ultimately, the significance of this handbook must be determined by you, the reader. Handled in humility, obedience and prayer, these studies will enhance your Christian life and increase your effectiveness as a witness for our Savior. In this case, possession is a mere formality; active use holds the only key to value.

Kenneth O. Gangel, Ph.D.
Dallas, Texas

PREFACE

This *Handbook for Christian Living* answers a critical need in the evangelical community. It is a straightforward presentation of what the Scripture has to say and what Christian writers have to say about moral issues we all face almost every day.

The Christian community is to be commended for its efficiency in disseminating Bible information through a great variety of teaching programs. A child from the average Christian family has a fair grasp of details about Bible personalities and Bible events. There is, however, a woeful shortfall of information on what the Bible has to say about the serious moral issues of our day. In other words, we evangelicals are strong on Bible information and weak on Bible application.

Consider this powerful admonition from the Psalmist David:

We will not hide them from their children,
Telling to the generation to come the praises of the Lord,
And His strength and His wonderful works that He has done.

For He established a testimony in Jacob,
And appointed a law in Israel,
Which He commanded our fathers,
That they should make them known to their children;

That the generation to come might know them,
The children who would be born,
That they may arise and declare them to their children.

That they may set their hope in God,
And not forget the works of God,
But keep His commandments;

And may not be like their fathers,
A stubborn and rebellious generation,
A generation that did not set its heart aright,
And whose spirit was not faithful to God.

Psalm 78:4–8

David said that God established a law in Israel that He wanted taught consistently from generation to generation. A law is a clear statement of right and wrong on a given issue. It is more than a salient bit of Bible information, as valuable as Bible information is. A law handed to us by God, revealed in His word, is a line in the sand, so to speak, which states, if you step over the line you are violating the Law of God. Christians are looking for straightforward answers on the moral issues. They want to know, for example, what the Bible teaches about abortion, homosexuality, unwed mothers, gambling and a host of other topics as common as your daily newspaper. That is what this book is about.

While the *Handbook for Christian Living* is an attempt to answer questions commonly raised by teenagers and young adults it is, in reality, a valuable guide for all Christians. Christians of every age level confront these issues and each of us needs a ready reference to what the Bible says about them.

This volume has been in "the works" for four years. It has involved scores of Christian writers, located in several countries, many of whom have told me they are anxious to own their own copy of this book for their personal reference.

I am grateful to Connie Mena, my able secretary, and to my family who have assisted me in this vital project.

—**Paul A. Kienel**

ABORTION

WHAT DOES THE BIBLE SAY ABOUT ABORTION?

The Issue: Prior to the mid-sixties, abortion was illegal in all of our states, except when the life of the mother was endangered. In 1971, the state of New York passed an abortion law making it possible for women to obtain an abortion on demand for any reason during the first twenty-four weeks of pregnancy.

The United States Supreme Court decision of 1973 (Roe vs. Wade) struck down all existing state laws prohibiting abortion, stating that a woman has control over her body and the life of the unborn child. The woman could then choose not to bear the child and she had the right to obtain an abortion on demand at any time between the conception and delivery. The feminist movement hailed this landmark decision and proclaimed that women had achieved reproductive freedom at last.

Christians believe that God is the originator of all life and the right to bestow or end life is in the providence of God alone. A key concern in this issue is, "When does life begin?" The pro-abortion community believes that an unborn child in its early stages of development is a mass of fetal tissue, not a person. The Bible indicates that human life **begins** at conception.

Key Bible References:

"Before I formed you in the womb I knew you; before you were born I sanctified you; and I ordained you a prophet to the nations." Jeremiah 1:5

For You have formed my inward parts; You have covered me in my mother's womb.

I will praise You, for I am fearfully and *wonderfully made; marvelous are your works, and that my soul knows very well.*

My frame was not hidden from You, when I was made in secret, and skillfully wrought in the lowest parts of the earth.

Your eyes saw my substance, being yet unformed. And in Your book they all were written, the days fashioned for me, when as yet there were *none of them.* Psalm 139:13–16

Additional References: Genesis 1:26; Exodus 20:13, 21:22; Judges 13:7; Psalm 127:3.

1

What Others Say: Bernard N. Nathanson, M.D., former director of the Center for Reproductive and Sexual Health in New York; Rev. Donald Shoemaker, assistant professor of Biblical Studies at Biola University; and Dr. John MacArthur, pastor, Grace Community Church, Sun Valley, California.

Bernard N. Nathanson, M.D.

There is no longer serious doubt in my mind that human life exists within the womb from the very onset of pregnancy, despite the fact that the nature of the intrauterine life has been the subject of considerable dispute in the past. Electrocardiographic evidence of heart function has been established in embryos as early as six weeks. Electroencephalographic recordings of human brain activity have been noted in embryos at eight weeks.[1]

. . . Here I would agree with one of the most fervent right-to-life physicians, C. Everett Koop . . . "It has been my constant experience that disability and unhappiness do not necessarily go together. Some of the most unhappy children whom I have known have all their physical and mental faculties, and on the other hand some of the happiest youngsters have borne burdens which I myself would find very difficult to bear."[2]

Donald Shoemaker

The whole moral system which God has given is fulfilled when men love God above all else and when they love their neighbors as themselves. When men truly love their neighbors, they do not covet or kill or violate other moral laws against their fellow man. Abortion ethics at its heart is a selfish grasping at personal rights to the exclusion of others. It is a bold overpowering of the weak by the strong. Jesus said this must not be—the neighbor must be endeared by every man. And no one is more a neighbor to another than the unborn child whose heart beats in the bosom of its mother.[3]

John MacArthur

Abortion . . . brutally challenges the fundamental determination of a person's right to live and contradicts God's declaration of life's sanctity.[4]

---

[1]Bernard N. Nathanson, M.D., *Aborting America,* Doubleday & Company, Inc., Garden City, New York, 1979, pp. 164–165.

[2]Ibid., pp. 235–236.

[3]Donald Shoemaker, *Abortion, The Bible, and The Christian,* Hayes Publishing Company, Inc., Cincinnati, Ohio, 1976, p. 48.

[4]John MacArthur, *The Biblical Position on Abortion,* Grace Community Church, Sun Valley, California, 1980, p. 1.

Because personhood begins at conception and because abortion involves taking the life of one who exists in the image of God, abortion is nothing short of killing. Abortionists have rejected God's gift of human life (Psalm 127:3) and God's gift of truth.[5]

Application: When faced with an unwanted pregnancy, is abortion a biblical solution? The answer is—a thousand times NO! We are created in the image of God (Genesis 1:26) and this includes the embryo growing in the mother's womb. Women claim that they have a right to determine what happens to their bodies and in a measure this is true, but the time to exercise control is before a pregnancy occurs.

Are deformities or other severe handicaps grounds for ending the life of an unborn child? The answer to this question is the same as for a normal child. Every life is precious in the sight of God, **without exception.**

Perhaps someone will read this who has had an abortion and is wondering if there is any redemptive love for herself. God is gracious, merciful, and forgiving (I John 1:9, 2:1–2). There is no sin so great that God cannot forgive. Confess the sin to God and then accept His forgiveness. Confession implies repentance, which is a turning away from sin and walking in fellowship with God.

—Dan Graves

ABORTION

WHAT IS THE CHRISTIAN ALTERNATIVE TO ABORTION?

The Issue: When a young woman is faced with an unplanned pregnancy, the world's answer is to terminate the pregnancy and allow the mother to go on with her life. Many Christians, realizing that God has given life to this child, are choosing the option of placing their child for adoption by loving Christians.

---

[5]Ibid., p. 13.

Key Bible References:

So the woman conceived and bore a son. And when she saw that he was a beautiful child, she hid him three months.

And the child grew, and she brought him to Pharaoh's daughter, and he became her son. Exodus 2:2, 10a

. . . just as He chose us in Him before the foundation of the world, that we should be holy and without blame before Him in love, having predestined us to adoption as sons by Jesus Christ to Himself, according to the good pleasure of His will, to the praise of the glory of His grace, by which He has made us accepted in the Beloved. Ephesians 1:4–6

Additional References: Psalms 22:9–10, 139:13–14; Galatians 4:7.

What Others Say: Charles R. Swindoll is the senior pastor of the First Evangelical Free Church in Fullerton, California; and Kay Marshall Strom is a schoolteacher and free-lance writer in Santa Barbara, California.

Charles R. Swindoll
First: God sets apart human life as unique and valuable since it bears His image. Second: Because this is true, God commands that all human life be preserved and protected. Third: Human life begins within the womb, where God personally and sovereignly superintends the development and maturation of the fetus before birth. Fourth: Therefore, since it is God's will that every child's life be protected after birth, it is certainly His will that such protection apply to the child in his or her prenatal state.[1]

Kay Marshall Strom
A Christian view of adoption . . . is unique in several ways. It is a concept authored by God and demonstrated by Him in its most perfect and complete sense by His adoption of all Christian believers into His own family.[2]

Application: Although great efforts are made to convince us that early pregnancy yields only a lump of fetal tissue, God makes it very clear that every life that is begun has been planned and created by Him. By choosing to carry and give birth to her baby, the birthmother spares the life of the child that God has created.

---

[1]Charles R. Swindoll, *The Sanctity of Life,* Word, Inc., Dallas, Texas, 1990, p. 25.
[2]Kay Marshall Strom, *Chosen Families,* Zondervan, Grand Rapids, Michigan, 1985, p. 28.

Some single mothers choose to raise a baby alone. However, most young women find themselves unable to support and care for a newborn child. Another option is to place her child for adoption. There are examples of adoption in the scripture going back to the book of Genesis. Abraham was prepared to adopt Eliezer, son of his head-servant, in order to have an heir. Moses' mother allowed him to be adopted by Pharaoh's daughter because she knew she would not be able to protect him herself. God even speaks of our position as His sons through adoption.

A birthmother today has the opportunity to choose the family into which her child will be placed. This allows her to have an active part in giving her child a chance to grow up in a Christian family consisting of a mother and father, which is the pattern we see throughout scriptures of God's design for a family.

—Linda Elam

ACTIVISTS

SHOULD CHRISTIANS BE INVOLVED IN SOCIAL ACTION?

The Issue: We live in the age of spectator sports. Spectators sit on the sidelines or in front of TVs *watching* the action. All too many Christians view their role in social issues much the same. To be a spectator does not require discipline, knowledge, effort or commitment. Effective social action demands these qualities. Also, many Christians view "ministry" as being directly connected to their church activity. Is social action ministry? Does God call His people to the arena of civic life in order to participate in a ministry of social action?

Key Bible References:

By the blessing of the upright the city is exalted, but it is overthrown by the mouth of the wicked. Proverbs 11:11

You are the salt of the earth; but if the salt loses its flavor, how shall it be seasoned? It is then good for nothing but to be thrown out and tramped under foot by men.

You are the light of the world. A city that is set on a hill cannot be hidden.

Nor do they light a lamp and put it under a basket, but on a lampstand, and it gives light to all who are *in the house.*

Let your light shine before men, that they may see your good works and glorify your Father in heaven." Matthew 5:13–16

. . . be filled with the knowledge of His will in all wisdom and spiritual understanding; that you may have a walk worthy of the Lord, fully pleasing Him, *being fruitful in every good work and increasing in the knowledge of God.* Colossians 1:9–10

Additional References: Deuteronomy 30:19–20; Job 36:7; Proverbs 14:19, 34, 25:19, 29:2; Isaiah 62.

What Others Say: John Ashcroft, governor of Missouri; Abraham Kuiper, pastor, theologian, author and prime minister of Holland; and Edmund Burke, English statesman.

John Ashcroft
It is the job of government to help maintain a circumstance in which people reach the maximum of their God-given potential.[1]

Abraham Kuiper
We may not sit back, separating ourselves from national life, and expect the Lord to deliver us from oppression by a miracle from heaven. He could do so, but that is not his pleasure. . . . Our God works by means. He uses men . . . . Therefore in the affairs of the nation, as well as in all other spheres of life, the Christian is called upon to fight the fight of faith, to be a soldier of Jesus Christ.[2]

Edmund Burke
All that is necessary for the triumph of evil is for good men to do nothing.[3]

Application: Does God specifically say anywhere in His word for Christians to be involved in social action? No, nowhere. Does God say anywhere in His word for Christians to be involved in social action? Yes, everywhere.

Social action is a question of righteousness. Righteousness is being in right-relationship with God. It is *acted* out daily, in words and

---

[1]John Ashcroft, "Created to Help God Create," *WORLD Magazine,* May 20, 1989, p. 5.
[2]Abraham Kuiper, "Needed Today: Some Prophets Like Jonah and Jeremiah," *WORLD Magazine,* October 20, 1990, p. 21.
[3]Edmund Burke, *The Rebirth of America,* Arthur S. DeMoss Foundation, 1986, p. 213.

deeds. The question then arises, how do I choose which activities to become involved in? Christians are exhorted many times in scripture (Colossians 1:9; Ephesians 1:17–18) to be filled with the knowledge of His will, in all wisdom and spiritual understanding. Before getting involved, the Christian must first collect the pertinent information (knowledge). Second, the Christian compares the information to scripture and seeks godly counsel. This moves raw knowledge from the brain (intellect) to the heart (understanding). Lastly, equipped with knowledge and understanding, and girded with prayer, the Christian exercises wisdom. Wisdom is demonstrated by correct *action* based on sound understanding. There are many levels of action. James 5:16b tells us: "The effective, fervent prayer of a righteous man avails much." With this world view, the Christian can launch into social action, reclaiming ground stolen by Satan, our adversary. This is not a spectator sport!

—Rohn J. Ritzema

ADULTERY AND FORNICATION

WHAT DOES THE BIBLE SAY ABOUT ADULTERY AND FORNICATION?

The Issue: Adultery, from the Greek word *moicheia* and fornication, from the Greek word *porneia* both refer to illicit, immoral sexual conduct. Of the two terms, fornication is the more general, and may be used to denote all kinds of illicit sexual intercourse including adultery. Adultery, on the other hand, is a more specific term used to denote illicit sexual intercourse with another's spouse.

In the Bible, these terms are used:
  (1) naturally—to describe actual physical sexual misconduct; and
  (2) metaphorically—to describe the spiritual sin of turning from God to idolatry, paganism, and worldly pursuits.

Regardless of the context in which they appear, both terms are used to describe the sin of turning from God to the world and the flesh, consequently taking the love that rightfully belongs to God and/or one's spouse and giving it to another.

7

Key Bible References:

You shall not commit adultery. Exodus 20:14

For this is the will of God, your sanctification; that you should abstain from sexual immorality. . . . I Thessalonians 4:3

Marriage is *honorable among all, and the bed undefiled; but fornicators and adulterers God will judge.* Hebrews 13:4

Adulterers and adulteresses! Do you not know that friendship with the world is enmity with God? Whoever therefore wants to be a friend of the world makes himself an enemy of God. James 4:4

Additional References: Romans 13:9; I Corinthians 6:9–10, 13b, 7:2; Galatians 5:19; Ephesians 5:3–5; Colossians 3:5; Jude 7; Revelation 2:14, 20, 17:1–2.

What Others Say: The late Dr. Francis A. Schaeffer, minister, missionary, philosopher, and author; and Dr. Tim LaHaye, pastor, counselor, author, president and founder of Family Life Seminars.

Francis A. Schaeffer

In our generation people are asking why promiscuous sexual relationships are wrong. I would say that there are three reasons . . . The first one, of course, is simply because God says so. God is the creator and the judge of the universe; his character is the law of the universe, and when he tells us a thing is wrong, it *is* wrong—if we are going to have a God at all of the kind the Scripture portrays.

Second, however, we must never forget that God has made us in our relationships to really fulfill that which he made us to be, and therefore, too, a right sexual relationship is for our good as we are made. . . . Promiscuity tries to force something into a form which God never made it for, and in which it cannot be fulfilled.

The third reason: . . . we know promiscuous sexual relationships are wrong because they break the picture of what God means marriage, the relationship of man and woman, to be. Marriage is set forth to be the illustration of the relationship of God and his people, and of Christ and his church. . . . The relationship of God with his people rests upon his character, and sexual relationships outside of marriage breaks this parallel which the Bible draws between marriage and the relationship of God with his people. . . . Both in the Old and New Testaments the Bible speaks out strongly against all sexual promiscuity. . . .[1]

---

[1]Francis A. Schaeffer, *The Church at the End of the 20th Century,* Inter-Varsity Press, Downers Grove, Illinois, 1970, p. 118.

Adultery is a sin that the church of Jesus Christ doesn't take lightly. Scripture so frequently castigates the sin of becoming "one flesh" with anyone other than one's own wife or husband that it labels it a sin against the person's own body (I Corinthians 6:18). Other passages identify it as a sin against the soul, meaning literally, "your life" (Proverbs 6:32).[2]

Application: American society has increasingly come to look upon sexual relationships from an amoral perspective. The results have been devastating: marriages breaking up at a rate of better than fifty percent; sexually transmitted diseases rampant and some, such as AIDS, with no known cure; teen pregnancies at an all-time high, and children indoctrinated with "sex education" from kindergarten through senior high school. Today more than ever Christians need both to understand and obey God's word with regard to sexual relationships and teach their children to do likewise. To maintain personal purity in sexual relationships should be among the highest priorities for a modern day Christian, being careful always to ". . . possess his own vessel in sanctification and honor" (I Thessalonians 4:4).

—**Robert T. Gallagher**

AGING

WHAT IS OUR RESPONSIBILITY
TO OUR ELDERS?

The Issue: Aging is universal and normal. We are increasingly aware of the fact that the problems of old age have economic, social and psychological consequences for everyone. Over 25 million Americans (16%) are over 60 years old and because of extended life expectancy, this number is expected to double by the year 2000.

Many elderly are self-sufficient, active, and lead productive lives. Others are disabled, lonely, isolated, feel useless or have other needs. In our youth-oriented society, little emphasis is placed on helping the elderly.

---

[2]Tim LaHaye, *If Ministers Fall, Can They Be Restored?*, Zondervan Publishing House, Grand Rapids, Michigan, 1990, p. 18.

As we face the growing "gray" population, we need to learn what the Bible has to say about our responsibility to our elders. All of us have a stake in reaching out to them—for if God grants the privilege, we will all one day be old.

Key Bible References:

Do not rebuke an older man, but exhort him *as a father,* the *younger men as brothers.*

Honor widows who are really widows. But if any widow has children or grandchildren, let them first learn to show piety at home and to repay their parents; for this is good and acceptable before God.

But if anyone does not provide for his own, and especially for those of his household, he has denied the faith and is worse than an unbeliever. I Timothy 5:1, 3–4, 8

Do not cast me off in the time of old age. . . . Psalm 71:9

"Honor your father and your mother, that your days may be long upon the land which the LORD *your God is giving you."* Exodus 20:12

Additional References: Leviticus 19:32; Job 12:12; Proverbs 23:22; James 1:27.

What Others Say: Dr. Olga Knopf, former member of the Senate Special Committee on Aging and a member of the faculty at Mt. Sinai School of Medicine; and Horace L. Kerr, former supervisor of Senior Adult Ministries for the Southern Baptist Sunday School Board, and executive director of the Mississippi Governor's council on Aging.

Dr. Olga Knopf
As long as a person lives, he has feelings, desires, and needs that are no different from those he had when young. To be pushed aside . . . is just as painful at eighty as it is at twenty.[1]

Horace L. Kerr
Our challenge is to be aware, understanding, concerned, and action-oriented toward the end that all senior adults may experience the abundant life promised by our Lord (John 10:10) and live with dignity and meaning in relation to others.[2]

---

[1]Dr. Olga Knopf, *Successful Aging: The Facts and Fallacies of Growing Old,* Viking Press, New York, New York, 1975, p. 189.
[2]Horace L. Kerr, *How to Minister to Senior Adults in Your Church,* Broadman Press, Nashville, Tennessee, 1980, p. 123.

Application: The context in I Timothy 5 is often overlooked. Paul writes to Timothy, explaining our obligation to care for aged parents. Verse 4 tells us to show piety (devotion or duty), to them, as well as to repay them—in care and provisions. Notice that verse 8 reprimands anyone who does not provide for those in the household, including elderly parents!

Several times, we are told to *honor* our parents. They deserve our respect, admiration and recognition. They would appreciate being asked their opinion, or having the opportunity to share their wisdom, accumulated from years of valuable experience. They can be important members of committees, and valuable volunteers.

We need to offer emotional support as well. Elderly people need compassion and understanding as they deal with physical problems and other changes in their life. They need to feel needed, useful, and included. They need to feel loved, and will appreciate gestures of affection and tenderness.

Admonition concerning widows (James 1:27), would show us a practical teaching. We should watch for opportunities to assist them, whether chores in and around the house, helping with errands, or providing food. We need to be aware of their financial burdens. Contact, through letters and phone calls is very important.

We need to see the elderly as individuals with diverse traits and needs. We also need to see them as men and women for whom Christ died, and has promised a glorious future with Him.

–Donald F. Cole

AGNOSTIC

WHAT IS THE CHRISTIAN RESPONSE TO THOSE WHO CLAIM TO BE AGNOSTICS?

The Issue: The word "agnostic" was introduced by British evolutionist Thomas H. Huxley in 1869 to promote the idea that man does not and cannot know whether God exists. He based his premise on John Locke's statement that man should not accept "propositions with more certainty than the evidence warrants." This, of course, put Huxley in good standing with Charles Darwin but he found himself at serious odds with the Bible-believing church community. An agnostic is not to be confused with an atheist. An atheist denies

11

the existence of God, an agnostic agrees that God exists but He can not be known.

Key Bible References:

Then Paul stood in the midst of the Areopagus and said, "Men of Athens, I perceive that in all things you are very religious; for as I was passing through and considering the objects of your worship, I even found an altar with this inscription: TO THE UNKNOWN GOD. Therefore, the One whom you worship without knowing, Him I proclaim to you." Acts 17:22–23

For to this end we both labor and suffer reproach, because we trust in the living God, who is the Savior of all men, especially of those who believe. I Timothy 4:10

"Men, why are you doing these things? We also are men with the same nature as you, and preach to you that you should turn from these vain things to the living God, who made the heaven, the earth, the sea, and all things that are in them, who in bygone generations allowed all nations to walk in their own ways.

"Nevertheless, He did not leave Himself without witness, in that He did good, gave us rain from heaven and fruitful seasons, filling our hearts with food and gladness." Acts 14:15–17

Additional References: Psalm 135:6; Matthew 22:23–32; I Timothy 1:17; Hebrews 10:30–31.

What Others Say: Dr. David L. Hocking, pastor, author and Bible scholar; Dr. David A. DeWitt, Search Ministries in Dallas, Texas; and Billy Graham, evangelist and author.

David L. Hocking
Some people with whom I have talked about God seem to know one thing: That you can't know if there is a God or not! They seem to ignore the fact that we are often ignorant of what others may know. This agnostic attitude is understandable. Our struggle with the known may cause us at times to deny that something exists, simply because we cannot see it or understand it. I believe in electricity, but I have never seen it. If you stick a wet finger in a socket, however, it might make you a believer.[1]

---

[1]David L. Hocking, *The Nature of God in Plain Language,* Word Books, Publishers, Waco, Texas, 1984, p. 18.

David A. DeWitt

It is common to find people who believe in the word "God." It is also increasingly common to find that many—probably most—of those same people who believe in something called "God" do not believe in a personal God. What I mean is: They do not believe in the existence of a real live person who created the universe and remains in sovereign control of it.

Hebrews 11:6 reads, "And without faith it is impossible to please Him, for he who comes to God *must believe that He is,* and that He is a rewarder of those who *seek Him*" (italics added). In other words, the first step in coming to God is to understand that there is a real, personal, ultimately sovereign being to come to.[2]

Billy Graham

The Bible says we can know God, because He has made Himself known to us. "No one has ever seen God, but God the only Son, who is at the Father's side, has made Him known" (John 1:18). The most important discovery you will ever make is that God loves you and you can know Him personally by committing your life to Jesus Christ.[3]

Application: The All Nations English Dictionary defines an agnostic as "a person who believes that nothing can be known about the existence of God or of anything except material things."[4] Such a position, of course, defies common logic. The existence of a beautiful painting implies an artist who painted it. Paintings do not paint themselves. Nothing in the world has ever been observed creating something from nothing. Nor is there a fossil anywhere in the world that shows a creature in transition from one species to another. There is a God and He can be known. To not acknowledge God as the great creator of all is like showing a painting and covering up the name of the artist. It is plagiarism of the worst sort.

—Paul A. Kienel

---

[2]David A. DeWitt, *Answering the Tough Ones,* Moody Press, Chicago, Illinois, 1980, pp. 121–122.

[3]Billy Graham, *Answers to Life's Problems,* Grason, Minnesota, 1960, pp. 283–284.

[4]Morris Watkins, *The All Nations English Dictionary,* All Nations, Pasadena, California, 1990, p. 12.

HOW SHOULD CHRISTIANS RESPOND
TO THOSE WITH AIDS?

The Issue: AIDS is one of a number of challenges facing society today. However, because it touches on sensitive areas such as sex, sexuality, morality and death, it can cause us to <u>react</u> out of deep-seated prejudices and fears. The key is to <u>respond</u> and not react—how do we do this? Jesus showed us the way in His attitude to the woman caught in adultery by displaying acceptance of her as a person combined with a call to go and sin no more.

Key Bible Reference:

And everyone went to his own house. But Jesus went to the Mount of Olives.

Now early in the morning He came again into the temple, and all the people came to Him; and He sat down and taught them.

Then the scribes and Pharisees brought to Him a woman caught in adultery. And when they had set her in the midst, they said to Him, "Teacher, this woman was caught in adultery, in the very act.

"Now Moses, in the law, commanded us that such should be stoned. But what do You say?"

This they said, testing Him, that they might have something of which to accuse Him. But Jesus stooped down and wrote on the ground with His finger, as though He did not hear.

So when they continued asking Him, He raised Himself up and said to them, "He who is without sin among you, let him throw a stone at her first."

And again He stooped down and wrote on the ground.

Then those who heard it, being convicted by their conscience, went out one by one, beginning with the oldest even to the last. And Jesus was left alone, and the woman standing in the midst.

When Jesus had raised Himself up and saw no one but the woman, He said to her, "Woman, where are those accusers of yours? Has no one condemned you?"

She said, "No one Lord." And Jesus said to her, "Neither do I condemn you; go and sin no more." John 8:1–11

Additional References: Matthew 22:37–39; John 13:34; I Corinthians 13:1–13.

What Others Say: Dr. Tim LaHaye, Christian author.

Tim LaHaye

Dr. James Curran, head of the AIDS task force at the Centers for Disease Control in Atlanta, recently made this sobering comment: "It's not just a 'gay' disease. It is spreading fast and all of us can get it. At this point we can't say when it will end. We have no cure. I think thousands more people will die of this disease before it's over." Mervyn Silverman, former head of San Francisco's health department, has called AIDS "the most devastating epidemic of the century."[1]

Application: Christians have always been called to be at the forefront of care and compassion for all who are ill, regardless of the cause of illness or any other factor. As Christians we should have only one response—to unconditionally love and care for those infected while clearly teaching how to avoid infection. At the same time we must live our lives according to God's standards. We often find this very hard because we either emphasize love and our own frailty or we emphasize teaching about moral behavior and God's standards. We can fall into traps of sentimentalism or harshness.

We have a responsibility to be aware and understand the ethical teaching of the Bible on sexuality, homosexuality, morality, life, and death. Not only do we need to get involved in our communities with people who are shunned and rejected and show them God's love, but also we need to respond to people within our own churches who may become sick with AIDS. With an average of ten years from infection to illness, growing churches may well have infected members due to previous lifestyles—we need to be able to reach out to them and embrace them as part of God's family and not be yet another source of rejection.

AIDS brings many difficulties into the open; it forces us to think through again what we believe and teach about sex, sexuality, lifestyles, death, and dying.

---

[1]Dr. Tim LaHaye, *Sex Education is for the Family,* Pyranee Books (Zondervan), Grand Rapids, Michigan, 1985, p. 166.

AIDS also presents a unique opportunity for church members to become more involved in society and to have a real impact on our nation by caring for those who are shunned and rejected.

—Patrick Dixon

ALCOHOL

SHOULD CHRISTIANS DRINK ALCOHOL?

The Issue: Do Scriptures support the practice of Christians drinking alcohol? The answer is a resounding **no,** if one accepts the admonitions in the Old Testament and wants to live in accordance with the character of our Lord Jesus Christ, who was sinless and who gave us a perfect example.

Key Bible References:

Wine is a mocker, strong drink is *a brawler, and whoever is led astray by it is not wise.* Proverbs 20:1

Do not look on the wine when it is red, when it sparkles in the cup, when it swirls around smoothly; at the last it bites like a serpent, and stings like a viper.

Your eyes will see strange things, and your heart will utter perverse things. Proverbs 23:31–33

Do not drink wine or intoxicating drink, you, nor your sons with you, when you go into the tabernacle of meeting, lest you die. It shall be *a statute forever throughout your generations,* . . . Leviticus 10:9

Additional References: Isaiah 5:22; Jeremiah 35:6; Daniel 1:5, 10:3; Ephesians 5:18; I Timothy 3:3.

What Others Say: Billy Graham, evangelist and author.

Billy Graham
The scourge of alcoholism and the hurt it causes relatives, friends, and colleagues is growing. It is now being considered as a disease and the emphasis seems to be on teaching people how to drink in moderation. As I see it, under present conditions, there is but one safe and Christian solution—total abstinence. Liquor is not neces-

sary either for health or for so-called gracious living. On the other hand, it is the cause of untold sorrow, suffering, and material loss, not to mention the spiritual implications of drinking.[1]

Application: We should remember that Jesus Christ was our High Priest and He applied the law of the priest to Himself because He was the High Priest after the order of Melchizadek. The Scriptures admonish us to pattern our lives after Christ. But someone will say, "Jesus Christ made wine at the wedding feast of the Canaan of Galilee."

This is a misunderstanding of the Greek word which was used. In our culture when we use the word wine it invariably implies that this is fermented grape juice but the Greek word is "oinos," or "oinon," which means "the fruit of the vine" or the "grape plant." The great Greek scholar Richard Jeb of Cambridge University defines "oinos" as a general term which includes all kinds of beverages. But in the Septuagint, the Greek version of the Hebrew Scriptures, used in Christ's day the Hebrew word for grape juice is translated 33 times by the Greek word "oinos."

But somebody will say, "How would they preserve it?" They preserved it in six or seven different ways. Fermentation will not set up if the grape juice has boiled because boiling kills the wild yeast germ just like our parents preserved fruit and vegetables in jars and they killed the yeast germ by boiling it. In Bible times people boiled grape juice down until it was a thick liquid called, "must" or "mustim." Aristotle talks about this. Virgil in 70 B.C. talks about how sweet "must" was boiled down until the luscious juice was so thick that they would scrape it out of the wine skins at times and they would dissolve it and they would use it for a drink.

Someone might ask, "doesn't Paul say, 'use a little wine for your stomach's sake' when he was admonishing Timothy about his frequent infirmities?" (I Timothy 5:23). Yes, he did, but Greek medicine called it "stomach wine." It was grape juice prepared as a thick, unfermented syrup and was much in use as a medicant for dispeptic and weak persons, which Timothy apparently was. Grape sugar is very close to blood sugar. There simply is no biblical justification at all for Christians to drink fermented beverage of any sort.

—**Bob Smith**

---

[1]Billy Graham, *Answers to Life's Problems,* Word Books, Publishers, Waco, Texas, 1960, p. 70.

ALCOHOLISM

HOW SHOULD CHRISTIANS RESPOND TO THOSE WHO ARE TRAPPED BY ALCOHOLISM?

The Issue: Alcoholism can be looked at in two ways. One way to view it is to identify it as a habit, choosing to make use of a substance to escape or soften the trials of one's experience and then becoming enslaved to the substance. A second way of viewing alcoholism comes from our present society, which has identified it as an illness, a disease. Certain individuals are more susceptible to being controlled by alcohol, and thus become entrapped in its use. It really doesn't matter which view is taken. The central fact is that alcoholics are slaves to their habit or weakness. Some Christians have difficulty responding to certain problems other people have, and alcoholism is one of these problems. It is easy for Christians to become "self-righteous" and judgmental, looking at the alcoholic through "legalistic" eyes, seeing only the shortcoming (or sin) and not seeing the need of the individual.

Somehow, we need to see the alcoholic as someone in need, and then see the Savior as One Who meets needs and assists in "healing" people of things which entrap them, either physically or spiritually. Somehow, we must get to the place where we can find the "sin" distasteful, but feel a need to minister to the "sinner." Either the alcoholic is not a believer and needs the Savior, or he is a believer who is dependent on something other than his Lord, and needs the restoration which can be provided by the Savior through believers. God's admonition to us is to "restore such a one."

Key Bible References:

Do not be overcome by evil, but overcome evil with good. Romans 12:21

Brethren, if a man is overtaken in any trespass, you who are spiritual restore such a one in a spirit of gentleness, considering yourself lest you also be tempted. Bear one another's burdens, and so fulfill the law of Christ. Galatians 6:1–2

Additional Reference: I Corinthians 8:12.

What Others Say: Harry Blamires, teacher, administrator and writer; Ken Gage, pastor, teacher and author and Joy Gage, teacher, writer and lecturer; and Bob and Pauline Bartosch, workers with Overcomers Outreach, a Christian ministry to alcoholics.

Harry Blamires

Calling us to a balanced view. . . . Indeed one may question whether deep compassion for the sinner can possibly exist without a correspondingly fierce hatred of the sins which disfigure him. This is a general principle of human relationships.

It is of course a matter of simple logic that the Church, in so far as She condemns sin plainly and firmly, to that extent can extend the maximum sympathy, compassion, and unquestioning acceptance to the sinner without the slightest possibility of misunderstanding or betrayal. Only in so far as the Church clearly identifies what is sinful can She open her arms to all sinners. Clear identification and condemnation of sin is the very precondition of mercy and forgiveness. . . . What is the value of forgiveness if there is nothing to forgive?[1]

Ken and Joy Gage

A crucial problem with the wine question is one of sensitivity toward Christians whose past includes alcoholism. Certainly most of us know at least one Christian who daily looks into the mirror and admits "I am an alcoholic. I cannot drink." Coping with the problem means having no liquor in the house and staying away from office parties. Must such Christians also be tempted from the least expected source—their circle of Christian friends? In accepting an invitation to dinner will they place themselves in a high risk area of temptation because the fare includes wine (or other alcohol)?[2] (parentheses mine)

Bob and Pauline Bartosch

The good news is—YES—it is possible to be FREED from the disease of chemical dependency! God has supplied tools for us to use to find peace and power against the enemy through this special fellowship and study of His Word. Hurting family members can be FREED from their obsessions with their loved one's dilemma, and can learn to completely turn them over to the Lord. It all seems to start with a willingness to be open to God's power through the many sources of help He provides. Our mutual openness provides a channel through which His love can flow and healing can begin.[3]

---

[1]Harry Blamires, *Where Do We Stand?*, Servant Books, Ann Arbor, Michigan, 1980, p. 102.

[2]Ken and Joy Gage, *Restoring Fellowship, Judgment and Church Discipline,* Moody Press, Chicago, Illinois, 1984, p. 72.

[3]Bob and Pauline Bartosch, *FREED,* Overcomers Outreach, La Habra, California, 1985, p. 4.

Application: The church is presently awakening to the challenge to reach out and minister to those in need. Christians can no longer pull their robes around them and walk away from those who have fallen along the way. The Bible is clear regarding sin and forgiveness. And it is also very clear that Christians have a responsibility to minister in the name of Christ to those in need. When Christian brothers are taken with a disease or failure, spiritual correction is in order and Christians are directed to "restore such a one."

New ministries have arisen, such as Overcomers Outreach, which have begun to reach out to those who have been imprisoned by alcohol or drugs. With proven measures, the strength of God's Word and the work of the Holy Spirit, people are finding that God has deliverance for them and the possibility of future growth and ministry. Christians need to develop a clear view on the harm alcohol and drugs can do and be wise in their decisions. It is clear that God holds us responsible for our brothers and sisters. We must take care not to cause others to stumble. And, when a brother or sister has stumbled and fallen, we are to minister so that healing can take place and a life can be restored to wholeness and the possibility of ministry.

Our desire should be to see that no one is captured by this destroying vice; but when we meet those who have already been taken in, the ministering Christian should find ways to reach out and firmly work toward restoration and wholeness.

—James W. Braley, Jr.

AMBITION

WHAT DOES THE BIBLE TEACH ABOUT AMBITION?

The Issue: What role does ambition play in the life of a Christian? Are we to be ambitious? Webster's dictionary defines ambition as "an ardent or strong desire for rank, fame or power; a desire to achieve a particular end." In worldly ambition one is rarely seeking the will of God, only personal advancement. In godly ambition the will of God is paramount. Ambition for righteousness is strongly encouraged throughout the Bible.

Two Avenues

Selfish ambition	*Unselfish ambition*
Babel builders (Gen. 11:1–9)	Abraham (Gen. 12:1–3,
Aaron & Miriam (Num. 12)	15:18–21)
Absalom (II Sam. 15:1–18,	Moses (Ex. 3—4, 32:7–14)
18)	David (I Sam. 16:1–13,
Adonijah (I Kin. 1)	24:1–22, 26:1–25)
Haman (Esth. 5:9–13, 6:6–9)	Jesus Christ (John 5:30–36,
James & John (Matt. 20:20;	6:38, 7:16)
Mark 10:35–45)	Paul (Rom. 9:3; Gal. 2:20;
Simon the sorcerer	Phil. 1:13)
(Acts 8:9–10)	Peter (I Peter 2:11–16, 5:1–9)

Selfish ambition leads to:	*Unselfish ambition leads to:*
Strife (James 4:1–2)	Cooperation
Vain glory (Gal. 5:26)	Exaltation of God
Conceit (Isa. 14:12–15)	Spiritual growth (Phil.
Haughty attitude	3:12–14)
(Matt. 18:1–6)	Extension of the gospel
Self-centered	(Rom. 15:17–20)
Jealousy (Num. 12:2)	Quietness (I Thess. 4:11)
Discouragement	Peace
Depression	Joy
Suicide	Acceptance before God

Key Bible References:

Let *nothing* be done *through selfish ambition or conceit, but in lowliness of mind let each esteem others better than himself.* Philippians 2:3

I press toward the goal for the prize of the upward call of God in Christ Jesus.

Therefore let us, as many as are mature, have this mind; and if in anything you think otherwise, God will reveal even this to you. Philippians 3:14–15

What Others Say: Ethel Barrett, Bible teacher and author.

Ethel Barrett

Selfish Ambition. This one is deadly because it has so many cover-ups. Assuming responsibility is one. This could mean riding rough-shod over anybody who happens to be in the way to assume responsibility in an area where you weren't invited. Resourceful-ness is another. This could mean finding devious methods of getting your way when you're blocked. Contributing is another. This coul mean forcing your ideas on the chairman of the committee you are *not* on and sulking if you can't have your way. The list lengthens, interminably. Initiative and assuming responsibility and resourcefulness and contributing are noble attributes if they are done with the right motive. But if your motive is selfish ambition, you are wrong even when you're right. You can't win.[1]

Application: Self evaluation is always in order. We must constantly be honest about our intent and purpose when seeking a position of following our desires. Am I pursuing this for my fame, power, glory? Am I a living sacrifice or am I sacrificing others? Is this the will of God or my will?

God desires that we do have ambition, and that our ambition is channeled in the right direction, which is to glorify God and edify the church and be a testimony to the unbeliever. Our prayers should always include: Keep me sensitive to your will for my life. Make me to be content where you have placed me that I might be of help to others and that I might glorify you.

The Bible teaches that if we are to be ambitious; let us be ambitious for the glory of God.

—**Anne Landry**

ANGELS

WHAT DOES THE BIBLE SAY ABOUT ANGELS?

The Issue: God's Word, the Bible, speaks of angels 273 times. Angels are created beings that:

      (1) Serve as messengers of God (Genesis 22:1; Luke 1:19);
      (2) Dr. Billy Graham refers to angels as "God's Secret Agents" who help to complete the will of the Ruler of the Universe and fulfill His judgment (Psalm 103:19–21);
      (3) Cannot be numbered (Revelation 5:11);
      (4) Function as "ministering spirits sent forth to minister for those who will inherit salvation" (Hebrews 1:14).

---

[1]Ethel Barrett, *Will the Real Phony Please Stand Up?*, Regal Books, Glendale, California, 1969, p. 120.

Each angel, no matter what rank, worships God and calls attention in the spiritual realm as to the great things God is doing. For example, an angel announced the Incarnation of Christ to Mary (Luke 1:26–38) and the Shepherds (Luke 2:8–15). Then an angel chorus sang "Glory to God in the highest," . . . Angels are at the disposal of Christ (Matthew 26:53). At His resurrection an angel rolled back the tombstone (Matthew 28:2). One day soon, angels will come with Christ in His Second Coming (II Thessalonians 1:7) and an angel of God will cast Satan into the bottomless pit (Revelation 20:1–3).

"Everlasting fire" was originally designed by God for the devil and those angels who rebelled against God (Matthew 25:41). Revelation 12:7–9 tells how Satan and his angels were cast out of heaven for their sin. Angels do not have the ability to experience the grace of God or forgiveness of sin as humans can. Human beings can be saved from their sin by believing on Christ as Savior. God's angels look on in awe of God's plan of redemption for mankind. They rejoice in the presence of God when a sinner repents. (Luke 15:10)

Key Bible References:

And the Angel of God, who went before the camp of Israel, moved and went behind them; and the pillar of cloud went from before them and stood behind them. Exodus 14:19

"My God sent His angel and shut the lions' mouths, so that they have not hurt me, because I was found innocent before Him; and also, O king, I have done no wrong before you." Daniel 6:22

Peter was sleeping, bound with two chains between two soldiers; and the guards before the door were keeping the prison.

Now behold, an angel of the Lord stood by him, *and a light shone in the prison; and he struck Peter on the side and raised him up, saying, "Arise quickly!" And his chains fell off* his hands. Acts 12:6b–7

Additional References: Numbers 22:22–35; Psalm 91:11–12; Matthew 13:41, 22:30, 24:31, 36, 25:31; Luke 2:13, 16:22; John 1:51, 20:12; Revelation 5:11–12, 19:17.

What Others Say: Dr. Billy Graham, evangelist and publisher of *Decision* magazine; Dr. John MacArthur, Jr., pastor of Grace Community Church and national radio speaker; and Dr. C. Fred Dickason, chairman of theology at Moody Bible Institute.

Billy Graham

I am convinced that these heavenly beings exist and that they provide unseen aid on our behalf. . . .

I believe in angels because the Bible says there are angels; and I believe the Bible to be the true Word of God.

I also believe in angels because I have sensed their presence in my life on special occasions.[1]

John MacArthur, Jr.

One thing I have gained out of [the] study of angels is the tremendous care that God has taken to assure His children of their security in a physical sense. Such assurance has alleviated a lot of the burden that I might normally bear over anxieties for physical accident, disease, or any kind of danger, knowing that God's angels are ministering to the physical care, protection, and guidance of His children . . . God's angels [are] amazing beings, and I'm sure that we'll never fully understand them until we meet them.[2]

C. Fred Dickason

Scripture indicates that the ministry of angels to men is primarily external and physical, whereas the ministry of the Holy Spirit is internal and spiritual. Angels minister for us; the Holy Spirit ministers *in* us (John 14:16–17; Heb. 1:13–14). They guard our bodies and pathway; He guards our spirits and guides us in the right way. They may be agents to answer prayer, but He is the Prompter and Director of our prayers (Rom. 8:26–27; Jude 20).[3]

Application: Most Christians will never realize how much help and protection they receive from God's angels during their lifetime. Even the apostle Peter didn't comprehend that he was being rescued from prison by an angel *until* he was out on the city street (Acts 12:9–11). He thought it was a vision (v. 9)! If we are children of God, we have the protection of the angels of God.

We, like angels, are created beings. We are ordered not to worship angels, although we might think we should if they reveal themselves to us in their splendor. When the apostle John saw one, he fell to worship the angel. But the angel said, "See *that you do* not *do that!* I am your fellow servant, and of your brethren who have the

[1]Billy Graham, *ANGELS: God's Secret Agents*, Doubleday, Garden City, New York, 1975, pp. 14–15.

[2]John MacArthur, Jr., *God, Satan and Angels*, Word of Grace Communications, Parorama City, California, 1983, p. 163.

[3]C. Fred Dickason, *Angels: Elect & Evil*, Moody Press, Chicago, 1975, p. 101.

testimony of Jesus. Worship God! For the testimony of Jesus is the spirit of prophecy" (Revelation 19:10). All created creatures, including we who are humans, should worship God, just as the angels do.

—John C. Holmes

ANGER

WHAT DOES THE BIBLE SAY ABOUT ANGER?

The Issue: Christians are taught to be kind, loving, and forgiving and to avoid anger, frustration, and resentment. However, the Bible clearly teaches that there are acceptable and unacceptable forms of anger. Knowing when anger is appropriate or inappropriate is a matter of great spiritual discernment and maturity.

Key Bible References:

"Be angry, and do not sin": *do not let the sun go down on your wrath, nor give place to the devil.* Ephesians 4:26–27

The discretion of a man makes him slow to anger, And his glory is *to overlook a transgression.* Proverbs 19:11

"You have heard that it was said to those of old, 'You shall not murder,' *and whoever murders will be in danger of the judgment.*

"But I say to you that whoever is angry with his brother without a cause shall be in danger of the judgment. . . ." Matthew 5:21–22

Additional References: Psalm 7:11; Proverbs 22:24–25, 29:20, 22; Romans 12:18; Galatians 5:20.

What Others Say: Jay E. Adams, Christian Counseling and Education Foundation; Tim LaHaye, President of Family Life Seminars; and James Dobson, founder and president of Focus on the Family.

Jay E. Adams
All sorts of problems arise in the Christian enterprise which may lead to angry feelings, since the body is composed of sinful members. Yet these problems can be solved. Anger need not persist so that it drives new rifts between believers or enlarges old ones. In-

stead there is a way of handling anger. Paul says it must be dealt with daily: "Do not let the sun go down on your anger."[1]

Tim LaHaye

Suppressed anger and bitterness can make a person emotionally upset until he is "not himself." In this state he often makes decisions that are harmful, wasteful or embarrassing. We are intensely emotional creatures, designed so by God, but if we permit anger to dominate us, it will squelch the richer emotion of love. Many a man takes his office grudges and irritations home and unconsciously lets his anger curtail what could be a free-flowing expression of love for his wife and children. Instead of enjoying his family and being enjoyed by them, he allows his mind and emotions to mull over the vexations of the day. Life is too short and our moments at home too brief to pay such a price for anger.[2]

James Dobson

When we sullenly "replay" the agitating event over and over in our minds, grinding our teeth in hostility and seeking opportunity for revenge, or lash out in some overt act of violence, then it is logical to assume that we cross over the line into sinfulness.[3]

Application: The emphasis placed on personal rights by modern society has affected the Christian community. The desire to assert ourselves and debase others is an outgrowth of selfishness. Ventilating our frustrations and anger on others is selfish and denies the dignity which was created in each of us. Christians are to engage in self-control and restraint when dealing with others. Some are more successful than others based on personal temperament and spiritual maturity. The Holy Spirit guides believers as they submit to God's will on a daily basis. God demands obedience in our reactions to the pressures of life.

—Daniel A. Bright

[1]Jay E. Adams, *Competent to Counsel,* Baker Book House, Grand Rapids, Michigan, 1970, p. 220.

[2]Tim LaHaye, *Spirit-Controlled Temperament,* Tyndale House Publishers, Wheaton, Illinois, 1966, p. 71.

[3]Dr. James Dobson, *Dr. James Dobson Answers Your Questions,* Tyndale House Publishers, Wheaton, Illinois, 1982, p. 317.

ASTROLOGY

DO THE STARS RULE OVER OUR LIVES?

The Issue: Since ancient times mankind has held a special fascination for predicting the future. The study of the stars and their influences in the guiding of human affairs has been of intense interest. God's original purpose in creating the stars and placing them in the heavens was so they might give light on earth and be for signs (Genesis 1:14, 17). Satan, however, has twisted this truth and successfully deceived many into believing that the zodiac is to be consulted when making short range and long range plans. This practice is in direct violation of God's command that we are to trust in Him to guide our ways. The Scripture is very clear that it is a sin to practice astrology.

Key Bible References:

"And take heed, lest you lift your eyes to heaven, and when you see the sun, the moon, and the stars, all the host of heaven, you feel driven to worship them and serve them, which the LORD your God has given all the peoples under the whole heaven as a heritage." Deuteronomy 4:19

So they left all the commandments of the LORD their God . . . and worshiped all the host of heaven, and served Baal.

Therefore the LORD was very angry with Israel, and removed them from His sight. . . . II Kings 17:16, 18

Praise Him, sun and moon; praise Him, all you stars of light! Psalm 148:3

Additional References: Genesis 1:16–17; Deuteronomy 17:2–5; II Kings 23:5; Isaiah 47:12–15; Jeremiah 31:35.

What Others Say: Dr. Henry M. Morris, Bible scholar and author.

Henry M. Morris

The term *Mazzaroth* (coming "in his season") is agreed by all scholars to refer to the famous zodiac, with its season-by-season procession of twelve great key signs in the heavens. These signs are certain constellations of stars, with each constellation appearing to an observer on earth to be a number of stars grouped together in an association bearing the name of a certain object. . . . the signs go back to the beginning of history and are essentially the same in all ancient nations. . . . The evidence seems compelling. . . . that the astrological meaning of these signs dates from the rebellion at Babel and its association with the "host of heaven."

. . . .Astrology has, ever since Babel, been associated with pantheism and occultism, and therefore firmly condemned by God, but it was *God* who established these stars in the first place to "be for signs"![1]

Application: God's Word teaches that we are to rely on Him to give us direction for the future as well as for our daily living. Christians should avoid reading horoscopes in the daily newspaper, making references to the signs of the zodiac or assigning any other symbolic attributes to the stars. Satan desires to keep us from seeking God's wisdom and truth, however, this places us in a position of displeasing our Creator.

Christians have the responsibility to speak out boldly against astrology. They must help those who may be deceived into believing that the stars may rule their lives. In the Old Testament, God forbade, condemned and punished the practice of astrology. His views on this subject are still the same!

—Loreen L. Ittermann

ATHEISM

WHAT IS THE CHRISTIAN RESPONSE TO THOSE WHO CLAIM THEY DO NOT BELIEVE IN GOD?

The Issue: We are increasingly facing secular and naturalistic philosophies and world views which either deny the existence of the God Who is revealed in the Bible or of His involvement in the lives of people. Many people, though not theoretical atheists, have become practical atheists—those for whom God is not real in their everyday experience. The affirmation of the Bible is that God has revealed Himself and can be experienced by those who choose to seek Him and to obey Him.

---

[1]Henry M. Morris, *The Long War Against God,* Baker Book House, Grand Rapids, Michigan, 1989, p. 266.

Key Bible References:

The fool has said in his heart, "There is no God." Psalm 14:1

Jesus said to him, "You shall love the LORD your God with all your heart, with all your soul, and with all your mind." Matthew 22:37

"And this is eternal life, that they may know You, the only true God, and Jesus Christ whom You have sent." John 17:3

But without faith it is impossible to please Him, for he who comes to God must believe that He is, and that He is a rewarder of those who diligently seek Him." Hebrews 11:6

Additional References: Job 38:2–3; Psalm 34:8; Proverbs 1:7, 2:1–6; Isaiah 43:10–13; John 1:1–4; Romans 1:18–20, 25.

What Others Say: Francis A. Schaeffer, a great student of the Bible and of man's philosophies and Josh McDowell, who has defended the Christian faith on countless college and university campuses offer the following counsel:

Francis A. Schaeffer

A man can only love a God who exists and who is personal and about whom he has knowledge. So the fact that God has communicated is also of supreme importance.[1]

Josh McDowell

If God is alive today, then one should be able to see His influence in the course of history as well as in individual lives. The account of God's continued influence is seen in fulfilled (Bible) prophecies.[2]

Application: Atheism or knowing God, which will it be? The first step is to consciously commit oneself to the conviction that God truly exists and to seek Him. Not to take this step is to commit oneself to agnosticism or atheism. Next, one must approach the Bible as a revelation from God about Himself, believing that He will reveal Himself to you as you seek Him. In the Bible one will discover Jesus and the eternal life which begins when one comes to know Him (John 17:3).

Committing oneself to God through Christ does not ensure that one will not face doubts, trials, defeats, and the effects of evil. However,

---

[1]Francis A. Schaeffer, *The God Who is There,* Inter-Varsity Press, Downers Grove, Illinois, 1968, p. 147.

[2]Josh McDowell, compiler, *Evidence That Demands a Verdict: Historical Evidences for the Christian Faith,* Campus Crusade for Christ, 1972, p. 275.

as Job ultimately discovered, God will reveal His power and His grace. Then one can say with Job, "I had heard of you by the hearing of the ear, but now my eye sees You" (Job 42:5). As the ancient but relevant psalmist exhorts us: "Taste and see . . ." (Psalm 34:8)—resolve to personally experience God in your life.

—**Raymond E. Martin**

BEAUTY

WHAT DOES THE BIBLE SAY TO THOSE WHO ARE PREOCCUPIED WITH THEIR PHYSICAL APPEARANCE?

The Issue: One of the best examples in the Bible of an individual who was preoccupied with his physical appearance was Absalom, the handsome son of David. The Bible says:

Now in all Israel there was no one who was praised as much as Absalom for his good looks. From the sole of his foot to the crown of his head there was no blemish in him.

And when he cut the hair of his head—at the end of every year he cut it because *it* was heavy on him—when he cut it, he weighed the hair of his head at two hundred shekels [approximately 3 lbs.] according to the king's standard (II Samuel 14:25–26).

Absalom had an enviable position as the King's son. He was popular. He stole the hearts of the people of Israel with his winning personality and his handsome appearance. The Scripture says, "there was no blemish in him." It is ironic that the beautiful hair that adorned Absalom's head ultimately led to his death when his hair became entangled in the branches of a tree. Thankfully, most people preoccupied with their appearance do not reach such an ignoble end. Regrettably, however, many people pay dearly for their vanity.

Key Bible References:

Do not let your beauty be that outward adorning *of arranging the hair, of wearing gold, or of putting on* fine *apparel; but let it be the hidden person of the heart, with the incorruptible ornament of a gentle and quiet spirit, which is very precious in the sight of God.* I Peter 3:3–4

"Therefore I say to you, do not worry about your life, what you will eat or what you will drink; nor about your body, what you will put on. Is not life more than food and the body more than clothing?

"Look at the birds of the air, for they neither sow nor reap nor gather into barns; yet your heavenly Father feeds them. Are you not of more value than they?" Matthew 6:25–26

Charm is deceitful and beauty is vain, but a woman who fears the LORD, she shall be praised. Proverbs 31:30

But the LORD said to Samuel, "Do not look at his appearance or at the height of his stature, because I have refused him. For the LORD does not see as man sees; for man looks at the outward appearance, but the LORD looks at the heart." I Samuel 16:7

Additional References: Ecclesiastes 1:2; I Corinthians 6:19–20; I Timothy 2:9–10.

What Others Say: Charles R. Swindoll, pastor of the Evangelical Free Church in Fullerton, California.

Charles R. Swindoll

Most of us have better sight than insight. There's nothing wrong with our vision; it's perspective that throws us the curve. And that is especially true when it comes to people. We tend to see only the obvious, but we overlook the significant. We focus on the surface while we fail to sense what is deep down inside. It is at this point that we humans are so unlike God.[1]

Application: Christ is our divine mentor in all aspects of Christian living including the way we appear to others. Isaiah, in his prophetic description of Christ, wrote, ". . . He has no form or comeliness; and when we see Him, *there is* no beauty that we should desire Him" (Isaiah 53:2b). In other words Christ's manner of dress, His outward appearance, did not distract from His ministry on earth. The Bible clearly stresses that we are not to be consumed with our outward appearance.

—Sandra Ann Mustin

---

[1]Charles R. Swindoll, *Living on the Ragged Edge,* Word Books, Publishers, Waco, Texas, 1985, p. 53.

BEREAVEMENT

HOW DO CHRISTIANS HANDLE BEREAVEMENT?

The Issue: When one experiences the loss of a loved one in death, one's emotions often turn to grief and loneliness which brings horrendous pain and a flood of tears. Thoughts and feelings of despair and anger may be triggered as a result of this loss.

However, for the Christian no matter how great the loss, God promises to bring comfort through the presence of the Holy Spirit and He promises to provide strength each day.

Key Bible References:

" . . . *for the LORD your God, He is the One who goes with You. He will not leave you nor forsake you.*" Deuteronomy 31:6b

"Let not your heart be troubled; you believe in God, believe also in Me." John 14:1

"I am the resurrection and the life. He who believes in Me, though he may die, he shall live." John 11:25

"And God will wipe away every tear from their eyes; there shall be no more death, nor sorrow, nor crying; there shall be no more pain, for the former things have passed away." Revelation 21:4

Additional References: Psalm 23:66; I Peter 5:7.

What Others Say: Dr. Lawrence J. Crabb, Jr., Christian psychologist and author; Dr. Robert Hemfelt, Dr. Frank Minirth, and Dr. Paul Meier, Christian clinical psychologists from the Minirth-Meier Clinic in Texas; and Dr. Theodore H. Epp, "Back to the Bible" broadcast.

Lawrence J. Crabb, Jr.
If my mind is fixed on the staggering truth that the Sovereign God of the universe loves me and has pledged himself to provide me with everything I need, if I really believe that, then I will sincerely bow my knees in thanksgiving. . . .[1]

---

[1]Lawrence J. Crabb, Jr., *Basic Principles of Biblical Counseling,* Zondervan Corporation, Grand Rapids, Michigan, 1975, p. 67.

Robert Hemfelt, Frank Minirth and Paul Meier

The grief process is built into us, which is reason enough to suggest that it is the way God planned for us to deal with loss, emotional turmoil and pain . . . "Jesus wept" (John 11:35).[2]

Theodore H. Epp

God's gracious purposes toward us persist through all time, even through the most painful trials.[3]

Application: Christians experiencing bereavement have the same emotions and loss as non-believers. However, a believer's response to bereavement is often quite different from unbelievers. After the shock, denial, anger, depression and sadness, the Christian should come to the final stage of forgiveness, resolution and acceptance. At that moment, the Christian accepts God's provision of love, joy, and peace through Jesus Christ for his or her body, mind and spirit. These fruits of the Holy Spirit accelerate the healing process through the bereavement period.

"Peace I leave with you, My peace I give to you; not as the world gives do I give to you. Let not your heart be troubled, neither let it be afraid" (John 14:27).

—Alex Ward

THE BIBLE

SHOULD CHRISTIANS BE BIBLE DEPENDENT?

The Issue: Non-Christians often accuse Christians of using the Bible as a crutch, implying that they are weak and not capable of standing on their own. The issue of Bible dependency by Christians brings humanism head-to-head with Christianity. The humanist community believes there is no higher authority, no greater source of strength, than man himself. He is, and should be, self-sufficient. Christians believe that man *is* weak and that acknowledging one's own human weakness is the first step toward receiving Christ as personal Savior, and a life of total dependency on the authority of God's Word, the Bible.

---

[2]Robert Hemfelt; Frank Minirth; Paul Meier, *Love is a Choice—Recovery for Co-Dependent Relationships,* Thomas Nelson Publishers, Nashville, Tennessee, 1989, p. 232.

[3]Theodore H. Epp, *Job, a Man Tried as Gold,* Back to the Bible broadcast publication, Lincoln, Nebraska, 1967, p. 194.

Key Bible References:

"All flesh is as grass, and all the glory of man as the flower of the grass. The grass withers, and its flower falls away.

"But the word of the LORD endures forever." I Peter 1:24–25

"Sanctify them by Your truth. Your word is truth." John 17:17

For this reason we also thank God without ceasing, because when you received the word of God which you heard from us, you welcomed it not as the word of men, but as it is in truth, the word of God, which also effectively works in you who believe. I Thessalonians 2:13

Additional References: Psalm 119; John 8:32; II Timothy 3:14–16; II Peter 1:19–21.

What Others Say: Charles R. Swindoll, pastor of the Evangelical Free Church in Fullerton, California; and Dr. Paul Feinberg, professor of Systematic Theology at Trinity Evangelical Seminary in Deerfield, Illinois.

Charles R. Swindoll

If I could have only one wish for God's people, it would be that all of us would return to the Word of God, that we would realize once and for all that His Book has the answers. The Bible IS the authority, the final resting place of our cares, our worries, our griefs, our tragedies, our sorrows, and our surprises. It is the final answer to our questions, our search. Turning back to the Scriptures will provide something that nothing else on the entire earth will provide.[1]

Paul Feinberg

Inerrancy means that when all facts are known, the Scriptures, in their original autographs and properly interpreted, will be shown to be wholly true in everything that they affirm, whether that has to do with doctrine or morality or with the social, physical, or life sciences. . . .[2]

Application: There are essentially two kinds of people in the world—those who believe in the inerrancy and complete authority of the Scriptures, and those who do not. Those who do not believe in the Bible place their trust in themselves and the general wisdom of man, or in a false deity. God's claim that His words as recorded in

---

[1]Charles R. Swindoll, *Growing Deep in the Christian Life,* Multnomah Press, Portland, Oregon, 1986, p. 56.

[2]Paul Feinberg, "The Meaning of Inerrancy," *Inerrancy,* Norman Geisler, Editor, Zondervan Publishers, Grand Rapids, Michigan, 1980, p. 294.

the Scriptures are absolutely true, represents an issue that cannot be ignored. People the world over have a major choice to make, with eternal consequences. Bible-dependent Christians have obviously opted to believe in Jesus Christ and the authority of God's Word.

—**Paul A. Kienel**

BORROWING

WHAT DOES THE BIBLE SAY ABOUT BORROWING?

The Issue: Is it right for a Christian to go into debt? Can Christians borrow money and remain in the will of God? Jesus and the apostles say very little about borrowing. What standard should the Christian use when borrowing money?

Key Bible References:

"If you lend money to any *of My people* who *are poor among you, you shall not be like a moneylender to him; you shall not charge him interest."* Exodus 22:25

The rich rules over the poor, and the borrower is *servant to the lender.* Proverbs 22:7

"Give to him who asks you, and from him who wants to borrow from you do not turn away." Matthew 5:42

Additional References: Deuteronomy 15:1–3; Matthew 18:23–35; Luke 7:41–43, 16:1–12; I Corinthians 16:2.

What Others Say: Dr. Gene A. Getz, senior pastor, Fellowship Bible Church North, Plano, Texas and adjunct teacher in pastoral studies at Dallas Theological Seminary.

Gene A. Getz
Several guidelines will help us to avoid irresponsible decisions that lead us to sin against God.
- We are out of God's will when we borrow money to buy things to glorify ourselves and not God (Matthew 6:3–4).
- We are out of God's will when we borrow because we are in bondage to materialism (Matthew 6:24), when our treasures are on earth rather than in heaven.

- We are out of God's will when any form of dishonesty is involved in borrowing money (I Timothy 6:10).
- We are out of God's will when we use borrowed money to achieve any goals that are out of the will of God (Romans 12:1–2).[1]

Application: We are to be faithful stewards of material possessions as a sacred trust from God. Therefore the way in which we handle our money is a reflection of our faithfulness to God. If we owe money, we should pay what we owe. In addition, we are to pay whatever we owe, whether it be love and good works, taxes to the government, or the firstfruit offering from our labor. Our responsibility is to utilize God's trust in a prudent and responsible way.

When we borrow we place ourselves in a certain amount of bondage. This may limit our ability to respond to the call of God. It may also limit our ability to put God first since we are bound to fulfill our obligations to creditors. And we may be limited in our ability to give to God's work on a regular, systematic, and proportional basis.

The economy of the New Testament world was highly integrated with financial dealings that involved indebtedness. We should be on guard against rationalization while living in an affluent society. Material possessions should be used to further the kingdom of God. The way we use our material possessions is an important criterion for determining whether or not we are living in the will of God.

—**Stephen E. Burris**

BURNOUT

WHAT IS THE BIBLE'S ANSWER TO EMOTIONAL BURNOUT?

The Issue: Burnout has been defined as a state of physical or psychological exhaustion that is related to chronic unrelieved pressures.[1] It may be described as a loss of enthusiasm, energy, perspective,

---

[1]Gene A. Getz, *Real Prosperity: Biblical Principles of Material Possessions,* Moody Press, Chicago, Illinois, 1990, p. 139.

---

[1]Keith W. Sehnert, M.D., *Stress/Unstress,* Augsburg Publishing House, Minneapolis, Minnesota, 1981, p. 55.

and purpose. Burnout results from stress that goes "unchecked" for an extended period of time. It is best characterized as a feeling of extreme weariness and hopelessness.

Key Bible References:

Therefore I hated life because the work that was done under the sun was distressing to me, for all is vanity and grasping for the wind.

Then I hated all my labor in which I had toiled under the sun, because I must leave it to the man who will come after me.

And who knows whether he will be wise or a fool? Yet he will rule over all my labor in which I toiled and in which I have shown myself wise under the sun. This also is vanity.

Therefore I turned my heart and despaired of all the labor in which I had toiled under the sun.

For there is a man whose labor is with wisdom, knowledge, and skill; yet he must leave his heritage to a man who has not labored for it. This also is vanity and a great evil.

For what has man for all his labor, and for striving of his heart with which he has toiled under the sun?

For all his days are sorrowful, and his work burdensome; even in the night his heart takes no rest. This also is vanity. Ecclesiastes 2:17–23

He gives power to the weak, and to those who have no might He increases strength.

But those who wait on the LORD shall renew their strength; they shall mount up with wings like eagles, they shall run and not be weary, they shall walk and not faint. Isaiah 40:29, 31

"Come to Me, all you who labor and are heavy laden, and I will give you rest." Matthew 11:28

And let us not grow weary while doing good, for in due season we shall reap if we do not lose heart. Galatians 6:9

Additional References: Psalm 69:1–3; Proverbs 23:4; Ecclesiastes 12:2.

What Others Say: Frank Minirth, M.D., psychiatrist; Don Hawkins, executive producer; Paul Meier, M.D., psychiatrist; Richard Flournoy, Ph.D., psychologist; and Lloyd J. Ogilvie, pastor and author.

Frank Minirth   **Don Hawkins**
Paul Meier   **Richard Flournoy**

Too much stress and burnout affect the whole person—physically, emotionally, and spiritually. Physical symptoms can include anything from ulcers and digestive upsets to coronary problems. Often a burnout victim experiences a constant sense of fatigue, coupled with an inability to sleep. Emotionally, a burnout victim often suffers from depression. That results from being angry with oneself because of an inability to function at one's previous high performance level. Spiritually, burnout victims often reflect . . . extreme anxiety over proving one's self-worth by serving God and others.[2]

Even though circumstances may have our "face in the dust," when we focus beyond our circumstances we will be able to say, "I have hope." Although the characteristics of burnout may vary in intensity and combination, although they may be cyclical or progressive, although they may come over weeks, months, or even years—whatever the case—through focusing on God and hoping in Him, burnout can be reversed.[3]

Lloyd J. Ogilvie

Some of us have the idea that our worth is related to how much we do. But we can never do enough to fill that bottomless pit of trying to earn our self-esteem. Then, some of us have the attitude that no one can do the job right except us. And the most defeating of all is trying to live on our own strength without allowing God to help us.[4]

I've never known a person to have a nervous breakdown doing what the Lord wills. He never asks us to do more than He is willing to provide strength for us to do. He does not guide us into a burnout.[5]

Application: The result of burnout is that the person no longer can produce effectively and no longer enjoys what he or she is doing. This is caused by taking on too much for the wrong reasons. The burned out person may ask: "Why am I doing all this? Who cares as much as I do? Is what I'm doing making any difference? Who am I trying to impress with all this? Who cares?" These are questions we ask when we lose track of why we are doing so much, when the results seem minimal.[6]

---

[2]Frank Minirth, M.D., Don Hawkins, Th.M., Paul Meier, M.D., and Richard Flournoy, Ph.D., *How to Beat Burnout,* Moody Press, Chicago, Illinois, 1986, p. 16.

[3]Ibid., p. 141.

[4]Lloyd J. Ogilvie, *Making Stress Work for You,* Word Books, Publishers, Waco, Texas, 1984, p. 115.

[5]Ibid., p. 131.

[6]Ibid., p. 119.

The solution is not just doing less, but doing the right things for the right reasons. It's having the freedom to say "yes" to some things and "no" to others because we have a clear understanding of our central goal.[7]

God has given us sufficient time to do the things He wants us to do. We must be realistic in our assessment of the things that consume our time and energy. Every Christian should determine priorities based on God's will for his or her life. James 4:15 summarizes it well with these words: ". . . you *ought* to say, 'If the Lord wills, we shall live and do this or that.'"

—**Jerry L. Haddock**

BUSINESS

WHAT IS THE BIBLICAL ETHIC OF BUSINESS?

The Issue: Our society places a great emphasis on taking care of yourself and getting ahead in life. Scripture places the emphasis on faithfulness, carefulness, and diligence. The challenge is for the Christian to be trustworthy, his mind set on God.

Key Bible References:

"So he called ten of his servants, delivered to them ten minas, and said to them, 'Do business till I come.'

"But his citizens hated him, and sent a delegation after him, saying, 'We will not have this man *to reign over us.'*

"And so it was that when he returned, having received the kingdom, he then commanded these servants, to whom he had given the money, to be called to him, that he might know how much every man had gained by trading." Luke 19:13–15

Additional References: Matthew 6:19–21, 19:16–26, 20:1–16, 25:14–30; Philippians 4:19; I Timothy 6:17–19.

What Others Say: Dr. David W. Gill, president of New College Berkeley.

---

[7]Ibid., p. 121.

David W. Gill
A business entrepreneur who develops habits of holistic, unified thinking, may well leave society, neighbors and the next generation much better off; he or she would be inclined to consider environmental impact, long-term consequences, and so on—not just a short-term marketing strategy aiming at maximum profits.[1]

Application: The standard for the Christian business stands in stark contrast to the cut-throat rat-race environment in which it must operate. The high premium that is placed on personal freedom is contrasted with the servant's heart. The Bible is clear that the businessman is to treat his Christian employees as brothers in Christ.

In addition, the Christian ethic of business is one of fairness and integrity. There is no place for making a profit or padding the bottom line by defrauding or exploiting others. In contrast to greed the Bible talks about diligence, generosity, peace, happiness, love, and satisfaction.

There is nothing anti-Christian about prosperity. The Bible emphasis is equally on the means and the ends. There is to be no compromise on biblical standards in order to gain prosperity.

—Stephen E. Burris

BUSYBODIES

WHAT DOES THE BIBLE SAY ABOUT BUSYBODIES?

The Issue: The tools of the busybody's trade are gossip, negative reports, slander and resentment. With an ungrateful, judgmental spirit he tries to do the Lord's work for Him, and the results can be disastrous. His discontent, habit of taking up the offenses of others and desire to get even are like a poison within any group of people, and he leaves a path of confusion, misunderstanding and hurt behind him. The busybody assumes rights he does not have and gets into the middle of situations where he does not belong. God reminds

---

[1]David W. Gill, *The Opening of the Christian Mind,* Inter-Varsity Press, Downers Grove, Illinois, 1989, p. 29.

us that we are to be busy in well-doing, stirring up peace rather than bitterness!

Key Bible References:

For we hear that there are some who walk among you in a disorderly manner, not working at all, but are busybodies. II Thessalonians 3:11

And besides they learn to be *idle, wandering about from house to house; and not only idle, but gossips also and busybodies, saying things which they ought not.* I Timothy 5:13

But let none of you suffer as a murderer, a thief, an evildoer, or as a busybody in other people's matters. I Peter 4:15

Additional References: Proverbs 15:2; Romans 12:17–19; Hebrews 12:14–15; James 3:6, 8, 13–18; I Peter 2:21–24.

What Others Say: Charles R. Swindoll, pastor and prolific writer.

Charles R. Swindoll

Information is powerful. The person who receives it and dispenses it bit by bit often does so that others might be impressed because he or she is "in the know." Few things are more satisfying to the old ego than having others stare wide-eyed, drop open the jaw, and say, "My, I didn't know that!" or "Why, that's hard to believe!" or "How in the world did you find that out?"

From now on, let's establish four practical ground rules:
(1) Whatever you're told in confidence, do not repeat.
(2) Whenever you're tempted to talk, do not yield.
(3) Whenever you're discussing people, do not gossip.
(4) However you're prone to disagree, do not slander.[1]

Application: There is no place for gossip, slander, or backbiting within the Christian life. The destructive potential of these negative habits is so great that God lists busybodies in Scripture along with murderers, thieves and evil-doers. The busybody needs to grow up and stop gossiping about others. He needs to realize that vengeance and judgment belong to the Lord, and that by controlling his tongue he learns to control his whole body.

---

[1]Charles R. Swindoll, *Come before Winter and . . . Share My Hope,* Tyndale House Publishers, Inc., Wheaton, Illinois, 1985, pp. 137–139.

If only the busybody could realize that the Lord has a wonderful plan which He is accomplishing through difficult situations! If only he could enlarge his view of God's work and power, perhaps he would stop meddling in the Holy Spirit's business.

Under what condition is the busybody most tempted to wrongdoing? It is idleness! What is the best remedy for tale-bearing and gossiping? It is staying so active serving and showing mercy to others that there isn't time to meddle in the affairs of others.

—Gary and Andra Foss

CAPITAL PUNISHMENT

WHAT DOES THE BIBLE SAY ABOUT CAPITAL PUNISHMENT?

The Issue: Those issues that involve life and death are perhaps the most serious ethical problems. Unfortunately they also tend to be the very issues over which there is the most intense disagreement. This is especially true of capital punishment. There are sincere Christians on both sides of this issue claiming biblical support. Still others would prefer not to think about such a controversial issue. This is not a responsible attitude when we consider that any one of us might someday be on a jury dealing with a capital case.

Key Bible References:

"He who strikes a man so that he dies shall surely be put to death." Exodus 21:12

". . . then you shall bring out to your gates that man or woman who has committed that wicked thing, and shall stone to death that man or woman with stones." Deuteronomy 17:5

Beloved, do not avenge yourselves, but rather *give place to wrath; for it is written,* "Vengeance is Mine, I will repay," *says the Lord.* Romans 12:19

For he is God's minister to you for good. But if you do evil, be afraid; for he does not bear the sword in vain; for he is God's minister, an avenger to execute *wrath on him who practices evil.* Romans 13:4

Additional References: Genesis 4:15; Exodus 21:22–23; Leviticus 17:11; Deuteronomy 13:6–10, 19:16–21, 32:35; Matthew 5:17–18; John 19:11; Acts 25:11; Ephesians 2:15.

What Others Say: Dr. Norman L. Geisler, dean of the Liberty Center for Christian Scholarship, Liberty University.

Norman L. Geisler

There are three basic views on capital punishment held by Christians: rehabilitationism, reconstructionism, and retributionism. Rehabilitationism opposes capital punishment for any crime. Reconstructionism insists on capital punishment for all major crimes, whether moral or religious. Retributionism holds that capital punishment is appropriate for some crimes, namely, capital offenses.

Rehabilitationism is based on a remedial (reformatory) view of justice. The criminal is seen as a patient who is sick in need of treatment. The other two views believe that justice is retributive. They view the criminal as a morally responsible person who deserves punishment. Retributionism differs from reconstructionism in that the former does not believe that the offenses calling for capital punishment under Moses' law are still binding today. Rather, retributionism contends that capital punishment is based on the biblically stated principle of a life for a life that is applicable to all persons in all places and all times.[1]

Application: Some claim that the sanctity of human life prohibits capital punishment. In fact, the principle of the sanctity of human life is the very thing that establishes the priority of the death penalty. This is why murder is so heinous: The murderer destroys the life of another. Human life is so sacred that whoever murders another forfeits his own right to live; this is the just punishment for his crime. A lesser punishment is less than just.

Capital punishment, like any other civil punishment, should and will be a deterrent if justly, swiftly, and openly applied.

An objection is that capital punishment is wrong because it cannot be administered fairly; at times even an innocent person might be killed. True, perfect administration may not be possible, but it is not necessary if certain safeguards are followed. Besides, this is not an argument against capital punishment as such, but against poor administration of it.

---

[1]Norman L. Geisler, *Christian Ethics Options and Issues,* Baker Book House, Grand Rapids, Michigan, 1989, p. 213.

A heavy responsibility lies upon lawmakers and law-enforcers. Each Christian must determine who to vote for based upon a candidate's stand for or against capital punishment. Who will represent a biblical perspective on human life, punishment, and a crime worthy of death?

—Stephen E. Burris

CHEATING

WHAT DOES THE BIBLE SAY ABOUT CHEATING?

The Issue: Cheating is the act or practice of dishonesty. It is the willful disregard of the law or rules, stated or morally determined, for one's personal gain or advancement. The new Webster's dictionary states, "one cheats by direct and gross falsehood." Also, a cheat is "a deceiver, a swindler." Cheating involves lying ("What I am doing is honest and proper"), and stealing (improperly and dishonestly obtaining that which is not one's own), and is, therefore, in complete opposition to God's biblical standards of truth and personal behavior. Simply stated, cheating is sin.

Key Bible References:

"You shall not steal, nor deal falsely, nor lie to one another.

"You shall not defraud your neighbor, nor rob him.

"You shall do not injustice in judgment, in measurement of length, weight, or volume.

"You shall have just balances, just weights. . . ." Leviticus 19:11, 13a, 35–36a

A false balance is *an abomination to the* LORD, *but a just weight* is *His delight.* Proverbs 11:1.

Lying lips are *an abomination to the* LORD, *but those who deal truthfully* are *His delight.* Proverbs 12:22

Additional References: Proverbs 16:11, 20:23, 21:6; Jeremiah 17:11; Ezekiel 45:10.

What Others Say: Charles Colson, Christian philosopher and author; and Erwin W. Lutzer (quoting Keith Miller).

Charles Colson

(When sin is in control) . . . there are no moral absolutes, there are no value-associated reasons to make one decision over another. We may as readily choose to ignore a neighbor rather than help him, to cheat rather than be honest . . .

Gone are any notions of duty to our fellow man and to the Creator. As a result, there is no straight edge of truth by which one can measure one's life. Truth is pliable and relative; it can take whatever shape we want.[1]

Erwin W. Lutzer

"Sin is the universal addiction to self that develops when individuals put themselves in the center of their personal world in a way that leads to abuse of others . . . Sin causes sinners to seek instant gratification, to be first, and to get more than their share now."[2]

Application: The difficulties generated by the decline of moral virtue and the increase of moral relativism (resulting in the "it all depends" philosophy of situation ethics) certainly include cheating! As society's moral standards have lowered, cheating has become a major problem—even affecting the Christian community. Not uncommon are: cadets suspended from military academies for cheating on exams; the savings and loan industry "collapse" because of illegal insider deals; tele-evangelists' fall because of dishonesty—cheating, moral and financial. Cheating is clearly a problem of putting one's self at the center of one's own values and priorities. Charles Swindoll agrees: "Don't forget our depraved track record: cheating on exams, taking a towel from a hotel, not working a full eight hours, bold-face lies and half-truths, exaggerated statements, hedging on reports of losses covered by insurance companies, broken financial promises, domestic deceit, and (dare I mention) ye olde I.R.S. reports we sign as being the truth."[3]

The Bible gives a clear solution: "These *are* the things you shall do: Speak each man the truth to his neighbor; give judgment in your gates for truth, justice, and peace . . . And do not love a false oath." Zechariah 8:16–17b. God's people must resolve to obey God and pattern themselves after God's way—the Truth.

–Paul M. House

---

[1]Charles Colson, *Against the Night,* Servant Publications, Ann Arbor, Michigan, 1989, pp. 39, 41.

[2]Erwin W. Lutzer, *Putting Your Past Behind You,* Here's Life Publishers, San Bernadino, California, 1990, p. 63.

[3]Charles R. Swindoll, *The Quest for Character,* Multnomah Press, Portland, Oregon, 1987, p. 70.

CHILD ABUSE

WHAT DO THE SCRIPTURES SAY ABOUT CHILD ABUSE?

The Issue: There is no universally accepted definition of child abuse. In its broadest interpretation, child abuse is defined as any intentional physical, emotional, or sexual injury or neglect (including abduction) of a child by an adult.

The occurrence of child abuse among school-age children is estimated to be as many as two million incidences per year in the United States.[1] Many abusers were themselves victims of child abuse. All states have laws requiring educators to report suspected abuse to civil authorities.

Key Bible References:

Let all bitterness, wrath, anger, clamor, and evil speaking be put away from you, with all malice.

And be kind to one another, tenderhearted, forgiving one another, just as God in Christ also has forgiven you. Ephesians 4:31–32

And you, fathers, do not provoke your children to wrath, but bring them up in the training and admonition of the Lord. Ephesians 6:4

Additional References: Psalm 127:3a; Isaiah 54:13.

What Others Say: Dr. Clyde M. Narramore, founder and president of the Narramore Christian Foundation and Christian psychologist.

Clyde M. Narramore

As children grow up, there are basic emotional needs such as feeling loved and feeling worthwhile. If these are not met, a person enters adulthood with negative feelings inside himself. The Bible says that if a child is raised by a father who is angry, the child will grow up with a snare to his own soul (hangups of the personality) (Proverbs 22:24–25). Many people who show violence and abuse in their homes are ones who were raised where basic emotional needs were never met. THEREFORE THEY ARE ANGRY. This anger erupts in violence and abuse of their own children.[1]

---

[1]Clyde M. Narramore, *Violence and Abuse in the Home,* Narramore Christian Foundation, Rosemead, California, 1978, p. 10.

Through the years, many children who have been abused, have found great strength and comfort from an understanding neighbor, Sunday school teacher or some other adult who encouraged the child to talk and understand why his folks have acted as they have. If a child can get a perspective as to why his parents are hostile and abusive, it will help tremendously. Instead of "absorbing" the hurt, the child can <u>understand</u> the dynamics, and feel differently about the condition.[2]

Application: Christians live in an increasingly violent and secular society. While the Bible counsels that discipline is to be part of child rearing, there are those who may misinterpret balanced correction to be abusive. A note of caution is appropriate. Discipline <u>can</u> be abusive if excessive and/or if it is administered in anger.

Children are a godly heritage, divine gifts from a loving God. Christians need to handle these young lives as stewards with loving care and reverence. They are to be nurtured, supported, and treated with affection in a warm and caring environment. To use them as objects of self-gratification as in sexual abuse is sin. Likewise, to vent one's own anger and frustration through physical or emotional injury is contrary to the Word of God.

Adults who are abusers should seek professional help from trained godly counselors. Many larger churches have psychologists on staff who will be able to assist the believer in finding the help they need. The sooner help is found, the sooner the answer will come.

—**Raymond E. White**

CHILDREN

WHAT IS THE BIBLICAL ROLE OF CHILDREN TO THEIR PARENTS?

The Issue: God has a design for the Christian family which gives authority and responsibilities to each member. When each member properly carries out Biblical responsibilities, the family will be internally healthy and able to be a productive building block in society. Unless families are strong, churches, civil governments, and

---

[2]Ibid., p. 21.

vocational institutions will reflect family weaknesses, and society as a whole will suffer. One consequence of the unbiblical exercise of family responsibilities is that other institutions, especially the civil state, will tend to assume responsibilities belonging to family members.

Children have responsibilities in the family that work in harmony with spousal and parental responsibilities. While the nature of a child's role toward parents changes over time, it continues for a lifetime. Initially, the child should respond to godly parental guidance with honor, respect, love, submission, and obedience. In a sense, the child is to cooperate with a parent's responsibility to lead the child into Christian maturity. The responsible child's role fundamentally serves his own interests as his development toward adulthood brings great satisfaction and joy to his parents. When the mature child leaves parental authority to cleave unto a spouse and develop a new extension of the family, honor, respect, and love for parents is a continuing responsibility. Finally, when parents develop a need for economic and emotional support in their elderly years, the child is to appropriately respond in the same manner that he would want his own children to respond to his needs when elderly.

Key Bible References:

Children, obey your parents in the Lord, for this is right.

"Honor your father and mother," which is the first commandment with promise: "that it may be well with you and you may live long on the earth." And you, fathers, do not provoke your children to wrath, but bring them up in the training and admonition of the Lord. Ephesians 6:1–4

"Cursed is the one who treats his father or his mother with contempt." And all the people shall say, "Amen!" Deuteronomy 27:16

My son, hear the instruction of your father, and do not forsake the law of your mother;

My son, if sinners entice you, do not consent.

My son, do not walk in the way with them, keep your foot from their path. . . . Proverbs 1:8, 10, 15

But if any widow has children or grandchildren, let them first learn to show piety at home and to repay their parents; for this is good and acceptable before God. I Timothy 5:4

Additional References: Exodus 20:12, 21:15; Leviticus 19:32; Deuteronomy 5:16; Ruth 2:11, 4:15; Proverbs 2:1–22, 4:1–7, 8:32–33, 17:6, 25, 19:13a, 26–27, 23:22–26; Micah 7:6; Malachi 1:6; Mark 7:9–13; John 19:26–27.

What Others Say: Gerald Regier, past president of the Family Research Council in Washington, D.C.

Gerald Regier

The rewards of Christian parenting are not in the momentary pleasures sought by so many in our society, but in the privilege of passing on God's love to our children and our children's children, and the privilege of producing godly children who will be productive and creative citizens in society.

My own grandfather illustrates this well. At thirty-five, he came to know the Lord in a little rural church in Oklahoma. He then decided that following Christ meant a change in lifestyle and priorities. He shut down the homemade whisky still, and said to the family, "We're going to follow the Lord." At his funeral almost sixty years later, all of his six children and twenty grandchildren were following the Lord. He left a godly heritage which can be a blessing to society rather than a drain on society.[1]

Application: Children who accept their responsibilities to grow to Christian maturity by honoring, respecting, loving, and submissively obeying their parents bring joy to their parents and cause others no harm. Rebellious fools can ruin the peaceful and productive atmosphere of the home, generate a juvenile criminal justice system, and carry irresponsibility into adulthood. Children who despise parental counsel after leaving home, or depart from the biblical principles taught during childhood, deprive their own children of the training they should receive. When children fail to provide emotional and economic support to parents as necessary, the inefficient civil state attempts to assume the child's responsibility through various welfare schemes, and society again suffers because children fail to carry out their biblical life-long role to parents.

—Robert L. Grete

---

[1]Gerald Regier, "Society's Attitude Toward Children," quoted in *Parents and Children,* edited by Jay Kesler, Ron Beers and LaVonne Neff, Victor Books, Wheaton, Illinois, 1986, p. 41.

CHILDREN

HOW SHOULD CHILDREN BE TRAINED?

The Issue: Educators disagree sharply about the philosophy, purposes, objectives, content, and methods of education. The reason is that education is an art, not a science. Nonchristian educators reject the Christian philosophy of education, which is based on truth revealed by God in nature, in the Bible, and in Jesus Christ. They view man as a higher form of animal life and that children can be conditioned to think and act properly.

The Bible teaches that children are precious in the sight of God and are God's gift to their parents. Created in the image of God, they have minds, emotions, and wills. They are more than natural bodies, for they have souls and spirits as well. The Bible affirms Christian learning by instructing children, setting a Christian example for them, and providing consistent discipline in love.

Key Bible References:

"Hear, O Israel: The LORD our God, the LORD is one!

"You shall love the LORD your God with all your heart, with all your soul, and with all your might.

"And these words which I command you today shall be in your heart; you shall teach them diligently to your children, . . ." Deuteronomy 6:4–7a

Train up a child in the way he should go, and when he is old he will not depart from it. Proverbs 22:6

And you, fathers, do not provoke your children to wrath, but bring them up in the training and admonition of the Lord. Ephesians 6:4

"A disciple is not above his teacher, but everyone who is perfectly trained will be like his teacher." Luke 6:40

Additional References: Proverbs 1:7; I Corinthians 11:1; Philippians 4:9; Hebrews 12:11.

What Others Say: Mrs. Jane Schimmer, educational consultant, Trinity Christian Academy, Dallas, Texas; Dr. Kenneth O. Gangel, chairman of the Christian Education Department, Dallas Theological Seminary, Dallas, Texas and Dr. Warren S. Benson, vice president of Academic Administration, Trinity Evangelical Divinity School, Deerfield, Illinois; and Dr. James Dobson, president of Focus on the Family, Pomona, California.

Jane Schimmer

From the earliest times when Moses instructed fathers to teach their sons "by the way," the example of the teacher and the message seemed inextricably intertwined. The Abrahamic Covenant showed the responsibility of each Hebrew to educate his family about God and His ways.[1]

Kenneth O. Gangel and Warren S. Benson

But how was the obligation to be communicated? . . . Perhaps it survived because that most crucial of all educational elements—aim, or objective—was never distorted or diminished in the minds of Hebrew parents. Theirs was the task of training the next generation, and failure in that task would not be taken lightly by the God who had called them to it.

Hebrew education always placed the vertical before the horizontal, relating man to God before concerning itself with the human level.[2]

James Dobson

Respectful and responsible children result from families where the proper combination of love and discipline is present. Both these ingredients must be applied in the necessary quantities.[3]

Application: Training children according to the Bible involves teaching by word and example, as well as consistent discipline. When Solomon declared that parents were to "train up a child in the way he should go," it was in the context of teaching spiritual truth and encouraging godly living (Proverbs 22:6). Jesus valued teaching by example and made it clear that "everyone who is perfectly trained will be like his teacher" (Luke 6:40b). When parents provide discipline, it is "in love" and for the purposes of correcting children and teaching them to do that which is pleasing to God. Training children in this way is much more rewarding than teaching dogs to obey!

—Robert W. Siemens

---

[1]Jane Schimmer, *Mate, Mother, Teacher, Me,* Association of Christian Schools International, Whittier, California, 1985, p. 59.

[2]Kenneth O. Gangel and Warren S. Benson, *Christian Education: Its History and Philosophy,* Moody Press, Chicago, Illinois, 1983, pp. 22, 20.

[3]James Dobson, *Dare to Discipline,* Tyndale Press, Wheaton, Illinois, 1981, p. 11.

CHRISTIAN COLLEGES

WHAT IS THE BIBLICAL BASIS FOR CHRISTIAN COLLEGES AND UNIVERSITIES?

The Issue: A significant segment of contemporary society sees little or no need for private education, and especially Christian schools. These opponents of Christian education contend that a single, uniform system is the greatest assurance of quality education. But Christian parents and educators respond that the most important element of quality—moral and biblical instruction—is omitted from a secular education. Furthermore, the academic quality in Christian schools, from elementary through university levels, is in many instances equal or superior to that of secular schools.

Key Bible References:

"Gather the people together, men and women and little ones, and the stranger who is within your gates, that they may hear and that they may learn to fear the LORD your God and carefully observe all the words of this law, and that their children, who have not known it, may hear and learn to fear the LORD your God as long as you live in the land. . . ." Deuteronomy 31:12–13

But solid food belongs to those who are of full age, that is, those who by reason of use have their senses exercised to discern both good and evil.

Therefore, leaving the discussion of the elementary principles *of Christ, let us go on to perfection, not laying again the foundation of repentance from dead works and of faith toward God. . . .* Hebrews 5:14, 6:1

Additional References: I Corinthians 2:6–16; Philippians 4:8–9; Colossians 1:9–10.

What Others Say: J. Edwin Orr; Joel A. Carpenter and Kenneth W. Shipps; and Robert W. Pazmiño.

J. Edwin Orr

Some today consider the Christian college with students numbered in the hundreds as a back number. It is wise to recall that in the United States, as in other countries, there was a time when all higher education, not to mention elementary education, consisted of such Christian colleges with student bodies in the hundreds. The Christian college has no need to apologize for its existence. It was the pioneer.[1]

Joel A. Carpenter and Kenneth W. Shipps

These colleges have a unique strength, however, in their commitment to engender a distinctly Christian worldview in their students and communities. This stands out in contrast to trends elsewhere, as a variety of critics have accused contemporary higher education of failing at the most critical of its cultural tasks, the transmission of a coherent set of values. Evangelical scholars, after several generations of second-class academic citizenship, are thus growing more confident now that their thoughts about seeking, importing, and living the truth may be of interest to the larger world of higher learning.[2]

Robert W. Pazmiño

Christian educators discern the readiness of students and teachers to deal with the various areas of the Christian faith selected for teaching. Chronological age and spiritual maturity are factors to consider. A sense of timing is important in relation to previous and anticipated learnings and in relation to unanticipated events.[3]

Application: Christian education begins in the home, continues in the church and church school, and is advanced in the halls of Christian higher education. In this age of secular humanism, the importance of Christian higher education becomes particularly momentous. Paying the cost of Christian education often represents a double payment for Christian parents who must support public education and then pay tuition at a Christian school. But no price is too high to keep our youth in the Church. Losing them to the world through exposure to secular education underscores the high value of a soul (Mark 8:36).

—Zenas J. Bicket

---

[1]J. Edwin Orr, *Campus Aflame,* Regal Books, G/L Publications, Glendale, California, 1971, p. 1.

[2]Joel A. Carpenter and Kenneth W. Shipps, editors, "Preface," *Making Higher Education Christian: the History and Mission of Evangelical Colleges in America,* Wm. B. Eerdmans Publishing Co., Grand Rapids, Michigan, 1987, pp. xii–xiii.

[3]Robert W. Pazmiño, *Foundational Issues in Christian Education,* Baker Book House, Grand Rapids, Michigan, 1988, p. 208.

CHRISTIAN SCHOOL EDUCATION

WHAT IS THE BIBLICAL BASE FOR CHRISTIAN SCHOOLS?

The Issue: Secular means "without God." Secular education means "knowledge without God." In sharp contrast, Christian education is "knowledge with God." The failure to mention or to teach subjects without God and His standards is to separate truth and education. It gives the idea that God isn't important and His standards are optional. It divides knowledge into sacred and secular sections. This is clearly a very dangerous way of producing a society who does not understand the role of truth and knowledge . . . however, the Bible teaches very strongly that students are to be taught knowledge based on God's truth and standards. All individuals are made by Him and the purpose of life is to live by the standards as written in the Bible. Successful education is totally based on the Word of God and then to have it reinforced daily in each subject by staff who openly live their lives based on the Christian truths they teach. Christian students do not become stronger Christians by leaving God out of education. Education and God must be together. Christian education brings the two together.

Key Bible References:

"Sanctify them by Your truth. Your word is truth." John 17:17

"And these words which I command you today shall be in your heart; you shall teach them diligently to your children, and shall talk of them when you sit in your house, when you walk by the way, when you lie down, and when you rise up." Deuteronomy 6:6–7

The law of the LORD is perfect, converting the soul; the testimony of the LORD is sure, making wise the simple; the statutes of the LORD are right, rejoicing the heart; the commandment of the LORD is pure, enlightening the eyes. Psalm 19:7–8

Additional References: Psalm 78:1–8; Proverbs 19:27; I Corinthians 1:17–25; Colossians 2:3, 8; II Timothy 2:15–17a.

What Others Say: Tim LaHaye, founder and president of Family Life Seminars, pastor, founder of San Diego Christian Unified School System and Christian Heritage College, author; Harry Blamires, author of *The Christian Mind;* and Frank E. Gaebelien, headmaster of the Stony Brook School and former co-editor of *Christianity Today.*

Tim LaHaye

In this world, there are two basic lines of reasoning that determine the morals, values, life-style, and activities of mankind—the wisdom of man or the wisdom of God. Today they take the form of atheistic humanism or Christianity. What this life is all about is the battle for your mind, whether you will live your life guided by man's wisdom (humanism) or God's wisdom (Christianity). Either one will affect the way you live and where you spend eternity.[1]

Harry Blamires

There is no longer a Christian mind. It is commonplace that the mind of modern man has been secularized. For instance, it has been deprived of any orientation towards the supernatural. The modern Christian accepts religion—its morality, its worship, its spiritual culture—but rejects the religious view of life: the view which sets all earthly issues within the context of the eternal, the view which relates all human problems—social, political, cultural—to the doctrinal foundations of the Christian faith, the view which sees all things here below in terms of God's supremacy and earth's transitoriness in terms of Heaven and Hell.[2]

Frank E. Gaebelien

The fact is inescapable: the world view of the teacher, in so far as he is effective, gradually conditions the world view of the pupil. No man teaches out of a philosophical vacuum. In one way or another, every teacher expresses the convictions he lives by, whether they be spiritually positive or negative.[3]

Application: The job of the Christian school is to teach correct doctrine, change wrong behavior, and develop sound convictions for righteous conduct. This can be accomplished by integrating biblical truths into each academic subject, into each extracurricular activity, and into each disciplinary procedure used. The Bible is the foundation for this life-developing style of education. In II Timothy 3:16 and 17 we read, "All Scripture is given by inspiration of God, and *is* profitable for doctrine (correct belief), for reproof (wrong behavior), for correction (wrong belief), for instruction in righteous-

---

[1]Tim LaHaye, *The Battle for the Mind,* Fleming H. Revell Co., Old Tappan, New Jersey, 1980, p. 11.

[2]Harry Blamires, *The Christian Mind,* Servant Books, Ann Arbor, Michigan, n.d., pp. 1–33.

[3]Frank E. Gaebelein, *The Pattern of God's Truth,* Moody Press, Chicago, Illinois, 1968, p. 37.

ness (correct behavior), that the man of God may be complete (correct convictions), thoroughly equipped for every good work (correct conduct)." To do this on a daily basis and to reinforce it year after year results in the development of a strong foundation for successful Christian living. Christian schools are not an option. They are a must! God and education cannot be separated.

—Thomas A. Scott

CHRISTIAN SCIENCE

WHAT IS THE CHRISTIAN'S ANSWER TO CHRISTIAN SCIENTISTS?

The Issue: Christian Science, founded by Mary Baker Eddy (1821–1910) in 1879 claims to "reinstate primitive Christianity and its lost element of healing" to the world. In contrast to the Bible she asserts the "revelation" God supposedly gave was "higher, clearer, and more permanent than before."

Mrs. Eddy published her "superior," metaphysical reinterpretation of the Bible in 1875 and entitled it *Science and Health With Key to the Scriptures.* In this textbook and in her other writings, while Mrs. Eddy claims to be restoring true Christianity, she at the same time flatly denies and contradicts the basic, core doctrines of historic Christian faith as found in the Holy Scriptures. Christian Science appears on the surface to be in harmony with the Bible because of its use of scriptural terms, yet the deception is that while using these orthodox terms Mrs. Eddy has filled them with unbiblical, metaphysical meanings that directly contradict their original context.

Christian Science and the other "Mind Sciences" (i.e. Religious Science, Unity School of Christianity, Divine Science, New Thought) are modern revivals of the ancient gnostic heresies which were soundly condemned during the first centuries of the Christian church. Among other essential doctrines Christian Science denies the Trinity, the Deity of Jesus Christ, the identity of Jesus as the Christ, His bodily resurrection, and salvation by grace through faith in Him alone.

Key Bible References:
Who is a liar but he who denies that Jesus is the Christ? He is antichrist who denies the Father and the Son,

56

Whoever denies the Son does not have the Father either; he who acknowledges the Son has the Father also. I John 2:22–23

Again the high priest asked Him, saying to Him, "Are You the Christ, the Son of the Blessed?" Jesus said, "I am." Mark 14:61b–62a

Beloved, do not believe every spirit, but test the spirits, whether they are of God; because many false prophets have gone out into the world.

By this you know the Spirit of God: Every spirit that confesses that Jesus Christ has come in the flesh is of God, and every spirit that does not confess that Jesus Christ has come in the flesh is not of God. And this is the spirit *of the Antichrist, which you have heard was coming, and is now already in the world.* I John 4:1–3

For many deceivers have gone out into the world who do not confess Jesus Christ as coming in the flesh. This is a deceiver and an antichrist. II John 7

Additional References: Genesis 1:26, 11:7; Numbers 23:19; Psalms 102:25–27, 119:89; Jeremiah 31:30; Matthew 3:17, 27:50–60; Romans 3:23; Ephesians 2:8–9; Hebrews 1:3, 8–12; I John 1:8–10, 3:4, 5:17.

What Others Say: Dr. Anthony Hoekema, professor of Systematic Theology and author; and the late Dr. Walter R. Martin, leading authority on cults, the occult, and comparative religion.

Anthony Hoekema
. . . Christian Scientists flatly reject every major doctrine of historic Christianity. Christian Scientists, therefore, have no more right to apply to themselves the title "Christian" than have Buddhists or Hindus—with whose teachings, indeed, Christian Science has greater affinity than with those of Christianity. We conclude that, strictly speaking, Christian Science is neither Christian nor a science.[1]

Walter R. Martin
. . . seemingly verifiable cases of healings by Christian Scientists, . . . which apparently defy contradiction and are, I believe a direct fulfillment of what Christ warned us of in His famous discourse as recorded in Matthew 7:15–23. Contrary to popular

---

[1]Anthony Hoekema, *Christian Science,* Eerdmans Publishing, Grand Rapids, Michigan, 1972, p. 64.

opinion, healing is not always a sign of divine favor, and never so when it is effected by those who deny the authority of the Scriptures and the very Christ in whose name they claim to heal. The Bible clearly teaches that Satan's emissaries can also duplicate miracles, as in the case of Moses and the Egyptian magicians as recorded in the book of Exodus (7:11, 22; 8:7, 18). Wonders do not always mean that God is working, for he works only to the glory of Jesus Christ and in perfect accord with biblical doctrine. The same kinds of miracles spoken of in a godly sense in Hebrews 2:4 are counterfeited by Satan in II Thessalonians 2:9. Mind Scientists, modern-day gnostics, deny both the authority of Scripture and the deity of Christ, and therefore it is of them, among others, that Jesus warned His disciples and us. Let us therefore be diligent lest we be deceived by those whose powers are after the workings of Satan, with "signs and [lying] wonders."[2]

Application: The Christian is called to share his or her faith with Christian Scientists and other "Mind Scientists" as the opportunity presents itself. The following guidelines will be helpful:

    (1) Pray for the person and listen to God for guidance on how to proceed.

    (2) Be loving, kind, respectful, and patient in attitude and manner. Set the person at ease.

    (3) Ask questions to determine where they are in their understanding of their faith. Don't readily assume they believe everything Mrs. Eddy taught.

    (4) Emphasize your equality before God to guard against a "spiritual superiority" on either side.

    (5) Stress the folly of self-salvation through "special spiritual knowledge" or "understanding."

    (6) Be ready to explain the reality of personal sin.

    (7) Contrast the God, Jesus, and salvation of the Bible with the teachings of Mrs. Eddy in her textbook "Science and Health."

    (8) Know what Christian Science teaches and where in the Bible you can find answers to their false teaching.

    (9) Be ready to explain how we know the Bible is completely trustworthy.

    (10) Ask them to define their terms and you do the same.

    (11) As the Holy Spirit leads you, at the right time give a concise, clear presentation of the Gospel of Jesus Christ using Scriptures to support it. Invite the person to trust

---

[2]Walter Martin, *Martin Speaks Out on the Cults,* Regal Books, Ventura, California, 1983, pp. 76–77.

in Jesus Christ alone for their eternal life and not in some special metaphysical knowledge or understanding.

(12) Follow up on the person and continue to pray for him or her.

—Todd Ehrenborg

THE CHURCH

WHAT IS THE VALUE OF THE CHURCH IN OUR LIVES?

The Issue: In our very busy age when almost everything may be calculated and printed on a home computer system with our never having to lift a pencil; learned from a television set or a radio with our never having to read a book; or ordered from a telephone and delivered to our door with our never having to leave our home, social interdependence appears to be less valued than ever before. Not unexpectedly, some believe the Church is no longer relevant and has failed to keep current with the rapidly changing values of our technological society. Why should Christians leave home and spend the money and effort to attend Church when such fine Christian programming is available through electronic media? Would discarding regular church attendance not be better stewardship of our time and our natural environmental resources, both of which are limited and disappearing?

Key Bible References:

And let us consider how one another in order to stir up love and good works, not forsaking the assembling of ourselves together, as is the manner of some, but exhorting one another, *and so much the more as you see the Day (of Christ's return) approaching.* Hebrew 10:24–25

And He put all things *under His feet, and gave Him to be head over all* things *to the church, which is His body, the fullness of Him who fills all in all.* Ephesians 1:22–23

. . . endeavoring to keep the unity of the Spirit in the bond of peace.

59

There is *one body and one Spirit, just as you were called in one hope of your calling;*

And He Himself gave some to be *apostles, some prophets, some evangelists, and some pastors and teachers, for the equipping of the saints for the work of ministry, for the edifying of the body of Christ,*

*. . . but, speaking the truth in love, may grow up in all things into Him who is the head—Christ—*Ephesians 4:3–4, 11–12, 15

Additional References: Psalm 95:6; Hebrews 12:22–23.

What Others Say: Howard Snyder, internationally recognized expert in the area of church structure and author.

Howard Snyder
Spiritual growth occurs best in a caring community. There are spiritual truths (the Christian) will never grasp and Christian standards (he) will never attain except as (he) shares in community with other believers—and this is God's plan. The Holy Spirit ministers to us, in large measure, through each other.[1]

Application: Our society is turning increasingly inward and many feel estranged from others, as though they really do not belong. Yet, most of us like to feel we are individuals, making our own decisions and not just following the pack. The church is in place to teach us to be more like Jesus Christ, not only so that we may teach others, though that is very important, but so that we be uniquely fitted as a part of His body. In this way, Christians each fill a special position in the church and are at the same time united with one another through the Holy Spirit with Jesus Christ as the head. How wonderful that we can all be so different and yet so much alike!

But how can this be accomplished unless we regularly gather together physically? The Word of God clearly teaches that we are to come together and spiritually stimulate one another. True, we can be stimulated by many media, but we can only stimulate others and maintain spontaneity when we share together face to face. It is in this way that we can discover and exercise the ministry gifts which God gives us to help each other "grow up" or mature into the image of Christ.

---

[1]Howard A. Snyder, *Community of the King,* Inter-Varsity Press, Madison, Wisconsin, 1977, p. 75.

Finally, we are called to unity. Unity presupposes understanding, and understanding requires communication. Only when we gather together do we have the opportunity to communicate our joys, beliefs, questions, needs and desires with one another. In so doing, we are not merely *communicating* with each other but *building* mutual understanding and trust. In this atmosphere of mutual understanding we can truly communicate love with each other and create the unity necessary for us to truly commune with Jesus Christ.

—Jeff D. Vermeer

CLOTHING

WHAT BIBLICAL STANDARDS SHOULD CHRISTIANS FOLLOW CONCERNING CLOTHING?

The Issue: There has always been a debate on what is considered proper dress for Christians. Many Christians have actually developed "dress codes" trying to clarify the issue. Styles and fashions are constantly in a state of flux and Christians are trapped in the dilemma of what they should wear. There are some biblical principles that can be followed to give one a sense of direction in the area of our outward appearance.

Key Bible References:

"Woe to you, scribes and Pharisees, hypocrites! For you cleanse the outside of the cup and dish, but inside they are full of extortion and self-indulgence.

"Blind Pharisee, first cleanse the inside of the cup and dish, that the outside of them may be clean also." Matthew 23:25–26.

But now you must also put off all these: anger, wrath, malice, blasphemy, filthy language out of your mouth.

Do not lie to one another, since you have put off the old man with his deeds, and have put on the new man who is renewed in knowledge according to the image of Him who created him,

Therefore, as the *elect of God, holy and beloved, put on tender mercies, kindness, humbleness of mind, meekness, longsuffering; bearing with one another, and forgiving one another, if anyone has a complaint against another; even as Christ forgave you, so you also* must do.

But above all these things put on love, which is the bond of perfection. Colossians 3:8–10, 12–14

Or do you not know that your body is the temple of the Holy Spirit who is *in you, whom you have from God, and you are not your own?*

For you were bought at a price; therefore glorify God in your body and in your spirit, which are God's. I Corinthians 6:19–20

Additional References: Psalm 101:3; Matthew 6:22–23, 13:1–23; Mark 4:24; Luke 8:18; I Corinthians 10:31.

What Others Say: President Bell of Saint Stephens College.

President Bell
They (our graduates) have little or no perception of standards—of truth, beauty, or goodness . . . All things are to them relative—relative not to absolutes but to expediency. Truth means to them little more than a body of observable facts: *beauty, conformity to fashion;* goodness, doing the things that will make one comfortable or popular.[1]

Application: Dress is a reflection of the attitude of the heart. It is true that a person can alter the outward appearance to hide the heart's condition once in awhile. But this will not be a consistent situation. This was the case when Jesus rebuked the Pharisees. He taught that if one's heart (the inside of the cup) was pure, the outside of the cup (one's appearance) would become clean also. If a Christian is to dress in accordance to God's design, he or she must first make the heart right.

Christians must *put off* the inward garments of the old nature (Colossians 3:8–9) and *put on* the garments of the new nature (Colossians 3:12–14). It is amazing what changes will take place, even in a person's dress, when the heart attitude is pure and clean.

---

[1]W. A. Harper, *Character Building in Colleges,* Abingdon Press, New York, New York, 1927, pp. 13–14.

Scripture makes it clear that our heart is greatly influenced by what we see and hear. Therefore, it is crucial that Christians guard our eyes and ears. Study the passages listed that deal with these areas to make sure your heart is right so that the outward appearance can be properly directed.

A Christian's body is God's temple. Whatever a Christian does with the body must glorify God. Glorifying God means to always reflect the true nature of God. What one puts in the body, puts out from the body, does with the body and *puts on the body* must reflect the nature of God Himself. What should a Christian wear? To have a proper dress standard, one must ask two questions. Is my heart right with God? Does my dress glorify God rather than self? If one's answer to both questions is yes, the person is within God's dress code.

—Glen L. Schultz

CORPORAL PUNISHMENT

SHOULD PARENTS SPANK THEIR CHILDREN?

The Issue: Spanking children has long been understood by parents as both a biblical and effective means of controlling the child's willful disobedience. However, in recent years corporal punishment has come under attack as the forerunner of violence and child abuse. There are many who believe that the way to stop violence in America is to stop spanking children. These same individuals believe that spanking is followed by hitting and ultimately by rape, murder, and assassination.

What does the Bible say about corporal punishment? Is there a relationship between corporal punishment, violence, and child abuse?

Key Bible References:

Children, obey your parents in the Lord, for this is right.

And you, fathers, do not provoke your children to wrath, but bring them up in the training and admonition of the Lord. Ephesians 6:1, 4

Do not withhold correction from a child, for if you beat him with a rod, he will not die.

You shall beat him with a rod, and deliver his soul from hell. Proverbs 23:13–14

He who spares his rod hates his son, but he who loves him disciplines him promptly. Proverbs 13:24

Additional References: Proverbs 4:1–4, 22:6, 29:17.

What Others Say: Dr. James Dobson, founder of Focus on the Family in Pomona, California.

James Dobson

Specialists also say that a spanking teaches your child to hit others, making him a more violent person. Nonsense! If your child has ever bumped his arm against a hot stove, you can bet he'll never deliberately do that again. He does not become a more violent person because the stove burnt him. In fact, he learned a valuable lesson from the pain. Similarly, when he falls out of his high chair or smashes his finger in the door or is bitten by a grumpy dog, he learns about the physical dangers in his world. These bumps and bruises throughout childhood are nature's way of teaching him that the physical world around him must be respected. They do not damage his self-esteem. They do not make him vicious. They merely acquaint him with reality. In like manner, an appropriate spanking from a loving parent in a moment of defiance provides the same service. It tells him there are not only physical dangers to be avoided, but he must steer clear of some social traps as well (selfishness, defiance, dishonesty, unprovoked aggression, etc.).[1]

Application: With many psychologists today, it's in vogue to say that all you can do by spanking children is teach them that power is important, that you're bigger than they are, and that you can force your will on them. Some psychologists even say that in order to stop violence in America, we must stop spanking children. It is ridiculous to blame America's obsession with violence on the disciplinary efforts of loving parents.

Spanking is for disobedience. The Bible says, "Children, obey your parents in the Lord, for this is right" (Ephesians 6:1). When a child disobeys, spanking is a possible disciplinary measure—and a very good one! But it has to be done right. Spanking is to be reserved for use in response to willful defiance.

---

[1]James Dobson, *Hide or Seek, Self-Esteem for the Child,* Fleming H. Revell Company, Old Tappan, New Jersey, 1974, p. 95.

However, let me hasten to emphasize that spanking is not the only tool for use in shaping the will, nor is it appropriate at all ages and for all situations. The wise parent must understand the physical and emotional characteristics of each stage in childhood, and then fit the discipline to a boy's or girl's individual needs.

—Ollie E. Gibbs

COUNSELING

SHOULD CHRISTIANS SEEK PROFESSIONAL COUNSELING?

The Issue: Many Christians have been propagandized by the media and educators into thinking that unless a counselor has a Ph.D. in some form of humanistic psychology or is a psychiatrist, he is not "qualified" to counsel hurting people. The truth is, Christians who know their Bible are often much better counselors than those who only know the wisdom of man in its many forms of humanism. Sigmund Freud, Carl Rogers (from whom much of my early training came), B. F. Skinner, and Benjamin Spock have had an awesome influence on the field of "professional counseling," and most of it is wrong and harmful.

Humanistic psychology is based on many serious errors. Consider: (1) They do not understand the nature of man. He is a "fallen" creature—they think he is "perfectable." (2) That humans have an inborn conscience that either accuses them or excuses them based on their behavior. Consequently, they tend to look on religion and strict Christian parents as harmful rather than helpful. (3) They do not recognize a fixed moral standard of behavior; instead they think people should be permitted to do whatever they want if it doesn't hurt others. (4) They do not accept a personal God to whom mankind can turn for help at times of need. (5) They usually have no respect for the Bible and are often hostile to it. (6) They reject the eternity of the soul which makes personal sacrifice in this life worthwhile in deference to a better eternal life.

Christians put their confidence in such thinkers at their own peril.

It is more than coincidental that the highest educated secular counselor of our day, the psychiatrist who holds both an M.D. and Ph.D.

degree, consistently scores as number one in suicides each year—hardly a recommendation for helping others with their problems.

Key Bible References:

Blessed (happy) is the man who walks not in the counsel of the ungodly. . . . Psalm 1:1

The fool has said in his heart, "There is *no God."* Psalm 14:1

The way of a fool (one who rejects God) is right in his own eyes, but he who heeds counsel (divine counsel) is wise. Proverbs 12:15

Additional References: Psalm 119:1–2; Luke 11:28.

What Others Say: Dr. Jay E. Adams, counselor, author, professor.

Jay E. Adams

"Pastor-counselors should stop sending their hard cases to secular psychologists. That's like saying Jesus Christ does not have the answer to their problems." Dr. Henry Brandt, Christian psychologist.

Psychologists—with neither warrant nor standard from God by which to do so—should get out of the business of trying to change persons. Psychology may be descriptive, but transgresses its boundaries whenever it becomes prescriptive. It can tell us many things about what man does, but not about what he should do.[1]

Application: The Bible has the answers to the problems of life and addresses almost every non-physical problem faced by humankind. Counselors who do not know the Bible are limited to human resources in their ability to help people, consequently they are unqualified to help the Christian. If a person's problem is physical, he should see his medical doctor. If it is emotional or spiritual (which most counseling problems are), he should see a Christian counselor who will use the Word of God to help him. Trying to help emotionally or spiritually upset people without the Bible is like trying to repair a car without guidance from the manufacturer's manual. There are two keys to happiness: Finding the will of God and doing it.

—Tim LaHaye

---

[1]Jay E. Adams, *Lectures on Counseling*, Presbyterian Reformed Publishing, Phillipsburg, New Jersey, 1977, p. 70.

CREATION

WHAT IS THE BIBLICAL ACCOUNT OF CREATION?

The Issue: Evangelical Christians are sharply divided on the foundational issue of creation. Traditionally, most Bible-believing Christians have held to the literal view that God created and made all things in six natural days, as described in Genesis 1. The 19th century rise of uniformitarianism, however, with its concept of the evolution of life over long geological ages, has persuaded many to reinterpret the Genesis record to accommodate this modern view of earth history.

Some Christians hold to theistic evolution and an allegorical view of Genesis, some prefer the day-age theory and "progressive creationism," while others place the geological ages in a supposed "gap" between the first two verses of Genesis. All these accommodations require also that the Noahic flood be a local flood rather than a universal flood, since the latter would have destroyed all geological evidences of the supposed ages of evolution. Modern "scientific creationists" argue on the other hand, that the scientific facts are best explained in the context of the literal-day, worldwide-flood narrative of Genesis.

Key Bible References:

God called the light Day, and the darkness He called Night. So the evening and the morning were the first day. Genesis 1:5

Thus the heavens and the earth, and all the host of them, were finished. And on the seventh day God ended His work which He had done, and He rested on the seventh day from all His work which He had done. Then God blessed the seventh day and sanctified it, because in it He rested from all His work which God had created and made. Genesis 2:1–3

For in six days the LORD made the heavens and the earth, the sea, and all that is in them, and rested the seventh day. Therefore the LORD blessed the Sabbath day, and hallowed it. Exodus 20:11

Additional References: Genesis 6:13, 7:17–22; Mark 10:6–9; I Corinthians 15:21–22, 39; Hebrews 11:3; II Peter 3:3–6.

What Others Say: Dr. Pattle P. T. Pun, biology professor at Wheaton College.

Pattle P. T. Pun

It is apparent that the most straightforward understanding of the Genesis record, without regard to all of the hermeneutical considerations suggested by science, is that God created heaven and earth in six solar days, that man was created in the sixth day, that death and chaos entered the world after the fall of Adam and Eve, that all of the fossils were the result of the catastrophic universal deluge which spared only Noah's family and the animals therewith.

(But he then adds.)

However, the recent Creationist position—has denied and belittled the vast amount of scientific evidence amassed to support the theory of evolution and the antiquity of the earth.[1]

He then, unfortunately, elects the second alternative, as do many other modern evangelicals.

Application: Although scientific/academic "peer pressure" makes it difficult to reject the evolutionary ages of geology, the inerrant record of Scripture constrains us to do so. The geological ages cannot be pigeon-holed between the first two verses of Genesis, because this would imply a worldwide cataclysm which would necessarily destroy all the supposed geological evidence for these ages. Neither can they be equated with the creation week of Genesis 1, for the contextual discussion of the six days, in both Genesis and Exodus 20:8–11, requires the literal interpretation.

Furthermore, there are only a few thousand years of written history anywhere in the records of even the oldest nations. The earth can only be made to look "old" by the unscriptural premise of uniformitarianism (note the warning against this assumption in II Peter 3:3–6), but the fact is that evidences of geologic catastrophe (e.g., the global fossil graveyard in the earth's sedimentary crust) abound everywhere, answering to the great Deluge, as recorded in Scripture and reflected in "flood traditions" all over the world. The Noahic deluge precludes the geological age system, and vice versa, and the false premise of uniformitarianism precludes true biblical creation and vice versa.

We should find assurance in the fact that there does exist strong scientific evidence supporting the biblical revelation of recent special creation of all things.

—Henry M. Morris

---

[1]Pattle P. T. Pun, "A Theory of Progressive Creationism," *Journal of the American Scientific American Affiliation,* Volume 39, March 1987, p. 14.

CRIME

WHAT IS THE BIBLE'S ANSWER TO CRIME?

The Issue: Crime is defined as a gross violation of human law—an aggravated offense against morality. Our holy God has much to say about the sinful nature of crime. His ten commandments indict all kinds of criminal acts, including murder, stealing, immorality, falsehoods that are generally involved in all crime and the fallen nature of man that covets and worships the idols of materialism, greed, pride and lust among others. The Bible has clear safeguards and cautions to keep us from tumbling into crime.

Key Bible References:

But know this, that in the last days perilous times will come:

For men will be lovers of themselves, lovers of money, boasters, proud, blasphemers, disobedient to parents, unthankful, unholy, unloving, unforgiving, slanderers, without self-control, brutal, despisers of good, traitors, headstrong, haughty, lovers of pleasure rather than lovers of God, having a form of godliness but denying its power. And from such people turn away! II Timothy 3:1–5

Therefore take up the whole armor of God, that you may be able to withstand in the evil day, and having done all, to stand. Ephesians 6:13

Your word have I hidden in my heart, that I may not sin against You. Psalm 119:11

Additional References: Exodus 20:1–17; Matthew 15:16–20; Romans 13:1–3, 8–10.

What Others Say: *World Almanac 1990;* and Charles Colson.

World Almanac 1990
The crime rate rose 2.1% in 1988, according to the FBI Uniform Crime Reports. From 1987 to 1988 overall violent crime increased by 4.5%, property crime increased by 1.8%.

Overall the number of crimes committed nationwide rose to 13.9 million in 1988. (And the upward spiral continues.)

Charles Colson

These are violent days in America, and wherever I go, I'm asked about it. Why is the crime rate out of control? Why is common decency so uncommon? When mayhem becomes mundane in a so-called civilized land, what can stem the tide?

Violent tendencies are not an illness. Criminal behaviors are not symptoms of a disease. We cannot explain away awful acts through sociological factors or odd chromosones. or poverty or germs or drugs. While these can surely be factors in criminal behavior, the root cause of crime has not changed since Cain. It is sin![1]

Application: God clearly condemns sin and warns us to flee youthful lusts as Joseph did; to walk circumspectly close to God's protective shadow (Psalm 91:1), to live in the scriptures for there we find the standards of holy living and the source, God's power, for overcoming sinful temptations and the allurements of Satan. God is merciful to repentant sinners. It is significant that Jesus forgave a repentant criminal who was impaled at his side at the crucifixion.

—**Anthony C. Fortosis**

CRITICISM

HOW DO WE SUCCESSFULLY COPE WITH CRITICISM?

The Issue: The Bible is replete with godly men and women on the receiving end of criticism. Even Jesus, perfect as a human being, was the target of many individuals' criticism. In one portion of scripture, Luke 7:33–34, Jesus and John each took an opposite course of action and yet each was criticized. Walking in close fellowship with the Lord and striving to please Him daily is no guarantee that one will be above criticism. When two or more different personalities merge to work on or through an issue, criticism in one form or another commonly rears its head. How is one to accept criticism? Is there a way to cope with criticism successfully?

---

[1]Charles Colson, "You Can't Cure the Wilding Sickness," *Christianity Today,* V.33:2, September 8, 1989.

Key Bible References:

Bless those who persecute you; bless and do not curse.

Do not be overcome by evil, but overcome evil with good. Romans 12:14, 21

Let all bitterness, wrath, anger, clamor, and evil speaking be put away from you, with all malice. Ephesians 4:31

See that no one renders evil for evil to anyone, but always pursue what is good both for yourselves and for all. I Thessalonians 5:15

Remind them to be subject to rulers and authorities, to obey, to be ready for every good work, to speak evil of no one, to be peaceable, gentle, showing all humility to all men. Titus 3:1–2

Additional References: II Corinthians 6:4, 8; I Peter 3:17; James 4:11.

What Others Say: Charles "T" Jones, motivational speaker, Bible teacher and author.

Charles "T" Jones

Did you ever notice how quickly our minds jump to negative conclusions about things we see and hear?

I believe that one of the most important habits for us to cultivate is to find something positive in everything that happens. You may think it's foolish to look for something that isn't there. You're right on that score, but I'm urging you to cultivate being a positive realist and see the positive thing that is already there.

You see, if a man really wants to find something positive in any situation, he can. The problem with most of us is we don't want to. The best things in life don't come easy; they come free, but not easy. Developing this attitude is worth all your effort.[1]

Application: One's view of criticism has a great deal to do with how successfully he will cope with it. James gives a wonderful clue when he states in James 1:2–3, "My brethren, count it all joy when you fall into various trials, knowing that the testing of your faith produces patience." The principle here is that one is to view each negative experience with a joy knowing that God has a specific purpose

---

[1]Charles "T" Jones, *Life Is Tremendous,* Executive Books, Harrisburg, Pennsylvania, 1968, pp. 14–15.

for it in our lives. If one submits properly to each test, the beautiful quality of patience results. We should welcome trials as friends.

The principle is the same when dealing with criticism; we must first see criticism as friend. If what is being said is true, then thank God He has brought something important to our attention to be corrected. If the criticism is not true, then we must search ourselves to see what it is about us that is giving rise to this criticism. In either situation we have the opportunity to make positive changes for God's glory.

If the criticism is purely vicious and we sense the person is just trying to deliberately hurt us, then we must implement the Matthew 18 principle or absorb the slander, without comment, as Jesus did!

—Art Nazigian

CULTS

WHAT IS THE BIBLICAL CRITERIA FOR DETERMINING WHEN A RELIGIOUS GROUP IS A CULT?

The Issue: The Bible fully recognizes the existence of other religions, all of which the Bible says are destructive, evil and not true to the Word of God. The Old Testament gives numerous references to idols, images and other gods. These religions are known as cults. Cults are a man-made system of religion claiming authorization yet distorting the Bible. There are many cults in the world and all of them are worshiping false gods and all of them say they are speaking the truth. Behind these religions are the operating forces of Satan, leading astray as many people as they possibly can. The Bible has the criteria for determining if a religion is a cult. The Bible most definitely reveals the true God and explicitly considers all other systems of worship as an abomination.

Key Bible References:

Lord, You have been our dwelling place in all generations.

Before the mountains were brought forth, or ever You had formed the earth and the world, even from everlasting to everlasting, You are God. Psalm 90:1–2

"To you it was shown, that you might know that the LORD Himself is God; there is none other besides Him." Deuteronomy 4:35

For there is one God and one Mediator between God and men, the Man Christ Jesus, who gave Himself a ransom for all, to be testified in due time. I Timothy 2:5–6

As you have therefore received Christ Jesus the Lord, so walk in Him, rooted and built up in Him and established in the faith, as you have been taught, abounding in it with thanksgiving.

Beware lest anyone cheat you through philosophy and empty deceit, according to the tradition of men, according to the basic principles of the world, and not according to Christ.

For in Him dwells all the fullness of the Godhead bodily; and you are complete in Him, who is the head of all principality and power. Colossians 2:6–10

Additional References: Deuteronomy 10:17; Psalm 96:5; John 1:14–18, 10:30.

What Others Say: Gordon R. Lewis, author and Bible scholar.

Gordon R. Lewis

Adherents of the cults sincerely claim to be devoted followers of Christ. The cults have Sunday schools, church services, radio programs, telecasts, revival services, prophetic conferences, Bible correspondence schools, attractive magazines, and challenging youth activities. Counterfeits always look genuine.

But the appearance of many marks of Christianity does not guarantee the validity of their claims. Jesus Christ, in the Sermon on the Mount, warned "Beware of false prophets which come to you in sheep's clothing but are inwardly ravening wolves" (Matthew 7:15).

How, then, can anyone know whom to believe? Allegiance to the heart of Biblical revelation! The crucial test of Christian integrity is the Christian gospel.[1]

Application: The Bible says always be ready to give an answer to anyone who asks you a reason on why you believe what you believe (I Peter 3:15). What you know about the Bible mentally and spiritually will help stabilize you, giving you confidence in what you believe. Timothy exhorts us to, "Be diligent to present yourself

---

[1]Gordon R. Lewis, *Confronting The Cults,* Presbyterian and Reformed Publishing Company, Phillipsburg, New Jersey, 1966, pp. 4–5.

approved to God, a worker who does not need to be ashamed, rightly dividing the word of truth" (II Timothy 2:15). Here are some practical questions to ask when confronted by a cult. Do they believe that Christ's death on the cross alone is the only basis for salvation? Do they believe that Christ was buried and rose from the dead? Do they trust Christ as their Savior or do they rely on their own works for salvation? Is their first task to preach the gospel or to teach on writings or revelations other than the Bible?

What is your answer to these questions and are you prepared to give an answer when confronted by someone from a religious cult? The Christian has a great Teacher, the Holy Spirit. When confronted by a cult remember, you may find it difficult to change their beliefs to that of the Bible. It is never too difficult for the Holy Spirit. God can transform anyone to become a follower of Him.

—Glenn A. Meeter

DANCING

SHOULD CHRISTIANS DANCE?

The Issue: Most Christians are offended by dancing when defined as rhythmic body movement to secular music giving a sense of undisciplined lifestyle and sexual innuendos. Additionally, popular dancing generally occurs in environments and with music that would be unacceptable to conservative Christians.

Key Bible References:

So it was, as soon as he came near the camp, that he saw the calf and *the dancing.* Exodus 32:19

And when Herodias's daughter herself came in and danced, and pleased Herod . . . the king sent an executioner . . . brought his head on a platter, and gave it to the girl; . . . Mark 6:22–28

For we have spent *enough of our past lifetime in doing the will of the Gentiles—when we walked in licentiousness, lusts, drunkenness, revelries, drinking parties, and abominable idolatries.* I Peter 4:3

Additional References: Exodus 15:19–21; Judges 11:30–39; I Samuel 18:6–7; II Samuel 6:14; Psalms 30:11, 150:4; Ecclesiastes 3:4; Matthew 11:17, 14:6–12.

What Others Say: J. Edwin Orr; and Robertson McQuilkin.

J. Edwin Orr

I do not believe that anyone can contradict that the dance destroys modesty. It promotes impure thinking. In many cases it soils lives and could cause immorality of the worst sort. The dance crowd is definitely the worldly crowd, and the worst of bad company for the child of God.[1]

Robertson McQuilkin

For the one who takes seriously New Testament teaching on purity of mind, to choose to dance with someone other than one's mate is to deliberately choose to "make provision for the flesh," either for oneself or for one's dance partner.[2]

Application: Simply defined, dance is the rhythmic movement of the body usually to music. It can be as harmless as roller skating to music and as sensual and lewd as today's "dirty dancing." The Bible makes many references to dancing associated with praise and historically, the Jews included folk dancing as a part of festivals and weddings. These types of dancing are very different from the modern, popular types of dancing. For the purposes of this article, aerobics, gymnastics, skating, ballet, folk and square dancing are not being discussed although a strong argument exists that acceptance of any type of dance eases the way into more sensual forms of dancing that are not acceptable.

Why has there been such opposition to dancing? Probably because two of the most horrendous crimes of the Bible are associated with dancing. The first is the children of Israel dancing naked around the image of a golden calf while Moses was receiving the Ten Commandments on Mount Sinai. The second was the beheading of John the Baptist after the daughter of Herodias displayed her talents. This type of lewd dancing was a regular practice in the temples of the day and was associated with temple prostitution. No wonder that the early church fathers and conscientious Christians through the ages have had great objections to dancing.

In the New Testament, Christians are taught to put away lewdness, revellings, carousings, licentiousness, adulteries, etc., and instead allow the Spirit of God to develop a self-disciplined lifestyle. Thus the problem with dancing is more than body movements. It includes questions concerning the setting, the music, the person's associa-

---

[1]J. Edwin Orr, *The Christian and Amusements,* Moody Press, Chicago, Illinois, 1960.
[2]Robertson McQuilkin, *An Introduction to Biblical Ethics,* Tyndale House Publishers, Inc., Wheaton, Illinois, 1989.

tions, the type of dress, the purpose, and the issue of Christian witness. Are the dress and manner of movement sexually suggestive even though there may be little physical contact between partners? What about the provocative lyrics common for these dances? Are the movements making the person oblivious to his hurts and problems? Is this the way Christians should solve problems? What about the assent to the worldly lifestyles of the unsaved? Would this be the place of open door to witness for Christ? Is there a question of offense to Christian brothers and sisters? The answers to these questions do not support dancing as an acceptable practice among Christians.

Should Christians dance? The answer is "No." It simply does not meet the test that whatever is done, must be done for the glory of God.

—Sharon R. Berry

DATING

WHAT ARE THE BIBLICAL GUIDELINES
FOR CHRISTIANS WHO DATE?

The Issue: Dating has become the method for young people to develop relationships with the opposite sex. It is also the basis for selecting a marital partner. Christians may accept the cultural method of dating, but the standards, goals, and dating activities should be distinctly different. The Bible is eminently clear in presenting principles that are to govern all relationships, and that includes the dating relationship.

Key Bible References:

Do not be unequally yoked together with unbelievers. For what fellowship has righteousness with lawlessness? And what communion has light with darkness? And what accord has Christ with Belial? Or what part has a believer with an unbeliever? II Corinthians 6:14–15

Oh, magnify the LORD with me, and let us exalt His name together. Psalm 34:3

For the LORD God is a sun and shield; the LORD will give grace and glory; no good thing will He withhold from them who walk uprightly. Psalm 84:11

Let no one despise your youth, but be an example to the believers in word, in conduct, in love, in spirit, in faith, in purity. I Timothy 4:12

Additional References: Deuteronomy 10:12–13; Proverbs 23:22, 24:1–6; Matthew 5:8.

What Others Say: Josh McDowell, speaker and author; and Barry St. Clair, Reach Out Ministeries, Atlanta, Georgia.

Josh McDowell

Everyone a person dates is, however remotely, a candidate for marriage. And there's no question but that a believer should never marry an unbeliever. Since if a person gets married it will be to someone he has dated, it only makes sense that the people one dates should meet at least the most basic requirement of a marriage partner—that of being a Christian. There are moral non-Christians, to be sure, but even with the best intentions, dating non-Christians can lead to immorality. It's a significant dilemma for the Christian teen that can best be handled by avoiding the situation altogether by not dating non-Christians.

No young person should assume he or she is strong enough to handle temptation and thus put himself in temptation's way. Rather, the assumption should be that we are all capable of sinning, and therefore the plan for a date should specifically avoid places and circumstances where temptation to immorality is likely.[1]

Barry St. Clair

It is important to stress to teens that their purpose in life is to glorify God. (Psalm 34:3) Teens should be taught that their worship of God should permeate every area of their lives—including dating. Christians and non-Christians can never reach complete unity. We are light, righteousness, and have the Spirit of God; they are darkness, lawlessness, and of the flesh. Because our purposes in life are different, we can never achieve partnership and harmony.

When a teen is seeking guidance concerning a relationship with the opposite sex, there are three things he or she should consider: (1) God's peace (Colossians 3:15), (2) God's Word (Colossians 3:16), and (3) advice from parents (Colossians 3:20).[2]

---

[1]Josh, McDowell, *How to Help Your Child Say No to Sexual Pressure,* Word Books, Publishers, Waco, Texas, 1987, Chapter 12.

[2]Barry St. Clair, Jay Kesler, Editor, *Parents and Teenagers,* Victor Books, Wheaton, Illinois, 1984.

Application: The faith of a Christian is to permeate every area of life. The acceptance of Christ as Savior is an eternal commitment that is to be lived out while here on earth. Christians, including Christian teenagers and young adults, are to live a biblical lifestyle that is honoring to God. The principles of Scripture are foremost in establishing relationships.

To date a non-Christian is to set a course that will develop into either conflict or compromise. Neither is pleasing to God. The differences in standards and convictions will set the individuals at odds with one another, or the Christian young person will compromise his or her biblical standards. To compromise on biblical standards is to break fellowship with the Lord, and that is the most important relationship that anyone can have.

Any relationship that is not honoring to God is a tool for Satan to use. Christians are to seek to live godly in Christ Jesus, and therefore must establish, structure, and cultivate all relationships with that goal in mind.

—**Derek J. Keenan**

DEATH

HOW CAN CHRISTIANS COPE WITH THE DEATH OF LOVED ONES?

The Issue: The death of a loved one, especially an immediate family member, such as a parent, grandparent, sibling or mate often is extremely difficult or even highly traumatic. Ideally the Christian should respond in a manner which honors the Lord, sets a good example for others, counts the trial all joy because of its maturing and refining value, and trusts God for comfort and strength throughout the bereavement period however long it may take. What is true ideally frequently is not the case in practical daily living. In the practical sense just how is the Christian to cope in the every day settings of life?

Key Bible References:

To everything there is *a season, a time for every purpose under heaven:*

A time to be born, and a time to die; . . .

He has made everything beautiful in its time. . . . Ecclesiastes 3:1–2, 11

And as it is appointed for men to die once, but after this the judgment, so Christ was offered once to bear the sins of many. . . . Hebrews 9:27–28

For to me, to live is *Christ, and to die* is *gain.*

For I am hard pressed between the two, having a desire to depart and be with Christ, which is *far better.* Philippians 1:21, 23

Therefore we are *always confident, knowing that while we are at home in the body we are absent from the Lord.*

For we walk by faith, not by sight.

We are confident, yes, well pleased rather to be absent from the body and to be present with the Lord. II Corinthians 5:6–8

Additional References: Psalms 31:14–15, 116:15; Acts 17:26; Romans 5:12, 6:23; Colossians 3:23–24; I Thessalonians 4:13–18.

What Others Say: Dr. Lehman Strauss, Bible teacher and writer; and Dr. Warren W. Wiersbe, author and Bible expositor.

Lehman Strauss
Preparation for death must be made in life, whether that death be your own or a loved one dear to you. Most people are unwilling to think seriously about death until it is forced upon them. But sooner or later death is certain to come into the experience of each of us. When it does come, the best course of action is to face it squarely in the light of the Scripture. Surely it is the part of wisdom to be prepared for this new and strange experience.[1]

Warren W. Wiersbe
Since death is unavoidable and life is unpredictable, the only course we can safely take is to yield ourselves into the hands of God and walk by faith in His Word. We don't live by explanations; we live by promises. We don't depend on luck but on the providential working of our loving Father as we trust His promises and obey His will.

As we walk by faith, we need not fear our "last enemy," because Jesus Christ has conquered death. "Fear not; I am the first and the

---

[1]Lehman Strauss, *When Loved Ones are Taken in Death,* Scripture Truth Book Co., Inc., Fincastle, Virginia, p. 7.

last; I am He that liveth, and was dead; and, behold, I am alive for evermore" (Rev. 1:17, 18).[2]

Application: To successfully cope with the death of a loved one the Christian must face the reality of death including its meaning and cause. The Scripture is the only source of guiding truth. Physical death cannot be dismissed as something other than the actual separation of the spirit and soul from the body. The cause of physical death is nothing less than sin and is the result of God's judgment (Genesis 3:3 and Romans 5:12). For the departed Christian the spirit and soul are transported into the very presence of the Lord in heaven. The body or shell decays and awaits the resurrection. God has appointed people once to death and we must understand the stark reality of this truth.

Human comprehension and effort will not yield understanding of the experience of death and the loss of a loved one. This will only lead to frustration and confusion which falls far short of success in coping. Faith is the dimension that surpasses all human understanding and yields the wisdom that brings forth maturing, coping, and peace. Faith in the eternal God and the undergirding promises of the Scripture produces an enduring strength that results in knowing that it is only the true God who will work good out of disaster.

Comfort is what the Christian seeks. This experience is found through reading the Bible. Continued exposure to passages of solace will relieve the all encompassing grief that accompanies death. The mind, will, and emotions require the bathing and renewing produced by reading and meditating on God's Word.

The Christian's times are in the hand of God. Implicit trust in the Heavenly Father who will make all things beautiful in due time is the key to coping with the death of loved ones.

—**Walter F. Garland**

---

[2]Warren W. Wiersbe, *Be Satisfied*, Victor Books, Wheaton, Illinois, 1990, p. 114.

DEBT

WHAT DOES THE BIBLE SAY ABOUT DEBT?

The Issue: The world tells us to get all we can by whatever means available and get it *now*. We learn from the world that our success will be measured, to a large degree, by how much we have. We hear early in life how easy it is to buy on credit and how difficult it is to have all we "should have" without going into debt. Jesus said that while Christians must live "in" the world, they are not to be "of" the world. Christians differ widely, however, in the way they interpret and apply these words of Jesus in the area of debt. Most would agree that to follow this command means rejecting the world's view and trusting God to meet our needs. While this does not necessarily mean Christians are never to incur debt, it does mean that they must consider the matter carefully and prayerfully, seeking wise counsel and following biblical guidelines. Debt should not be accepted by Christians as necessary, automatic, normal, or right just because it is "the American way."

Key Bible References:

The wicked borrows and does not repay, but the righteous shows mercy and gives. Psalm 37:21

The rich rules over the poor, and the borrower is *servant to the lender.* Proverbs 22:7

And He said to them, "Take heed and beware of covetousness, for one's life does not consist in the abundance of the things he possesses." Luke 12:15

Let your *conduct* be *without covetousness,* and be *content with such things as you have. For He Himself has said,* "I will never leave you nor forsake you." Hebrews 13:5

Additional References: Deuteronomy 15:1–3, 24:6; Proverbs 6:1–5, 11:15; Matthew 6:25–33; I Timothy 5:8; James 4:13–15.

What Others Say: Larry Burkett, writer, financial counselor, host of the radio program, "How to Manage Your Money" and founder of Christian Financial Concepts; and Ron Blue, financial planner and managing partner of a financial advisory firm.

Larry Burkett
It makes a lot of sense to be debt free. It can be done. Granted, the average couple can't buy a home debt free, but if they're willing to

discipline themselves and pay off that mortgage, almost any couple in the United States can be debt free in ten to fifteen years.[1]

Borrowing is a manifestation of a lack of understanding of God's promises, because God has committed Himself to provide us with everything we need, and even an abundance above that for every good deed.[2]

Ron Blue

I'm concerned that trouble with debt is *always and only* a symptom of something else. There are four common causes of problem debt: a lack of discipline; a lack of contentment; a search for security; a search for significance.[3]

Debt may violate two biblical principles: it almost always presumes upon the future, and it may deny God the opportunity to do what He really wants to do in our lives.[4]

Application: Debt is not a sin, but Scripture warns that it can become an insidious, destructive force that increases stress, alters relationships, and hinders effective service for Christ. Most importantly, it may indicate a lack of trust in God's care and provision. Before Christians incur any debt they should be sure they understand all the costs and economic consequences involved in order to be certain that it makes good economic sense. They must be sure, also, that it can be repaid. Any debt that results from a need for recognition or a greedy desire for possessions is certain to affect the debtor negatively. Christians must examine the alternatives and consequences carefully and go before the Lord in fervent prayer. Counsel from older, wiser Christians is helpful. Only after these steps have been taken and all concerned are in complete agreement and are experiencing inner peace about the debt, should it be incurred. Jesus came to set us free. Christians should not be in bondage to debt.

—Ron and Carol Sipus

---

[1] Larry Burkett, *Answers To Your Family's Financial Questions,* Focus on the Family Press, Pomona, California, 1987, p. 83.

[2] Ibid., p. 98.

[3] Ron Blue, *The Debt Squeeze: How Your Family Can Become Financially Free,* Focus on the Family Press, Pomona, California, 1989, p. 10.

[4] Ibid., p. 47.

DEMONS

WHAT DOES THE BIBLE SAY ABOUT DEMONS?

The Issue: The Scriptures present a rather clear picture of Satan and his "angels." These demons were worshiped in Old Testament times and much of Jesus' ministry dealt with demons, their work and power. He made it clear to His disciples that Satan was a powerful spiritual enemy and demons were doing Satan's work. They continue to do his bidding today.

The Bible presents two great spiritual powers working against each other. The one power is the One True God, creator of the universe and all of life; the other is Satan, a fallen angel who desired to be as great as God, who is the Prince of the Power of the Air, and holds dominion over the earth.

The Bible makes it clear who will win in this battle and calls upon all people to accept the work of Jesus Christ on their behalf. In that way they will become "changed people" who have moved from death to life and will experience eternal life with Jesus Christ. Believers are called upon to put on "the whole armor of God" so they can withstand the attacks of the devil and his angels. There is no reason why believers should have difficulty with demons if they are trusting and following the Lord as He has taught.

Key Bible References:

They sacrificed to demons, not to God, to gods they did not know, to new gods, new arrivals that your fathers did not fear. Deuteronomy 32:17.

Now when He rose early on the first day of the week, He appeared first to Mary Magdalene, out of whom He had cast seven devils. Mark 16:9

Rather that the things which the Gentiles sacrifice they sacrifice to demons, and not to God, and I do not want you to have fellowship with demons.

You cannot drink the cup of the Lord and the cup of demons; you cannot partake of the Lord's table and of the table of demons. I Corinthians 10:20–21

You believe that there is one God. You do well. Even the demons believe—and tremble! James 2:19

83

Additional References: Psalm 106:37; Matthew 7:22, 10:8; Mark 1:34; Luke 4:41, 8:30; I Timothy 4:1; Revelation 9:20, 16:14, 18:2.

What Others Say: C. Fred Dickason, faculty member and chairman of the theology department at Moody Bible Institute; and Neil T. Anderson, chairman of the Practical Theology Department at Talbot School of Theology.

C. Fred Dickason

Demons are fallen angels and therefore Satan's subjects and helpers in his program of opposition to God and His people. Demons are persons with intellect, sensibility, and will, just as angels. They are spirit beings who are morally perverted in their personality, in their doctrine, and in their conduct.

Basically they promote Satan's program of the lie, extending his power and promoting his philosophy. They promote rebellion, slander, idolatry, and false religions and cults. They oppress mankind by affecting the body causing mental problems, destroying life, and dominating through possession.

They seek defeat of believers by waging spiritual warfare on all fronts. Demons attack confidence; tempting to sin and inflicting maladies. They seek defeat of the church through creating divisions, counteracting the gospel ministry and causing persecution.[1]

Neil T. Anderson

It was an eye-opening experience for the disciples to discover that "the demons are subject to us in Your name" (Luke 10:17). "Subject" (hupotasso) is a military term meaning "to arrange under." It pictures a group of soldiers snapping to attention and following precisely the orders of their commanding officer.

Perhaps the disciples suffered under the same misconception which blinds many Christians today. We see God and His kingdom on one side and Satan and his kingdom on the other side. Both kingdoms seem to be very powerful, and here we are, stuck in the middle between the two, like the rope in a tug of war. On some days God seems to be winning, and on other days the devil appears to have the upper hand. And we don't seem to have anything to say about who wins the battle.

But, the disciples came back from their mission with a new perspective, a true perspective. Spiritual authority is not a tug-of-war on a horizontal plane; it is a vertical chain of command. Jesus Christ has

---

[1]C. Fred Dickason, *Angels Elect and Evil*, Moody Press, Chicago, Illinois, 1975. pp. 161–168.

all authority in heaven and on earth (Matthew 28:18); He's at the top. He has given His authority and power to His servants to be exercised in His name (Luke 10:17); we're underneath Him. And Satan and his demons? They're at the bottom, subject to the authority Christ has invested in us. They have no more right to rule your life than a buck private has to order a general to clean the latrine.[2]

Application: The Christian must come to the realization that there are demon powers. Jesus has made it clear that the Devil and his angels are at work in the world today. But, Jesus has not left us helpless! He has provided the power and authority needed to deal with the attacks of demons. He has given believers power and authority which leads to real freedom in Jesus Christ.

Yes, there are powers and principalities that are great and awesome, these powers are destructive and will attempt to attack God's plan and purposes, but the ultimate victory is with Jesus Christ. He has not left us defenseless. He still has the authority and power to overcome evil and has given us the right to claim His authority. He has also provided the "armor of God" (Ephesians 6:11) so we can stand against the powers of the devil and his angels.

We have great freedom and power in Christ and He challenges us to appropriate that freedom and power!

—James W. Braley

DISCERNMENT

WHAT IS BIBLICAL DISCERNMENT?

The Issue: The need for spiritual discernment to perceive good and evil has always been great. With deception getting greater as we get closer to the end time and false teachers more abundant, we need divine enablement to distinguish between truth and error. Scripture says that even some of the elect will be deceived in the latter days. We must learn to see through the surface problem to the root cause. We must not have knowledge and lack wise discernment. We must learn to know what to look for when evaluating peo-

---

[2]Neil T. Anderson, *T-H-E Bondage Breaker,* Harvest House Publishers, Eugene, Oregon, 1990. p. 61.

ple, problems, and things. Are we using Scripture as our guide to discern between right and wrong? The truth of Scripture must be paramount and we must never believe what man preaches unless it has been filtered through God's Holy Word.

Key Bible References:

"For the LORD does *not* see *as man sees; for man looks at the outward appearance, but the LORD looks at the heart."* I Samuel 16:7b

"Therefore, give to Your servant an understanding heart to judge Your people, that I may discern between good and evil. For who is able to judge this great people of Yours?" I Kings 3:9

For we do not wrestle against flesh and blood, but against principalities, against powers, against the rulers of the darkness of this age, against spiritual hosts *of wickedness in the heavenly* places. Ephesians 6:12

But solid food belongs to those who are of full age, that is, *those who by reason of use have their senses exercised to discern both good and evil.* Hebrews 5:14

Additional References: Isaiah 11:3; I Corinthians 2:14; II Corinthians 11:13-15, 13:5; Galatians 6:4; Ephesians 4:14–16; I Thessalonians 5:19–22; I John 4:1–4.

What Others Say: Charles R. Swindoll, pastor of the Evangelical Free Church in Fullerton, California; and Kenneth O. Gangel, professor and chairman of the Department of Christian Education at Dallas Theological Seminary.

Charles R. Swindoll

Discernment is the ability to detect, to recognize, to perceive beyond what is said. Discernment is the ability to "sense" by means of intuition. It is insight apart from the obvious, outside the realm of facts. Discernment isn't taught as much as it is caught. Paul wrote, "I pray that you will grow in full knowledge and discernment." There is a third term we need to define. . . . balance as I have in mind remaining free of extremes, being able to see the whole picture not just one side or a small part of it. Apollos in Acts 18 is a positive example of the balance of knowledge and discernment. Three principles we must never forget:

    (1) No one person has all the truth.
    (2) No single church or minister owns exclusive rights to your mind.

(3) No specific interpretation is correct just because a gifted teacher says so.

Don't miss it. Add a full cup of discernment to your knowledge. Mix it well and you'll never lose your balance.[1]

Kenneth O. Gangel

Natural Discernment is possible for every man, Christian or not. Sometimes we call it good judgment or horse sense—the ability to make wise decisions by observing and understanding. Some people have more of this than others, but it can be learned. All of us should be alert to do this.

Spiritual Discernment comes to a believer as he grows in Christ (Ephesians 4:14–15). It is connected to a great extent with knowledge of the Bible and with spiritual growth in our lives. It comes with a sensitivity to the Holy Spirit.

Gifted Discernment is that which the Holy Spirit gives to some believers as a special gift, enabling them to serve the Church as watchman, to identify by super-natural insight what is not truth. Like many of the other gifts, this one can lead to pride and perverted use resulting in character assassination and harsh criticism. This will not happen if we remember that all gifts are of grace and for the benefit of the Church and must be exercised in love.[2]

Application: Discernment is needed daily in the "little" things of life. Sometimes we call it common sense, but we will be more in tune with what God wants for us day by day if we bathe the decisions of the day in prayer. An old expression "haste makes waste" has a biblical partner called "Wait on the Lord." Other decisions of a deeper nature require more spiritual depth which comes as we spiritually mature. We must always seek a biblical balance in our wise discernment.

We are in an age where Satan is very active and cannot be defeated on a day by day basis without the supernatural power of God. Occult activity, the New Age Movement, Secular Humanism, and even some of God's leaders setting themselves up as "mini-gods," all require a special measure of discernment.

—J. Douglas Yoder

[1]Charles R. Swindoll, *Growing Deep in the Christian Life,* Multnomah Press, Portland, Oregon, 1986, pp. 38–40, 44–45, 47, 49.

[2]Kenneth O. Gangel, *Unwrap Your Spiritual Gifts,* Victor Books, Wheaton, Illinois, 1983, p. 94.

DISCIPLESHIP

WHAT DOES THE BIBLE TEACH ABOUT CHRISTIAN DISCIPLESHIP?

The Issue: Just as Jesus called twelve men to be His disciples during His earthly ministry, He has called every Christian to not only be His disciple, but also to make disciples of all nations. The first step in discipleship is to personally accept Jesus Christ as Savior. The next step which covers the remainder of a Christian's life is to make Jesus Christ the Lord of your life.

Key Bible References:

"Go therefore and make disciples of all nations, baptizing them in the name of the Father and of the Son and of the Holy Spirit, teaching them to observe all things that I have commanded you; and lo, I am with you always, even to the end of the age." Amen. Matthew 28:19–20

Then He said to them all, "If any one desires to come after Me, let him deny himself, and take up his cross daily, and follow Me.

"For whoever desires to save his life will lose it, but whoever loses his life for my sake will save it.

"For what advantage is it to a man if he gains the whole world, and is himself destroyed or lost?

"For whoever is ashamed of Me and My words, of him the Son of Man will be ashamed when He comes in His own glory, and in His Father's, and of the holy angels." Luke 9:23–26

"By this all will know that you are My disciples, if you have love for one another." John 13:35

"So likewise, whoever of you does not forsake all that he has cannot be My disciple." Luke 14:33

Additional References: Deuteronomy 6:5; Psalm 1:1–3; Ecclesiastes 12:13; Jeremiah 9:24; Matthew 5:13-16, 6:33; Luke 10:27; John 12:24–26.

What Others Say: Dr. V. Raymond Edmond, former president of Wheaton College; Charles W. Colson; and Charles R. Swindoll.

V. Raymond Edmond

Discipleship means "discipline"! The disciple is that one who has been taught or trained by the Master, who has come with his ignorance, superstition and sin, to find learning, truth and forgiveness from the Savior. Without discipline we are not disciples, even though we profess His name and pass for a follower of the lowly Nazarene. In an undisciplined age when liberty and license have replaced law and loyalty, there is greater need than ever before that we be disciplined to be His disciples.[1]

Charles W. Colson

To believe Jesus means we follow Him and join what He called the "Kingdom of God," which He said was "at hand." This is a new commitment . . . new companionship, a new community established by conversion.[2]

Charles R. Swindoll

My permanent theme in life? "To God be the glory for the things He has done." How does this occur?

First, by cultivating the habit of including the Lord God in every segment of your life.

Second, by refusing to expect or accept any of the glory that belongs to God.

Third, by maintaining a priority relationship with Him that is more important than any other on earth.[3]

Application: The process of discipleship is a two-step process which begins with salvation. The second step is to become mature in Christ through a lifetime of spiritual growth. This growth can only happen as the Christian allows the Spirit of God to control every area of his or her life through the disciplines of: meditating on the Word of God, communicating with God through prayer, and making disciples of others. This is the life that was modeled by Jesus Christ and the Christian is to become more like Christ on a daily basis. This is what the Bible teaches about discipleship.

—Randall A. Ross

---

[1]V. Raymond Edmond, *The Disciplines of Life*, Harvest House Publishers, Eugene, Oregon, 1982, p. 9.

[2]Charles W. Colson, *Loving God*, Zondervan Publishing, Grand Rapids, Michigan, 1983, p. 176.

[3]Charles R. Swindoll, *Rise and Shine*, Multnomah Press, Portland, Oregon, 1989, pp. 29–31.

DISPUTES

HOW ARE DISPUTES RESOLVED AMONG CHRISTIANS?

The Issue: Satan would like to destroy the normal flow of harmony and good fellowship among Christians. Even as Christians, we may at times irritate other Christians and other Christians may irritate us, resulting in a misunderstanding or a full-blown dispute. God's ways are best and He has provided a way for Christians to settle their differences in what many call "The Matthew 18 Principle." It is profoundly simple.

Key Bible References:

"Moreover if your brother sins against you, go and tell him his fault between you and him alone. If he hears you, you have gained your brother.

"But if he will not hear you, take with you one or two more, that 'by the mouth of two or three witnesses every word may be established.'

"And if he refuses to hear them, tell it to the church. But if he refuses even to hear the church, let him be to you like a heathen and a tax collector." Matthew 18:15–17

Dare any of you, having a matter against another, go to law before the unrighteous, and not before the saints?

Now therefore, it is already an utter failure for you that you go to law against one another. Why do you not rather accept wrong? Why do you not rather let yourselves be defrauded? I Corinthians 6:1, 7

And do not grieve the Holy Spirit of God, by whom you were sealed for the day of redemption.

Let all bitterness, wrath, anger, clamor, and evil speaking be put away from you, with all malice.

And be kind to one another, tenderhearted, forgiving one another, just as God in Christ also forgave you. Ephesians 4:30–32

Additional References: Proverbs 11:9, 27:6; John 13:34-35; Galatians 6:1.

What Others Say: Dr. Henry M. Morris, Bible scholar and author.

Henry M. Morris

Few things hinder the cause of Christ as much as personal disagreements between Christians. Christ told His disciples that their relationship to Him would be obvious to the world when the world saw their unique love for one another. (John 13:35) The opposite is likewise true—Christians who feud among themselves bring disgrace upon their Lord and His church.

The Apostle Paul addressed himself to this problem when it existed in the church at Corinth. He expressed amazement that members of the church were hauling one another into court because of personal differences. (I Corinthians 6:1) Inspired by the Holy Spirit, the apostle reasoned with them along the following lines. Christians will one day judge the world and the angels. The truth of their glorious future should have a present application—they should have enough spiritual discernment to settle their relatively petty squabbles. Furthermore, those who professed to be spiritual should not resort to the judgment of those who were antagonistic to spiritual truths in an effort to seek justice. (I Corinthians 6:2–4)[1]

Application: The "me generation" philosophy of "I'll do it my way" sometimes spills over into the Christian community. This is often true when it comes to resolving disputes among Christians. The first step, and most often the only step needed in solving Christian to Christian disputes, is for one of the two Christians to initiate face-to-face dialogue. Most Christian to Christian disputes are resolved at the two people level. If, on the other hand, as Matthew 18:16 says, one Christian will not "hear" the other Christian or does not agree on the solution to the problem, then God's Matthew 18 principle requires that the Christian who is attempting to resolve the problem take one or two others with him or her to meet with the other Christian so that "every word may be established." If the problem is not solved at the small group level, then the disagreement is to be brought before the church. If the church determines that one of the Christians is wrong and if he or she (verse 17) "refuses even to hear the church," then that individual is to be regarded as a "heathen" who has rejected the body of believers.

It is clearly stated in the Bible that Christians are not to sue other Christians or otherwise take fellow Christians to civil court to resolve disputes. I Corinthians 6:1 says, "Dare any of you having a

---

[1]Henry M. Morris and Martin E. Clark, *The Bible Has the Answer,* Creation Life Publishers, San Diego, California, 1976, p. 191.

matter against another, go to law before the unrighteous, and not before the saints?" God's people must resolve their disputes in God-ordained, orderly fashion within the church, not in the secular world.

—Paul A. Kienel

┌─────────────┐ DIVORCE └─────────────┘

WHAT IS THE BIBLICAL PERSPECTIVE OF DIVORCE?

The Issue: At one time, divorce was looked upon with great disdain in the church. However, over the years we have seen an increase in the number of divorces involving Christian homes. Today divorce has become the accepted way to work out problems in a marriage. Satan knows that the home is the foundational cornerstone for a stable society. Divorce is a major symptom of a diseased view of what God considers so vital to the human race—marriage. God's Word gives us specific principles by which Christians can ensure a secure and happy marriage.

Key Bible References:

The Pharisees also came to Him, testing Him, and saying to Him, "Is it lawful for a man to divorce his wife for just any reason?"

And He answered and said to them, "Have you not read that He who made them at the beginning 'made them male and female,' and said, 'For this reason a man shall leave his father and mother and be joined to his wife, and the two shall become one flesh'?

"So then, they are no longer two but one flesh. Therefore what God has joined together, let not man separate."

They said to Him, "Why then did Moses command to give a certificate of divorce, and to put her away?"

He said to them, "Moses, because of the hardness of your hearts, permitted you to divorce your wives, but from the beginning it was not so.

"And I say to you, whoever divorces his wife, except for sexual immorality, and marries another, commits adultery; and whoever marries her who is divorced commits adultery." Matthew 19:3–9

Additional References: Genesis 1:27–28; Exodus 20:14, 17b; Malachi 2:14–16; I Corinthians 7:1–7; II Corinthians 6:14; Ephesians 5:22–23.

What Others Say: John MacArthur, pastor, author and radio minister; Warren Wiersbe, pastor and author; and Stanley Baldwin, author.

John MacArthur
When God created one man for one woman, He set that standard in motion for all of human history. . . . Marriage is a consecration of two people to each other . . . that says I am totally separated unto you . . . a husband and wife actually become the personal possession of one another. When two people come together, in God's view they literally become one person.[1]

Warren Wiersbe
Since marriage is basically a physical relationship (one flesh), it can only be broken by a physical cause. Adultery and death would be two such causes. . . . It is God's will that the marriage be permanent, a lifetime commitment . . . divorce can never be God's first choice for a couple. God hates divorce.[2]

Stanley Baldwin
None of this divorce business was in the will and plan of God. If we are going to talk about what's right, divorce is excluded. That was Jesus' teaching.[3]

Application: Today's youth face difficult days when preparing for family life. God's ideal is constantly being attacked from every side. However, marriage is still a marvelous God-ordained institution that provides the greatest joys a man and woman can ever experience here on earth. In order to establish a sound Christian home, Christians must follow the principles found in God's Word. First, a Christian is only to marry another Christian. Over the years pas-

---

[1] John MacArthur, *John MacArthur's Bible Studies on Divorce,* Moody Press, Chicago, Illinois, 1985, pp. 11–13.
[2] Warren Wiersbe, *Be Wise,* Victor Books, Wheaton, Illinois, 1985, pp. 78, 84–85.
[3] Stanley Baldwin, *What Did Jesus Say About That?,* Victor Books, Wheaton Illinois, 1978, p. 127.

tors and evangelists have preached, "If you are a child of God and you marry a child of the devil, you are sure to have trouble with your father-in-law."

Second, two people should never marry if they are not willing to make this a lifetime commitment. Marriage is not a contract or a 50-50 arrangement. It requires the giving of 100% of yourself to your spouse and expecting nothing in return. Christ, the bridegroom, gave His life for the church, the bride.

Young people should not focus on whether or not there are ever legitimate reasons for divorce. Their focus should be on marrying in the will of God and entering this union for life with divorce never being an option. This will ensure the founding of sound Christian homes which will provide for a strong society.

—Glen L. Schultz

DOUBLEMINDEDNESS

WHAT DOES THE BIBLE SAY ABOUT DOUBLEMINDEDNESS?

The Issue: Certainly much has been said about the confused state of young people today. While there is sufficient evil bombardment upon every aspect of their daily lives, doublemindedness on the part of adult leaders has greatly contributed to the dilemma. It is past time to hear what God's Word has to say about this matter.

Key Biblical References:

> . . . *a double-minded man, unstable in all his ways.* James 1:8

> *They feared the LORD, yet served their own gods—according to the rituals of the nations from among whom they were carried away.* II Kings 17:33

> *You cannot drink the cup of the Lord and the cup of demons; you cannot partake of the Lord's table and the table of demons.* I Corinthians 10:21

Additional References: Zephaniah 1:4–5; Luke 16:13; James 4:8.

What Others Say: Dr. Roy W. Lowrie, Jr., author and Christian educator; and Bill Glass, evangelist and sports figure.

Roy W. Lowrie, Jr.

A godly schoolteacher whose life is an example to his students is of great worth. Great damage is done by those teachers whose lives are a wrong example before impressionable children during the plastic years when their values, which will affect eternity, are being formed.[1]

Bill Glass

Obviously you need to feel concerned about who has control of your mind. Either Satan or the Holy Spirit is in charge. Check who dominates by asking if your thoughts are positive or negative—of faith or unbelief. A humorist suggested that two dogs fight for control of your life. Only one wins at any given time. Which? "The one you say 'sick 'em' to."[2]

Application: If our goal is to help young people be conformed to the image of Christ, then we must teach as only He would.

Doublemindedness can have no rightful place in the process.

—Wayne Freeman

DRUGS

WHAT IS THE CHRISTIAN RESPONSE TO THE DILEMMA OF DRUGS?

The Issue: Of all the problems of American life today, few are more disturbing than the problem of drug use. America's reliance on drugs is unequaled in the history of mankind. Drugs are a two-edged sword, capable of both saving lives and ruining them. The real problem is that drugs are "selling promises," that cannot be kept, to millions of people searching for happiness and a life with meaning. The Bible clearly outlines the road to happiness and meaning as well as the way of escape from drugs.

---

[1]Roy W. Lowrie, Jr., *To Those Who Teach in Christian Schools,* Association for Christian Schools International, Whittier, California, 1978, p. 26.

[2]Bill Glass, *How to Win When the Roof Caves In,* Fleming H. Revell Company, Old Tappan, New Jersey, 1988, p. 184.

Key Bible References:

Do you not know that you are the temple of God and that *the Spirit of God dwells in you?*

If anyone defiles the temple of God, God will destroy him. For the temple of God is holy, which temple *you are.* I Corinthians 3:16–17

Do you not know that to whom you present yourselves slaves to obey, you are that one's slaves whom you obey, whether of sin to death, or of obedience to righteousness?

I speak in human terms *because of the weakness of your flesh. For just as you presented your members* as *slaves of uncleanness, and of lawlessness* leading *to* more *lawlessness, so now present your members* as *slaves* of *righteousness for holiness.* Romans 6:16, 19

Additional References: Mark 7:15–23; Romans 12:1–2; II Corinthians 5:17; Galatians 6:7.

What Others Say: George Bush, President of the United States; and William J. Bennett, former director of the Office of National Drug Control Policy.

George Bush
America's fight against epidemic illegal drug use cannot be won on any single front alone; it must be waged *everywhere*—at every level of Federal, State, and local government and by every citizen in every community across the country. On behalf of those Americans most directly suffering from the scourge of drugs—and all the many more who must be further protected from it—I ask for your help and support.[1]

William J. Bennett
People take drugs for many complicated reasons that we do not yet fully understand. But most drug users share an attitude toward their drugs that we would do well to acknowledge openly: At least at first, they find drugs intensely pleasurable. It is a hollow, degrading, and deceptive pleasure, of course, and pursuing it is an appallingly self-destructive impulse. But self-destructive behavior is a human flaw that has always been with us—and always will. And drug addiction is a particularly tenacious form of self-destruction,

---

[1]President George Bush, *National Drug Control Strategy,* U.S. Government Printing Office, Washington, D.C., September, 1989. (Introduction)

one which its victims very often cannot simply choose to correct on their own.[2]

Application: The contemporary drug scene presents a paradox: Those who are weekend users are doing all they can to get into the scene, while those in the scene would like to be out. Obviously, this is the age of disillusionment. Everyone wants to be happy; everyone is searching for peace. No matter what part of the world you travel, you will find people caught up in this relentless search.

There is hope! By offering the drug user a personal relationship with God through His Son, Jesus Christ, we can offer him a solution that will meet every need in his life—even the very needs that caused him to turn to drugs in the first place. The supernatural power of God can set the captured free.

The drug user must admit that he or she is hooked and that there is no easy way out. There is no simple cure. Only by turning to God and believing in His Son, Jesus Christ, can the drug user find the power to be set free from sin. "And you shall know the truth, and the truth shall make you free" (John 8:32).

—Ollie E. Gibbs

EMOTIONAL ABUSE

WHAT IS THE BIBLICAL ANSWER TO THOSE WHO ABUSE OTHERS EMOTIONALLY?

The Issue: As Christians we are in daily contact with others at home, work, and church. We find ourselves involved in both intimate and casual relationships. In all relationships conflict inevitably occurs. During conflict one person may resort to emotional abuse. By actions or words the offender rejects, "puts down," and makes others feel inferior or inadequate. The Bible commands the person who is being abused to forgive and pray for the offender. What words of command and warning does God give to those who emotionally abuse others?

---

[2]William J. Bennett, *National Drug Control Strategy,* U.S. Government Printing Office, Washington, D.C., September, 1989, p. 9.

Key Bible References:

Do not be deceived, God is not mocked; for whatever a man sows, that he will also reap. Galatians 6:7

And this commandment we have from Him: that he who loves God must *love his brother also.* I John 4:21

"But I say to you that for every idle word men may speak, they will give account of it in the day of judgment.

"For by your words you will be justified and by your words you will be condemned." Matthew 12:36–37

Let *nothing* be done *through selfish ambition or conceit, but in lowliness of mind let each esteem others better than himself.*

Let each of you look out not only for his own interests, but also for the interests of others. Philippians 2:3–4

Additional References: Proverbs 8:13, 11:17, 13:3, 18:6–7, 29:11; Matthew 5:22; Ephesians 4:29, 31–32; James 3:6, 8–10, 4:11; I John 4:7–8, 20–21.

What Others Say: William Backus, Ph.D., Christian psychologist and pastor.

William Backus

If you are a habitual "zapper," you may find that omitting put-downs is not as much fun as including them in your conversations with others. There is a certain wicked satisfaction in verbally "creaming" the other person, especially when you are upset by his actions. Because of that, you will have to work extra hard to tell yourself the truth about personalizing and "zapping"—namely that, in the long run, they create trouble for the relationship and for the "zapper." That is because God has so ordered the universe that the fruits of "zapping" come back on the "zapper's" own head.

Jesus made clear that this untruthful and unloving speech is fraught with danger to the person who indulges in it. . . .[1]

Loving speech doesn't put down. Instead of put-downs, loving speech will contain positive, rewarding phrases and words. . . .

---

[1]William Backus, *Telling Each Other the Truth,* Bethany House Publishers, Minneapolis, Minnesota, 1985, p. 129.
[2]Ibid., p. 161.

Name-calling, put-downs, and zaps, on the other hand, are attempts to hurt others, or to revel in wrong.[2]

Application: The person who emotionally abuses others can often list real or imagined wrongs. They themselves often feel unhappy or angry; they want their own way or feel their rights have been violated. In order to solve the conflict or vent their feelings, they attack. They choose by actions or words to reject the other person or make them feel inadequate or inferior. The person who resorts to this kind of abuse, for whatever reason, must heed the commands and warnings of Scripture.

God's command to us is: whatever a person is or may do to us, we are to treat them with the kind of love and consideration found in I Corinthians 13. We are to put others first and look out for their interests not only our own. If the other person's welfare is put ahead of our own, abuse would be eliminated. Love does not abuse another.

If the command to love is disregarded, the offender must then become acutely aware of God's warnings. God hears and takes account of every hurtful and careless word or action that harms another. God, whose judgment should never be taken lightly, hates a perverse mouth or action and He will discipline. In fact, Scripture says that whoever does not love, does not know God (I John 4:8). The abuser should examine the validity of his or her relationship with God. God's love rather than selfishness *must* be the motivation that guides our words and actions when dealing with others.

—Barbara C. Williams

║ END TIMES ║

WHAT DOES THE BIBLE SAY ABOUT END TIMES?

The Issue: The "end times" is generally defined as the period between the first coming of Jesus Christ as the babe in a manger and His second advent to set up His earthly kingdom. Conservative Christians believe and teach that the Bible predicts with infallible accuracy the events that will take place during this period. Liberal theologians (Schweitzer, Dodd, Cullmann, and others) question the accuracy of Bible prophecy and deny that it is possible to know the details of future events. It is evident that the Bible contains many passages on the subject of the end times. In the New Testament much of the teaching by the apostles as well as by Christ Himself deals with His return and the end of time.

Key Bible References:

"But of that day and hour no one knows, no, not even the angels of heaven, but My Father only.

"Therefore you also be ready, for the Son of Man is coming at an hour when you do not expect Him." Matthew 24:36, 44

"But when you hear of wars and commotions, do not be terrified; for these things must come to pass first, but the end will not come *immediately."*

Then He said to them, "Nation will rise against nation, and kingdom against kingdom.

"And there will be great earthquakes in various places, and famines and pestilences; and there will be fearful sights and great signs from heaven." Luke 21:9–11

Let no one deceive you by any means, for that day will not come *unless the falling away comes first, and the man of sin is revealed, the son of perdition, who opposes and exalts himself above all that is called God or that is worshiped, so that he sits as God in the temple of God, showing himself that he is God.* II Thessalonians 2:3–4

Additional References: Matthew 24, 25; I Thessalonians 4:13–18, 5:1–11; II Thessalonians 2:1–17; II Timothy 3:1–9; II Peter 3:1–18; I John 3:2–3.

What Others Say: Charles R. Swindoll, pastor of the Evangelical Free Church in Fullerton, California; and Dr. John F. Walvoord, former president of Dallas Theological Seminary in Dallas, Texas.

Charles R. Swindoll

Here are some facts about prophecy that will surprise most people:
—One out of every 30 verses in the Bible mentions the subject of Christ's return or the end of time.
—Of the 216 chapters in the New Testament, there are well over 300 references to the return of Jesus Christ.
—Only 4 of the 27 New Testament books fail to mention Christ's return.
—That means one-twentieth of the entire New Testament is dedicated to the subject of our Lord's return.

—In the Old Testament, such well-known and reliable men of God as Job, Moses, David, Isaiah, Jeremiah, Daniel, and most of the minor prophets, fixed at least part of their attention on the Lord's return.

—Christ spoke of His return often, especially after He had revealed His death. He never did so in vague or uncertain terms.

—Those who lived on following His teaching, who established the churches and wrote the Scriptures in the first century frequently mentioned His return in their preaching and in their writings.[1]

John F. Walvoord

Eschatology [especially the study of end times] is not designed to satisfy curiosity but to provide an intelligent comprehension of the future as a guide for a present program, and a sure ground for hope.[2]

Application: The main event of the "end times" as prophesied in the New Testament is the second coming of Jesus Christ. End time prophecies are given as both a warning to the unbeliever and an encouragement to the believer. These prophecies include: (1) a general decline in morality (II Timothy 3); (2) a widespread decline of the Christian faith (II Peter 3:1–4); (3) a rebellious attitude of young people (II Timothy 3:2); (4) the identification and establishment of the Antichrist (man of sin) (II Thessalonians 2:3–4); (5) a notable increase in the number of anti-Christian political leaders (I John 2:18); (6) a tragic increase of preachers, teachers and other leaders in the church who teach false doctrines (Jude 4, 16–18); (7) worldwide preaching of the gospel (Matthew 24:3, 7); (8) an increase in wars and threats of war (Matthew 24:3, 6); (9) an unusual increase of natural disasters (Matthew 24:3, 7); and (10) the reestablishment of Israel as a nation with the subsequent return of Jews from around the world (Ezekiel 37:21–22).

Christian scholars disagree concerning the great tribulation and time of trouble prophesied to take place during the end times. Pretribulationists believe and teach that Christ will gather all believers to Himself before this time of trouble. Post-tribulationists believe that this gathering of the saints and the time of tribulation will take place after the second advent of Christ. It is left to the reader to search the scriptures to determine to his personal satisfaction the sequence of these end time events.

---

[1]Charles R. Swindoll, *Growing Deep in the Christian Life,* Multnomah Press, Portland, Oregon, 1986, p. 268.

[2]Dr. John F. Walvoord, "Eschatology," *Zondervan Pictorial Bible Dictionary,* Merrill C. Tenney, Editor, Zondervan Publishing, Grand Rapids, Michigan, 1963, p. 259.

While it is evident from Scripture that we do not know "... the day nor the hour in which the Son of Man is coming" (Matthew 25:13b), these and many other prophecies in the Bible are given to Christians that they might be prepared for these events, warn others, and be strengthened in their belief and hope.

—Eugene J. Fadel

ENTERTAINMENT

WHAT ARE THE BIBLICAL GUIDELINES FOR THE ENTERTAINMENT OF CHRISTIANS?

The Issue: In a pleasure pursuing world are there types of entertainment that the committed Christian can participate in without compromising his convictions or violating biblical principles? Certainly, leisure and recreation are credible activities for the revitalization of any individual. Life in the fast-paced Twentieth Century demands it. However, the world says, "You owe it to yourself," and, "If it feels good, do it!" In response to these secular suggestions, what form should Christian entertainment take and what should be its guiding principle?

Key Bible References:

Do not forget to entertain strangers, for by so doing *some have unwittingly entertained angels.* Hebrews 13:2

It is *good neither to eat meat nor drink wine or* do anything *by which your brother stumbles or is offended or is made weak.* Romans 14:21

Or do you not know that your body is the temple of the Holy Spirit who is *in you, whom you have from God, and you are not your own?*

For you were bought at a price; therefore glorify God in your body and in your spirit, which are God's. I Corinthians 6:19–20

Do not be unequally yoked together with unbelievers. For what fellowship has righteousness with lawlessness? And what communion has light with darkness? II Corinthians 6:14

Additional References: Romans 12:2, 10, 13; I Corinthians 3:16–17, 10:31; II Corinthians 6:17; I Timothy 4:12; Hebrews 10:24–25; I Peter 4:9–11.

What Others Say: Dr. John MacArthur, pastor, author, Bible teacher.

John MacArthur

Can the church fight apathy and materialism by feeding people's appetite for entertainment? Evidently many in the church believe the answer is yes, as church after church jumps on the show-business bandwagon. It is a troubling trend that is luring many otherwise orthodox churches away from biblical priorities.

The idea is to give the audience what they want. Tailor the church service to whatever will draw a crowd. As a result pastors are more like politicians than shepherds, looking to appeal to the public rather than leading and building the flock God gave them.

The flock is served a slick, professional show, where drama, pop music, and maybe a soft-sell sermon constitute the worship service. But the emphasis isn't on worship, it's on entertainment.

Our society is filled with people who want what they want when they want it. They are into their own lifestyle, recreation and entertainment. When churches appeal to those selfish desires, they only fuel that fire and hinder true godliness![1]

Application: Perhaps the most noted form of entertainment in the Bible is hospitality. It was used by Abraham to the angels (Genesis 18:1–8), Joseph to his brethren (Genesis 43:31–34), Rahab to the spies (Joshua 2:1–21), David to Mephibosheth (II Samuel 9:7–13), Zacchaeus to Jesus (Luke 19:1–10), and by a host of others throughout Scripture. In almost every recorded instance the hospitality honored God and carried its own reward.

Other appropriate forms of entertainment for Christians are:

Family activities	Travel	Swimming
Church socials	Reading	Skiing
Fellowship	Dining out	Golfing
Picnics	Select music	Tennis
Camping/hiking	Hobbies	Select theme parks
Walking/jogging	Fishing	Select sports events

---

[1]John MacArthur, "Gimme That Showtime Religion," *Masterpiece,* September/ October, 1990, pp. 2–3.

103

Whether participating in the church or using world entertainment sources, the Christian should be selective, use good discretion, and be a godly example. Christian involvement in any activity should have as its supreme goal the glory of God. Now, "That's Entertainment!"

—Dan L. Shedd

ENVIRONMENT

WHAT IS THE CHRISTIAN'S RESPONSIBILITY TO THE EARTH'S ENVIRONMENT?

The Issue: In what theologians often refer to as the "dominion (or cultural) mandate" in Genesis, God gives man rule over all of the earth. But what does this mandate mean in an industrialized world? Does man have free reign to do whatever he pleases, or does the biblical mandate also command man to be environmentally responsible? Today there is a growing fascination among Christians and non-Christians alike with the environment, and man's use of the earth's natural resources. Biblical stewardship of the earth is increasingly becoming a hotly debated issue as Christians grapple with the problems of resource management, industrialization, and population growth. A balanced and thoughtful approach to man's role in his natural environment needs to begin with a biblical foundation.

Key Bible References:

Then God said, "Let Us make man in Our image, according to Our likeness; let them have dominion over the fish of the sea, over the birds of the air, and over the cattle, over all the earth and over every creeping thing that creeps on the earth." Genesis 1:26

The earth is the LORD's, and all its fullness, the world and those who dwell therein. Psalm 24:1

Additional References: Genesis 1:26–30, 2:15; Psalm 104; Romans 8:20–22; Colossians 1:16.

What Others Say: Dr. Lawrence Adams, director of Economic Studies at the Institute on Religion and Democracy in Washington, D.C.; and E. Calvin Beisner, writer and lecturer.

Lawrence Adams

Today's growing concern for the environment among Christians is commendable. The mandate to rule over the earth involves cultivation, and is summed up as "responsible stewardship." However, it is necessary to guard against this concern becoming a preoccupation, and thus the "guiding principle" of our theology. The recent environmental movement has elements which suggest sacredness and purity of the earth, and which deny the effects of sin. This thinking can erode the Christian's sense of both God's nature and the nature of creation.

As stated in the Oxford Declaration, a biblical perspective sees that while humans were given dominion over the earth, they do not have license to abuse it. This implies the need to maintain a healthy ecological system over time. Failure in exercising this careful stewardship usually results from either selfish individualism that neglects human community or a rigid collectivism that stifles human freedom.[1]

E. Calvin Beisner

. . . the earth, with everything in it—though it belongs to God—was intended by God to serve man's needs. Man was not made for the earth; the earth was made for man. It is man, not the earth or anything in it, who was created in the image of God. To make man subservient to the earth is to turn the purpose of God in creation on its head. Certainly the environment should be protected, but it must be protected for the sake of man, not for its own sake. Anything else is idolatry of nature.

The goal of resource management should be to increase the degree to which the world serves man. Since, however, different people have different needs and desires, no generalization is possible regarding what particular uses serve that goal and what ones don't. Within the limits of God's moral Law, any use of resources that serves people is permissible.[2]

Application: Christians need to understand fully that God is creator, and that all things, including man, are created by Him and for Him. Further, all things are being redeemed by Him (Colossians 1:20). The purpose of creation is to glorify God. Men and women, being in God's image, are to be wise stewards of what the Lord has given them dominion over.

---

[1]Lawrence Adams, and Fredrick Jones, "Stewardship in the 90's: Two Views," *Economic Studies Briefing Paper,* no. 1, The Institute on Religion and Democracy, Washington, D.C., July, 1990, p. 6.

[2]E. Calvin Beisner, *Prospects for Growth,* Crossway Books, Westchester, Illinois, 1990, pp. 163, 168.

Consequently, man is given the authority to use his natural environment. However, man is ultimately responsible to God for the decisions he makes regarding the use of what has been given to him. Because man is sinful, he has damaged God's creation and produced a variety of ecological problems through bad stewardship (Romans 8:20–22). If Christians are not objective and humble in their approach to the use of the earth's resources and the role of man in his environment, they risk mistakenly imposing on others their own standards rather than God's. Human beings are created to be a part of a larger community, and therefore have a responsibility to exercise dominion over creation in a way which is responsible not only to God, but to all mankind, including future generations.

—**Lonni K. Jackson**

ETHICS

IS IT POSSIBLE TO HAVE ETHICS WITHOUT A BIBLICAL MORAL BASE?

The Issue: Modern secular societies have tried to eradicate religion from the public square and yet at the same time establish a system of ethics that keeps their societies from falling into moral anarchy. But history has no record of any society that has been successful in maintaining a moral code without a strong religious base. Moreover, no society has been able to have both freedom and morality apart from Christianity.

Perhaps the most graphic example of a modern society that has tried to remove all vestiges of religion and still maintain an ethical system was the Soviet Union. But by the early 1990's it became clear this system was failing. Millions of Bibles—for the first time since 1917—were being distributed in the country to counteract the effects of atheism.

Western democracies have fared little better. A 1990 Josephson Institute for the Advancement of Ethics study observed that "American youth lack commitment to core moral values like honesty, personal responsibility, respect for others, and civic duty."

Increasingly, it is becoming apparent that a thorough-going system of ethics can come only from the Bible.

Key Bible References:

How can a young man cleanse his way? By taking heed according to Your word. Psalm 119:9

All Scripture is *given by inspiration of God, and* is *profitable for doctrine, for reproof, for correction, for instruction in righteousness, that the man of God may be complete, thoroughly equipped for every good work.* II Timothy 3:16-17

... by which have been given to us exceedingly great and precious promises, that through these you may be partakers of the divine nature, having escaped the corruption that is *in the world through lust.*

But also for this very reason, giving all diligence, add to your faith virtue, to virtue knowledge, to knowledge self-control, to self-control perseverance, to perseverance godliness, to godliness brotherly kindness, and to brotherly kindness love. II Peter 1:4–7

There is a way which seems right to a man, but its end is *the way of death.* Proverbs 14:12

Additional References: Judges 17:6; Psalm 119; Proverbs 16:25; Romans 1:18–32; II Peter 1:3–8.

What Others Say: Charles Colson, contemporary Christian author; John Witherspoon, evangelical signer of the Declaration of Independence; and George Washington, first United States President.

Charles Colson
Our nation demands ethics, but abandons the objective moral base on which any real standard of ethics must logically rest. . . . in Western civilization that foundation has been twenty-three centuries of accumulated wisdom, natural law, and the Judeo-Christian tradition based on Biblical revelation.[1]

John Witherspoon
Nothing is more certain, than that a general profligacy and corruption of manners make a people ripe for destruction. A good form of government may hold the rotten materials together for a time, but beyond a certain pitch, even the best constitution will be ineffectual, and slavery must ensue.[2]

---

[1]Charles Colson, *The God of Stones and Spiders,* Crossway Books, Wheaton, Illinois, 1990.
[2]James Witherspoon, *Works,* Vol. V. , p. 209.

George Washington

Of all the disposition and habits which lead to political prosperity, religion, and morality are indispensable supports. . . . And let us with caution indulge the supposition that morality can be maintained without religion. Whatever may be conceded to the influence of refined education on minds of peculiar structure, reason and experience both forbid us to expect that national morality can prevail in exclusion of religious principle.[3]

Application: Modern societies will continue to sink into moral decay—and develop governments with ever-increasing police powers to deal with the consequences—unless there is a revival of true Christianity. With biblical Christianity comes true peace, moral order, and freedom. Conscience may uphold civilization for a time (Romans 2) but even that becomes distorted without an objective standard of righteousness (II Timothy 4:2).

To restore ethics to our society, it is the duty of every Christian to conduct his or her professional and personal affairs in such a way as will bring honor and glory to Jesus Christ. Through personal piety, public witness, Christian service, and the application of biblical principles to politics, education, and business, Christians can help re-establish ethics on a proper biblical foundation.

—Robert A. Peterson

EUTHANASIA

WHAT DOES THE BIBLE SAY ABOUT EUTHANASIA?

The Issue: Euthanasia is defined as, "the act or practice of killing or permitting death of hopelessly sick or injured individuals in a relatively painless way for reasons of mercy," in Webster's Ninth New Collegiate Dictionary. A popular term for euthanasia is "mercy killing." The word euthanasia comes from the Greek (eu + thanatos) and its literal meaning is "good death." The belief in euthanasia has led to killing patients thought to be terminally ill, the aged who appear to be useless drains on society, or the assisting of older and

---

[3]James D. Richardson, *A Compilation of the Messages and Papers of the Presidents,* I, Washington: Government Printing Office, 1896, p. 220.

infirmed people to kill themselves. Usually this is done with poisons or overdoses of drugs or certain medications. Related to these practices are the concerns about how long to attempt to sustain life through artificial means and when to terminate those practices if evidence shows that death would occur without them.

Key Bible References:

"You shall not murder." Exodus 20:13

Then God said, "Let Us make man in Our image, according to Our likeness; let them have dominion over... all the earth...."

So God created man in His own image; in the image of God He created him; male and female He created them.

Then God blessed them, and God said to them, "Be fruitful and multiply; fill the earth and subdue it, . . ." Genesis 1:26–28

Determining the moment of death is God's prerogative. "Man who is born of woman is of few days.

Since his days are determined, the number of his months is with You; You have appointed his limits, so that he cannot pass." Job 14:1, 5

A time to be born, and a time to die; . . . Ecclesiastes 3:2

Additional References: Genesis 9:6–7; Psalm 139:13–16; Romans 6:23; I Corinthians 15:26, 56; Hebrews 9:27.

What Others Say: Francis A. Schaeffer, Bible scholar and Christian philosopher and C. Everett Koop, M.D., Christian medical doctor and former Surgeon General of the United States; and John Jefferson Davis, Bible scholar and seminary professor.

Francis A. Schaeffer and C. Everett Koop
. . . we must say that we are proponents of the sanctity of human life—all human life—born and unborn; old and young; black, white, brown and yellow. We fear the attitude of the medical profession in sanctioning abortion and in moving inexorably down the road from abortion to infanticide and finally further on to what might be unthinkable today but acceptable in a very few years—such as a widespread euthanasia program.[1]

---

[1]Francis A. Schaeffer and C. Everett Koop, M.D., *Whatever Happened To the Human Race?*, Fleming H. Revell Company, Old Tappan, New Jersey, 1979, p. 110.

Our concern is more than not killing the elderly and the ill. It is giving them real life.[2]

John Jefferson Davis

According to the Bible, death is unnatural, inevitable and for the Christian, not final. Death is an unnatural intrusion into God's good universe. It is a direct consequence of man's sin (Genesis 2:17 "On the day you eat of it, you will surely die"; Romans 6:23, "for the wages of sin is death"). Death is the "last enemy," an enemy of man that will be finally overcome at the time of Christ's return and the final resurrection (I Corinthians 15:26–56). Because death is unnatural, the Christian will reject humanistic philosophies that see death and dying as only a "natural" transition to either oblivion or to some higher stage of existence. According to the Bible, for the unbeliever death is in fact a prelude to final judgment in the presence of God (Hebrews 9:27).[3]

Showing mercy to a dog or to a horse suffering great pain is likewise not a good argument of euthanasia . . . the Christian view of man's immortal soul precludes any consideration of man's death that leaves out the question of his eternal destiny.[4]

While the Bible never explicitly condemns suicide, every instance of suicide in the Bible is directly associated with the person's spiritual collapse, from Saul to Judas (I Samuel 31:4; II Samuel 17:23; I Kings 16:18–20; Matthew 27:5; Acts 1:18). The Biblical attitude toward human life is so affirmative that an explicit condemnation of suicide is unnecessary; its evil is self-evident.[5]

There is also the important distinction between "sustaining life" and "prolonging dying," or as Paul Ramsey states it, between "saving life by prolonging the living of it and only prolonging a patient's dying." There is no moral obligation to prolong artificially a truly terminal patient's irreversible and imminent process of dying. This is sometimes called employing "useless means" of treatment. The point of any form of medical treatment is to cure the patient, or if curing is not possible, at least to contribute to a reasonable expectation of life and level of comfort. A form of treatment with no reasonable expectation of accomplishing these ends is not therapy in any meaningful sense of the word, but may in fact represent an inappropriate imposition upon the dying patient.[6]

---

[2]Ibid., p. 117.

[3]John Jefferson Davis, *Evangelical Ethics, Issues Facing the Church Today,* Presbyterian and Reformed Publishing Company, Phillipsburg, New Jersey, 1985, p. 182.

[4]Ibid., p. 188.

[5]Ibid., p. 188.

[6]Ibid., p. 182.

Application: Secular man looks at human life the same way he would look at animal life and thus makes pragmatic decisions that do not take into consideration God's special creative acts or God's direct teaching regarding the purpose and sanctity of life. It is possible for man to make wrong judgments about the worth of the elderly or the value of the individual. Some groups in our society today would like to see euthanasia legalized. However, this would certainly strain the "ethics" of the medical profession because they would move from "healer" to society's "executioner." Christians need to view life as sacred and death as God's prerogative. We must see that there is no such thing as a life not worthy to be lived.

We must also be realistic and realize that we will need to not merely stand against the killing of the aged and/or infirmed, but we must be willing to sacrifice to provide for their care and assist them in living a full, complete and productive life wherever and however possible. Some day each of us will be in the same place, needing the assistance of loving individuals dedicated to our care.

The issue of sustaining life by artificial means may need to be decided case by case, but the principles remain the same. Any treatment should either point towards a cure for the patient or to providing a level of comfort during the process of dying.

—James W. Braley

EVOLUTION

IS THERE A BIBLICAL FOUNDATION FOR EVOLUTION?

The Issue: Many Christians believe they can accept the basic tenets of evolutionary theory and "harmonize" this with the biblical account of origins as recorded in the book of Genesis. This particular "harmonization" is called "theistic evolution," of which there are many variants. This position, as well as others that accept major aspects of evolutionary theory, such as "progressive creation," are considered by strict creationists to be compromise positions that undermine the Gospel and the authority of God's Word.

Key Bible References:

Also for Adam and his wife the LORD God made tunics of skin, and clothed them.

Then the LORD God said, "Behold, the man has become like one of Us, to know good and evil. And now, lest he put out his hand and take also of the tree of life, and eat, and live forever"—therefore the LORD God sent him out of the garden of Eden to till the ground from which he was taken. Genesis 3:21–23

*Therefore, just as through one man sin entered the world, and death through sin, and thus death spread to all men, because all sinned—*Romans 5:12

For we know that the whole creation groans and labors with birth pangs together until now. Romans 8:22

For since by man came death, by Man also came the resurrection of the dead.

For as in Adam all die, even so in Christ all shall be made alive.

The last enemy that will be destroyed is death. I Corinthians 15:21–22, 26

Additional References: Genesis 1:29–30; Exodus 20:11; Matthew 19:4–6, 24:37–39; Luke 16:27–31, 24:25–27; John 5:45–47; Acts 3:21; I Timothy 2:13–14.

What Others Say: Jacques Monod (deceased), atheist, and Nobel prize-winning French biologist; G. Richard Bozarth, atheist, and writer for *The American Atheist;* and Dr. Henry Morris, creation scientist, author, and president of the Institute for Creation Research.

Jacques Monod

(Natural) selection is the blindest, and most cruel way of evolving new species, . . . The struggle for life and elimination of the weakest is a horrible process, against which our whole modern ethics revolts. An ideal society is a non-selective society, is one where the weak is protected; which is exactly the reverse of the so-called natural law. I am surprised that a Christian would defend the idea that this is the process which God more or less set up in order to have evolution.[1]

G. Richard Bozarth

. . . Christianity is—must be!—totally committed to the special creation as described in Genesis, and Christianity must fight with its full might, fair or foul, against the theory of evolution. . . . It be-

---

[1]Jacques Monod, "Jacques Monod and 'Theistic Evolution'" *Ex Nihilo,* Creation Science Foundation Ltd., Australia, Vol. 3, No. 2, 1980, p. 19.

comes clear now that the whole justification of Jesus' life and death is predicated on the existence of Adam and the forbidden fruit he and Eve ate. Without the original sin, who needs to be redeemed? Without Adam's fall into a life of constant sin terminated by death, what purpose is there to Christianity? None.[2]

Henry Morris

The book of Genesis thus is in reality the foundation of all true history, as well as of true science and true philosophy. . . . It is quite impossible, therefore, for one to reject the historicity and divine authority of the book of Genesis without undermining, and in effect, repudiating, the authority of the entire Bible. If the first Adam is only an allegory, then by all logic, so is the second Adam. If man did not really fall into sin from his state of created innocency, there is no reason for him to need a Savior.[3]

Application: In reality, theistic evolution is no different scientifically from atheistic evolution. God is simply added to the story. Christians who believe that God used evolution in creation accept what the atheistic view tells them, and then add God to the situation and reinterpret the Bible.

Evolution teaches that death and bloodshed existed virtually from the beginning. The Bible teaches that God introduced death and bloodshed as a consequence of sin—the penalty which Christ, the last Adam, bore by His death and shedding of blood on the cross but triumphed over in His glorious resurrection for the redemption of man. If death and bloodshed existed before man sinned (as theistic evolution requires), the redemption message (and thus the reason for death) is nonsense. God Himself was the first One to shed blood, because He gave Adam and Eve coats of skin to cover their nakedness. Cain's offering was rejected because it did not involve the shedding of blood.

Accepting evolution destroys the redemption message and means that Genesis cannot be taken literally. In fact, Genesis must be taken literally as all major doctrines of Christianity, directly or indirectly, have their basis in the book of Genesis. If Genesis cannot be taken literally, there is no foundation for Christian doctrine; therefore, Christian doctrine no longer has meaning. There is certainly no biblical foundation for evolution!

—Ken Ham

[2]G. Richard Bozarth, "The Meaning of Evolution," *The American Atheist,* September, 1978, p. 19.

[3]Henry M. Morris, *The Genesis Record,* Creation Life Publishers, San Diego, California, 1976, pp. 21–22.

EXCELLENCE

WHAT DOES THE SCRIPTURE SAY ABOUT EXCELLENCE?

The Issue: Christians are too often accused of being second-rate in the way they dress, the literature they publish, the schools they run, the standards of quality they maintain. Yet, we understand from the Scripture that excellence of life is a definite outworking of the presence of God in the life of a believer. The essence of excellence resides in God and should be reflected in those created in the image of God and called the children of God. The more we are in God and He in us, the more excellent we become. Philippians 4:13 promises "I can do all things through Christ who strengthens me." Christ did not enable us for mediocrity but for excellence.

Key Bible References:

O LORD, our Lord, how excellent is Your name in all the earth! Psalm 8:9

...They shall see the glory of the LORD, the excellency of our God. Isaiah 35:2c

But indeed I also count all things loss for the excellence of the knowledge of Christ Jesus my Lord, ... Philippians 3:8

Even so you, since you are zealous for spiritual gifts, let it be for the edification of the church that you seek to excel. I Corinthians 14:12

Additional References: Exodus 15:7; Job 37:23; Psalm 150:2; Isaiah 12:5, 28:29; I Corinthians 12:31.

What Others Say: Ted Engstrom, author on corporate and personal life management.

Ted Engstrom

Lasting success, true excellence seldom comes overnight. And it always has a price. One night after he had given one of the greatest concerts of his brilliant career, Paderewski was greeted by an over-eager fan who said, "Oh, I'd give my life to be able to play like you do." Paderewski replied quietly, "I did."[1]

---

[1] Ted W. Engstrom, *The Pursuit of Excellence,* Zondervan Publishing, Grand Rapids, Michigan, 1982, p. 85.

Excellence is a process that should occupy all our days, whether it is tied to a specific piece of work done or not. Just as you must work at life, so you must work at the spirit of excellence. It will become a part of you only through a singleness of purpose and a determination to see your goals through to the end.[2]

Application: There is no excuse for shoddiness on the part of Christians. Our values and goals may not always call for the use of cutting-edge technology or Madison Avenue techniques, but there is never an excuse for short-sheeted quality in a work that claims the name of Christ.

Excellence is not a state which we attain; it is a trait of God which we reflect by His gracious spirit working in us. An excellent spirit was found in Daniel (Daniel 5:12). The apostle Paul made it clear, however, that we should not depend on our excellence but on God. "And I, brethren, when I came to you, did not come with excellence of speech . . . but in demonstration of the Spirit and of power, that your faith should not be in the wisdom of men but in the power of God" (I Corinthians 2:1, 4–5).

Excellence in the life of a believer is not a trait designed to draw attention to oneself. Then what is the motivation for us to excel? ". . . *let it be* for the edification of the church *that* you seek to excel" (I Corinthians 14:12). Christ will build His church with Christians of excellence.

Excellent Christian living is not automatic. Excellence is the glove on the hand of diligence. It is hard work and there are no clip-out coupons for a special deal. We must say as David did, ". . . nor will I offer burnt offerings to the LORD my God with that which costs me nothing (II Samuel 24:24). Christian excellence is living life "heartily, as to the Lord" (Colossians 3:23), approving "the things that are excellent" (Philippians 1:9–11).

—Philip H. Graybeal

---

[2]Ibid., p. 89.

FAITH

HOW CAN A PERSON INCREASE
ONE'S FAITH DAILY?

The Issue: Extending love to others develops one's relationship to man while exercising faith deepens one's relationship to God. For this reason, God states clearly that it is impossible to please Him without faith. Many Christians are in a spiritual rut today because they have stopped living by faith and are now guided by fear and apprehension. If one is obedient to God's Word, he will be continually taking steps of faith. Knowing this truth, why is it so difficult to voluntarily exercise faith day by day? How can the Christian increase his faith?

Key Bible References:

Now faith is the substance of things hoped for, the evidence of things not seen.

For by it the elders obtained a good *testimony.*

But without faith it is impossible to please Him, *for he who comes to God must believe that He is, and that He is a rewarder of those who diligently seek Him.* Hebrews 11:1–2, 6

So then faith comes by hearing, and hearing by the word of God. Romans 10:17

Additional References: Luke 17:5–6; II Corinthians 5:7; Ephesians 6:16.

What Others Say: Dwight L. Moody, evangelist and Bible teacher.

Dwight L. Moody
I prayed for faith, and thought that someday faith would come down and strike me like lightning. But faith did not come. One day I read in the tenth chapter of Romans, "Now faith comes by hearing, and hearing by the Word of God." I had closed my Bible and prayed for faith. Now I opened my Bible and began to study, and faith has been growing ever since.[1]

---

[1]Quotation from one of Dwight L. Moody's messages on faith.

116

Application: As an earthly father who loves his children and is alert to ways to show his love, our heavenly Father is equally attentive to us. His desire is to do mighty things for us on a daily basis. God works through our steps of faith. There are many biblical examples to indicate that God's power was released only after man voluntarily did something requiring faith. Another critical value of faith is that it quenches the fiery darts of doubt that come from Satan (Ephesians 6:16).

Hebrews reminds us it is impossible to please God without exercising faith. How can one increase his faith daily? In Romans 10:17 it is clear that faith is interwoven with God's Word. The key is to real-ize what God says is true. Memorizing verses is good but realizing these truths is greater. The more of the Bible we implicitly believe and use, the more our faith grows. Realization of the Word means the truth drops from our head into our hearts and we *really* believe enough to act. This gives one the courage to step out to test God. The more we try God . . . the more He responds. . . .

—**Art Nazigian**

FAMILY

WHAT IS THE BASIC VALUE OF FAMILY IN OUR LIVES?

The Issue: God planned and ordained the family to be the basic unit of society, to provide care, cultivation, and companionship, and for procreation. It is to be a training ground for nurturing children and conforming adults into godly men and women who can bless the world and glorify their Creator. The family is an illustration of our relationship to God and as such is vehemently opposed and attacked by Satan.

Key Bible References:

And the LORD God said, "It is not good that man should be alone; I will make him a helper comparable to him."

And Adam said: "This is now bone of my bones and flesh of my flesh; she shall be called Woman, because she was taken out of Man."

Therefore a man shall leave his father and mother and be joined to his wife, and they shall become one flesh. Genesis 2:18, 23–24

"And these words which I command you today shall be in your heart; you shall teach them diligently to your children, and shall talk of them when you sit in your house, when you walk by the way, when you lie down, and when you rise up." Deuteronomy 6:6–7

Husbands, love your wives, just as Christ also loved the church and gave Himself for it, that He might sanctify and cleanse it with the washing of water by the word, that He might present it to Himself a glorious church, not having spot or wrinkle or any such thing, but that it should be holy and without blemish.

So husbands ought to love their own wives as their own bodies; he who loves his wife loves himself.

For no one ever hated his own flesh, but nourishes and cherishes it, just as the Lord does *the church.*

For we are members of His body, of His flesh and of His bones.

"For this reason a man shall leave his father and mother and be joined to his wife, and the two shall become one flesh." Ephesians 5:25–31

Children, obey your parents in the Lord, for this is right.

"Honor your father and mother," *which is the first commandment with promise:* "that it may be well with you and you may live long on the earth."

And you, fathers, do not provoke your children to wrath, but bring them up in the training and admonition of the Lord. Ephesians 6:1–4

Additional References: Genesis 1:28; Deuteronomy 6:1–2; Psalms 68:6a, 107:40–43; Proverbs 6:20–23; I Thessalonians 2:11–12; I Timothy 5:4, 8; I Peter 3:1–9.

What Others Say: Charles R. Swindoll, pastor of First Evangelical Free Church in Fullerton, California.

Charles R. Swindoll

Immediately after the Lord God created the first man and woman, He blessed them (placed His favor upon them), and then He spoke to them. In fact, the first command in all the Scripture appears in this section. Interestingly, it had to do with the family: "Be fruitful and multiply; fill the earth . . ." (Genesis 1:28).

In the final verses of Genesis 2, the zoom lens of Scripture again picks up the subject of the family as God planned it. Look closely. Woven into the fabric of those two sentences are four timeless one-word principles that give a marriage (as well as a family) its strength:

Severance	"leave his father and mother"
Permanence	"cleave to his wife"
Unity	"they shall become one flesh"
Intimacy	"both naked and were not ashamed"

From earliest time God has cared so much about the family that He provided the foundational guidelines that would make it solid and keep it strong. Stop and think. Before He said much about work or anything at all about civil government, the church, the school, the law, the races, or maintaining our health, God spelled out the primary principles of domestic health and happiness. To Him, that deserved top priority. And He didn't forget about it once He set everything in motion.[1]

Application: Colleagues, friends, neighbors, and fellow-church members often change throughout our lives but the weave of our family tapestry is always a part of us. Throughout the Bible, God identifies people by their families. While the man and woman are to leave and cleave when forming a new family, the ties to the extended family form an inescapable chain of continuity and a network of care and accountability. The extended family often forms a safety net not easily broken. For example, youths, and adults, who may be tempted to make unwise and hurtful decisions, perhaps in rebellion against parents, may think twice before disappointing extended family members like grandparents or aunts and uncles.

To accurately represent God's relationship to man and Christ's relationship to His bride, the church, and to reproduce Christians, to bring the lost into the family of God, Christians must reflect God's love in their own earthly families, follow God's divine order of authority in the home, and heed His command to leave and be joined (Genesis 2:24–25). Because the family is under attack, believers must "close ranks" by drawing closer to God who will draw the family circle tighter together.

—A. Pierre Guillermin

---

[1]Charles R. Swindoll, *Growing Wise in Family Life,* Multnomah Press, Portland, Oregon, 1988, pp. 37–38.

FAMILY PRAYER TIME

WHICH BIBLICAL PRINCIPLES SUPPORT FAMILY PRAYER TIME?

The Issue: No serious Christian would dispute the value of collective family prayer. That's why it is so surprising to find no biblical commands to do so and no clear-cut examples of families praying together in Scripture. Perhaps it is so obvious a requirement for spiritual training that the heavenly Father assumes His children will observe it joyfully.

Several biblical principles apply, however, like the recognition that spiritual growth is impossible without prayer. The passages cited below indicate that parents have an absolute responsibility to share God's truth with their children and the reality and vitality of prayer is surely a significant portion of that truth.

Key Bible References:

"You shall teach them diligently to your children, and shall talk of them when you sit in your house, when you walk by the way, when you lie down, and when you rise up.

"You shall bind them as a sign on your hand, and they shall be as frontlets between your eyes.

"You shall write them on the doorposts of your house and on your gates." Deuteronomy 6:7–9

"The secret things belong to the LORD our God, but those things which are revealed belong to us and to our children forever, that we may do all the words of this law." Deuteronomy 29:29

And you, fathers, do not provoke your children to wrath, but bring them up in the training and admonition of the Lord. Ephesians 6:4

Husbands, likewise dwell with them with understanding, giving honor to the wife, as to the weaker vessel, and as being heirs together of the grace of life, that your prayers may not be hindered. I Peter 3:7–12

Additional References: I Samuel 12:23; Psalms 127, 128; Proverbs 4:1–4; Hebrews 4:16.

What Others Say: Dr. V. Gilbert Beers, president of Scripture Press Publications; and Dr. Robert A. Cook, former president of Kings College in Briarcliff Manor, New York.

V. Gilbert Beers

Prayer is perhaps the most important ingredient in Christian living. It deserves loving role-modeling so that our children become enthusiastic about those times when they can talk to their Heavenly Father.[1]

Robert A. Cook

My authority in my home is exactly proportional to what I got fresh from God that day. I don't even have to talk about it—there is a heavenly aura when Dad's met God. When I backslide, every thing at home falls apart.[2]

Application: The family prayer which our Lord taught His disciples reminds us all of the absolute dependence we have upon the Lord for every thing in life, both physical and spiritual needs. Praying for and with our children is productive in at least three ways. It fulfills God's command to parents to nurture their children in the things of the Lord; it calls down from heaven the grace for daily living which every member of every family needs; and it offers a model of prayer which our children can reproduce in their own lives and ultimately as parents with their own children. Individual spiritual growth is impossible without prayer and corporate family spiritual growth falls under this same restriction.

—Kenneth O. Gangel

FATHERHOOD

WHAT IS THE BIBLICAL ROLE OF A FATHER?

The Issue: Since God's creation of the earth, men have struggled to adequately fulfill the role of fatherhood. Moreover, it seems that time has only served to further erode the standing of a father in relation to his children. In today's fast-paced, pressure-laden, "me-

---

[1]V. Gilbert Beers, "Teaching Children to Pray," *Parents and Children,* Jay Kesler, Ron Beers and LaVonne Neff, Editors, Victor Books, Wheaton, Illinois, 1986, p. 668.
[2]Lloyd Cory, *Quotable Quotations,* Victor Books, Wheaton, Illinois, 1985, p. 132.

oriented" society, many people view fatherhood as passé, a bothersome intrusion into other self-oriented priorities. But through Scripture, God has given us a clear-cut, balanced view of who we are to be as fathers: Men who teach, encourage, discipline, comfort, and love our children.

Key Bible References:

... as you know how we exhorted, and comforted, and charged every one of you, as a father does *his own children, that you would walk worthy of God who calls you into His own kingdom and glory.* I Thessalonians 2:11–12

And you, fathers, do not provoke your children to wrath, but bring them up in the training and admonition of the Lord. Ephesians 6:4

He who spares his rod hates his son, but he who loves him disciplines him promptly. Proverbs 13:24

Additional References: Proverbs 22:6, 15; I Corinthians 11:1; Galatians 6:7; Hebrews 12:5–9.

What Others Say: Charles R. Swindoll, pastor of the Evangelical Free Church in Fullerton, California.

Charles R. Swindoll

Instead of challenging fathers to give of themselves, the system encourages them to give the stuff their increased salaries can buy—a better education, a membership at the club, material possessions, nicer homes, extra cars, personal TVs, credit cards, and computers; the list goes on. But what about dad himself?

Oh, dads, when will we learn? How long will it take? Each day of our lives we make deposits into the memory banks of our children. By remembering that, I find I am more likely to work on the qualities that build a lasting relationship between my children and me.[1]

Application: As believers, we are called to focus every day in renewed spiritual warfare as Christian soldiers battling Satan and the worldview of life he has promoted. We need to recognize the lures of this world for what they are, make a decision to stand for what God would have us to do, and then stick to our commitment to serve Him. All of which means that as fathers, we must be willing to sac-

---

[1]Charles R. Swindoll, *Growing Wise In Family Life,* Multnomah Press, Portland, Oregon, 1988, pp. 64, 66.

rifice our own pleasures for the sake of our children, putting our time, attention and efforts into "training them up in the way they should go"—not an easy task when we ourselves have been so bombarded, brainwashed, and trained by Satan and his spokesmen here on earth.

As Christians, we are called to personify Christ to a lost world. We need to fulfill the Great Commission by beginning with our own children, making their spiritual growth and personal development our first priority in life—so that one day soon we will have taught them to have a walk worthy of the calling God has extended to us all.

—Ken Lee

FATHERLESS

WHAT IS OUR CHRISTIAN RESPONSIBILITY TO THE FATHERLESS?

The Issue: It is easy for Christians, particularly those of us who live in an affluent society, to become caught up in our own lives and to neglect our responsibility to help others. The fatherless are a special concern of our heavenly Father, often associated with the Bible with widows and the weak, oppressed, lonely, bereaved and afflicted. Clearly our God expects us to actively work in His name on their behalf.

Key Bible References:

Pure and undefiled religion before God and the Father is this: to visit orphans and widows in their trouble, . . . James 1:27

Learn to do good; seek justice, reprove the oppressor; defend the fatherless, plead for the widow. Isaiah 1:17

Defend the poor and fatherless; do justice to the afflicted and needy.

Deliver the poor and needy; free them from the hand of the wicked. Psalm 82:3–4

"And I will come near you for judgment; I will be a swift witness against sorcerers, against adulterers, against perjurers,

against those who exploit wage earners and widows and fatherless, and against those who turn away an alien—because they do not fear Me," says the LORD of hosts. Malachi 3:5

Additional References: Exodus 22:24; Deuteronomy 10:18, 24:17–22; Psalms 10:14, 18, 146:9; Matthew 25:35–44; John 14:18; Colossians 3:12–14; I Timothy 5:10.

What Others Say: W. Stanley Mooneyham, past president of World Vision; and Manfred George Gutzke, former seminary professor and preacher in the Southern Presbyterian Church.

W. Stanley Mooneyham
When the Athenian philosopher Aristides was called upon to defend his fellow Christians before Emperor Hadrian in A.D. 125, he said, "They love one another. The widow's needs are not ignored, and they rescue the orphan from the person who does him violence. . . ."

Caring for the needs of deprived children is both a moral responsibility and an ethical imperative . . . commanded by God in the Scripture.[1]

Manfred George Gutzke
All through the history of the church . . . , wherever the Gospel has gone there followed kindness and help for the poor and needy. Hospitals have been built, old folks home have been organized and orphanages have been set up. No other name in the world has ever been associated with helping the poor and the weak, the fatherless and those in distress like the name of the Lord Jesus Christ.[2]

Application: Whether we come from good and complete homes, or from troubled family backgrounds, every Christian has the joy and comfort of being an adopted child of God, of being able to say each day, "Our Father in heaven." In turn, our heavenly Father calls us to exercise the same kind of love and compassion we have received from Him to others. To do that we need to be aware of legitimate needs and to open our hearts, homes, and bank accounts.

—**Jack Layman**

---

[1]W. Stanley Mooneyham, *Baker's Dictionary of Christian Ethics,* Carl F. H. Henry, Editor, Baker Book House, Grand Rapids, Michigan, 1973, p. 477.

[2]Manford George Gutzke, *Plain Talk on James,* Zondervan Publishing, Grand Rapids, Michigan, 1969, pp. 58–59.

FEAR

WHAT DOES THE BIBLE TEACH ABOUT OVERCOMING FEAR?

The Issue: Fear is any of a variety of degrees of anxiety associated with social disgrace or bodily harm. This emotional reaction can be in response to real or imagined dangers or misfortunes. Uncontrolled, this emotion can cause us to have fears and anxieties which can hinder us in our relationship with God and with our fellowman. Fear can undermine our trust in God and can cause us to doubt that He is able to help us through the difficult time we are facing.

Just as it is not God's plan for man to live in fear, it is Satan's goal to cause us to be pulled down and to be paralyzed by the anxieties of life.

Key Bible References:

". . . Let not your heart be troubled, neither let it be afraid." John 14:27b

. . . He who is in you is greater than he who is in the world.

There is no fear in love; but perfect love casts out fear. . . . I John 4:4b, 18a

I sought the LORD, and He heard me, and delivered me from all my fears. Psalm 34:4

. . . casting all your care upon Him, for He cares for you. I Peter 5:7

Additional References: Psalms 23:4, 27:1, 46:2; Proverbs 1:7, 10:27; Isaiah 43:1; Ecclesiastes 12:13; Matthew 10:28; Luke 1:50; Philippians 2:12; II Timothy 1:7; Hebrews 12:28.

What Others Say: Dr. Kenneth Chafin, long-time pastor of the South Main Baptist Church in Houston, Texas; and Dr. Charles E. Blair, pastor of Calvary Temple in Denver, Colorado.

Kenneth Chafin

The list of what fear can do to our lives seems endless. In its mildest form it can create a kind of uneasiness about our lives which diminishes everything, and in its most savage form, fear is capable of immobilizing us and rendering us incapable of functioning in any area of our lives. This is why it is so important that each of us learn to look carefully at those things we are afraid of and find ways of managing them. I purposely used the word "manage" in preference to "solve," because we never completely get rid of fear in our lives. Like temptation, it will always be with us, and we must learn to cope with it.

I have found great help in managing fears and anxieties from some counsel which Jesus Christ gave. Many of my friends are surprised to discover that Jesus spent a lot of time talking to people about their fears and anxieties. Again and again in the Gospel stories, Jesus speaks to his listeners about their fears, and then He gives us this assurance, "Peace I leave with you; my peace I give to you; not as the world gives do I give to you. Let not your hearts be troubled, neither let them be afraid." (John 14:27)[1]

Charles E. Blair

The more fear Satan tried to dump on me, the more I countered with the promises of God. Fear and torment left because the love of God is released when we act upon the promises of God and love drives out fear.

In that experience I discovered four steps to coping with fear. They are: (1) Face your fear, (2) Review your resources, (3) Replace your fears with praise, and (4) Give your fear to God.[2]

Application: There are two sides to fear. There is the reverent and worshipful fear of the Lord, which is spoken of in Proverbs 1:7, as the beginning of knowledge. There is also the fear spoken of in Romans 8:15 which leads to bondage.

The fear of the Lord is necessary in the Christian's life because it leads to peace that passes all our understanding. Peace that allows the Christian to live above the bondage of fear. Peace that gives us the knowledge that "He who is in you is greater than he who is in the world" (I John 4:4). Those fears which bring bondage are of the world. We are not of the world but we are in the world. Even Christians are sometimes touched by those worldly fears. Eight of the ten spies sent in to spy out the promised land returned with a report that said, "We were like grasshoppers in our own sight and in theirs," when they told of the giants (Numbers 13:33). That sense of fear spread throughout the people and because of fear they were

---

[1]Kenneth Chafin, *How To Know When You've Got It Made,* Word Books, Publishers, Waco, Texas, 1986, pp. 113, 119.

[2]Charles E. Blair, *When The Journey Seems Too Great,* Tyndale House, Wheaton, Illinois, 1988, p. 137.

required, of God, to wander in the wilderness for forty years. Because of fear they were not allowed to enter the promised land. Peter was so afraid that he denied he even knew Jesus. Thousands of Gideon's army were afraid and left the troop.

The secret to living above fear is to "seek first the Kingdom of God and His righteousness" because "God is love." First John 4:18 reminds us that "There is no fear in love; but perfect love casts out fear. . . ." First Peter 5:7 assures each of us that we can and should cast "all our cares upon Him, for he cares for you." Psalm 34:4 says "I sought the LORD, and He heard me, and delivered me from all my fears."

God's word gives us the guidelines for living above fear. It does not promise that we will not be confronted with fearful situations but it does give the promise that no problem is too great for us to overcome through Him.

—**Edra J. Hudson**

FLIRTING

WHAT DOES THE BIBLE SAY TO THOSE WHO FLIRT?

The Issue: So often "flirting" is considered as being cute at an early age and as one grows older, it becomes a normal, acceptable practice by many. Since flirting is non-tangible, many feel there can be nothing wrong with it. Webster's New World Dictionary defines flirt as "making insincere advances, to play at love without serious intentions."

Some Christians have even considered flirting as not being mentioned or referenced in Scripture as a concern and thereby overlook the inherent dangers of it.

Key Bible References:

Can a man take fire to his bosom, and his clothes not be burned?

Can one walk on hot coals, and his feet not be seared? Proverbs 6:27–28

Or do you not know that your body is the temple of the Holy Spirit who is in you, whom you have from God, and you are not your own?

For you were bought at a price; therefore glorify God in your body .... I Corinthians 6:19-20

No temptation has overtaken you except such as is common to man; but God is faithful, who will not allow you to be tempted beyond what you are able, but with the temptation will also make the way of escape. .... I Corinthians 10:13

Additional References: Proverbs 2:10-22, 11:22, 16:2, 18, 21:4, 31:30; Isaiah 3:16; I Peter 3:4; I John 2:16.

What Others Say: Josh McDowell; and Barry Wood, authors.

Josh McDowell

I do not believe most Christians make a single, willful decision to commit fornication. Rather, it is a series of smaller decisions which allow for improper thinking to enter in. Once the mind has become contaminated with impure thoughts and desires, it becomes much easier for us to make wrong decisions.[1]

Barry Wood

Flirting sexually can be done by the guys as well as girls. There is a difference between being friendly, winsome, or outgoing—and flirting. Flirting says, "I'm available to you in other ways than just friends." What both guys and gals need to understand is that we're not to separate the body from the spirit (I Peter 3:4).[2]

Application: Men and women flirt to fulfill an inward desire to be accepted by the person he or she is attracted to. It is self pride that initially causes one to acquire another's attention, and everyone who is proud in heart is an abomination to the Lord. Through the subtle use of suggestive body language, especially the eyes, or direct verbal flirtation, individuals toy with the desires of the flesh. Proverbs 6:27-28 warns that if we play with the fires of passion, we will get burned.

Flirting has no place in Christian lives unless it is done in private with the one God has given through marriage.

—Ernest C. Rebstock

---

[1]Josh McDowell, *What I Wish My Parents Knew About My Sexuality,* Here's Life Publishers, San Bernadino, California, 1986, p. 160.

[2]Barry Wood, *Questions Teenagers Ask About Dating and Sex,* Fleming H. Revell Company, Old Tappan, New Jersey, 1981, p. 46.

FORGIVENESS

WHAT DOES THE BIBLE SAY ABOUT FORGIVENESS?

The Issue: Anger is an emotion that all people, even great saints of God, contend with in their lives. Anger is Satan's strategy to create bitterness, stress, illness and broken relationships among people. God's Word is very clear to state that the Christian response to anger must be forgiveness. That God feels so strongly about forgiveness is evidenced by the fact that it is a conditional principle of the Bible—"For if you forgive men their trespasses, your heavenly Father will also forgive you. But if you do not forgive men their trespasses, neither will your Father forgive your trespasses" (Matthew 6:14–15).

Key Bible References:

Then Peter came to Him and said, "Lord, how often shall my brother sin against me, and I forgive him? Up to seven times?"

Jesus said to him, "I do not say to you, up to seven times, but up to seventy times seven." Matthew 18:21–22

In Him we have redemption through His blood, the forgiveness of sins, according to the riches of His grace. Ephesians 1:7

And do not grieve the Holy Spirit of God, by whom you were sealed for the day of redemption.

Let all bitterness, wrath, anger, clamor, and evil speaking be put away from you, with all malice. Ephesians 4:30-31

. . . even as Christ forgave you, so you also must do. Colossians 3:13

Additional References: Proverbs 14:29, 29:11; Matthew 18:21–35; Acts 2:38; Ephesians 4:26–27; James 1:19; I John 1:9.

What Others Say: Jerry Cook, pastor of East Hill Church in Gresham, Oregon; Charles R. Swindoll, pastor of the Evangelical Free Church in Fullerton, California; and William Barclay, Scottish New Testament interpreter and author.

Jerry Cook
Forgive, and you'll be forgiven. Judge not, and you'll not be judged. That's in the Word (see Luke 6:37). Release people from your per-

sonal judgment! For unless I can be assured of your forgiveness, I cannot really open myself to you. You see, I know that sooner or later I will disappoint you and fail you. Not by design or desire, but I am imperfect; I'm still under construction. I must know that you will not condemn me when my weakness and flaws and sins begin to show. I need the assurance of your forgiveness—a forgiveness with no bitter aftertaste.[1]

Charles R. Swindoll

Hebrews 12:15 states that a root of bitterness can spring up and cause trouble, causing many to be defiled. You cannot nurture the bitterness plant and at the same time keep it concealed. The bitter root bears bitter fruit. You may think you can hide it . . . live with it . . . "grin and bear it," but you cannot. Slowly, inexorably, that sharp, cutting edge of unforgiveness will work its way to the surface. The poison seedling will find insidious ways to cut into others. Ironically, the one who suffers most is the one who lashes out at those around him. . . . If we nurture feelings of bitterness we are little better than inmates of an internal concentration camp. We lock ourselves in a lonely isolation chamber, walled in by our own refusal to forgive.[2]

William Barclay

If we say, "I will never forgive so-and-so for what he or she has done to me," if we say, "I will never forget what so-and-so did to me," and then go and take this petition on our lips, we are quite deliberately asking God not to forgive us. As someone has put it: "Forgiveness, like peace, is one and indivisible." Human forgiveness and divine forgiveness are inextricably intercombined. Our forgiveness of our fellow-men and God's forgiveness of us cannot be separated; they are interlinked and interdependent. If we remember what we are doing when we take this petition on our lips, there would be times when we would not dare to pray it.[3]

Application: In today's "rights-oriented" society, one needs to know that anger results when a person feels a personal right has been violated. Job 1:21 encourages an attitude of heart that yields personal rights to God—"Naked I came from my mother's womb, and naked shall I return there. The LORD gave, and the LORD has taken away; blessed be the name of the LORD."

---

[1]Jerry Cook, *Love, Acceptance and Forgiveness,* Regal Books, Ventura, California, 1979, pp. 20–21.

[2]Charles R. Swindoll, *Growing Strong in the Seasons of Life,* Multnomah Press, Portland, Oregon, 1983, p. 167.

[3]William Barclay, *The Gospel of Matthew,* The Westminster Press, Philadelphia, Pennsylvania, 1975, p. 222.

There is no bigger hindrance to a person's surrender to Christ than unresolved anger, which the Bible calls bitterness. The consequences of unresolved anger are well-known to counselors and doctors—physical illness, emotional stress and depression, and spiritual apathy. The largest toll is paid by the angry person and not the recipient of the anger.

The natural response to anger is revenge. The Christian response to anger is forgiveness. Literally, biblical forgiveness refers to sending away and letting go of anger. To extend true forgiveness to another requires a biblical understanding of one's own sinful condition before God (Romans 3:23), Jesus Christ's finished work on the cross (Ephesians 1:7) and God's forgiveness toward sin confessed (I John 1:9). The simplicity of the Gospel is that Jesus Christ forgives sin. It is not acceptable, nor will God tolerate it when one whom he has forgiven refuses to forgive another.

—**David Rhodes**

FRIENDS

WHAT KIND OF FRIENDSHIPS SHOULD CHRISTIANS MAINTAIN?

The Issue: The topic of friendship illustrates the need for biblical wisdom and balance in our lives. On the one hand we can see the need to be (like Jesus) "friends of sinners," but those kinds of friends can also pull us down. And even Christian friendships can result in bad attitudes toward other people and toward the Lord. How can we be friends to others, have the friends we need, and develop a friendship with God—all at the same time?

Key Bible References:

"This is My commandment, that you love one another as I have loved you.

"Greater love has no one than this, than to lay down one's life for his friends.

"You are My friends if you do whatever I command you.

"No longer do I call you servants, for a servant does not know what his master is doing; but I have called you friends, . . ."
John 15:12–15

... Do you not know that friendship with the world is enmity with God? Whoever therefore wants to be a friend of the world makes himself an enemy of God. James 4:4

Do not be deceived: "Evil company corrupts good habits." I Corinthians 15:33

He who walks with wise men will be wise, but the companion of fools will be destroyed. Proverbs 13:20

Additional References: Exodus 33:4; Deuteronomy 13:6–8; Proverbs 17:17, 19:4–7, 27:6, 9–10, 17; Matthew 11:19; Luke 5:30–32, 7:34, 12:4–7, 21:16–17; John 11:11, 35–36; II Corinthians 6:14–15; James 2:23; III John 14.

What Others Say: Don Posterski has done a landmark study in Canada; Josh McDowell and Bill Jones are popular and effective youth speakers.

Don Posterski

Teenagers (are) clustering together and finding fulfillment with each other as never before. A friendship cluster is more than just a circle of relationships. It is heart and soul of being young today. It is a place to belong. There is no formal membership. You are either in or out. Members of friendship clusters would rather spend their time feeling intimacy and acceptance from their few choice friends than receiving recognition individually. . . . For today's teenagers friendship is an end in itself.[1]

Josh McDowell and Bill Jones

So you can know lots of people, or rather have lots of casual friendships, but feel lonely because you don't have any committed friendships. It is that third and deepest level (after casual and close friendships) where your needs for love and acceptance are met. It is your committed friends who take away your loneliness.[2]

Application: There is no question that friendship groups are a key element in teenage society, although the friendships obviously range from casual and shallow to deep loyalty, sharing and commitment. (If you are an "outsider," ask for help in how to be accepted, but you can begin by being a friend to others.) We ought to be friendly to those outside of Christ, but must choose our closest

---

[1]Don Posterski, *Friendship: A Window On Ministry to Youth,* Project Teen Canada, distributed by Inter-Varsity Press, Markham, Ontario, Canada, 1986, pp. 7–8.

[2]Josh McDowell and Bill Jones, *The Teenager Q and A Book,* Word Books, Dallas, Texas, 1990, p. 103.

friends wisely, encourage our group to be loyal to Christ as well as to one another, and not allow any friendships to keep us from being loyal, sharing, and committed friends of Jesus.

—Jack Layman

FRUGALITY

WHAT DOES THE BIBLE TEACH ABOUT FRUGALITY?

The Issue: The Bible clearly teaches that God would have His own use all resources (money, natural resources, food, strength, etc.) very carefully and avoid wastefulness. Scriptures endorse a "no waste" economic system. When one wastes little, he is considered a good and wise steward. As the Christian exercises frugality he includes giving, supporting his family, meeting the demands of civil government and planning for the next generation.

Key Bible References:

"And let them gather all the food of those good years that are coming, and store up grain under the authority of Pharaoh, and let them keep food in the cities.

"Then that food shall be for a reserve for the land for the seven years of famine which shall be in the land of Egypt, that the land may not perish during the famine." Genesis 41:35–36

There is *desirable treasure, and oil in the dwelling of the wise, but a foolish man squanders it.* Proverbs 21:20

So when they were filled, He said to His disciples, "Gather up the fragments that remain, so that nothing is lost." John 6:12

Additional References: I Kings 17:5–16; Proverbs 11:16, 12:27, 13:22, 18:9; Matthew 14:20; Mark 7:28; Luke 16:1.

What Others Say: Gary Demar; Ron Blue; and Larry Burkett, Christian money management experts.

Gary Demar
At this point a word of caution is in order. The Christian does not have to deny material wealth in order to obtain wisdom and righ-

133

teousness. Scripture compares wisdom and righteousness with gold, silver and jewels. The Bible nowhere states that you cannot have one (riches) without the other (wisdom). The truly wise man will understand how to accumulate wealth, make it available to those in need, support worthwhile businesses and charitable organizations and avoid the allurement of riches.[1]

Ron Blue
A wise person will desire no more than he may get justly, use soberly, distribute cheerfully and leave contendedly.[2]

Larry Burkett
An indulgence can be defined as anything we buy that has little or no utility to us. To determine if something is an indulgence, we have to look into our lives and say, "Am I missing something as a result of not having this? Does this thing enhance my spiritual life, my family life or my business life?" The cost of the item is not a key factor.[3]

Application: A modern, popular theme in America is "make all you can, save some as you can, spend all you can on the good life." In contrast, John Wesley offers a biblical response to the question how can Christians exercise frugality, "make all you can, save all you can, give all you can."[4] Through proper planning the individual, family, local church, business and/or governmental agency can avoid excessive waste.

Several principles will help us in the day-to-day decision-making process:
   (1) God has been clear to promise sufficient provision for His own.
   (2) All that is was created by Him. Charged with dominion, man has watchcare over His creation.
   (3) As Christians bring honor and glory to the Father through obedience, the Father is faithful to bless.

Man should covenant to heed the Scripture to avoid wasting, to be prudent and wise in the distribution of resources under his control.

---

[1]Gary Demar, *God and Government: Issues in Biblical Perspective*, American Vision Press, Atlanta, Georgia, 1984, p. 153.

[2]Ron Blue, *Master Your Money*, Word Books, Dallas, Texas, 1990, p. 26.

[3]Larry Burkett, *Answers to Your Family's Financial Questions*, Focus on the Family Publishing, Pomona, California, 1987, p. 9.

[4]Thomas Schmidt, "The Evils of Wealth: the Hard Sayings of Jesus," *Christianity Today*, Carol Stream, Illinois, May 12, 1989, p. 38.

Such will allow one to minister effectively as an example for his family, his church, and the world.

—Jerald B. Hubbard

GAMBLING

WHAT DOES THE BIBLE SAY ABOUT GAMBLING?

The Issue: Gambling is a pervasive growth industry in North America. According to a recent Gallup poll, 82% of Americans approve of gambling in some form. In 1989 Americans wagered about $265 billion both legally and illegally, a figure that is growing at a rate of 10% annually. Government sponsored lotteries continue to initiate increasing numbers of people into a gambling lifestyle.

Tragically ten million North Americans are compulsive gamblers, psychologically addicted to an activity that robs them of their money, their employment, and often their families. Many are driven to drug and alcohol addiction, crime, or suicide by their uncontrollable gambling lust.

Gambling is not simple risk taking, equated with operating a business or driving on a busy freeway. It devises artificial risks in pursuit of excessive and unearned gains based almost entirely on chance or "luck." For those who take the Scriptures seriously gambling cannot be an option.

Key Bible References:

He who is greedy for gain troubles his own house, . . . Proverbs 15:27

But those who desire to be rich fall into temptation and a snare, and into many foolish and harmful lusts which drown men in destruction and perdition.

For the love of money is a root of all kinds of evil for which some have strayed from the faith in their greediness and pierced themselves through with many sorrows. I Timothy 6:9–10

Wealth gained by dishonesty will be diminished, but he who gathers by labour will increase. Proverbs 13:11

"As a partridge that broods but does not hatch, so is he who gets riches, but not by right; it will leave him in the midst of his days, and at his end he will be a fool." Jeremiah 17:11

Additional References: Genesis 3:17–19; Proverbs 21:25–26; Matthew 6:19–21, 25:14–30; Romans 14:13–21; Philippians 2:4; II Thessalonians 3:12.

What Others Say: Dr. Larry Braidfoot, attorney; The Canadian Foundation on Compulsive Gambling; and the late William Temple, Archbishop of Canterbury and former head of the Anglican Church.

Larry Braidfoot
Gambling contributes nothing to the common good. It undermines values, mocks work, finances crime, robs children, enslaves its addicts, subverts governments and poisons whatever it touches.[1]

The Canadian Foundation on Compulsive Gambling
The compulsive gambler feels a need to gamble for the "high" he experiences; winning or losing has much less importance to him. He loses control over a passion for taking high financial risks and this leads to a chaotic life with gradual loss of financial and social support. The result usually leads to jail, suicide, alcohol or drug addiction and social ostracism.[2]

William Temple
Gambling challenges that view of life which the Christian Church exists to uphold and extend. Its glorification of mere chance is a denial of the divine order of nature. To risk money haphazardly is to disregard the insistence of the Church in every age of living faith that possessions are a trust and that men must account to God for their use. The persistent appeal to covetousness is fundamentally opposed to the unselfishness which was taught by Jesus Christ and by the New Testament as a whole. . . . The attempt (inseparable from gambling) to make profit out of inevitable loss and possible suffering of others is the antithesis of the love of one's neighbour on which our Lord insisted.[3]

Application: Should a Christian gamble? If a Christian sees a burning apartment building in which many of the tenants are being consumed by flames, should he step inside and toss a few branches into

---

[1]Dr. Larry Braidfoot, *Gambling: A Deadly Game*, Broadman Press, Nashville, Tennessee, 1985, p. 191.

[2]Canadian Foundation on Compulsive Gambling (Ontario) Information Pamphlet.

[3]William Temple, *Gambling and Ethics*, Issued by the Churches' Committee on Gambling, Abbey House, London, England, p. 8.

the fire to amuse himself? How can a believer be involved in gambling even in the smallest of ways when he realizes that he is adding fuel to the flames of suffering for so many? How can he ignore God's requirements of responsible stewardship? How can he risk his own well-being in such a destructive activity?

As gambling continues to proliferate in North America so will the ensuing misery of broken homes and broken lives. That, as the bookmakers say, is a "sure thing." Christians cannot afford to be part of it.

—Mark A. Kennedy

GENEROSITY

WHAT DOES THE BIBLE SAY ABOUT GENEROSITY?

The Issue: The Bible is full of examples of those who gave of themselves or their means to benefit others. Christians today should not be outdone by those in the world, who in their philanthropy bring honor to themselves or their organization. Believers should be marked by a generous spirit which will result in bringing honor to the Lord. The supreme example of a munificent spirit was given to us by God the Father as He magnanimously presented His only Son to die for the sins of mankind.

Key Bible References:

The foolish person will no longer be called generous, nor the miser said to be *bountiful;*

But a generous man devises generous things, and by generosity he shall stand. Isaiah 32:5, 8

The generous soul will be made rich, . . . Proverbs 11:25a

Command those who are rich in this present age not to be haughty, nor to trust in uncertain riches but in the living God, who gives us richly all things to enjoy.

Let them *do good, that they be rich in good works, ready to give, willing to share, . . .* I Timothy 6:17–18

But do not forget to do good and to share, for with such sacrifices God is well pleased. Hebrews 13:16

Additional References: Mark 10:21; Acts 10:2

What Others Say: Billy Graham, evangelist and author; Robert Gilmour LeTourneau, inventor, designer, manufacturer, and Christian philanthropist.

Billy Graham

There is no joy in life like the joy of sharing. Don't be content to have too much when millions in the world have too little.[1]

Robert Gilmour LeTourneau

Carlton Case, friend and legal adviser to R. G. LeTourneau, looked worried. "Bob," he was saying, "you surely do not appreciate the meaning of this word. It is not my business, even though I am your attorney, to dissuade you and Mrs. LeTourneau from giving your personal wealth for the promotion of Christian work, if that is your wish; but I do consider it my duty to point out the serious implications of this word 'irrevocable.' If you allow it to stand, it means that—"

"That I can't take it back again, even if I want to," broke in Mr. LeTourneau himself. "That if an emergency arises, and I am short of money, I cannot dip my hand into this fund. That my children will have no claim upon it. I know all that, but all the same, that word 'irrevocable' has to stand. Do you think that my wife and I want to give this to the Lord today, and take it back again tomorrow?"[2]

Application: In this materialistic, self-centered world, characterized by ungrateful and selfish mankind, we should recognize that God expects of Christians a different attitude towards what we possess and how we regard those who have genuine need. Galatians 6:6 says, "Let him who is taught the word share in all good things with him who teaches." God's children are certainly worthy of their hire, and pastors, missionaries, and other full-time workers are to be generously cared for by those who benefit from their ministry.

II Corthinians 9:6-7 sums up the true Christian's attitude: "But this *I say:* He who sows sparingly will also reap sparingly, and he who sows bountifully will also reap bountifully. So *let* each one *give* as he purposes in his heart, not grudgingly or of necessity; for God loves a cheerful giver."

---

[1]Billy Graham, *The Secret of Happiness,* Doubleday and Company, Garden City, New York, 1955, p. 110.

[2]Donald F. Ackland, *Moving Heaven and Earth,* The Iverson-Ford Associates, New York, New York, 1949, p. 155.

Our Lord considered the widow's two mites given from her poverty to be a more generous gift than the donation given by the rich who put large amounts in the treasury.

—Paul D. Montgomery

GIVING

WHAT ARE THE BIBLICAL PRINCIPLES OF GIVING?

The Issue: As litmus paper is the acid-base indicator for science, so is the attitude toward giving for a Christian of any age. Though it is painful to admit, even as Christians, we tend to be forgetful and to drift toward self-sufficiency. Our loving Father understands our weaknesses so He wisely provided a "string around our finger" (giving) to remind us of His character, His ownership, and His way of blessing us.

Key Bible References:

"For God so loved the world that He gave His only begotten Son, that whoever believes in Him should not perish but have everlasting life." John 3:16

"I have been crucified with Christ; it is no longer I who live, but Christ lives in me; and the life which I now live in the flesh I live by faith in the Son of God, who loved me and gave Himself for me." Galatians 2:20

Then He looked up and saw the rich putting their gifts into the treasury, and He saw also a certain poor widow putting in two mites.

So He said, "Truly I say to you that this poor widow has put in more than all; for all these out of their abundance have put in offerings for God, but she out of her poverty has put in all the livelihood that she had." Luke 21:1–4

Additional References: Numbers 18:8–20; Esther 9:22.

What Others Say: Larry Burkett, founder of Christian Financial Concepts; and Charles R. Swindoll, pastor and author.

Larry Burkett

Above all else, God is concerned with our attitude. The abundance or the lack of money does not affect our relationship to Him—only our attitude does. . . . Because of its tangibility, money is a testing ground before God of our true willingness to surrender self to Him.[1]

Charles R. Swindoll

The ideal gift is . . . yourself. In your quest for character, don't forget the value of unselfishness. That's right, give some of yourself away.[2]

Application: In a society that promotes "having it all now," the attitude of a giving heart is rare. For that reason, a young person who reflects the giving character of a loving Father is refreshingly distinctive.

A genuine giving heart does not just happen. It begins with an understanding of ownership. Though all of us are created by God, a Christian is His twice—once by creation and again by purchase with His life. Having responded to His love by acknowledging His ownership, giving is a natural, joyful expression of His character through us. The questions of "what" or "how much" to give can then be freely answered as a steward of His possessions, not ours.

A young person concluding that he does not have much to give needs only to remember the widow who gave all she had. The gift of self (time, care, counsel, help) is foundational to the development of a giving heart.

Unselfish giving is one of the steps of faith God chooses to bless in many ways. For the one with a giving heart, those blessings are not sought but are merely a by-product. The true reward is the fellowship with a Father who freely gives Himself to us every day.

—Len McWilliams

---

[1]Larry Burkett, *How to Manage Your Money,* Moody Press, Chicago, Illinois, 1975, p. 13.

[2]Charles R. Swindoll, *The Quest for Character,* Multnomah Press, Portland Oregon, 1987, p. 177.

GOD

WHAT DO THE SCRIPTURES SAY ABOUT KNOWING GOD?

The Issue: Who is God? What is God like? What does God do? Can a human really know God? Philosophers continually ask such questions. The answers are not found in the theories of man. They are found in the wisdom of the eternal Word of God. The truths exposed in God's Word provide the filling of this questioning void inherent in the hearts of all men. God wants us to know Him and to understand Him—His attributes, His thoughts, and His ways. Because God has given us His spirit, it is possible to know these things about God. And since we are made in His image, knowing God should direct our daily behavior.

Key Bible References:

For thus says the LORD, who created the heavens, who is God, who formed the earth and made it, who has established it, who did not create it in vain, who formed it to be inhabited: "I am the LORD, and there is no other.

"I have not spoken in secret, in a dark place of the earth; I did not say to the seed of Jacob, 'Seek Me in vain'; I, the LORD, speak righteousness, I declare things that are right." Isaiah 45:18–19

But we speak the wisdom of God in a mystery, the hidden wisdom which God ordained before the ages for our glory, which none of the rulers of this age knew; for had they known, they would not have crucified the Lord of glory.

But as it is written: "Eye has not seen, nor ear heard nor have entered into the heart of man the things which God has prepared for those who love Him." I Corinthians 2:7–9

Additional References: I Chronicles 29:10–13; Job 11:7–8; Hosea 6:3; John 17:3; Romans 1:18–22; II Corinthians 4:6.

What Others Say: Earl D. Radmacher, Bible scholar and author; A. W. Tozer, Bible scholar; and Charles R. Swindoll, pastor and author.

Earl D. Radmacher

People that take time to contemplate what God is like shall exchange their weakness for his strength. One who truly understands what God is like will find himself giving more and more attention to the spiritual and less and less importance to the material![1]

A. W. Tozer

Without doubt the mightiest thought the mind can entertain is the thought of God.[2]

Charles R. Swindoll

You need to know that God wants to be on a close and special basis with us. God wants our arms around Him. God wants to hear us say, "I love You, Father. I trust You. I adore You."

The better you get to know your God, the more comfortable you will be with that kind of response. And as you gain comfort in that kind of response, express it. Sing your songs. Lay your burdens on Him. Trust Him with all your heart and might. He'll be honored as you do that.[3]

Application: God has chosen to reveal Himself through the eternal truth of His precious Word. Each name for God helps us to know another of His attributes (Genesis 17:1, Psalm 95:6, Luke 11:2, I Timothy 6:15). Our God is all-powerful (Jeremiah 32:17). He is all-knowing (I John 3:20). He is everywhere at all times (Jeremiah 23:24). He is eternal (Psalm 90:2). He is sovereign (Isaiah 14:27). And He never changes (James 1:17). The Scriptures reveal His very nature. Therefore, as we grow in Him and as we learn to die to self, we can replace the lust of the flesh, the lust of the eyes, and the pride of life with the fruit of the Spirit. The insecurity of failing to understand God can be replaced with the peace of resting upon the everlasting and loving arms of our heavenly Father. He has allowed us to become joint heirs with Christ as His sons. It is worth the time and energy to search the Scriptures in order to better know and love our God. Knowing Him is the greatest of all things to know. Knowing Him gives our lives eternal meaning.

—Jon D. Hoey

---

[1]William F. Kerr, *God, What is He Like?*, Tyndale House Publishers, Inc., Wheaton, Illinois, 1977, p. 21.

[2]The Navigators, *Foundations for Faith—Design for Discipleship, Book 5*, NavPress, Colorado Springs, Colorado, 1973, p. 7.

[3]Charles R. Swindoll, *Growing Deep in the Christian Life*, Multnomah Press, Portland, Oregon, 1986, p. 116.

GOOD REPORT

WHAT DOES THE BIBLE SAY ABOUT GIVING A GOOD REPORT?

The Issue: In every organization there is a multitude of interpersonal relationships. If Satan can cut off any line of communication, he will score a victory. In a great many Christian organizations, that's exactly what is happening. People end up offending others and get offended themselves because of the gossip and slander that prevail. In such an atmosphere, it is impossible to enjoy the presence of God or to impress others with His love and power. Yet God in His Word demands that we demonstrate unity and love one for another. It is by this unity (the commitment to only give and receive good reports about others) that we demonstrate that Jesus Christ is who He said He was (John 17:21).

Key Bible References:

"Moreover if your brother sins against you, go and tell him his fault between you and him alone. If he hears you, you have gained your brother.

"But if he will not hear you, *take with you one or two more, that* 'by the mouth of two or three witnesses every word may be established.'

"And if he refuses to hear them, tell it *to the church.*

"But if he refuses even to hear the church, let him be to you like a heathen and a tax collector.

"Assuredly, I say to you, whatever you bind on earth will be bound in heaven, and whatever you loose on earth will be loosed in heaven." Matthew 18:15–17

Brethren, if a man is overtaken in any trespass, you who are *spiritual restore such a one in a spirit of gentleness, considering yourself lest you also be tempted.* Galatians 6:1

Debate your case with your neighbor himself, *and do not disclose the secret to another;* . . . Proverbs 25:9

Faithful are *the wounds of a friend, but the kisses of an enemy* are *deceitful.* Proverbs 27:6

Additional References: Proverbs 6:16–19, 11:9; John 13:35.

143

What Others Say: Bill Gothard, founder of The Institute in Basic Life Principles, Chicago, Illinois; and Dr. Paul A. Kienel, executive director, Association of Christian Schools, Inc., Whittier, California.

Bill Gothard

If every Christian were committed to the principle of a good report, three results would transform the Church into a dynamic force in our nation and in the world. (1) Disloyalty with its gossip and slander would cease and give way to rich fellowship among sincere Christians; (2) Christians would become a corrective and edifying force to each other with results that weaker Christians would be strengthened and false teachers would be exposed; and (3) the world would believe that God sent His Son with a message of hope for them.[1]

Paul A. Kienel

The Body of Christ is made up of people. Like any collection of earthly mortals, the people associated with the body of Christ have the potential for misunderstanding, disagreement and even wrongdoing. Nevertheless, it is God's will that we live and work together in harmony. Due to our human nature we may at times irritate others, resulting in misunderstandings or strong disagreements. In Matthew 18:15–17 Jesus gives His formula for solving person-to-person problems. It is called "the Matthew 18 Principle."[2]

Application: To maintain the unity which God desires in the body of Christ today, we must commit ourselves to the principle of only giving and listening to good reports unless we are being asked to go as a witness following the Matthew 18:15–17 sequence. We must remind ourselves that the mark of spirituality is not whether we are able to expose a brother but whether we are able to restore him (Galatians 6:1). Sometimes our lack of love for an offending Christian is a far greater detriment to the spread of the Gospel than whatever fault we try to expose or correct in his life. Christians need to be different; we need to be concerned about each other and our walk with our precious Lord and Savior Jesus Christ.

—Claude (Bud) Schindler, Jr.

---

[1]Bill Gothard, *Discovering a Forgotten Truth,* Institute in Basic Youth Conflicts, 1976, Chicago, Illinois, p. 1.
[2]Paul A. Kienel, "The Matthew 18 Principle for Solving School Problems," Association of Christian Schools, Int., *Christian School Comment,* Vol. 14, No. 1.

GOOD WORKS

WHAT DOES THE BIBLE TEACH ABOUT GOOD WORKS?

The Issue: The proper place of good works in the life of a Christian has been the subject of controversy since the earliest days of the church. There have been those who, in their zeal for good works, have declared such unselfish effort as essential to salvation. To the other extreme are those who so emphasize salvation by grace through faith alone that they neglect altogether the biblical truth concerning good works. The Scriptures teach that salvation is, indeed, God's work of grace on the part of a believing sinner and apart from any human effort; however, after salvation, the Scriptures teach that good works are to be a vital part of the life of a believer to the end that the unsaved will see them and glorify God.

Key Bible References:

For by grace you have been saved through faith, and that not of yourselves; it is the gift of God, not of works, lest anyone should boast.

For we are His workmanship, created in Christ Jesus for good works, which God prepared beforehand that we should walk in them. Ephesians 2:8–10

This is a faithful saying, and these things I want you to affirm constantly, that those who have believed in God should be careful to maintain good works. These things are good and profitable to men. Titus 3:8

. . . having your conduct honorable among the Gentiles, that when they speak against you as evildoers, they may, by your good works which they observe, glorify God in the day of visitation. I Peter 2:12

Additional References: Matthew 5:16; Colossians 1:10; II Timothy 2:21, 3:16–17; Titus 2:7; Hebrews 10:24.

What Others Say: The late Dr. J. Vernon McGee, pastor, author, and Bible teacher on "Thru The Bible Radio," Pasadena, California; and Dr. W. A. Criswell, former pastor of the First Baptist Church of Dallas, Texas.

J. Vernon McGee

The fact that the believer is saved by the grace of God does not excuse him from performing good works. . . . My friend, after you have been saved, God is going to talk to you about good works. Until that time, God is not even interested in your "good works" because what you call a good work, God calls dirty laundry. The righteousness of man is filthy rags in His sight (see Isaiah 64:6). He doesn't want any of that. He wants to *save* you. If you come to Him just as you are, He will save you, because He has *done* something for you. . . . After you are saved, after you are a child of God, then He wants to talk to you about producing good works. He wants you to get involved in getting out the Word of God to others.[1]

W. A. Criswell

The Christian man, the kingdom citizen, is . . . the light of the world. Whatever hope we may have in the destiny of the future is to be found in him and in the Saviour he follows . . . Jesus avows that the light of the life cannot be hid. It is like a city set on a hill or like a lamp which is never put under a bushel. Our Lord, therefore, admonishes His citizens to shine with all their might. Their lives and their deeds are sometimes the only God a lost world will ever know, and their testimony is sometimes the only message a lost world will ever hear. . . .[2]

Application: Good works are the product of lives that have been redeemed by the grace of God and consecrated to Him. As the miracles of Jesus authenticated His deity, the good works of Christians authenticate their witness and testimony. The verbal witness of believers is either enhanced or negated by the visible demonstration of their faith in the lives that they live. By good works and deeds that honor the Savior, Christians become living illustrations of the loving grace and saving power of the Lord Jesus Christ.

—**Robert T. Gallagher**

[1] J. Vernon McGee, *Thru The Bible With J. Vernon McGee,* Thomas Nelson, Inc., Nashville, Tennessee, 1983, p. 494.

[2] W. A. Criswell, *Expository Notes on the Gospel of Matthew,* Zondervan Publishing House, Grand Rapids, Michigan, 1961, pp. 33–34.

GOSSIP

WHAT DOES THE BIBLE SAY ABOUT FALSE REPORTS?

The Issue: We live at a time when gossip is not only a temptation, it is a featured segment on the evening news and the focus of entire magazines and tabloids. Gossip sells and offers a great financial benefit for the reporter. Unfortunately, it is not just the rich and famous who are the focus and force of gossip and slander. It is a temptation that we all face. Many a friendship, organization, church, and even family have been hurt or mortally wounded by gossip.

Key Bible References:

These six things the LORD hates, yes, seven are an abomination to Him: . . . A false witness who speaks lies, . . . Proverbs 6:16, 19a

Where there is no wood, the fire goes out; and where there is no talebearer, strife ceases. Proverbs 26:20

. . . and whoever spreads slander is a fool. Proverbs 10:18b

Do not speak evil of one another, brethren. James 4:11a

Additional References: Proverbs 11:13, 16:28, 17:9, 20:19, 26:22; Titus 3:1–2.

What Others Say: Dr. Charles R. Swindoll, pastor and author.

Charles R. Swindoll

(1) Identify the sources by name. If someone is determined to share information that is damaging or hurtful, request that the source be specifically stated.

(2) Support evidence with facts. Do not accept hearsay. Refuse to listen unless honest-to-goodness truth is being communicated. You can tell. Truth is rarely veiled or uncertain. Rumors fade when exposed to the light.

(3) Ask the person, "May I quote you?" It's remarkable how quickly rumor-spreaders can turn four shades of red! Equally remarkable is the speed with which they can backpedal.

(4) Openly admit, "I don't appreciate hearing that." This approach is for the strong. It might drive a wedge between

you and the guilty . . . but it's a sure way to halt the regular garbage delivery to your ears.[1]

Application: Gossip is not always a matter of false reporting. It can just be a case of idle talk or rumor that has no constructive goal. Someone defined gossip as "sharing information with those who are not part of the problem or part of the solution."

God identifies gossip as one of the seven things that He hates. He admonishes us to refrain from the act of useless chatter, strife, backbiting, and gossip. Since God has designed us as social beings, he gives us specific guidelines for our speech. We should be ". . . speaking to one another in psalms and hymns and spiritual songs, singing and making melody in your hearts to the Lord, giving thanks always for all things to God the Father in the name of our Lord Jesus Christ, submitting to one another in the fear of God" (Ephesians 5:19–21). Our words are to be that which "is good for necessary edification, that it may impart grace to the hearers" (Ephesians 4:29).

Christians must refuse to participate in a conversation that involves gossip. They can have no part in it either as the speaker or the hearer. God tells us that when we refrain from gossip there are numerous benefits.

(1) We demonstrate the qualities of a good friend (Proverbs 11:13, 16:28).

(2) We help to extinguish a flame that can be deadly and destructive to relationships (Proverbs 26:20).

(3) We show the evidence of faithfulness and trustworthiness (Proverbs 20:19).

More importantly, when we refrain from gossip, the act of sharing unnecessary information that could be hurtful, we show our obedience to our Lord. He has commanded us to refrain from "idle chatter."

—**Donna Marie Furrey**

---

[1]Charles R. Swindoll, *Growing Strong In The Seasons Of Life,* Multnomah Press, Portland, Oregon, 1984, p. 106.

GOVERNMENT

WHAT IS THE BIBLICAL BASIS
FOR CIVIL GOVERNMENT?

The Issue: The conflict between Divine and human authority has existed since the beginning of humanity. The twentieth century versions of this conflict have centered on separation of church and state. The Christian believes that its view of Government (and authority in general) must be based on the teachings of the Word of God—the Bible. The Bible very clearly teaches the sovereignty of God over all the affairs of mankind. A Christian world view teaches that reverence belongs to both God and human government and where a conflict exists between the two, the Christian must fear God first.

Key Bible References:

Let every soul be subject to the governing authorities. For there is no authority except from God, and the authorities that exist are appointed by God.

Therefore whoever resists the authority resists the ordinance of God, and those who resist will bring judgment on themselves.

For rulers are not a terror to good works, but to evil. Do you want to be unafraid of the authority? Do what is good, and you will have praise from the same.

For he is God's minister to you for good. But if you do evil, be afraid; for he does not bear the sword in vain; for he is God's minister, an avenger to execute *wrath on him who practices evil.*

Therefore you must be subject, not only because of wrath but also for conscience' sake.

For because of this you also pay taxes, for they are God's ministers attending continually to this very thing.

Render therefore to all their due: taxes to whom taxes are due, *customs to whom customs, fear to whom fear, honor to whom honor.* Romans 13:1–7

. . . "Render therefore to Caesar the things that are Caesar's, and to God the things that are God's." Luke 20:25

". . . that the Most High God rules in the kingdom of men, and appoints over it whomever He chooses." Daniel 5:21b

When the righteous are in authority, the people rejoice; but when a wicked man *rules, the people groan.* Proverbs 29:2

Additional References: Job 12:18–19; Psalm 102:15; Proverbs 14:34; Isaiah 40:13–26; I Timothy 2:1–2; Hebrews 13:17.

What Others Say: Dr. Francis A. Schaeffer, Christian philosopher and theologian; and Dr. Carl F. H. Henry, Bible scholar.

Francis A. Schaeffer
No truly authoritarian government can tolerate those who have a real absolute by which to judge its arbitrary absolutes and who speak out and act upon that absolute. For the Christian, the basic issue is having an absolute by which to judge the state and society.[1]

In *Lex Rex: Law is King,* 1644, Samuel Rutherford wrote of "a concept of freedom without chaos because there was form. There was a government of law rather than of the arbitrary decisions of men—because the Bible as the final authority was there as the base."[2]

Carl F. H. Henry
In New Testament perspective the state serves a limited function; it is not to be the source and stipulator of human liberties. Rather it is to preserve and promote divinely given rights in a political framework of justice and order, enabling human beings to voluntarily do what God requires.[3]

Application: The Bible clearly teaches the role of civil government in the lives of people. People are to be subject to the laws and principles of God as the highest priority. Christians are also commanded to be subject to those in authority over them because those authorities are acting as ministers of God. Only when human governmental authority violates the authority of the Word of God is the Christian allowed to be civilly disobedient. Great emphasis in Scripture is placed on obedience of those in authority and prayer for those who have the rule over mankind. This is the responsibility of the Christian in human government ordained by God.

—Randall A. Ross

---

[1]Francis A. Schaeffer, *How Should We Then Live?* Fleming H. Revell Company, Old Tappan, New Jersey, 1976, pp. 256–257.

[2]Ibid., p. 109.

[3]Carl F. H. Henry, *The Christian Mindset in a Secular Society,* Multnomah Press, Portland, Oregon, 1984, pp. 66–67.

GUILT

HOW DO CHRISTIANS HANDLE GUILT?

The Issue: Guilt presupposes a higher law to which a person is responsible. It is a mixture of many emotions and thoughts which destroy inner peace, bring shame and regret, and lead to a fear of punishment. It may also lead to alienation from others and from oneself, due to the difference between what one really is and what one wishes to be. It may also lead to feelings of loneliness, isolation and inferiority.

There are two kinds of guilt: real or true guilt, which comes as a result of breaking God's law; and unreal, false or neurotic guilt, which has no basis in reality, but is usually self-imposed.

Real guilt comes from sin, "missing the mark." The disobedience of Adam and Eve in the Garden of Eden broke their relationship with God. They knew they were guilty, and sought to deny their accountability. When the prophet Nathan confronted King David with his sins of adultery and murder, the king recognized his guilt. Upon confessing and repenting of his sin (see II Samuel 11 and 12, and Psalm 51), he was immediately relieved of his guilt.

Unreal guilt stems from a lack of understanding of God's forgiveness, or from guilt feelings which stem from negative experiences, many times in childhood. These people usually suffer from a low self-image, depression, and feelings of inadequacy. Sometimes this results in fatigue, self-punishment, criticism of self and others.

Key Bible References:

He who covers his sins will not prosper, but whoever confesses and forsakes them *will have mercy.* Proverbs 28:13

If we confess our sins, He is faithful and just to forgive us our *sins and to cleanse us from all unrighteousness.* I John 1:9

There is *therefore now no condemnation to those who are in Christ Jesus. . . .* Romans 8:1

"This being *so, I myself always strive to have a conscience without offense toward God and men."* Acts 24:16

Additional References: Psalm 51; Isaiah 53; Luke 18:9–14; John 18, 19; Romans 2:1–11, 3, 6, 7:18–25; I Peter 3:15–16.

What Others Say: Ralph W. Sockman; Billy Graham; Tim Timmons; and Clyde Narramore.

Ralph W. Sockman

The conscience is the source of our guilty feelings. It acts as a built-in voice of the Creator and not as the echo of the crowd. . . . To try to kill the conscience is to try to destroy something sacred to one's own individuality. To ignore the voice of conscience is to deceive the self, but to become burdened with a sense of unforgivable sin is also to deny the nature of Christ's mission. The mission of Christ was to free people of an unreasonable sense of guilt, for "He shall save His people from their sins" (Matthew 1:21).[1]

Billy Graham

The conscience of man is often beyond the grasp of a psychiatrist. With all his techniques, he cannot sound its depravity and depth. Man himself is helpless to detach himself from the gnawing guilt of a heart bowed down with the weight of sin. But where man has failed, God has succeeded.[2]

Tim Timmons and Stephen Arterburn

Guilt can be either appropriate or inappropriate. Appropriate guilt occurs when we do something in direct conflict with our system of values. . . . Inappropriate guilt comes from events beyond our control. When parents divorce, children feel a high level of inappropriate guilt because they feel that they are responsible. Such guilt often plagues children for years. . . . Appropriate or inappropriate, if guilt is unresolved, it results in obsessions of the mind.[3]

Clyde Narramore

The Bible reveals man's own personal guilt. . . . It is imperative that each person come to grips with his own sin. Until he realizes this, he is deceived about his depraved condition. Sin is a reality and it must be dealt with in a real way. Until sin is sought out, confessed and forgiven by Christ, it continues to linger like cancerous tissue, affecting the entire person.[4]

Application: A healthy conscience is of utmost value in the Christian's pursuit of holiness, ". . . without which no one will see the Lord" (Hebrews 12:14).

---

[1]Edgar N. Jackson, *How to Preach to People's Needs,* Baker Book House, 1972, pp. 26–27.

[2]Billy Graham, *The Billy Graham Christian Worker's Handbook,* edited by Charles G. Ward, World Wide Publications, 1984, pp. 117–118.

[3]Tim Timmons and Stephen Arterburn, *Hooked on Life,* Oliver-Nelson, 1985, p. 49.

[4]Clyde Narramore, *The Psychology of Counseling,* Zondervan Publishing House, 1960, p. 244.

True guilt alerts the Christian of sin, reminding him to confess it in prayer, truly repent, and turn from its practice. Anyone so turning to God, whether believer or unbeliever, is assured of the forgiveness of the Heavenly Father. He accepts God's forgiveness by faith, and then must forgive himself. The Word and the forgiving nature of God should dispel the sense of guilt.

Continued repeating of such sin, while forbidden in God's plan, will still be forgiven, if the person repents. But if sincerity turns to rebellion, it becomes more difficult to truly repent.

Satan, the "accuser of our brethren" (Revelation 12:10), tries to use false guilt to cause the believer to be ineffective in his Christian life. Satan says, "You have sinned, and there is nothing you can do about it." But God says, "You have sinned, and there IS something you can do about it." One should learn to respond to God's inner voice of the Holy Spirit, repent and forsake sin.

Such guilt feelings should be handled by (1) forgetting the past, (2) reaching forth to the future, and (3) pressing toward the mark in Christ Jesus (Philippians 3:13–14).

—Steve Asmuth

HANDICAPPED

WHAT SHOULD THE ATTITUDE OF CHRISTIANS BE TOWARD PEOPLE WHO ARE HANDICAPPED?

The Issue: If a person is a truly Christ-oriented Christian then love shows no difference in the treatment of a person with a disability than a person without. Love means helping those who cannot help themselves. We are instructed to help those with problem areas—no matter what kind of problem that might be. Love shows no boundaries. It offers no alternatives to total and complete acceptance of all those who are physically and/or emotionally handicapped.

Key Bible References:

"But when you do a charitable deed, do not let your left hand know what your right hand is doing, that your charitable deed may be in secret; and your Father who sees in secret will Himself reward you openly." Matthew 6:3–4

Though I speak with the tongues of men and of angels, but have not love, I have become as sounding brass or a clanging cymbal.

And though I bestow all my goods to feed the poor and though I give my body to be burned, but have not love, it profits me nothing.

Love never fails. But whether there are prophecies, they will fail; whether there are tongues, they will cease; whether there is knowledge, it will vanish away. I Corinthians 13:1, 3, 8

. . . always carrying about in the body the dying of the Lord Jesus, that the life of Jesus also may be manifested in our body. II Corinthians 4:10

Additional References: II Samuel 9:1–13; Acts 14:8–10.

What Others Say: Amy Carmichael, missionary and author; and Dale Evans Rogers, actress, singer, and author.

Amy Carmichael
Hereby perceive we the love of God, because He laid down His life for us, and we ought to lay down our lives for our brethren. How often I think of that *ought*. No sugary sentiment there. Just the stern, glorious trumpet call, OUGHT. But can words tell the joy buried deep within? Mine cannot. It laughs at words.—Amy Carmichael letter written in the Old Forest House 1922.[1]

Dale Evans Rogers
Our baby came into the world with an appalling handicap. I believe with all my heart that God sent her on a two-year mission to our household, to strengthen us spiritually and to draw us together in the knowledge and love of fellowship with God.[2]

Application: One must see the unique human being first, and only secondly, that this person has a disability. Only then can one show the person the unique quality of a true Christian and acting on that love. Compare your reaction and acceptability of this person with a trip. When going on a trip to Italy, for example, you get excited, you buy a guide book and make a wonderful plan. The Colosseum, The Michelangelo, David, the gondolas in Venice. After months of anticipation the day arrives. You pack and several hours later the plane

---

[1]Elisabeth Elliot, *The Life and Legacy of Amy Carmichael: A Chance to Die,* Fleming H. Revell Company, Old Tappan, New Jersey, 1987, p. 13.

[2]Dale Evans Rogers, *Angels Unaware,* Fleming H. Revell Company, Old Tappan, New Jersey, 1975, p. 3.

lands. The stewardess comes in and says, "Welcome to Holland." "Holland! What? I signed up for Italy, I am prepared and dreamed Italy for so long." A change in plans leaves you stranded in Holland. So you must go out and buy new guide books and learn a different language. And you'll meet a whole new group of people you would never have met.

It's just a different place. It's slower paced than Italy, less flashy than Italy, but after you've been there for a while and you catch your breath—you look around and you begin to notice that Holland has windmills, Holland has tulips, Holland even has Rembrandts!

If you spend your life mourning the fact that you didn't get to Italy, you may never be free to enjoy the very special, the very lovely things about Holland.

Don't miss the chance to incorporate the very special, the very lovely things about a handicapped person into your life. Put your LOVE into action.

—Diane Nason

HAPPINESS

WHAT DOES THE BIBLE TEACH ABOUT HAPPINESS?

The Issue: Most people are seeking happiness. The problem is that most people wouldn't recognize it because they are hoping for an existence with no trouble, no difficulty, no failure. Somehow people think they will find true happiness if there are no problems or challenges. The Scripture is clear that God wants us to be happy. He blesses us with eternal blessings.

Sometimes we make a distinction between happiness and joy; happiness being more dependent on circumstance and joy being an inner quality of contentment and peace. God has not promised that there would not be trials and difficulties. He has promised that we can find happiness and joy right in the middle of the difficulties! And, that is true happiness—true joy—because no matter what the circumstances are we can know the contentment of the presence of God in our lives and the great gift provided by Jesus Christ. We can know that through the difficulties and testings in our lives He is working it to our good and our growth.

His goal for us is that we would be "like Jesus Christ," "follow in His footsteps." There is where we find happiness—not in the temporary offerings of the things of the world, but in the eternal, consistent and constant provisions made for us in Jesus Christ.

Key Bible References:

He who heeds the word wisely will find good, and whoever trusts in the LORD, happy is he. Proverbs 16:20

Is anyone among you suffering? Let him pray. Is anyone cheerful? Let him sing psalms. James 5:13

But let the righteous be glad; let them rejoice before God; yes, let them rejoice exceedingly. Psalm 68:3

My brethren, count it all joy when you fall into various trials, knowing that the testing of your faith produces patience. But let patience have its perfect work, that you may be perfect and complete, lacking nothing. James 1:2–4

Additional References: I Kings 4:20; Psalm 10:6; Proverbs 15:13; Ecclesiastes 3:12, 5:19, 7:14; Romans 4:7–8; I Corinthians 7:9, 13.

What Others Say: Dr. Leith C. Anderson, pastor, Wooddale Church in Eden Prairie, Minnesota.

Leith C. Anderson

The ancient Greeks had insights into life which have stood the test of time. Their language is one of the most expressive and definitive on all the earth.

Eutuches was one of their words for happiness. It meant a "fleeting earthly happiness." It was the kind of happiness which was mostly on the outside and dependent on circumstances. Like us, they must have hoped that good happenings and good feelings on the outside would work their way inside until they became truly happy from the outside in.

Strange as it sounds, constant external happiness would probably make us all miserable! George Bernard Shaw figured it this way: "A lifetime of happiness! No man could bear it: It would be hell on earth." If everything went our way and life was free of problems, there would be no challenges. We wouldn't have anything to compare our happiness to until we might not recognize happiness if we had it.

Makarios was another Greek word for happiness. It was far better. The Greeks used this word when referring to the inner happiness which goes beyond circumstances. It is a deep-down happiness which does not depend on externals. Happiness which is from the inside out.

That's the kind of happiness most of us are after. We know that our earth is not a perfect place and that *eutuches* happiness is never a real possibility. But, if we could really live happily on the inside, we could endure anything on the outside. In fact, happiness on the inside would probably go a long way to change our circumstances on the outside.

Interestingly, the Bible (much of which was written in Greek) never uses the word *eutuches*. Every biblical reference to happiness is *makarios*. What's even better is that the Bible repeatedly talks in terms of offering and even expecting us to pursue and achieve the happiness of heaven while here on earth.[1]

Application: Discouragement and dissatisfaction usually come when we are focusing on the external conditions around us. We are threatened when we feel insecure, we are unhappy when we feel our needs are not being met. We withdraw from people when we don't feel approved or appreciated. Happiness, according to the Bible, is not based on such external issues. If we have been changed spiritually from the inside out by trusting the finished work of Jesus Christ, we can then begin to experience the happiness that works from the inside out. We can know true happiness—joy—which transcends all circumstances.

We read of those who were captives and found true happiness in their cells; we can hear the testimony of those dying with cancer and yet they express real happiness and contentment. We learn from those who have gone through "deep waters" that their happiness is centered in Jesus Christ and not in outward circumstances.

Jesus has also promised that if we will follow Him, live our lives as He has directed, and follow His commandments, then we will experience true happiness. Circumstances will not affect us negatively. When all kinds of trials and temptations crowd into our lives, we can either resent them, or we can "welcome them as friends" and allow them to work patience in our lives. Patience will have its perfect work in us, too, and we will find that even in the midst of our trials we can find real joy. That is the happiness that Jesus offers . . . happiness (joy) even during times of great testing and trial. He

---

[1] Leith C. Anderson, *Making Happiness Happen*, Victor Books, Wheaton, Illinois, 1985, pp. 9–10.

gives a peace that transcends circumstance and we can depend upon His happiness in our lives as it works from the inside out.

—James W. Braley

HEATHEN

DOES GOD HOLD PEOPLE ACCOUNTABLE WHO NEVER HEAR ABOUT THE GOSPEL OF CHRIST?

The Issue: Frequently the question is asked: What about those who have never heard the gospel of Jesus Christ? Are they lost? To answer quite simply, "Yes they are lost." We cannot fully appreciate the "lostness" of man without first acknowledging that man was created by God, in His image, and for fellowship with Himself. However, man deliberately chose to disobey God—sin came into his life and a God-shaped vacuum was created that nothing but His Spirit can fill. Without God, *All men are lost!*

Key Bible References:

"For God so loved the world that He gave His only begotten Son, that whoever believes in Him should not perish but have everlasting life.

"For God did not send His Son into the world to condemn the world, but that the world through Him might be saved.

"He who believes in Him is not condemned; but he who does not believe is condemned already, because he has not believed in the name of the only begotten Son of God.

"He who believes in the Son has everlasting life; and he who does not believe the Son shall not see life, but the wrath of God abides on him." John 3:16–18, 36

. . . because what may be known of God is manifest in them, for God has shown it to them.

For since the creation of the world His invisible attributes are clearly seen, being understood by the things that are made, even His eternal power and Godhead; so that they are without excuse, because, although they knew God, they did not glorify

Him as God, nor were thankful, but became futile in their thoughts, and their foolish hearts were darkened.

Professing to be wise, they became fools, and changed the glory of the incorruptible God into an image made like corruptible man—and birds and fourfooted beasts and creeping things.
Romans 1:19–23

Additional References: Acts 14:1–7; Romans 2:14–15, 3:23, 7:19–21; II Corinthians 4:4; II Thessalonians 1:9; I John 5:19.

What Others Say: J. Herbert Kane, author of *Wanted: World Christians.*

J. Herbert Kane

Regardless of whether we refer to the "pagans" in America or the "heathen" in Africa, *All men are lost.* However, when dealing with the so-called heathen—devotees of the non-Christian religions—there are four truths we must keep in mind.

(1) *The heathen were not "heathen" to begin with.* They *became* heathen when they deliberately gave up the knowledge of God. Romans 1:21–23.

(2) *In their progressive apostasy the heathen did not lose all knowledge of God.* They retained a knowledge of His eternal power and deity which reached them through creation. Romans 1:19–20.

(3) *The revelation of God through creation is supplemented by another revelation that comes through nature or providence.* Nearly every heathen society has some knowledge, however vague, of a great Spirit in the sky who has the power of life and death, who causes the sun to shine and the rain to fall. They observe religious rituals to celebrate a good harvest, giving thank offerings to the earth god, or the rain god, or the sun god, but not to the Creator God of heaven and earth. God has not left himself without witness. Acts 14:17.

(4) *There is still another form of light—the light of conscience.* The heathen have neither the light of the law or the light of the gospel, but they do have the light of conscience. Conscience is not a perfect measure, it can be abused so that it malfunctions, but it still remains as the divine monitor within the human breast. No individual is so low on the moral scale that his conscience fails to function. Romans 2:14–15.[1]

---

[1] J. Herbert Kane, *Wanted: World Christians,* Baker Book House, Grand Rapids, Michigan, 1986, pp. 52–53.

Application: As we approach the end of the Twentieth Century, it is estimated that nine out of every ten people in our world today are lost and that three out of four have <u>never</u> heard the Gospel of Jesus Christ unto salvation. The church needs to be awakened to the unfinished task of reaching a lost world for Christ. Individual believers need to have their heart broken with the lostness of man. However, as long as the church continues to place world missions at the bottom of its priority list, devoting only a small portion of its manpower and financial resources, the task will never be completed.

Scripture teaches that it is through a personal encounter with Jesus Christ that a person is saved. It is not through an encounter with creation, innate moral judgment, or belief in a righteous creator. Jesus said, "I am the way, the truth, and the life. No one comes to the Father except through me" John 14:6.

The challenge is quite clear. "How then shall they call on Him in whom they have not believed? And how shall they believe in Him of whom they have not heard? And how shall they hear without a preacher?" Romans 10:14.

And how shall they preach unless they are sent? As it is written; "How beautiful are the feet of those who preach the gospel of peace, who bring glad tidings of good things!" Romans 10:15.

—Phillip M. Renicks

HEAVEN

WHAT DOES THE BIBLE SAY ABOUT HEAVEN?

The Issue: People around the world have never wanted to believe that their death results in termination of their existence. For centuries mankind has either accepted what they have been told or created their own version of what will happen to them when their bodies die. Christians have available to them some of the answers to this question, but some of the answer is still a great mystery that will be revealed to us when we are ushered into the presence of God in the "likeness of Christ."

Heaven is the abode of God, heavenly beings He created, and of people found to be righteous in Christ at their physical death.

Key Bible References:

The LORD looks down from heaven upon the children of men, to see if there are any who understand, who seek God. Psalm 14:2

Do not be rash with your mouth, and let not your heart utter anything hastily before God. For God is in heaven, and you on earth; therefore let your words be few. Ecclesiastes 5:2

"But of that day and hour no one knows, no, not even the angels of heaven, but My Father only." Matthew 24:36

"In My Father's house are many mansions; if it were not so, I would have told you. I go to prepare a place for you." John 14:2

Additional References: Deuteronomy 10:14; II Kings 2:11; Psalms 11:4a, 20:6, 33:13; Matthew 5:12, 16; Revelation 19—22.

What Others Say: Lewis Sperry Chafer, Bible scholar.

Lewis Sperry Chafer

One has well said, "Heaven is a prepared place for a prepared people." Very definite preparation is required for those who would enter that celestial sphere (cf. Colossians 1:12). They must be like Christ both in standing and state (Romans 8:29; I John 3:2).

It remains to observe that heaven is a place of beauty (Revelation 21:1–22:7) with various inhabitants (Hebrews 12:22–24), of life (I Timothy 4:8), holiness (Revelation 21:27), service (Revelation 22:3), worship (Revelation 19:1–3), fellowship with God (II Timothy 4:8), and glory (II Corinthians 4:17. See Revelation 21:4–5).[1]

Application: It is obvious in the Scripture that much is written about the Lord and our response to Him as we live on this earth, while in comparison relatively little is written about heaven. It is evident that we are primarily to dwell on our obedient response in thanksgiving to our Savior, and a life-style of expression that the gospel is true and worthy of telling to others. At the same time, God has revealed some details about heaven as He has described His present and our future abode.

We anticipate the fact that there will be no more sorrow, no more trouble, no more fears. However, the most significant truth about heaven is that it will be the location in which we will have the privi-

---

[1]Lewis Sperry Chafer, *Chafer Systematic Theology,* Dallas Seminary Press, Dallas, Texas, 1948, p. 186.

lege of worshiping God in all His glory. His holiness will so dominate our existence that the location, even though magnificent in its splendor, will be insignificant in comparison. <u>Christians look forward to heaven because God is there to be worshiped!</u>

—Steven Longbrake

HEDONISM

WHAT DOES THE BIBLE SAY ABOUT THOSE WHO LIVE FOR PLEASURE?

The Issue: What comes first in our lives is at the heart of what it means to truly live the Christian life. Jesus said in Matthew 6:33, "But seek first the kingdom of God. . . ." Hedonism says that pleasure is the chief end of man. Contemporary society is increasingly buying into this philosophy which says that pursuit of pleasure in all its forms is the ultimate goal of life. Eat, drink, and be merry, go for the gusto, or do it if it feels good, embodies the concept of hedonism. Hedonism is a philosophy of life based on selfish indulgence. It is an approach to life which brings satisfaction for a brief season, but a trail of tears and regrets which last for a lifetime. Hedonism is in clear conflict with God's will. Only being in proper relationship with God through Jesus Christ brings true meaning and fulfillment.

Key Bible References:

You ask and do not receive, because you ask amiss, that you may spend it *on your pleasures.*

Adulterers and adulteresses! Do you not know that friendship with the world is enmity (hostility) with God? Whoever therefore wants to be a friend of the world makes himself an enemy of God. James 4:3–4

He who loves pleasure will be *a poor man;* . . . Proverbs 21:17

". . . therefore enjoy pleasure"; but surely, this also was *vanity.* Ecclesiastes 2:1b

For we ourselves were also once foolish, disobedient, deceived, serving various lusts and pleasures, living in malice and envy, hateful and hating one another. Titus 3:3

Additional References: Psalm 5:4; Proverbs 11:6; Romans 12:2; Galatians 5:16; I Thessalonians 4:3–7; II Timothy 3:4.

What Others Say: Richard W. DeHaan, author and radio Bible teacher; and Billy Graham, evangelist and author.

Richard W. DeHaan

The hedonistic attitude toward life is both inadequate and destructive . . . A society cannot flourish if people are always thinking in terms of "me" instead of "we". . . . If our nation continues to make a god out of pleasure, we will go the way of Greece and Rome.[1]

Billy Graham

The world (system) has a tendency to lead us into sin—evil companions, pleasures. . . . You will find in your born-again experience that your pleasures have been lifted into an entirely new and glorious reality.

Speaking on the Christian life, Graham states, "It is not a series of 'don'ts,' but a series of 'dos'."[2]

Application: All humans desire to be happy and to find meaning in life. Solomon pursued a hedonistic lifestyle. When it was all over, he said that the pursuit of pleasure was vanity, which basically means a vapor. Hedonism is reckless indulgence in the pleasures of this world without regard to moral or spiritual consequences. It is ignoring the boundaries and the limits that God has put in place for our own good. When pleasure is our god, it is a trap which enslaves. The very pleasures which bring thrills in time prove to be the very source of personal destruction (promiscuous sex, excessive drinking, gluttony, pornography, etc.). Pleasure as a goal is temporary, does not ultimately satisfy, crowds out God, and in time brings judgment (Luke 12:19).

The Christian life should not be the pursuit of pleasure, but on the other hand, the Christian life should not be characterized by the absence of pleasure. For example, some people seek to find pleasure in sex. But the problem is not with sex. Sex is a beautiful gift from God. The problem is the abuse and inappropriate use of sex. Sex in marriage is a wonderful and pleasureable gift from God. God's will brings fulfillment and great joy.

As Christians we may not hold a hedonistic view of life, but if our walk is not close with the Lord, we can begin to exhibit characteris-

---

[1]Richard W. DeHaan, *Happiness Is Not An Accident,* Zondervan Publishing, Grand Rapids, Michigan, 1971, pp. 58–59.

[2]Billy Graham, *Peace with God,* Grason, Minneapolis, Minnesota, 1984, p. 158.

tics of a hedonistic lifestyle. Believers who flirt with a hedonistic lifestyle do not honor the Lord, and limit their effectiveness as Christians. The solution to this problem is found in I John 2:15: "Do not love the world and the things of the world. If anyone loves the world, the love of the Father is not in Him."

—Robert H. Tennies

HELL

WHAT DOES THE BIBLE SAY ABOUT HELL?

The Issue: Satan, for obvious reasons, would have the world believe that Hell does not exist. Human reason would have man eliminate Hell by asking, "How can a God of love send anyone to a place of eternal punishment?" The existence of Hell, however, does not depend upon Satan's plans or man's reason but on the Word of the Living God. God has clearly revealed that He has created a place of eternal punishment and we label that place, Hell.

The Old Testament translates Hell from the Hebrew word sheol, meaning either the grave, a pit or the place of the dead. Hell in the New Testament is translated from either Hades, Tartaros, or Gehenna. Hades is equivalent to sheol. Tartaros, found only in II Peter 2:4, is the place where some fallen angels have been cast. Gehenna comes from the name of the Valley of Hinnom or "place of burning," a refuse dump of perpetual fire, illustrating and implying a place of torture.

Scripture's general usage of hell is in reference to a place of future punishment for the lost. Speaking in precise terms the terminal destiny of the lost will not be hell. The lost will appear before the great white throne of judgment to be condemned to the lake of fire where they will experience eternal damnation (Revelation 20:11–15). It is especially important to recognize that the lake of fire is a place, not merely a concept or state of being (Luke 16:28). The eternal character of the place is clearly taught in Matthew 18:8, 25:41 and Mark 9:43–48 where the fire is stated to be unquenchable.

Key Bible References:

The wicked shall be turned into hell, and all the nations that forget God. Psalm 9:17

"And if your hand makes you sin, cut it off. It is better for you to enter into life maimed, than having two hands, to go to hell, into the fire that shall never be quenched—where 'their worm does not die and the fire is not quenched.'" Mark 9:43–44

"And being in torments in Hades, he lifted up his eyes and saw Abraham afar off, and Lazarus in his bosom.

"Then he cried and said, 'Father Abraham, have mercy on me, and send Lazarus that he may dip the tip of his finger in water and cool my tongue; for I am tormented in this flame.'" Luke 16:23–24

Additional References: Proverbs 7:24–27; Isaiah 14:9–11.

What Others Say: Lewis Sperry Chafer, founder of Dallas Theological Seminary, author and theologian.

Lewis Sperry Chafer

As heaven is a place and not a mere state of mind, in like manner those reprobated go to a place. This truth is indicated by the words hades (Matthew 11:23, 16:18; Luke 10:15, 16:23; Revelation 1:18, 20:13–14) and gehenna (Matthew 5:22, 29–30, 10:28; James 3:6)—a place of "torment" (Luke 16:28). That it is a condition of unspeakable misery is indicated by the figurative terms used to describe its sufferings—"everlasting fire" (Matthew 25:41); "where the worm dieth not and the fire is not quenched" (Mark 9:44); "the lake which burneth with fire and brimstone" (Revelation 21:8); "bottomless pit" (Revelation 9:2); "outer darkness," a place of "weeping and gnashing of teeth" (Matthew 8:12); "fire unquenchable" (Luke 3:17); "furnace of fire" (Matthew 13:42); "blackness of darkness" (Jude 1:13); and "the smoke of their torment ascendeth up for ever and ever: and they have no rest day or night" (Revelation 14:11). In these instances a figure of speech is not a license to modify the thought which the figure expresses; it is rather to be recognized that a figure of speech, in these passages, is a feeble attempt to declare in language that which is beyond the power of words to describe. . . . It is well to observe, also, that nearly every one of these expressions fell from the lips of Christ. He alone has disclosed almost all that is revealed of this place of retribution. It is as though no human author could be depended upon to speak forth all of this terrible truth.[1]

---

[1]Lewis Sperry Chafer, *Systematic Theology,* Zondervan Publishing House, Grand Rapids, Michigan, 1947, Vol. IV, pp. 430–431.

Application: There is no way to question the reality of eternal punishment if one accepts the Scriptures as God's Truth. The actuality of hell must be faced. There are at least three vital issues that a study of hell brings to our consciousness. (1) God's nature includes a demand for justice in regards to His holiness. (2) If one is to be prepared for eternity that preparation must be completed today, for tomorrow is not certain. (3) Hell is the certain destiny of any who postpone repentance until they face judgment after death.

An awareness of the certainty of hell and its unspeakable eternal agony aligned with an accurate understanding of the truth that God "is not willing that any should perish" provides considerable motivation to seek God's salvation. The truth of hell is a vital aspect of the balance that exists in perfect harmony within the character of God. It is a point of creative tension for our finite capacities but serves, nevertheless, as a focal point in developing an accurate perspective of how infinite, divine balance plays itself out regarding our eternal destiny.

We live in an age in which many would have us see love as the only attribute of God. It is, therefore, of paramount importance that we gain a balanced biblical perspective on the nature of God. A place of eternal punishment is consistent with the character of the God of the Bible. We, therefore, must be willing to act on the Truth revealed by God.

—John Bole

HOME

WHAT DOES THE BIBLE SAY ABOUT HOME?

The Issue: Webster's dictionary says that "a home *is a* place where one likes to be: a place thought of as the center of one's affections: a restful or congenial place."

God Himself created Adam and Eve and placed them in their home, the Garden of Eden. They were cast out of that first home through sin, and established a home outside the garden. They were to be fruitful and multiply, and thus fulfill the historic definition of a family, "a group of people related by blood, marriage, or adoption." They of course were related by blood, but in today's world the definition of a family has changed drastically to "a group of people who love and care for one another." This can include all sorts of perversions of God's original intent when He created Adam and Eve.

Key Bible References:

"Therefore whoever hears these sayings of Mine, and does them, I will liken him to a wise man who built his house on the rock: and the rain descended, the floods came, and the winds blew and beat on that house; and it did not fall, for it was founded on the rock.

"Now everyone who hears these sayings of Mine, and does not do them, will be like a foolish man who built his house on the sand: and the rain descended, the floods came, and the winds blew and beat on that house; and it fell. And great was its fall." Matthew 7:24–27

But if anyone does not provide for his own, and especially for those of his household, he has denied the faith and is worse than an unbeliever. I Timothy 5:8

I will behave myself wisely in a perfect way. Oh, when will You come to me? I will walk within my house with a perfect heart.

I will set nothing wicked before my eyes; I hate the work of those who fall away; it shall not cling to me.

A perverse heart shall depart from me; I will not know wickedness.

Whosoever secretly slanders his neighbor, him I will destroy; the one who has a a haughty look and a proud heart, him I will not endure.

My eyes shall *be on the faithful of the land, that they may dwell with me; he who walks in a perfect way, he shall serve me. He who works deceit shall not dwell within my house; he who tells lies shall not continue in my presence.* Psalm 101:2–7

Additional References: Psalm 127; Proverbs 24:3–4; John 20:10; I Corinthians 11:34, 14:35; I Timothy 5:4; Titus 2:5.

What Others Say: Nick Stinnett, chairman of the Department of Human Development and the Family at the University of Nebraska, Lincoln; Dr. Warren W. Wiersbe, author and conference speaker; Dr. Howard Hendricks, retired professor, Dallas Theological Seminary; and Dr. Robert G. Lee, pastor emeritus, Bellevue Baptist Church, Memphis (deceased).

Nick Stinnett

All together we studied 3,000 families and collected a lot of information. But when we analyzed it all, we found six main qualities in strong families. Strong families

- are committed to the family.
- spend time together.
- have good family communication.
- express appreciation to one another.
- have a spiritual commitment.
- are able to solve problems in a crisis.[1]

Warren W. Wiersbe

A Christian family is built at home, not some place else. The Christian school and the church can only fortify what is built at home, and we thank God for their ministry.[2]

Howard Hendricks

The eight traits of a healthy home are communication, conviction, affirmation, trust, respect, care, responsibility, and initiative.[3]

Robert G. Lee

A man's home is a real fortress in a warring world, where a woman buckles on his armor in the morning as he goes forth to the battles of the day and soothes his wounds when he comes home at night. There is a vast difference between a house and a home. A house is built by human hands, but a home is built by human hearts.[4]

Application: Following a fire which destroyed their dwelling, someone said to a little boy, "Now you have no home." "Ah, but I do," he responded, "I just don't have a place to put it."

—Peter W. Teague

[1]Nick Stinnett, "Six Qualities that Make Families Strong," *Family Building: Six Qualities of a Strong Family,* Editor George Rekers, Regal Books, Ventura, California, 1985, p. 38.

[2]Warren W. Wiersbe, "Christianity in Concrete," *Confident Living Magazine,* May, 1984, p. 6.

[3]Howard Hendricks, Discovery Digest article from Radio Bible Class.

[4]Robert G. Lee, "Piety First In The Home" *Home Life,* May, 1950.

HOMOSEXUALS

WHAT DOES THE BIBLE SAY
ABOUT HOMOSEXUALS?

The Issue: There are eight Bible references to homosexuality. All eight condemn it as sinful, unnatural, and brand it a perversion. Whether we like to talk or think about it or not, homosexuality is weaving itself into the fabric of society. Unless we understand the problem and prepare ourselves and our children against the "Gay is Good" campaign, your family or my family could fall victim to this insidious evil.

Key Bible References:

You shall not lie with a male as with a woman. It is an abomination. Leviticus 18:22

For this reason God gave them up to vile passions. For even their women exchanged the natural use for what is against nature.

Likewise also the men, leaving the natural use of the woman, burned in their lust for one another, men with men committing what is shameful, and receiving in themselves the penalty of their error which was due. Romans 1:26–27

Do you not know that the unrighteous will not inherit the kingdom of God? Do not be deceived. Neither fornicators, nor idolaters, nor adulterers, nor homosexuals, nor sodomites, nor thieves, nor covetous, nor drunkards, nor revilers, nor extortioners will inherit the kingdom of God. I Corinthians 6:9–10

Additional References: Genesis 1:27, 19:4–5, 24; Leviticus 20:13; I Kings 14:24; I Timothy 1:9–11; II Peter 2:6; Jude 7.

What Others Say: Dr. Tim LaHaye, president of Family Life Seminars.

Tim LaHaye

Those who try to defend homosexuality usually maintain that condemnation of homosexuality is an Old Testament teaching. Because Christ came to free us from the Law, and since he did not discuss same-sex union, we are no longer under the Old Testament condemnatory policy, they insist. What they forget is that the Old Testament reveals God's attitude toward sin, so that the fact that we do not stone people for homosexual acts today does not change the fact that in God's eyes it is still an "abomination."[1]

Homosexuality is not just a sin against one's own body, but an offense against God. Therefore the phrase "a Christian homosexual" is really a contradiction of terms. A homosexual violates God's clearly prescribed will, thwarts his purpose for man, and has incurred "the wrath of God." If a man persists in this sin long enough, God will "give him up to a reprobate mind."[2]

Application: God has not left any room in His Word for the practice of homosexuality. The apostle Paul made it very clear that those who practice homosexuality will not inherit the Kingdom of God (I Corinthians 6:9–10). Though homosexuality may be an acceptable lifestyle for those in today's society, in God's eyes it is an "abomination."

—Kent Miller

HONESTY

WHAT IS THE BIBLICAL PERSPECTIVE ON HONESTY?

The Issue: In a day when all absolutes and virtues are under attack or at least questioned, the once valued trait of honesty is no exception. Is it old fashioned to be honest and in turn expect honesty from others in every situation? Does it really matter to God if pencils and papers from the office are taken home and used for personal reasons? Do IRS officials "expect" people not to declare all of their income? Would one today really conclude that honesty is the best policy? God's Word is crystal clear on this particular topic.

Key Bible References:

"Behold, therefore, I beat My fists at the dishonest profit which you have made, . . ." Ezekiel 22:13a

Finally, brethren, whatever things are true, whatever things are noble, whatever things are just, whatever things are pure,

---

[1]Tim LaHaye, *The Unhappy Gays,* Tyndale House Publishers, Inc., Wheaton, Illinois, 1978, p. 146.
[2]Ibid., p. 111.

whatever things are *lovely, whatever things* are *of good report, if* there is *any virtue and if* there is *anything praiseworthy— meditate on these things.* Philippians 4:8

Additional References: Acts 6:3; I Corinthians 4:2; II Corinthians 8:21.

What Others Say: *Attitudes Unlimited* Publication No. 12; and Dr. Ted W. Engstrom, pastor president of World Vision.

Attitudes Unlimited

Honesty, to be genuine, must have its roots in our soul. Unless it is buried that deep, we do not possess it, and we cannot manifest anything we do not actually have. If we are to give honest performance, we must first have it.

Honesty takes plenty of courage . . . but the rewards are tremendous. Folks will say of you . . . there is a person we can trust . . . on whom we can depend to act fairly, justly, considerately. This individual is worthy of promotion . . . recognition . . . success.[1]

Ted W. Engstrom

At the age of twenty-four, Abraham Lincoln served as the postmaster of New Salem, Illinois, for which he was paid an annual salary of $55.70.

Even then, twenty-four years before he entered the White House, the rail-splitter was showing the character that earned the title of "Honest Abe."

The New Salem post office was closed in 1836, but it was several years before an agent arrived from Washington to settle accounts with ex-postmaster Lincoln, who was a struggling lawyer not doing very well.

The agent informed him that $17 was due the government. Lincoln crossed the room, opened an old trunk and took out a yellowed cotton rag, bound with a string. Untying it, he spread out the cloth and there was the $17. He had been holding it untouched for all these years.[2]

Application: Honesty is simply being truthful at all times. As one looks at the life of Jesus Christ, does he ever see Jesus saying or doing anything other than what is honest, right, and true? Dishonesty is usually practiced when one is trying to unjustly claim some-

---

[1]Attitudes Unlimited, 840 Westchester Drive, Dallas, Texas, No. 12.
[2]Ted W. Engstrom, *Integrity,* Word Books, Publishers, Waco, Texas, 1987, p. 75.

thing, attempting to squeeze out of an unpleasant situation, or trying to give a false impression. If one properly realizes God's great love, he is usually motivated to trust Him fully under all circumstances. One must not seek what is not his; the Lord will provide every need. Cheating in any form is a pure lack of trust and confidence in God. Also, the principle of sowing and reaping is operative at all times. If one sows dishonesty, he can be sure he will reap dishonesty many, many times over.

There is no greater sign of one's love and devotion to God than following His Word every day. In turn, being obedient to God's directives is clear assurance of having an effective, productive, and joyful life.

What could be so important to cause us to be dishonest knowing full well that our heavenly Father sees everything? Honesty is not only the best policy of life, it's the only way of life.

—Art Nazigian

HUMANISM

WHAT IS THE BIBLICAL RESPONSE TO HUMANISM?

The Issue: Who determines the values and standards by which we live? Is the materialistic present world all there is? Does the answer to the violence, immorality, injustice, and corruption in the world reside in God or in man's ability to unleash his own innate goodness? These are some of the significant questions man needs to have answered in our day. The answer of humanistic thinkers is to begin with man alone to find a unified meaning to life. The supernatural is relegated to myth status. The materialistic present is all that ultimately matters. And our ultimate faith should be placed in man as the one who is able to bring order, beauty, and life-enhancing pleasure to this troubled world. Christians believe, however, that something altogether different is taught in the Bible.

Key Bible References:

"Therefore know this day, and consider it *in your heart, that the LORD Himself* is *God in heaven above and on the earth beneath; there is no other."* Deuteronomy 4:39

For the wrath of God is revealed from heaven against all ungodli-
ness and unrighteousness of men, who suppress the truth in un-
righteousness, because what may be known of God is manifest in
them, for God has shown it to them.

. . . although they knew God, they did not glorify Him *as God, nor*
were thankful, but became futile in their thoughts, and their fool-
ish hearts were darkened. Romans 1:18–19, 21

Additional References: Matthew 6:33; Acts 17:24–31; Romans 1:18–
2:3; I Corinthians 10:22; Hebrews 11:6.

What Others Say: Francis A. Schaeffer, theologian, philosopher, and
author; and Dr. Henry M. Morris, Bible scholar and author.

Francis A. Schaeffer

There is a death wish inherent in humanism—the impulsive drive
to beat to death the base which made our freedoms and our culture
possible. Humanists have been determined to beat to death the
knowledge of God and the knowledge that God has not been silent,
but has spoken in the Bible and through Christ—and they have
been determined to do this even though the death of values has
come with the death of knowledge.[1]

Henry M. Morris

In humanism, since there is no external creator and since man is
the highest achievement of the evolutionary process, man himself
becomes the only God there is. Evolutionary humanism either generates anarchism, in which each man is in effect his own God and
does his own thing, or else leads to collectivism, in which the state
becomes god, represented by man at its helm who receives its worship.[2]

Application: Man is involved in a frantic search for meaning and
hope. Thus, he experiences a desperate longing to center his life
around something of significant value. The answer of the humanist
is, "Look to yourself!" And man's confusion deepens.

It is to this environment of despair that the Christian brings a profound message of hope. There is a God who has spoken to our deepest need. He is the source of all meaning and value. And, best of all,
He will bring order where there is confusion, peace where there is

---

[1]Francis A. Schaeffer, *How Should We Then Live?*, Fleming H. Revell Company; Old
Tappan, New Jersey, 1976, p. 226.
[2]Henry M. Morris, *Education for the Real World*, Master Books, San Diego, California,
1977, p. 82.

turmoil, and life where there is death. This God will take His right-ful place at the center of your life when you come to Him by faith in the death of His Son Jesus Christ for your sins.

—**David H. Greiner**

HUMILITY

WHAT DOES THE BIBLE TEACH ABOUT HUMILITY?

The Issue: Humility is the opposite of pride. Man fights an internal battle with pride which is the result of his sin nature. Even as Satan, because of pride, sought to become equal with God so pride causes man to seek independence from God and have an improper opinion of himself. The humble have a realistic opinion of themselves and acknowledge their dependence upon God. Biblical humility is the basis for both salvation and exaltation by God.

Key Bible References:

"And whoever exalts himself will be abased, and he who humbles himself will be exalted." Matthew 23:12

Yes, all of you *be submissive to one another, and be clothed with humility, for*

"God resists the proud, but gives grace to the humble."

Therefore humble yourselves under the mighty hand of God, that He may exalt you in due time. I Peter 5:5b–6

Additional References: Proverbs 16:19, 29:23; Micah 6:8; Matthew 11:29, 18:4; John 13:14; Acts 20:18–19; Colossians 3:12; James 4:10.

What Others Say: Dr. Merrill F. Unger, professor emeritus, Dallas Theological Seminary in Dallas, Texas; and George J. C. Marchant, vicar of St. Nicholas, Durham, England.

Merrill F. Unger

Christian humility is that grace which makes one think of himself no more highly than he ought to think (Romans 12:3). It requires us to feel that in God's sight we have no merit, and in honor to prefer our brethren to ourselves (Romans 12:10), but does not demand undue self-deprecation or depressing views of one's self, but lowliness of self-estimation, freedom from vanity. The word is about equivalent to meekness (Psalm 25:9), and is essential to discipleship to Christ (Matthew 18:3, 4).[1]

George J. C. Marchant

Before God, man is humbled as creature (Genesis 18:27) and sinner (Luke 18:9–14) having nothing to boast in (Romans 7:18; Galatians 6:3). Corresponding to the humility of Christ in redemption (Philippians 2:8; II Corinthians 8:9), humility is the essence of saving faith (Romans 3:27). The Christian calling by the Holy Spirit (I Corinthians 1:29–31) excludes all pride of race or religion (Philippians 3:4–7), social status (Matthew 23:6–11; Mark 10:43–45) or person (I John 2:16).[2]

Application: All Christians are called to humility even as we are also called to holiness and to self crucifixion. True humility is only achievable with God's help as it is counter to man's own sin nature. Only by surrendering self and self-will to the perfect Will of God and becoming nothing before Him can we achieve true humility. Our holiness will always be seen most clearly in our humility before God and man. As pride can transform the highest angels into devils so pride must die in us before anything of heaven can live in us. Humility is the flower that only blossoms on the grave of self-will.

—Herbert L. Meeks III

INCEST

WHAT DOES THE BIBLE SAY ABOUT THE SERIOUS PROBLEM OF INCEST?

The Issue: Incest is one of the many schemes Satan uses to destroy families and lives. By incest we mean sexual abuse, molestation or intercourse by or with a close relative, parent or step-parent. Our society is so sexually oriented that even Christians can suffer from its damaging pain. Most, however, don't know what to do if they

---

[1]Merrill F. Unger, "Humility," *Unger's Bible Dictionary,* Moody Press, Chicago, Illinois, 1970, p. 507.

[2]George J. C. Marchant, "Humility," *Baker's Dictionary of Theology,* Everett F. Harrison, Editor, Baker Book House, Grand Rapids, Michigan, 1969, p. 274.

have been molested or discover that someone they love has been. The shame of incest is usually so great that the victim has an especially hard time accepting how precious and loved they are by Jesus. The Bible, however, is especially clear in offering His hope and healing to all who have experienced such wounding.

Key Bible References:

I sought the LORD, and He heard me, and delivered me from all my fears. Psalm 34:4

And have no fellowship with the unfruitful works of darkness, but rather expose them.

For it is shameful even to speak of those things which are done by them in secret. Ephesians 5:11–12

When my father and my mother forsake me, then the LORD will take care of me. Psalm 27:10

For I know the thoughts that I think toward you, says the LORD, thoughts of peace and not of evil, to give you a future and a hope. Jeremiah 29:11

Additional References: Psalm 17:6–9; Mark 11:25–26; John 14:27; Romans 8:38–39; II Corinthians 1:3–4; I John 4:15–16.

What Others Say: David B. Peters, family counselor, author and child protective services worker; Vicki Tanner, psychologist, and Lynda Elliott, licensed social worker.

David B. Peters
Literally millions of individuals across this nation have experienced the same pain and confusion that you have. What happened is not your fault. The blame belongs totally to the adult who chose to take advantage of an innocent child.

If you are still being molested, please tell someone about it. What is happening to you will not stop unless you tell and keep telling until someone believes you. Adults who sexually abuse children do not stop until someone makes them stop, no matter what they promise. You may very much love the person who is hurting you but you must remember that he is sick and needs help. He cannot get that help unless you tell someone what is happening. Start by telling your mother. If she does not believe you or won't protect you, tell a teacher, a policeman, or someone else you trust.[1]

---

[1]David B. Peters, *A Betrayal of Innocence,* Word Books, Publishers, Waco, Texas, 1986, p. 150.

Vickie Tanner and Lynda Elliott
In our work with men and women who have been victims of emotional, physical, and sexual abuse, we have found many traditional approaches to treatment—stress management, parenting skills, and insight-oriented approaches—valuable, though limited, in producing lasting change and healing. The hurt from abuse is too deep for any human being to heal another. We have found that the true hope for freedom from the pain of abuse is through a personal relationship with God the Father through Jesus Christ. Only He can heal the wounds.[2]

Application: The pain of incest is not God's desire for anyone. Victims of incest need the hope and healing that only God can bring. The first step is to face the reality of its occurrence and tell someone you trust. There is hope. Healing and change does come when you know what to do. Expose the situation and then seek out a knowledgeable pastor or professional who not only understands incest but knows how God brings healing. Above all else don't avoid the pain or the problem. Change comes when we face the problem with God. God promises you strength, healing and hope.

—Alfred H. Ells

INFANTICIDE

WHAT IS THE BIBLE'S ANSWER TO THOSE WHO DESTROY "NON-PERFECT" CHILDREN?

The Issue: Infanticide is the killing of a born child. It is the disposing of a child so that society does not have to face the responsibility of caring for the handicapped or mentally impaired. It is the ultimate selfishness and desperate means to neglect our first priority from God, to take care of a human life entrusted to someone's care. God has given all people the command to be stewards of human life. The Bible is emphatic that our children are to receive care and never be destroyed for another's gain.

---

[2]Vicki L. Tanner, Ph.D. and Lynda D. Elliott, *My Father's Child,* Wolgemuth & Hyatt, Publishers, Inc., Brentwood, Tennessee, 1988, p. xiii.

Key Bible References:

"Take heed that you do not despise one of these little ones, for I say to you that in heaven their angels always see the face of My Father who is in heaven.

"Even so it is not the will of your Father who is in heaven that one of these little ones should perish." Matthew 18:10, 14

Behold, children are *a heritage from the LORD, the fruit of the womb* is His *reward.* Psalm 127:3

"Then the righteous will answer Him, saying, 'Lord, when did we see You hungry and feed You, or thirsty and give You drink?

'When did we see You a Stranger and take You in, or naked and clothe You?

'Or when did we see You sick, or in prison, and come to You?'

"And the King will answer and say to them, 'Assuredly, I say to you, inasmuch as you did it to one of the least of these My brethren, you did it to Me.'" Matthew 25:37–40

Additional References: Genesis 33:5; II Kings 17:16–20; Psalm 82:3.

What Others Say: Francis A. Schaeffer and Dr. C. Everett Koop, authors of *Whatever Happened To The Human Race;* and Ron Jenson and Chuck MacDonald, authors of *Together We Can Deal With Life in the 80's.*

Francis A. Schaeffer and C. Everett Koop, M.D.

Putting pressure on the public and on legislators to accept a lower view of human beings, small groups of people often argue their case by using a few extreme examples to gain sympathy for ideas and practices that are not limited to extreme cases. These then become the common practice of the day. Abortion, for example, has moved from something once considered unusual and now in many cases is an accepted form of "birth control." Infanticide is following the same pattern. The argument begins with people who have a so-called vegetative existence. There then follows a tendency to expand the indications and eliminate almost any child who is unwanted for some reason.[1]

---

[1]Francis A. Schaeffer and C. Everett Koop, M.D., *Whatever Happened To The Human Race?*, Fleming H. Revell Company, Old Tappan, New Jersey, 1979, p. 68.

Ron Jenson and Chuck MacDonald

Doctors today justify allowing [disabled] children to die with a view that it saves the families crushing burdens and the child itself of a life not worth living. Yet disability and unhappiness do not necessarily go together. Some of the most unhappy children are in perfect health, while some of the happiest children have physical problems which most of us would find very difficult to endure.[2]

Application: The Bible instructs us to have respect and to care for life because it is a gracious gift from God. To forbid life is to murder and to prohibit a person from living a full life. What can you do to preserve life? First you must have God's view. God's view is that life has worth, because every human being is made in the image of God (Genesis 1:26). This will affect your life style and how you treat others. Infanticide will become increasingly popular in America because abortion is allowed, it is the next step downward. You can make a difference by following God's plan for respect and care for the human lives entrusted to your care.

—**Glenn A. Meeter**

INHERITANCE

SHOULD CHRISTIANS LEAVE AN INHERITANCE?

The Issue: With so many needy people in the world and worthy ministries and other groups requesting donations for their projects, can Christians set aside assets for bequests with a good conscience? What are some guidelines that Christians should consider when leaving an inheritance?

Key Bible References:

A good man *leaves an inheritance to his children's children, but the wealth of the sinner is stored up for the righteous.* Proverbs 13:22

And the LORD spoke to Moses, saying,

---

[2]Ron Jenson with Chuck MacDonald, *Together We Can Deal With Life in the 80's,* Here's Life Publishers, Inc., San Bernardino, California, 1982, p. 87.

179

"The daughters of Zelophehad speak what is right; you shall surely give them a possession of inheritance among their father's brothers, and cause the inheritance of their father to pass to them." Numbers 27:6–7

But if anyone does not provide for his own, and especially for those of his household, he has denied the faith and is worse than an unbeliever. I Timothy 5:8

Additional References: Proverbs 31:16–18; Matthew 6:19–21; Luke 12:13–34, 15:11–32; Acts 5:1–11; I Corinthians 16:2; I Timothy 6:6–8, 17–19.

What Others Say: Larry Burkett, founder and president of Christian Financial Concepts, writer, and radio talk-show host; Ron Blue, a Certified Public Accountant and founder of a personal financial planning firm; and Dr. Ruth Haycock, past chairman of the Department of Christian School Education at Piedmont Bible College and international speaker.

Larry Burkett

I believe that inheritance is proper. Generally in the Bible, it was given to adult children before the parent died. According to Jewish tradition, a father would begin to pass along his inheritance to his oldest son when he reached his mid-thirties. Eventually, he inherited most of the property that his father was going to give him while the father was still around to show him how to manage it. . . . The principle of inheritance is scriptural. The problem is that most parents wait until death and then have no opportunity to oversee the inheritance's use. Whatever you want to give to your children, give it while you're still living, if at all possible.[1]

Ron Blue

We are stewards of God's resources, and our last stewardship decision is to transfer God's resources to those who will handle them in accordance with His wishes. If one child has rebelled or is not walking in accordance with what God would have him to do, the last stewardship decision must be not to leave him any of God's resources. . . . you need to be willing to treat your children differently, and the only way you can do that is to remember whose resources you are passing on. Not only is godliness a consideration in terms of treating your children differently, but their needs may differ.[2]

---

[1]Larry Burkett, *Answers to Your Family's Financial Questions,* Focus on the Family Publishing, Pomona, California, 1987, pp. 126–127.

[2]Ron and Judy Blue, *Money Matters for Parents and Their Kids,* Oliver-Nelson, Nashville, Tennessee, 1988, pp. 170–171.

Application: The Bible clearly teaches that Christians are stewards over the resources God has placed in their hands. In the Old Testament He established inheritance laws for His people to follow. In the New Testament He placed an increased emphasis on a believer's motives of the heart in financial matters and on the necessity for sensitivity to the needs of others. Christians must seek God for discernment on how to meet the delicate balance that is required between present needs and future bequests.

According to Larry Burkett, over 80% of Americans die without leaving a will. This can greatly delay the settlement of the estate, and it leaves the government to decide how it is to be divided. In the loss of both parents, the government will also decide who will be the guardians of any minor children. The first step then is to take the time to make a will. Other points to consider: (1) Donors should evaluate to what extent children or other individuals should share in their assets. (2) Donors should consider dispersing assets during their lifetime to their adult children so that they will be able to guide and evaluate the successfulness of their initial bequests (Luke 15:11–32). (3) Donors should consider leaving a portion to worthy Christian ministries by stipulating a dollar amount or a percentage for them. (4) Donors will want to periodically update their wills since circumstances change over time.

—Burton Carney

INTEGRITY

CAN A CHRISTIAN LIVE A LIFE OF INTEGRITY IN TODAY'S SOCIETY?

The Issue: There is no single simple definition of integrity. It can be described in several ways. For example, integrity is doing what you said you would do. You are "genuine." You are not pretending to be anything other than what you are. You are for "real."

Several words are often used to define integrity, but each falls short. Consider a few of them: honesty, truth, candor, virtue, purity, uprightness, completeness, and soundness. Notice that these qualities are not the society norms of self-seeking or self-fulfillment goals.

Key Bible References:

He who *does not backbite with his tongue, nor does evil to his neighbor, nor does he take up a reproach against his friend; in*

181

whose eyes a vile person is despised, but he honors those who fear the LORD; he who swears to his own hurt and does change; he who does not put out his money at usury, nor does he take a bribe against the innocent. He who does these things shall never be moved. Psalm 15:3–5

A good name is to be chosen rather than great riches, loving favor rather than silver and gold. Proverbs 22:1

Additional References: Job 2:3, 9, 4:6; Psalm 26:1, 11; Romans 9:1; I Peter 1:3, 5.

What Others Say: Doug Sherman, founder and president of Career Impact Ministries (CIM); and Edgar Guest, American poet.

Doug Sherman
The overwhelming teaching of Scripture is that integrity is a treasure worth paying any price to preserve—any price, whether it be your job, career, reputation, savings, position, whatever. I can say this unequivocally because integrity is a value that is rooted in the very character of God![1]

Edgar Guest
"Myself"
I have to live with myself, and so
I want to be fit for myself to know,
I want to be able, as days go by,
Always to look myself straight in the eye;
I don't want to stand, with the setting sun,
And hate myself for things I have done.

I don't want to keep on a closet shelf
A lot of secrets about myself,
And fool myself, as I come and go,
Into thinking that nobody else will know
The kind of a man I really am;
I don't want to dress up myself in sham.

I want to go out with my head erect,
I want to deserve all men's respect;
But here in the struggle for fame and pelf
I want to be able to like myself.
I don't want to look at myself and know
That I'm bluster and bluff and empty show.

---

[1]Doug Sherman & William Hendricks, *Keeping Your Ethical Edge Sharp*, NavPress, Colorado Springs, Colorado, 1990, p. 37.

I can never hide myself from me;
I see what others may never see;
I know what others may never know,
I never can fool myself, and so,
Whatever happens, I want to be
*Self-respecting and conscience free.*²

Application: The world is looking for examples of personal integrity. They want to see a person who will give more than a simple day's work—one who will not compromise principle or character. A person who has the courage to stand for personal and biblical convictions, even under severe pressure. Whether we like it or not, people are judged by the friends they choose, the places they visit and the decisions they make. A person of personal integrity will study the Scripture to determine the biblical position on the issues of life. They will develop strong convictions that will allow them to resist the pressure to conform to wrong actions or speech. They will stand for rightness and oppose all appearance of evil.

—August C. Enderlin

JEHOVAH'S WITNESSES

WHAT IS THE BIBLE BELIEVER'S RESPONSE TO JEHOVAH'S WITNESSES?

The Issue: With an active membership of over 4,000,000 and more than 300,000 baptisms reported in the 1990 service year, most people have heard of Jehovah's Witnesses. Unfortunately, their teachings contradict most of the beliefs of Bible-believing Christians—denying such doctrines as: the Trinity, the deity of Christ, the personality of the Holy Spirit, the bodily resurrection of Christ, salvation by faith alone, and the "born again" experience for all but the 144,000. While the Witnesses affirm that the Bible is inspired and authoritative, they claim that the correct understanding of the Scriptures is only communicated through "God's organization." One's salvation depends on association with this organization with such requirements as: the studying and distrib-

---

²Ted Engstrom, *Integrity,* Word Books, Publishers, Waco, Texas, 1987, pp. 40–41.

uting of Watchtower materials, attending meetings, being baptized, and being in submission and faithful to it.[1]

Of the many approaches in response to the teachings and denials of this group, only one is presented.[2] Is salvation gained through works as a "reward," by "endurance," and "hard work" and not realized until sometime during the millennium, as the Witnesses teach? Or, is salvation a gift from God received through faith in Christ by one who acknowledges himself as a lost sinner (Romans 3:23, 6:23; Ephesians 2:1–10)? What does the Bible teach?

Key Bible References:

Then they said to Him, "What shall we do, that we may work the works of God?"

Jesus answered and said to them, "This is the work of God, that you believe in Him whom He sent." John 6:28–29

For by grace you have been saved through faith, and that not of yourselves; it is the gift of God, not of works, lest anyone should boast.

For we are His workmanship, created in Christ Jesus for good works, which God prepared beforehand that we should walk in them. Ephesians 2:8–10

. . . not by works of righteousness which we have done, but according to His mercy He saved us, through the washing of regeneration and renewing of the Holy Spirit, whom He poured out on us abundantly through Jesus Christ our Savior, that having been justified by His grace we shall become heirs according to the hope of eternal life. Titus 3:5–7

And this is the testimony: that God has given us eternal life, and this life is in His Son.

He who has the Son has life; he who does not have the Son of God does not have life.

These things I have written to you who believe in the name of the Son of God, that you may know that you have eternal life,

---

[1]*The Watchtower,* Aug. 15, 1972, pp. 491–497; July 15, 1979, p. 14; Nov. 15, 1981, p. 21; Dec. 1, 1981, p. 27; Feb. 15, 1983, pp. 12–13; *Life Everlasting—in Freedom of the Sons of God,* pp. 387–399.

[2]For those interested in further help and for tapes, books, tracts and other materials, Eric Pement's *Directory of Cult Research Organizations* (various editions since 1986) lists about 100 ministries which specialize on the Jehovah's Witnesses, Cornerstone Press, 4707 N. Malden St., Chicago, Illinois 60640.

and that you may continue to *believe in the name of the Son of God.* I John 5:11–13

Additional References: Matthew 11:28–30; John 1:12, 3:3–7, 16, 36, 5:24, 6:40, 10:27–30, 14:6; Romans 4:1–6, 5:1–21; II Timothy 1:9; I John 5:1.

What Others Say: David A. Reed, former Jehovah's Witness elder and presiding minister; and Kevin R. Quick, author of *Pilgrimage Through the Watchtower.*

David A. Reed

All those years as Jehovah's Witnesses, the Watchtower organization had taken us on a guided tour through the Bible. We gained a lot of knowledge about the Old Testament, and we could quote a lot of Scripture, but we never heard the gospel of salvation in Christ. We never learned to depend on Jesus for our salvation and to look to him personally as our Lord. Everything centered around the Watchtower's works program, and people were expected to come to Jehovah God through the organization.[3]

Kevin R. Quick

I thought of my own arrogance as I had gone from door to door preaching that no one could be saved who had rejected the Watchtower, God's organization. But now things were looking very different. It really wasn't we who were important, not the Watchtower, not any man, but Christ. It was Jesus who had died. It was Jesus who calls His sheep by name . . . (John 10:3).

Life as a Christian and life as a Jehovah's Witness are as different as day and night. The foundation of my new life, my personal relationship with Christ, is a glorious, immovable foundation (Matthew 7:24–25). My righteousness is no longer my own; I indeed have no righteousness in myself.[4]

Application: Why must Bible-believing Christians share Christ with Jehovah's Witnesses? Because they, like others who don't know Christ as their Savior, are lost. They normally will not read non-Witness religious literature, listen to Christian radio, watch Christian television or attend church services. Some have come to Christ through searching the Scriptures, but most Witnesses heard the

---

[3]David A. Reed, *Jehovah's Witnesses Answered Verse by Verse,* Baker Book House, Grand Rapids, Michigan, 1986, pp. 126–127.

[4]Kevin R. Quick, *Pilgrimage Through the Watchtower,* Baker Book House, Grand Rapids, Michigan, 1989, pp. 69, 84.

Gospel and accepted Christ through the testimony of concerned Christians.

Christians must be prayerful, prepared, persistent and patient. They may never see any results. "But don't despair; by God's grace seeds are being planted." Or, as in ex-Witness Kevin Quick's case, "it took seven years of witnessing by at least twelve different Christians before I finally came to Christ."[5]

"Christians have the opportunity to reach out in love to Jehovah's Witnesses. True, it is necessary to be prepared, so as not to become entangled in their web. But when a Witness knocks on our door, we can plant a seed of doubt or perhaps water what someone else has planted. Thousands of Witnesses have left the Watchtower and become Christians in the truest sense. We can find them in various churches and fellowships throughout the world."[6]

Thank God for the challenge, the opportunity, and His blessing!

—Edmond C. Gruss

JEWISH RELIGION

WHAT IS THE CHRISTIAN RESPONSE TO JUDAISM?

The Issue: In Judaism, Jewish people and proselytes to Judaism are taught that their Bible, which excludes the New Testament, presents that they can go directly to God for the forgiveness of sin, and that no mediator or sacrifice is needed. The Jewish Bible teaches, however, that the forgiveness of sin is contingent upon animal sacrifices, and then finally upon the sacrifice of The Messiah. The Law of Moses requires even today the blood sacrifice for the atonement of one's soul. The New Testament teaches that "the blood of Jesus Christ (The Messiah) cleanses us from all sin."

Key Bible References:

In Him we have redemption through His blood, the forgiveness of sins, according to the riches of His grace. . . . Ephesians 1:7

---

[5]Ibid., p. 98.
[6]Leonard and Marjorie Chretien, *Witnesses of Jehovah,* Harvest House Publishers, Eugene, Oregon, 1988, pp. 209–210.

For Christ also suffered once for sins, the just for the unjust, that He might bring us to God, being put to death in the flesh but made alive by the Spirit. I Peter 3:18

But Christ came as *High Priest of the good things to come, with the greater and more perfect tabernacle not made with hands, that is, not of this creation.*

Not with the blood of goats and calves, but with His own blood He entered the Most Holy Place once for all, having obtained eternal redemption. Hebrews 9:11–12

Additional References: Leviticus 17:11; Deuteronomy 27:1–6; Psalm 32:1–2, 5; Galatians 5:5.

What Others Say: Dr. Jerry Falwell, senior pastor of Thomas Road Baptist Church and chancellor of Liberty University.

Jerry Falwell

I believe the only ultimate help for this wicked world comes from Almighty God, the God of the Bible. He alone is the answer to all peoples: Jews, Gentiles, black, white. God had very little trouble helping the Jews in Old Testament times, and I believe He can do just as well today.[1]

In my mind a Jew converting to Christianity does not abandon in the slightest sense of the word his wonderful Old Testament heritage. In reality, a Christian Jew is simply a son of Abraham who, having studied the evidence, has concluded that Jesus Christ is indeed the Messiah so often promised in the Old Testament.[2]

Application: Since no form of Judaism results in salvation, Christians ought to comply with Romans 11:30–31: "For as you were once disobedient to God, yet have now obtained mercy through their disobedience, even so these also have now been disobedient, that through the mercy shown you they also may obtain mercy." II Corinthians 5:20: "Therefore we are ambassadors for Christ, as though God were pleading through us: we implore *you* on Christ's behalf, be reconciled to God." This should be the Christian response to Judaism!

—Myron "Mike" Perl

---

[1]Merrill Simon, *Jerry Falwell and the Jews,* Jonathan David Publishers, Inc., Middle Village, New York, 1984, p. 28.
[2]Ibid., p. 35.

187

JUSTICE

WHY DO BAD THINGS HAPPEN
TO GOOD PEOPLE?

The Issue: Webster defines justice as, "the quality of being just, impartial, or fair; to treat fairly or adequately." As Christians we are tempted to interpret that definition wrongly when we apply it to God. We tend to think that if He treats us justly and fairly nothing painful or negative will happen in our lives. We ask questions like "Why me, Lord?" and "Why do the righteous suffer?" when difficulties assail us or those around us. However, if we review the Bible we will see that there is much space given to the description of the difficulties of God's people. Even those He chose as special leaders or messengers experienced difficulties and challenges in their lives. According to the Scriptures, there seem to be two reasons for the negative things that happen in the world—sin and Satan.

Sin, according to J. B. Phillips, is "the breaking of rules"[1] and this leads to consequences and/or suffering. It doesn't necessarily mean that the suffering will be only for the one breaking the rules, but that others may also suffer because of it. As an example, wrong decisions by parents can affect children "to the third and fourth generations." Satan is a power for spiritual evil in our world and can cause immeasurable difficulty and pain. Jesus provided encouragement for us when He promised peace in the midst of tribulation, joy even when we are suffering, and deliverance. God's admonition in Psalm 50:15 is "Call upon Me in the day of trouble; I will deliver you, and you shall glorify Me."

Key Bible References:

Surely God will never do wickedly, nor will the Almighty pervert justice.

For He need not further consider a man, that he should go before God in judgment. Job 34:12, 23

No temptation has overtaken you except as is common to man; but God is faithful, who will not allow you to be tempted beyond what you are able, but with the temptation will also make the way of escape, that you may be able to bear it. I Corinthians 10:13

---

[1]J. B. Phillips, *You God Is Too Small,* The Macmillan Company, New York, New York, 1955, p. 104.

"Great and marvelous are *Your works, Lord God Almighty! Just and true* are *Your ways, O King of the saints!"* Revelation 15:3

Additional References: Job 13:15; Psalm 145:17.

What Others Say: J. B. Phillips, English pastor, theologian, translator and teacher; Charles R. Swindoll, pastor, writer and teacher; and Gordon McDonald, author, speaker and consultant.

J. B. Phillips
We find Jesus accepting these things, (pain, disease, injustice and evil) which many people advance as the greatest hindrance to religious faith, as part of the stuff of life. He did not pretend that they did not exist: He coped with them personally by restoring, wherever possible, the true order of health, sanity, and constructive goodness. He made no promise that those who followed Him in His plan of re-establishing life on its proper basic principles would enjoy special immunity from pain and sorrow—nor did He Himself experience such immunity.[2]

Charles R. Swindoll
No wonder our heavenly home has as its entrance pearly gates! Those who go through them need no explanation. They are the ones who have been wounded, bruised, and have responded to the sting of irritations with the pearl of adjustment. J. B. Phillips must have realized this as he paraphrased James 1:2–4:

"When all kinds of trials crowd into your lives, my brothers, don't resist them as intruders, but welcome them as friends! Realize that they have come to test your endurance. But let the process go on until that endurance is fully developed, and you will find you have become men (and women) of mature character. . . ."[3]

And so, we accept rather than explain. We trust rather than try to make it all fit together so perfectly it squeaks. It helps to remember that each generation has only a few of the pieces, none of which may fit into one another. So stop trying to wrap everything in neat boxes. Let's be illogical about this for a change. Otherwise, we try to play God's role. And most of us are fresh out of omniscience.[4]

Gordon McDonald
Our planet is rife with the sad stories of men and women who have been hit by something like a meteor or an imbedded explosive de-

---

[2]Ibid., p. 103.
[3]Charles R. Swindoll, *Growing Strong in the Seasons of Life,* Multnomah Press, Portland, Oregon, 1983, p. 164.
[4]Ibid., p. 162.

vice. Yesterday's world so bright and vigorous lies today in pieces. What happened?

Can a world under threat of breaking be defended? Yes, emphatically yes. Has it been done before? Many times. The precedents abound. But if my personal world breaks, is there still hope? Can that broken world be rebuilt? Again, the answer is yes. God has put all the pieces in place, and the process for rebuilding has been time-tested and proven authentic.[5]

Application: God is just! This He has revealed to us in His Word and it has been attested to by many experiences of those who wrote Scripture. Our problem is that we would prefer having no difficulty or problem enter our lives. God admonishes us to "welcome them as friends" so they can be used to build our lives. His purpose in our lives is for us to have quality and character like that of Jesus, our elder brother and perfect example. Problems are not always direct punishment for sin. The world order God has established allows for consequences to cause difficulties even for the innocent. The consequences of sin and of the work of Satan always affect human kind. The emphasis in Scripture is twofold:

(1) We are to trust the Lord and lean not on our own understanding. We must accept by faith the provision He has made for us when He promised joy in the midst of tribulation and peace in difficulty and allow it to do its work in us, drawing us to maturity and positive character. We cannot always understand the "whys" of life and trouble, but we can practice the principles He has given us to trust, accept, mature, and grow.

(2) There are times, too, when our difficulty is the natural consequence of our own sin. Then Scripture is clear that we must take care of this by asking forgiveness. We find it hard to accept when the righteous suffer. Somehow, to us, this doesn't seem fair or just. But God is looking at a much larger picture and we are seeing only part of that picture. He has not promised roses and carefree living. He has promised that He will not leave us or forsake us; that He will be there to provide the necessary endurance, and that His joy is sufficient for our needs.

---

[5]Gordon McDonald, *Rebuilding Your Broken World,* Oliver-Nelson Books, Nashville, Tennessee, 1988, p. 33.

We must remember what Charles Swindoll said: "Let's be illogical about this for a change. Otherwise, we try to play God's role. And most of us are fresh out of omniscience."[6]

—James W. Braley, Jr.

IS IT EVER RIGHT FOR CHRISTIANS TO DISOBEY THE LAW?

The Issue: From the earliest of times (Genesis 9), God ordained the institution of government. While He did not specify its form or type, He clearly gave it the responsibility to promote justice. In both the Old and New Testament people are taught to respect and obey their government. But is there ever a time when a Christian should disobey civil government? Yes, if the government ever commands something that God forbids, or forbids something that God commands, a Christian must disobey.

Key Bible References:

Let every soul be subject to the governing authorities. For there is no authority except from God, and the authorities that exist are appointed by God.

Therefore whoever resists the authority resists the ordinance of God, and those who resist will bring judgment on themselves.

For rulers are not a terror to good works, but to evil. Do you want to be unafraid of the authority? Do what is good, and you will have praise from the same.

For he is God's minister to you for good. But if you do evil, be afraid; for he does not bear the sword in vain; for he is God's minister, an avenger to execute *wrath on him who practices evil.* Romans 13:1–4

Therefore submit yourselves to every ordinance of man for the Lord's sake, whether to the king as supreme, or to governors, as to those who are sent by him for the punishment of evildoers and for *the praise of those who do good.* I Peter 2:13–14

---

[6]Swindoll, op. cit., p. 162.

And they (the Sanhedrin) called them and commanded them not to speak at all or teach in the name of Jesus.

But Peter and John answered and said to them, "Whether it is right in the sight of God to listen to you more than to God, you judge.

"For we cannot but speak the things which we have seen and heard." Acts 4:18–20

Additional References: Exodus 1:15–22, 2:1–3, 22:28; Esther 4:1–6; Daniel 3:1–30, 6:1–28; Mark 12:14–17; Acts 5:22–42, 23:2–5, 28:16, 30; Titus 3:1–2.

What Others Say: Vindiciae Contra Tyrannos—*"A Defense of Liberty Against Tyrants"* is considered to be one of the finest Huguenot writings. It was first published in 1597 during a time of severe persecution.

Vindiciae Contra Tyrannos

". . . it may well be demanded wherefore Christians have endured so many afflictions, but that they were always persuaded that God must be obeyed simply and absolutely, and kings with this exception, that they command not that which is repugnant to the law of God. Otherways wherefore should the apostles have answered, that God must rather be obeyed than men . . . we must always obey God's commandments without any exception, and man's ever with limitation . . ." (p. 65)[1]

Application: History has provided some excellent examples of persons who put their beliefs above the rules of government: **John Bunyan (1628–1688)**, an English lay-preacher, was imprisoned for twelve years for refusing to obtain a government license to preach. When offered his freedom on the condition that he no longer preach, his reply was: "If I am freed today, I will preach tomorrow." *Pilgrim's Progress* was written while he was imprisoned. **Jeremiah Moore,** a Baptist pastor, was jailed in Virginia in 1790 for preaching without a state license. Patrick Henry successfully defended him. **Corrie ten Boom** and her family hid Jewish people in their home in defiance of Nazi orders in the Netherlands during World War II.

Christians in the western world have enjoyed almost two hundred years of relative religious freedom. However many now sense signif-

---

[1] Rus Walton, "Concerning the Higher Powers," Letter from Plymouth Rock, The Plymouth Rock Foundation, Marlborough, New Hampshire, Vol. 9, No. 4.

icant changes taking place in the political climate as governments and cultures increasingly shift away from their Judeo-Christian roots. More and more laws are being passed and court decisions are being made that contradict God's higher law. It seems likely that Christians will face increased chances of having to make decisions of whether to obey God or their government. At such a time Christians must "count the cost" and make their decisions with care. Civil disobedience in both biblical and secular history often resulted in difficult circumstances or imprisonment. Yet God wonderfully proved Himself able to strengthen those that sought to do His will.

—Burton Carney

LEADERS

ARE LEADERS BORN OR MADE?

The Issue: We often hear the phrase, "He is a born leader." Is there a biblical basis for this assertion or is it merely a man-made slogan on which we can hang our inadequacies? As we examine God's word we find the biblical process for leadership. Throughout the Bible we see clearly demonstrated that leaders are developed through the example of others. Effective leaders do not emerge because of their effervescent personality, position power, financial status, or great intellectual endowments. They are effective leaders because they have learned certain principles that motivate others to follow them. Christ's entire ministry on earth was spent training leaders to train leaders.

Key Bible References:

And He said to them, "Follow Me, and I will make *you fishers of men."* Matthew 4:19

"Imitate me, just as I also imitate Christ." I Corinthians 11:1

Additional References: I Samuel 16:7; Philippians 4:9; II Thessalonians 3:7.

What Others Say: Dr. Mark Lee, educator, author, speaker, and management consultant; Leighton Ford, president of Leighton Ford Ministries; Dr. J. Robert Clinton, assistant professor of leadership and extension at the School of World Mission, Fuller Theological Seminary; and Dr. Eugene B. Habecker, president of Huntington College.

Mark Lee

Persons who lead *earn* the right to lead as they respond appropriately to meaningful opportunities. The young David seems to have *learned* leadership lessons at each juncture of his life reported in the Old Testament. His songs suggest that the knowledge he *gained* through his experiences was stored for a later period. . . . Even as a follower, dutifully serving the directives of his father, David *learned* skills he would utilize for leadership.

If I am to lead effectively, that leadership must *grow* out of the experiences I have had. . . . A person is *developing* leadership potential as he responds effectively to each venture in his life.[1]

Leighton Ford

I believe we can make either of two opposite mistakes in viewing leadership development. One is to attach a mystique to leadership that says in effect, "God calls leaders. Leaders are born. There is nothing we can do about it." The opposite is to say, "Leaders are made. With the right techniques, we can produce them."

It is always true that God gives leadership to His Church and His Kingdom: "Promotion cometh neither from the east, nor from the west, nor from the south. But God . . . putteth down one, and setteth up another," said the psalmist. (Psalm 75:6–7)

But it is also true that there are processes that God uses to *produce* His leaders. A study of Scripture shows the stages of *development* in a Moses, a David, or a Paul.[2]

J. Robert Clinton

Leadership is a dynamic *process* in which a man or woman with God-given capacity influences a specific group of God's people toward His purposes for the group. This is contrary to the popular notion that a leader must have a formal position, a formal title, or formal training.

Leaders are *shaped* by deliberate training and by experience.[3]

---

[1]Mark Lee, "The Possibility of Leadership: Opportunity," *Leadership/Followship,* Beaverlodge, Alberta, Canada, 1983, pp. 20, 24–25.

[2]Leighton Ford, Foreword, *The Making of a Leader,* J. Robert Clinton, NavPress, Colorado Springs, Colorado, 1988, p. 10.

[3]J. Robert Clinton, Preface, *The Making of a Leader,* NavPress, Colorado Springs, Colorado, 1988, pp. 14–15.

Eugene B. Habecker

The pattern in Scripture seems to be that as long as the leader *obeyed* the will of the Lord, God was prepared to use that person.[4]

Application: Although it is true that we are all born with various gifts and abilities, a thorough research of great leaders reveals one thing—they are all diverse in abilities, talents, intelligence, physical appearance and personality traits. Leaders are not born with a certain set of characteristics that assure effective leadership. While it is true many are born with superior talents and gifts, the extent to which we develop and wisely use the gifts we have been given by our Creator will determine the extent to which we become effective leaders. Down through the years many great leaders have emerged from the ranks of both the fortunate and the deprived. Many have emerged through poverty, handicapped circumstances, and educationally disadvantaged environments. The ministry of Christ centered heavily on developing leadership among individuals with such limitations. Regardless of their situations, as He called them, and they committed themselves to His discipleship, they too became "fishers of men."

While it may be true that God raises up individuals to do a specific task only for a season, He does not recall us to inactive duty. Different assignments? Yes! Different levels of responsibility? Yes! Lessons to be learned from mistakes and failures? Yes! But from effective leader to a leader of passivity? No! The great commission calls us to become disciples for Jesus Christ. The Scriptures challenge us to become leaders who train others to become leaders (Matthew 28:18–20). Despite our innate gifts and abilities, if we fail to have this impact on others, we fail to lead.

—Jerry L. Haddock

LIFE

WHAT IS GOD'S PURPOSE FOR EACH HUMAN LIFE?

The Issue: Each one of us is a sentient and rational being. We require purpose for our lives, whether explicit or implicit. Everything we do

---

[4]Eugene B. Habecker, "Chosen by God," *The Other Side of Leadership,* Victor Books, Wheaton, Illinois, 1987, p. 54.

195

is actuated by some motive or purpose. Each one of us may have outlined a clever and reasonable purpose for his or her life, but unless it agrees with the Creator's purpose it will ultimately be self-destructive.

Key Bible References:

... having made known to us the mystery of His will, according to His good pleasure which He purposed in Himself, that in the dispensation of the fullness of the times He might gather together in one all things in Christ, both which are in heaven and which are on earth—even in him, in whom also we have obtained an inheritance, being predestinated according to the purpose of Him who works all things according to the counsel of His will, ... Ephesians 1:9–11

Therefore do not be ashamed of the testimony of our Lord, nor of me His prisoner, but share with me in the sufferings for the gospel according to the power of God, who has saved us and called us *with a holy calling, not according to our works, but according to His own purpose and grace which was given to us in Christ Jesus before time began,* ... II Timothy 1:8–9

And we know that all things work together for good to those who love God, to those who are the called according to His *purpose.* Romans 8:28

Additional References: Genesis 1:28; Romans 9:11.

What Others Say: James Moffatt, Glasgow Bible scholar.

James Moffatt

God gives no men preferential treatment. He is "no respecter of persons." He has no favorites. He is fair and equal in his dealings. ... His purpose for, and offer to one, is his purpose for, and offer to all. His purpose in eternity past is joined to his purpose in eternity future, and men can lay hold of these tenses of his purpose where they lay hold of each other.[1]

Application: If I were to ask you individually what God's purpose for your life is, I would get numerous answers, all of which would suffer from one defect: they would all be partial.

There is an all-encompassing, impartial answer that centers around the two great mandates that God has given to the world.

---

[1]James Moffatt, *Predestination*, Loiseaux Bros., New York, Inc., New York, n.d.

The Cultural Mandate He gave at the beginning of the world, and the Great Commission He gave at the beginning of the Christian era after the resurrection of Jesus Christ. The former was at the dawn of creation, the latter at the dawn of the new creation.

The Cultural Mandate derives from God's initial instructions to the human race in Genesis 1:26–28. The Great Commission is expressed in Jesus' instructions to the disciples in Matthew 23:19, 20.

From these two orders—to subdue the world and have dominion over it, and to evangelize all nations in the name of Christ—we can draw three specific responsibilities which constitute God's purpose for each one of our lives.

(1) We are to be refashioned into God's image.
(2) In accordance with the Great Commission, we are given the purpose of bringing as many other people as possible into that same divine image.
(3) We are to take all the potentialities, spheres, and institutions of this world and surrender them at the foot of the cross.

Our lives and the works thereof, must be explicitly offered to God and to His glory. Only in this way can each of us discover God's purpose for individual lives.

—D. James Kennedy

LIFESTYLE

WHAT IS A CHRISTIAN LIFESTYLE FOR TEENAGERS?

The Issue: Lifestyle is best described as the typical way of living of an individual, group, or culture. It is a distinctive set of characteristics that are expressed in the way an individual or group lives. Lifestyle is the result of a series of decisions each individual or group makes on how a person should live his life, what is morally right (acceptable) and wrong (not acceptable), and the values on which these decisions are based.

A Christian lifestyle is one in which these values and decisions are based on the commands and principles of the Word of God. The Bible does not use the term "lifestyle," but the same concept is expressed by the term Christian "walk," and the Bible has much to say about this. The Bible gives us the directions for a Christian walk, or lifestyle, and God gives to each of us the responsibility to choose the kind of life we will live in relationship to these directions.

Key Bible References:

> . . .*walk worthy of the Lord, fully pleasing* Him, *being fruitful in every good work.* . . . Colossians 1:10

> . . . *as you received from us how you ought to walk and to please God; for you know what commandments we gave you through the Lord Jesus.* I Thessalonians 4:1–2

> *He who says he abides in Him ought himself also to walk just as He walked.* I John 2:6

> *For we are His workmanship, created in Christ Jesus for good works, which God prepared beforehand that we should walk in them.* Ephesians 2:10

Additional References: Romans 14; Galatians 2:20, 5:16; Ephesians 4:1, 5:15; Philippians 3:16–18; Colossians 2:6; I Thessalonians 2:12; I Timothy 4:12.

What Others Say: Dr. Garry Friesen, chairman of the Bible department at Multnomah School of the Bible, Portland, Oregon; and Paul Borthwick, missions director at Grace Chapel in Lexington, Massachusetts.

Garry Friesen

In those areas specifically addressed by the Bible, the revealed commands and principles of God (His moral will) are to be obeyed. In those areas where the Bible gives no command or principle (nonmoral decisions), the believer is free and responsible to choose his own course of action. Any decision made within the moral will of God is acceptable to God. In nonmoral decisions, the objective of the Christian is to make wise decisions on the basis of spiritual expediency. In all decisions, the believer should humbly submit, in advance, to the outworking of God's sovereign will as it touches each decision.[1]

Paul Borthwick

How we choose to live and set our personal priorities conditions our ability to build our personal world vision. . . . None of us want to

---

[1]Garry Friesen, *Decision Making and the Will of God,* Multnomah Press, Portland, Oregon, 1980, p. 257.

shrink—either as persons or as Christians who seek to see the world as God sees it. If we choose to grow, however, we have to make personal choices regarding lifestyle, values, and priorities that contradict those of our society. . . . If we are going to choose lifestyles that honor God in the light of the world in which we live, we, too, must consider separation. Simplifying our lifestyles is a counter-cultural choice. . . .[2]

Application: Everyone agrees that Christians should develop a style of life that is distinctively Christian, but there are many different options regarding what is acceptable or not acceptable in a Christian lifestyle. Individual opinions on the issue must give way to biblical absolutes. When the Bible clearly reveals the commands and principles of God on a particular issue such as sexual immorality, drunkenness, dishonesty, profanity, or selfish behavior, there can be no debate. Christians do not have choices in these areas.

On issues where the will of God is not clearly revealed, there are options left to each individual and Christians will inevitably make different decisions in these areas. Frequently people will conclude that their decision is the only correct one, or at least spiritually better than any of the other options, and will incorporate their opinion into a set of principles that they believe to be the "Christian lifestyle." Those who do not accept their version of the "Christian lifestyle" are viewed as less spiritual, carnal, or even non-Christians. This is a cause of much divisiveness in the Christian community. "Who are you to judge another's servant? To his own master he stands or falls. . . . So then each of us shall give account of himself to God. Therefore let us not judge one another anymore . . ." (Romans 14:4, 12–13).

Teenagers in particular must be taught:
  (1) the absolute standards of God's Word (John 17:17),
  (2) the value of separation from the standards of the world, a concept that is especially difficult for them, because teenagers are extremely reluctant to be "different" (I Peter 2:9),
  (3) the joy of lovingly surrendering liberties for the spiritual benefit of others (Romans 14:15).

These concepts are taught better by modeling than by lecturing. Teaching a Christian lifestyle to teenagers must be a laboratory course, not a lecture course.

—William R. McKinley, Jr.

---

[2]Paul Borthwick, *A Mind For Missions,* NavPress, Colorado Springs, Colorado, 1987, pp. 133–139.

LONELINESS

WHAT DO THE SCRIPTURES SAY
ABOUT LONELINESS?

The Issue: Every human being suffers from times of loneliness in his or her life. Loneliness is identified by feelings of desolation, sadness, lack of companionship or general lonesomeness. Satan would have us believe that we are without help and separated from God, but the Scriptures make it clear that the love of God and His very presence continually surrounds His children. Therefore, loneliness to the Christian can be an experience that will cause him or her to draw closer to the Lord.

Key Bible References:

"And the LORD, He is the one who goes before you. He will be with you, He will not leave you nor forsake you; do not fear nor be dismayed." Deuteronomy 31:8

And the LORD God said, "It is not good that man should be alone; I will make him a helper comparable to him." Genesis 2:18

For none of us lives to himself, and no one dies to himself. Romans 14:7

Additional References: Psalm 68:6; Ecclesiastes 4:10; Matthew 10:39, 28:20; John 14:17.

What Others Say: Dr. Steven S. Ivy, chief of the chaplain service, Veterans Administration Medical Center in Nashville, Tennessee; and Elisabeth Elliot, former missionary to Ecuador and wife of martyred missionary Jim Elliot.

Steven S. Ivy

First, loneliness is both painful and promising. It is painful to know how different I am from others. The prophet Elijah was sure he was all alone in his dedication to God's cause. He isolated himself and hid in a cave because of his conviction (I Kings 19). It is painful to feel isolation, self-hatred, meaninglessness.

But there is also promise. Abraham's willingness to leave his familiar home led into many lonely circumstances, yet his faith formed the basis of God's covenant with the people of Israel. Jesus frequently sought out "lonely places" for prayer and meditation. Loneliness may be turned to solitude when it is dedicated to a cause, a project, or God. When loneliness turns to solitude, its promise is fully experienced.[1]

Elisabeth Elliot

When we think of being lonely, we usually mean that there are no people around; no one with us, no one to talk to. Or else we find that the people around us are "not on our wavelength"—they don't understand us, and that can be worse than no company at all. So loneliness in my experience is not relieved by just anyone's company. It needs to be someone special—someone who understands me, someone who can listen and be there when I need them.

The giant scope of His [God's] power in world affairs does not cause Him to overlook our individual concerns. And He has come to earth to prove it. Because of that He can sympathize with our weakness. He understands our feelings because being human, He has experienced loneliness too.[2]

Application: While loneliness may be evidenced during every season of life, many researchers have concluded that it is during adolescence that it is most likely to be experienced. Adolescence is a time when friends are all important. When a friendship is broken the adolescent will most likely experience loneliness.

Loneliness, however, may come to both the adolescent and the adult as a result of many different experiences. A few of these experiences include loss of a loved one, illness, separation from others, singleness, being afraid to love, and depression. While there may be different solutions to loneliness, a scriptural key is to use loneliness as an opportunity to be *alone with God* and to experience His promise of Matthew 28:20, " . . . lo, I am with you always."

—Eugene J. Fadel

---

[1]Steven S. Ivy, *The Promise and Pain of Loneliness,* Broadman Press, Nashville, Tennessee, 1989, p. 16.

[2]Elisabeth Elliot, *Loneliness,* Oliver-Nelson Books, Nashville, Tennessee, 1988, p. 44.

LOVE

WHAT DOES THE BIBLE SAY ABOUT DIVINE LOVE?

The Issue: The term "divine love" is synonymous with the term "God's love." The original Greek language of the New Testament uses a special word, "agapao," to describe this love. Simply stated, it means a love that loves regardless of the object, and regardless of what is given in return. It is a love of esteem and approbation. The simplest and the most profound of all verses in which this word is used is in John 3:16.

Key Bible References:

"For God so loved the world that He gave His only begotten Son, that whoever believes in Him should not perish but have everlasting life." John 3:16

"As the Father loved Me, I also have loved you; abide in My love.

"If you keep My commandments, you will abide in My love, just as I have kept My Father's commandments and abide in His love.

Additional References: Romans 5:5, 8; I Corinthians 13; Ephesians 5:25; I John 4:7–5:3.

What Others Say: Kenneth S. Wuest, teacher of New Testament Greek at Moody Bible Institute; and Masumi Tayotome, Inter-Varsity Christian Fellowship.

Kenneth S. Wuest

God's love for a sinful and lost race springs from His heart in response to the high value He places on each human soul. Each sinner is most precious to God, first, because he bears the image of his Creator even though that image be marred by sin, and second, because through redemption, that sinner can be conformed into the very image of God's dear Son.[1]

---

[1]Kenneth S. Wuest, *Golden Nuggets from the Greek New Testament,* William B. Eerdmans Publishing Company, Grand Rapids, Michigan, 1940, p. 60.

Divine love is likened to the "in spite of" kind of love. The person is loved in spite of, not because of what he is. He does not have to deserve it and he does not have to earn it. He is simply loved as he is, in spite of the faults or ignorance or bad habits he may have. God's love is not a theory or a teaching, but a concrete demonstration in the person of Jesus Christ.[2]

Application: The singular meaning of "agapao" beautifully denotes divine love. Our Lord's cry on the cross when He said, "Father, forgive them, for they do not know what they do" (Luke 23:34), candidly demonstrates the essence of this love. Because of divine love, God the Father gave His Son, God the Son gave His life, and God the Holy Spirit empowers us, God's children, to so love in return.

—James A. Thiessen

LOVE

WHAT DOES THE BIBLE SAY ABOUT HUMAN LOVE?

The Issue: LOVE! Perhaps this word best describes the essence of human experience. Within it lies the full range of man's emotions and deepest longings. Who can replace a mother's enduring love? The love of a brother or sister remains true in times of greatest need. How about the lifetime love of a wife who bears the name and children of her husband? A father gazing upon the face of his newborn child has unspeakable love. In the complex battles of life such loves give meaning. Love is the brilliant noon sunshine in human relationships. God's Word contains the full range of human love relationships.

Key Bible References:

"You have heard that it was said, 'You shall love your neighbor *and hate your enemy.'*

---

[2]Masumi Tayotome, *Three Kinds of Love,* Inter-Varsity Press, Chicago, Illinois, 1968, p. 8.

"But I say to you, love your enemies, bless those who curse you, do good to those who hate you. . . ." Matthew 5:43–44

"A new commandment I give to you, that you love one another; as I have loved you, that you also love one another.

"By this all will know that you are My disciples, if you have love for one another." John 13:34–35

Husbands, love your wives, just as Christ also loved the church and gave Himself for it,

Additional References: Deuteronomy 10:19; I Samuel 20:17; Proverbs 10:12, 17:17; Matthew 25:35–40; Luke 10:28–37, 15:22–24; Romans 12:9, 14:13–17; Galatians 5:13–14; I Peter 4:8.

What Others Say: Charles R. Swindoll, pastor of the Evangelical Free Church in Fullerton, California; Paul A. Kienel, executive director of the Association of Christian Schools International in La Habra, California; William Shakespeare; and St. Augustine.

Charles R. Swindoll
But the world doesn't need phony love; or mushy, fickle, wimpy love; or conditional love that says "if you _____, then I'll love you"; or swap-meet love that says "Because you gave me this, I'll swap you love in return." No. What the world needs now is tough love, authentic love.[1]

Paul A. Kienel
Your children and my children can survive almost every emotional trauma in life if they have a strong home base where they know they have unconditional parental love. To provide that emotional stability, some things must remain constant and love in the family is one of them.[2]

William Shakespeare
Love comforteth like sunshine after rain.

St. Augustine
It has hands to help others. It has feet to hasten to the poor and needy. It has eyes to see misery and want. It has ears to hear the sighs and sorrows of men. That is what love looks like.

Application: In New Testament times when asked to give the greatest commandment, Jesus responded that "You shall love the LORD

---

[1]Charles R. Swindoll, "Dropping Your Guard," *Guideposts,* Carmel, New York, 1983, p. 115.

[2]Paul A. Kienel, *Love in the Family,* P. K. Books, La Habra, California, 1980, p. 13.

your God with all your heart, . . . soul, . . . mind." He quickly followed this statement with, "And the second *is* like it: 'You shall love your neighbor as yourself'" Matthew 22:37, 39. Believers like to speak of I Corinthians 13 as the "Love Chapter" in Scripture. These fifteen statements given by the Apostle Paul are the ideal measure of human love: "Love suffers long *and* is kind; love does not envy; love does not parade itself, (love) is not puffed up; (love) does not behave rudely, (love) does not seek its own, (love) is not provoked, (love) thinks no evil; (love) does not rejoice in iniquity, but (love) rejoices in the truth; (love) bears all things, (love) believes all things, (love) hopes all things, (love) endures all things. Love never fails." I Corinthains 13:4–8. "And now abide faith, hope, love, these three; but the greatest of these *is* love." I Corinthians 13:13.

—J. Wayne Temple

MARRIAGE

WHAT IS THE BIBLICAL FOUNDATION FOR MARRIAGE?

The Issue: God ordained the wondrous union of husband and wife in the Garden with Adam and Eve. In a momentous Scripture repeated four times in the Bible (Genesis 2:24; Matthew 19:5; Mark 10:7–8; and Ephesians 5:31) God says, "Therefore a man shall leave his father and mother and be joined to his wife, and they shall become one flesh." Each partner, unique and distinct, is to love the other in sickness or in health; in abundance or in poverty; for better or for worse; until death separates them. The key Scripture points to the strong bond of unity, of permanence, of breaking away from parental "apron strings," and of intimacy. Marriage is hard work and decries selfishness. Ephesians 5:22–30 gives the picture of the marriage union being a reflection of Christ's relationship to us. Marriage is the most significant human relationship God has given to mankind. The Song of Solomon gives a beautiful picture of the intimacy of marriage.

Key Bible References:

He who *finds a wife finds a good* thing, *and obtains favor from the* LORD. Proverbs 18:22

Her children rise up and call her blessed; her husband also, *and he praises her.* Proverbs 31:28

Unless the LORD builds the house, they labor in vain who build it, . . . Psalm 127:1

Wives, submit to your own husbands, as is fitting in the Lord. Husbands, love your wives and do not be bitter toward them. Colossians 3:18–19

Additional References: I Corinthians 7:1–5; Hebrews 13:4; I Peter 3:1–7.

What Others Say: Charles R. Swindoll; and Mike Mason.

Charles R. Swindoll
Singer Cliff Barrows of the Billy Graham team told me a few years ago about some of the ways he found to maintain delight and happiness in his own home. "I find marriages are held together by twelve words," he said. "These are, 'I am wrong,' 'I am sorry,' 'please forgive me,' and 'I love you.'"[1]

Mike Mason
In marriage we are afforded a small glimpse into what it actually must have meant for our Lord Jesus, the Son of God, really and truly to have "borne our sins." . . . The loved one with whom we dwell and share our whole life bears the full brunt of all of our sufferings, complaints, vices, and griefs to such an extent that it might almost be said that they pass through the same experiences that we ourselves do.[2]

Application: Marriage is in trouble in our society. God's plan for the unity of husband and wife is largely neglected. Divorce rates are ominous even among Christians, and for many marriages which do not break up they resign themselves far too often to a paltry coexistence. The only redeeming answer is to commit ourselves to God's clear plan in the Scripture for an enduring, fulfilling marital relationship.

—Anthony C. Fortosis

---

[1]Charles R. Swindoll, *Strike the Original Match,* Multnomah Press, Portland, Oregon, 1982, p. 82.

[2]Mike Mason, *The Mastery of Marriage,* Multnomah Press, Portland, Oregon, 1985, p. 162.

MATERIALISM

WHAT DOES THE BIBLE TEACH ABOUT MATERIALISM?

The Issue: Christians live with an on-going tension of being *in the world* and yet *not of it*. Being in the world requires of us that we use and interact with a material world. How does a Christian determine how much of his or her time, energy and talent to focus on material things? How do we live in a media-driven world without succumbing to the temptation to acquire and consume all the objects that are advertised to us? How do we exercise responsible stewardship of all that is available to us in our affluent American culture?

Key Bible References:

"Do not lay up for yourselves treasures on earth, where moth and rust destroy and where thieves break in and steal; but lay up for yourselves treasures in heaven, where neither moth nor rust destroys and where thieves do not break in and steal.

"For where your treasure is, there your heart will be also." Matthew 6:19–21

Command those who are rich in this present age not to be haughty, nor to trust in uncertain riches but in the living God, who gives us richly all things to enjoy. I Timothy 6:17

'For what is a man profited if he gains the whole world, and loses his own soul? Or what will a man give in exchange for his soul?" Matthew 16:26

And He said to them, "Take heed and beware of covetousness, for one's life does not consist in the abundance of the things he possesses." Luke 12:15

Additional References: Matthew 6:22–34; Luke 12:16–21; I Timothy 6:6–8.

What Others Say: John White, counselor, professor of psychiatry, author; and Frank E. Gaebelein, headmaster emeritus, Stoney Brook School and former co-editor of *Christianity Today*.

John White
It is not that riches, nice homes or luxuries of any kind are in themselves bad. They may in fact represent gifts of a loving God, given

for our enjoyment. They have their dangers of course. We get too used to them, too fond of them. Or they can become goals to be achieved. But in themselves they are in no way evil. If our attitude is right we shall inevitably, as I pointed out earlier, share our good homes with those in need of shelter, provided our churches are properly organized to spot and remedy human dilemmas around us quickly and effectively.[1]

Frank E. Gaebelein

The Old Testament sets wealth and prosperity in perspective. It hedges them about with restrictions and cautions. Wealth is not to be accumulated just for the sake of getting more and more, it must not be gained by oppression and injustice, it can and does lead to covetousness. Wealth does not belong to us but to God, who is the ultimate owner of all we have. We are stewards, not proprietors, of our wealth. In our use of it, we are sinning if we do not reflect God's special concern for the poor and hungry, the weak and oppressed. What we do with what we have must be in accord with the great command to love God with everything we are and have. Even our ability to gain wealth is a stewardship like any other talent.[2]

Application: At the center of materialism is the principle that *matter* is what really matters. As Christians we reject such a view of life yet we acknowledge that matter does matter. The Scriptures are full of instructions concerning our relationship to, and use of, money and resources. Wealth in itself is not condemned, it is the love of or obsession with wealth that receives God's judgment. God is just in His judgment because He is the rightful owner of all things. We are only stewards and caretakers of all that He has provided for our needs and pleasures. In the consumerism of our culture, it is important for Christians to prayerfully engage the battle for simple living and generous giving by carefully evaluating each financial decision that needs to be made. It has been said that the Christian should determine to keep his "standard of living" as constant as possible throughout life so that his "standard of giving" can continue to increase as resources permit.

—Kenneth H. Tanis

---

[1]John White, "The Golden Cow"—*Materialism in the Twentieth-Century Church*, Inter-Varsity Press, Downers Grove, Illinois, 1979, p. 93.

[2]Ronald J. Sider, "Living More Simply"—*Biblical Principles and Practical Models*, Inter-Varsity Press, Downers Grove, Illinois, 1980, p. 38.

THE MIND

HOW DOES A BELIEVER DEVELOP A CHRISTIAN MIND?

The Issue: The Bible states that Christians "have the mind of Christ" (I Corinthians 2:16). But many do not seem to think as Christ does nor live as He lived. Thinking rightly is the first step to living rightly. We have been taught from an early age that as a person thinks in his heart, so is he. In a world of conflicting ideas and secular thought plus the avalanche of words and images that assault us daily, how can the believer think Christian thoughts so that he may also live a Christ-like life? Secular philosophies seem in the ascendancy in education, business, entertainment, and government and Christians are greatly influenced by them, especially through the media. A God-centered way of looking at life and the world is needed by God's people to keep the world from casting us in its mold and to be a positive force for God in society, His salt and light.

Key Bible References:

And do not be conformed to this world, but be transformed by the renewing of your mind, that you may prove what is *that good and acceptable and perfect will of God.* Romans 12:2

Be anxious for nothing, but in everything by prayer and supplication, with thanksgiving, let your requests be made known to God; and the peace of God, which surpasses all understanding, will guard your hearts and minds through Christ Jesus.

Finally, brethren, whatever things are true, whatever things are noble, whatever things are *just, whatever things* are *pure, whatever things* are *lovely, whatever things* are *of good report, if* there is *any virtue and if* there is *anything praiseworthy— meditate on these things.* Philippians 4:6–8

Additional References: Isaiah 55:6–11; Matthew 11:28–30; Romans 8:1–11; I Corinthians 2:6–16; Ephesians 4:17–32; Philippians 2:5–11; Colossians 3:1–17.

What Others Say: Harry Blamires, English spokesman and writer; and Dr. John R. W. Stott, former rector of All Souls Church in London.

Harry Blamires

There is no longer a Christian mind. There is still, of course, a Christian ethic, a Christian practice, and a Christian spirituality. As a moral being, the modern Christian subscribes to a code other than that of the non-Christian. As a member of the Church, he undertakes obligations and observations ignored by the non-Christian. As a spiritual being, in prayer and meditation, he strives to cultivate a dimension of life unexplored by the non-Christian. But as a thinking being, the modern Christian has succumbed to secularization. He accepts religion—its morality, its worship, its spiritual culture; but he rejects the religious view of life, the view which sets all earthly issues within the context of the eternal, the view which relates all human problems—social, political, culture—to the doctrinal foundations of the Christian Faith, the view which sees all things here below in terms of God's supremacy and earth's transitoriness, in terms of Heaven and Hell.[1]

John R. W. Stott

Self-control is primarily mind-control. What we sow in our minds we reap in our actions. "Feed the Minds" is the slogan of a current campaign for the spread of Christian literature. It bears witness to the fact that men's minds need to be fed just as much as their bodies. And the kind of food our minds devour will determine the kind of person we become. Healthy minds have a healthy appetite. We must satisfy them with health-giving food and not with dangerous intellectual drugs and poisons.[2]

Application: Our way of thinking is molded from birth, the product of input from our families, friends, school, church, the media, the culture immediately surrounding us. In addition, we have what Scripture calls "the mind of the flesh," the inborn tendency to leave God and the spiritual world out of our thinking and center almost exclusively on our own concerns and the world around us. To understand how to develop the mind of Christ with all this adverse baggage, we must first know what His mind is. It means to know what He knows, to have His perspective, to share His values, to adopt His attitudes and responses, to copy His obedience to His Father and to possess His motives. These are the channels through which our Lord's thought flowed.

We have the mind of Christ, and yet we need to be renewed in our minds. This must start with a cleansing from sin which has led us

---

[1]Harry Blamires, *The Christian Mind,* S.P.C.K., London, 1966, pp. 3–4.
[2]John R. W. Stott, *Your Mind Matters,* Inter-Varsity Press, Downers Grove, Illinois, 1972, p. 41.

to wrong thinking. Then we must begin to form new thoughts from the Bible which will fill our minds with God's truth and will actually live in us as we read and obey it. Serious study of the Scriptures and hiding it in our hearts and minds is essential to developing a Christian mind. However, it is obedience which really enables us to think as a Christian.

To know the Word and not obey it deceives us into thinking that we please God, but obedience makes God's control over our minds a reality. It begins with our destroying wrong thoughts as we judge them by what God's Word says, then deliberately behaving as God commands and seeking to think through all areas of life based on this perspective. Thus we "put off the old man and put on the new man" and begin to "think on these things" as Paul directs. In this process we are "transformed by the renewing of our minds."

—H. Gene Garrick

MONEY

WHAT BIBLICAL PRINCIPLES APPLY TO PERSONAL FINANCES?

The Issue: Believe it or not, Satan is out to destroy God's first institution on earth—the home. Financial problems are one of the main causes for disharmony and eventual divorce among Christian couples. We can hardly live without money, but we often don't live wisely with it. In this day of economic instability, we Christians need to be careful stewards of all God has given us. It is up to each individual to judge whether or not he or she is following God's principles.

Key Bible References:

The blessing of the LORD makes one rich, and He adds no sorrow with it. Proverbs 10:22

And He said to them, "Take heed and beware of covetousness, for one's life does not consist in the abundance of the things which he possesses." Luke 12:15

"Do not labor for the food which perishes, but for the food which endures to everlasting life, which the Son of Man will give you. . . ." John 6:27

Do not love the world or the things in the world. If anyone loves the world, the love of the Father is not in him.

For all that is in the world—the lust of the flesh, the lust of the eyes, and the pride of life—is not of the Father but is of the world. I John 2:15–16

Additional References: Proverbs 21:20, 22:7; Malachi 3:10; II Corinthians 9:6, 10; Philippians 2:3–4.

What Others Say: Larry Burkett, director of Christian Financial Concepts, Inc., Dahlonega, Georgia; and Ronald W. Blue, director of Leadership Dynamics International, Atlanta, Georgia.

Larry Burkett

It is important for a Christian to be able to recognize financial bondage, but it is equally important to know how to achieve freedom. Financial freedom manifests itself in every aspect of the Christian life—relief from worry and tension about overdue bills, a clear conscience before God, before other men, and the absolute assurance that God is in control of his finances.[1]

Ronald W. Blue

I have been asked many times what is the biggest financial mistake I see, and the answer is easy—*a consumptive lifestyle.* A consumptive lifestyle is simply spending more than you can afford, or spending more than you should, given your other goals and priorities. Almost everyone in America falls victim to living a consumptive lifestyle.[2]

Application: Since money is an emotional subject for many people, I will list some biblical principles that apply to the personal finances of Christians:
- All we have and ever hope to have is given by God.
- It is His will that we devise and execute good stewardship.
- Good stewardship should include careful planning, budgeting, and giving.
- Accept God's provision and be content.
- Maintain a clear conscience in business practices and personal involvements.

---

[1]Larry Burkett, *A Guide to Family Budgeting* (brochure), Christian Financial Concepts, Dahlonega, Georgia, 1985.

[2]Ronald W. Blue, *Master Your Money,* Thomas Nelson Publishers, Nashville, Tennessee, 1986, p. 114.

- Financial bondage strangles; therefore, maintain checks and balances between your needs and your wants.

—James A. Thiessen

MORALITY

SHOULD CHRISTIANS IMPOSE THEIR MORALITY ON OTHERS?

The Issue: We live in a day in which established standards are being questioned. Even the Christian community is divided on many issues. Our society is faced with establishing a position on such issues as abortion, fetal experimentation, pain and suffering, and scores of other issues. Christians of various persuasions try to impose their interpretation and standards on the issue. The secularist brings his interpretation on the subject thus the conflict. God certainly knows the answer.

Key Bible References:

But Daniel purposed in his heart that he would not defile himself with the portion of the king's delicacies, nor with the wine which he drank; therefore he requested of the chief of the eunuchs that he might not defile himself.

And the chief of the eunuchs said to Daniel, "I fear my lord the king, who has appointed your food and drink. For why should he see your faces looking worse than the young men who are your age? Then you would endanger my head before the king."

"Please test your servants for ten days, and let them give us vegetables to eat and water to drink."

And at the end of ten days their countenance appeared better and fatter in flesh than all the young men who ate the portion of the king's delicacies. Daniel 1:8, 10, 12, 15

"I, the LORD, search the heart, I test the mind, even to give every man according to his ways, and according to the fruit of his doings." Jeremiah 17:10

"You are great in counsel and mighty in work, for your eyes are open to all the ways of the sons of men, to give everyone according to his ways and according to the fruit of his doings." Jeremiah 32:19

For we must all appear before the judgment seat of Christ, that each one may receive the things done *in the body, according to what he has done, whether good or bad.* II Corinthians 5:10

Additional References: Proverbs 20:3, 11; Matthew 5:13–16; Romans 14:12; Colossians 3:23–25; I Peter 2:11–17.

What Others Say: Alexander Solzhenitsyn, Russian novelist and Nobel laureate.

Alexander Solzhenitsyn

In addition to the grave political situation in the world today, we are witnessing the emergence of a wholly new situation, a crisis of unknown nature, one completely different, one entirely non-political. We're approaching a major turning point in world history, in the history of civilization. It can be seen in various areas by various specialists. I could compare it only with the turning point from the Middle Ages to the Modern Era, a whole shift of civilizations. It is a turning point at which settled concepts suddenly become hazy, lose their precise contours, at which our familiar and commonly used words lose their meaning, become empty shells, at which methods which have been reliable for many centuries no longer work. It's the sort of turning point at which the hierarchy of values to which we are dedicated all our lives, which we use to judge what is valuable and what is not, and which causes our lives and hearts to beat, is starting to waver and may perhaps collapse.

And these two crises: the political crisis of today's world and the oncoming spiritual crisis, are occurring at the same time. It is our generation that will have to confront them.[1]

Application: Christians have been arguing the rightness and wrongness of issues for centuries. Just when it appears an answer is at hand new information comes forth to cloud the final decision. Christ died that justice would be the final solution. Jesus Christ is our standard, our rule, our measure.

---

[1]Alexander Solzhenitsyn, speech at AFL-CIO meeting, July, 1975.

Authority rests in the Scripture; not in the church and Scripture or the state and Scripture. True morality comes from God's Word and is lived out in an individual life. Christians should never attempt to impose their personal morality on this generation or future generations. The only morality that has credibility for any generation is the moral standard of Christ as revealed in the Bible.

—August C. Enderlin

MORMONISM

WHAT IS THE BIBLICAL RESPONSE TO MORMONISM?

The Issue: The Church of Jesus Christ of Latter-day Saints (Mormon Church) was founded by the "Prophet" Joseph Smith, Jr., who claimed the Father and the Son spoke to him in an 1820 vision near his parents' New York home. "Jesus" told the teenaged Smith that all the current churches were wrong. Later, he supposedly translated the Book of Mormon from certain gold plates received from the angel Moroni. The book heavily plagiarizes the King James Bible however, and contradicts a number of major modern Mormon teachings. Also, Smith had many "revelations," among which are sprinkled heresies and false prophecies.

The Mormon Church claims to be the one true church, but actually it is a non-Christian cult with radically anti-biblical teachings such as a belief in the existence of many Gods; the Father, Son, and Holy Ghost are three Gods; and each God was once a man with a God over him. "God the Father" over this earth is neither omnipotent nor omnipresent, but has a body of flesh and bones and is a resurrected, exalted Man who is married to a "Heavenly Mother." "Jesus" is a spirit-brother of Lucifer, who sweat for our sins in the Garden of Gethsemane. He was not begotten by the Holy Ghost in Mary, but the Father himself sired Jesus. By obeying the "laws and ordinances" of the Mormon gospel, we too can earn the highest salvation and become Gods and Goddesses over our own worlds. A "testimony" of Mormonism's truthfulness primarily rests upon subjective/supernatural experience. When Mormonism and the Bible disagree, it is the Bible that must be wrong, according to Mormon belief.

Key Bible References:

"And the Father Himself, who sent Me, has testified of Me. You have neither heard His voice at any time, nor seen His form." John 5:37

"When a prophet speaks in the name of the LORD, if the thing does not happen or come to pass, that is the thing which the LORD has not spoken; the prophet has spoken it presumptuously; you shall not be afraid of him." Deuteronomy 18:22

For by grace you have been saved through faith, and that not of yourselves; it is the gift of God, not of works, lest anyone should boast. Ephesians 2:8–9

Additional References: Numbers 23:19; Deuteronomy 13:1–3; Psalm 90:2; Isaiah 8:20, 43:10; Hosea 11:9; Mark 12:32, 34; Luke 1:35; John 3:16, 4:24, 6:28–29; I Corinthians 15:3; Colossians 1:20; Revelation 1:8.

What Others Say: Jerald and Sandra Tanner, Salt Lake City-based Christian authorities in the area of Mormonism.

Jerald and Sandra Tanner

Mormon leaders have made the tragic mistake of pointing their people toward a church instead of toward the Saviour. They claim that their church is the only true church and that all others are false and have no authority. This tends to make people more concerned about an organization than about their relationship with Christ.

Mormonism teaches that shortly after the death of Christ, the whole Christian world fell into a state of apostasy. In the Bible, however, Jesus said ". . . upon this rock I will build my church; and the gates of hell shall not prevail against it" (Matthew 16:18).[1]

Application: Mormonism presents many challenges to orthodox, Bible-based Christianity. A major part of the problem is the fact that most believers simply don't know the Bible with its major doctrines well enough. For instance, when a Christian witness tells a Mormon we're saved by grace through faith (Ephesians 2:8) the Mormon may counter with ". . . faith without works is dead" (James 2:20). A prepared believer might answer, "Yes, faith without works is dead, but you're still saved by a <u>saving</u> faith alone. Faith alone saves, but given time, a saving faith is never alone. The witness could illustrate the danger and futility of relying upon one's good

---

[1]Jerald and Sandra Tanner, *The Changing World of Mormonism*, Moody Press, Chicago, Illinois, 1980, pp. 554–555.

works by using the parable of the self-righteous Pharisee and the humble tax-gatherer (Luke 18:9–14), followed by a reference to Isaiah 64:6 ("all our righteousnesses *are* like filthy rags").

Discussions on the nature of God offer great opportunities for a prepared Christian to biblically expose the Mormon "Gods" for the utter error that they are while pointing the Mormon toward the one true God. Mormons tend to ridicule Christian belief in the Trinity, by asking, "Was Jesus a ventriloquist at His baptism when the voice came from heaven saying 'Thou art my beloved Son; in thee I am well pleased'?" The Christian can respond with, "Can God be in more than one place at the same time?" Mormonism says "No," the Bible, of course, says "Yes" (see Jeremiah 23:24). The Christian should be prepared to show from the Bible that although the Father, Son and Holy Ghost are all described as God, there is only one true God (cf. Isaiah 44:8) and the relationship between the Father and the Son for instance, is far more than mere "oneness of purpose" as the Mormon Church claims (see John 14:10–11). Pray earnestly that God who is merciful will redeem those who are caught in the cult of Mormonism.

—**Wally Tope**

MOTHERHOOD

WHAT IS THE BIBLICAL ROLE OF A MOTHER?

The Issue: The Bible talks about ". . . a joyful mother of children" (Psalm 113:9b). Motherhood is presented in the Bible as an enviable, rewarding experience. In contrast, secular thinkers view motherhood in ways that are demeaning and not fulfilling. For example:

"Babies are not sweet little things. They wet and dirty themselves, they get sick, they're very expensive to take care of," warns a Planned Parenthood pamphlet distributed for student use. One local public school curriculum guide warns that "it is estimated that it takes $70,000 to $100,000 (not including mother's loss of income) to raise a child these days," that "babies need attention and care 24 hours a day," and that they often spoil marriages by making their father "jealous" and rendering their mothers "depleted."[1]

---

[1]Paul A. Kienel, *Love in the Family,* PK Publications, La Habra, California, 1980, p. 14.

The Christian community must not allow non-biblical thinking to destroy God's purpose for motherhood. The writer of Proverbs 31 describes a mother as a fulfilled woman, a woman of achievement and as a loving parent whose children "rise up and call her blessed" (Proverbs 31:28). What a contrast to the world's view of motherhood!

Key Bible References:

"A woman, when she is in labor, has sorrow because her hour has come; but as soon as she has given birth to the child, she no longer remembers the anguish, for joy that a human being has been born into the world." John 16:21

But if anyone does not provide for his own, and especially for those of his household, he has denied the faith and is worse than an unbeliever. I Timothy 5:8

My son, keep your father's command, and do not forsake the law of your mother.

Bind them continually upon your heart; tie them around your neck.

When you roam, they will lead you; when you sleep, they will keep you; and when *you awake, they will speak with you.*

For the commandment is *a lamp, and the law* is *light; reproofs of instruction* are *the way of life,* . . . Proverbs 6:20–23

Additional References: Judges 13:8; Psalm 127:3; Isaiah 49:1; Ephesians 5:31–32, 6:1–4.

What Others Say: Dr. James C. Dobson, Christian psychologist, author, and family advocate; and Patricia H. Rushford, author and mother.

James C. Dobson
A message to the husbands of Christian homemakers:

It is high time you realized that your wives are under attack today! Everything they have been taught from earliest childhood is being subjected to ridicule and scorn. Hardly a day passes when the traditional values of the Judeo-Christian heritage are not blatantly mocked and undermined.

—The notion that motherhood is a worthwhile investment of a woman's time suffers unrelenting bombardment.
—And the idea that wives should yield to the leadership of their husbands, as commanded in Ephesians 5:21–33 is considered almost medieval in its stupidity.

—And the concept that a man and woman should become one flesh, finding their identity in each other rather than as separate and competing individuals, is said to be intolerably insulting to women.

All of these deeply ingrained values, which many of your wives are trying desperately to sustain, are continually exposed to the wrath of hell itself. The Western media—radio, television and the press—are working relentlessly to shred the last vestiges of Christian tradition. And your wives who believe in that spiritual heritage are virtually hanging by their thumbs![2]

Patricia H. Rushford
The world is full of riches, but none of them can compare with the treasures that lie within a mother's heart. The greatest thing about all these treasures is that they are free. God has given us the keys. Now all we have to do is use them.[3]

Application: You often hear the phrase "motherhood, apple pie and the American flag." Americans continue to have a reverence for apple pie and the American flag but motherhood, in the traditional sense, is in jeopardy. For those of us who are believers in Jesus Christ we must hold firmly to the biblical concepts of motherhood.

—Colleen M. Kausrud

MUSIC

WHAT BIBLICAL CRITERIA SHOULD CHRISTIANS FOLLOW WHEN LISTENING TO, OR PERFORMING MUSIC?

The Issue: There is probably no other human cultural activity which reaches into, shapes, and even controls so much of behavior as listening to or performing music. Music is a beautiful gift of God, but not all musicians glorify God with their music. Ideas in music, for the Christian, may weaken or strengthen their faith. Christians be-

---

[2]James C. Dobson, *Straight Talk to Men and Their Wives,* Word Books, Publishers, Waco, Texas, 1980, pp. 101–102.
[3]Patricia H. Rushford, *What Kids Need Most in a Mom,* Fleming H. Revell Company, Old Tappan, New Jersey, 1986, p. 49.

lieve that they have much freedom in Christ (even musically), but not everything is helpful to the believer.

Key Bible References:

And have no fellowship with the unfruitful works of darkness, but rather expose them. Ephesians 5:11

All things are lawful for me, but all things are not helpful. All things are lawful for me, but I will not be brought under the power of any. I Corinthians 6:12

Test all things; hold fast what is good.

Abstain from every form of evil. I Thessalonians 5:21–22

Beware lest anyone cheat you through philosophy and empty deceit, according to the tradition of men, according to the basic principles of the world, and not according to Christ. Colossians 2:8

Additional References: Exodus 32:18; I Samuel 16:23; II Samuel 1:17–27; Psalms 33:2–3, 40:3; Isaiah 12:5; Luke 6:43–45; Ephesians 5:18–19; Colossians 3:16.

What Others Say: Martin Luther (1483–1546), German reformer and composer; Larnelle Harris, Christian contemporary musician; and Michael W. Smith, singer, songwriter.

Martin Luther

Music is a beautiful and lovely gift of God, a queen over every stirring of the human heart. Nothing on earth is more powerful than noble music in making the sad joyful, the arrogant discreet, the despondent valiant; in charming the haughty to humility, and in mitigating envy and hatred. . . . I give musica the next place after theologia, and the highest honor.[1]

Larnelle Harris

We need to expose people to the Gospel, and some have difficulty at first hearing it from a pulpit. Music is a way of getting God's Word to those who might not listen to it in another form.[2]

---

[1]Richard Viladesau, "Music As An Approach to God," *The Catholic World,* Vol. 232, No. 1387, Jan/Feb 1989, pp. 4–9.

[2]Audrey T. Hingley, "A Parent's Guide To Contemporary Christian Music," *Christian Herald,* Vol. 110, No. 5, May 1987, p. 46.

Research the lyrics and find out what we are saying in our songs. Read what we say in interviews, and talk to people who have attended our concerts.[3]

Application: A Christian vocal artist recently sang: "You got to know who to/who not to listen to." That is a good guideline for those who believe in Christ. Music is more than lyrics, rhythm, melody, and harmony. It also includes the listener's personality and perception of the attitudes and lifestyle of the performer. Music is expressed differently in every culture and subculture of every age in recorded history. The Bible provides criteria for Christians to follow when listening to or performing music. We are to test all things for truth. We are to examine everything carefully, holding to the good and abstaining from every form of evil. As Christians, we are called to be critics in testing and seeing what is good. Scripture, however, also alerts us that not everything we listen to or perform is a profitable activity for us.

God created us in such a way that we do respond to music. That response may please God, or grieve Him. Saul's "evil spirit" departed from him after David's instrumental solo. Jeremiah musically lamented over Josiah's death. When Moses and Joshua descended from the mount, it was music to which the idolatrous worshipers were responding.

As Christians, we are warned not to participate in evil. If some music or performers are identified with nihilism, violence, sexual promiscuity, and drugs, we are to avoid them.

–Dennis W. Mills

NEW AGE

WHAT IS THE CHRISTIAN'S RESPONSE TO THE NEW AGE MOVEMENT?

The Issue: The New Age Movement is a powerful spiritual force ultimately orchestrated by Satan in an attempt to deceive mankind into believing that a perfect world order is possible as we discover

---

[3]Ibid., p. 46.

the "godhood" within us. By appealing to the pride of sinful nature, Satan works as an angel of light to promote Eastern mysticism, the embracing of spirit guides, and a belief that all is divine: human-kind, nature and the cosmos. The true Christian, however, holds fast to the premise that we have been created by a personal God, and have no hope as sinners outside of His provision for our redemption through Jesus Christ, His Son. Therefore, Christians should be aware of the New Age Movement heresy, and test the spirits according to the truth of the Scriptures.

Key Bible References:

And for this reason God will send them strong delusion, that they should believe the lie, that they all may be condemned who did not believe the truth but had pleasure in unrighteousness. II Thessalonians 2:11–12

. . . because, although they knew God, they did not glorify Him *as God, nor were thankful, but became futile in their thoughts, and their foolish hearts were darkened.*

Professing to be wise, they became fools, . . . Romans 1:21–22

Beloved, do not believe every spirit, but test the spirits, whether they are of God; because many false prophets have gone out into the world. I John 4:1

Additional References: Genesis 3:1–5; Exodus 20:3; Acts 17:22–31; Ephesians 6:10–18.

What Others Say: Randall N. Baer, former New Age leader and author; and Texe Marrs, director of Living Truth Ministries in Austin, Texas and author.

Randall N. Baer

Let me tell you what the New Age Movement is really like, from the perspective of one who has lived it, breathed it, and worshipped it for 15 years. By holding up the serpent's original temptation to partake of the forbidden fruit, the New Age Movement has seduced many millions of people into accepting the promises of personal godhood, unlimited power, and immortality through reincarnation.[1]

---

[1]Randall N. Baer, *Inside the New Age Nightmare,* Huntington House, Inc., Lafayette, Louisiana, 1989, p. 78.

By keeping up with the current trends in the New Age, many of these forces' movements and strategies lay exposed, and Christians may be forewarned and forearmed regarding the lurking danger of tomorrow's impending titanic world events.[2]

Texe Marrs

This is an unheralded, most unimaginable, religious, political, economic, social, cultural, and scientific movement that has already dramatically changed this planet whether you know it or not.[3]

The most important question in the universe is this: When Jesus returns will you be ready? Jesus is Lord.[4]

Application: The New Age philosophy must be recognized as a lie designed by Satan, and contrary to the truth. Ultimate truth resides in Jesus Christ alone who claimed to be the Way, the Truth, and the Life (John 14:6). Christians are to carefully study the Scriptures to discern truth from error and be better equipped to test the spirits.

—**Loreen L. Ittermann**

OBEDIENCE

WHY IS OBEDIENCE IMPORTANT TO THE CHRISTIAN?

The Issue: Obedience is submission to someone of higher authority. Because the Christian recognizes God's authority, he willingly learns and obeys God's scriptural commands. Most of the world's population are not Christians and are unconcerned with God's standards revealed in the Scripture. The Christian, however, is God's child and he or she is concerned about what God says about lifestyle and behavior. Instead of ignoring God's standards he or she obeys them.

---

[2]Ibid., p. 76.

[3]Texe Marrs, *Mystery Mark of the New Age,* Crossway Books, Westchester, Illinois, 1988, p. 16.

[4]Ibid., p. 248.

Key Bible References:

"He who has My commandments and keeps them, it is he who loves Me. And he who loves Me will be loved by My Father, and I will love him and manifest Myself to him."

Judas (not Iscariot) said to Him, "Lord, how is it that You will manifest Yourself to us, and not to the world?"

Jesus answered and said to him, "If anyone loves Me, he will keep My word; and My Father will love him, and We will come to him and make Our home with him.

"He who does not love Me does not keep My words; and the word which you hear is not Mine but the Father's who sent Me."
John 14:21–24

Now by this we know that we know Him, if we keep His commandments.

He who says, "I know Him," and does not keep His commandments, is a liar, and the truth is not in him.

But whoever keeps His word, truly the love of God is perfected in him. By this we know that we are in Him.

He who says he abides in Him ought himself also to walk just as He walked. I John 2:3–6

Additional References: I Samuel 15:12–23; Matthew 21:28–31; Luke 6:46–49; Acts 5:25–31; Hebrews 5:8, 12:5–11.

What Others Say: J. Oswald Sanders; Alan Redpath; and Oswald Chambers.

J. Oswald Sanders

"I do like to do what I like," said the little daughter of a friend. We all like to run our lives, and in most of us there is an inherent tendency to resent any authority imposed from without. Even regeneration does not eradicate the desire to "turn every one to his own way." The characteristic of the sons of God is that they are led by the Spirit of God, and sons here indicates not children but those who share the rank, character, likeness, and privilege of their Father. Independence of spirit is a mark of spiritual immaturity or decadence. Submission to the leading of the Holy Spirit is a sign of mature Christian character. The Spirit will gladly lead us when we place the reins of our lives in His hands, and will deliver us from this disability.[1]

---

[1] J. Oswald Sanders, *A Spiritual Clinic,* Moody Press, Chicago, Illinois, 1958, p. 74.

Alan Redpath

I admit I do not always like the sovereignty of Jesus Christ. Often, alas, I have disputed it; but every time I have disputed it, that act of resistance has been followed by weeks and months of spiritual stagnation and failure when, although I did not lose my relationship with Him, I lost something almost as wonderful—the sense of His presence and the reality of His fellowship. I lived for weeks and months, alas, even sometimes for over a year in darkness, because I had again raised myself and said, "No!" at some point to the sovereignty of my Lord.

At any point in life you can resist His sovereignty, but at that moment God puts you on the shelf: you are useless to Him. Oh, you can carry on preaching sermons, teaching a Sunday school class, using the same pious language and singing the same hymns, but the unction and the uplift have gone. The liberty of the Holy Ghost has gone; the reality has gone. The Lord is in your heart, but you have quenched His Spirit.[2]

Oswald Chambers

The golden rule for understanding spiritually is not intellect, but obedience. If a man wants scientific knowledge, intellectual curiosity is his guide; but if he wants insight into what Jesus Christ teaches, he can only get it by obedience. If things are dark to me, then I may be sure there is something I will not do. Intellectual darkness comes through ignorance; spiritual darkness comes because of something I do not intend to obey.[3]

Application: Those who claim to be Christians recognize Jesus Christ—the Son of God—as their personal Savior. However, Jesus Christ throughout the Scriptures claims to be the Lord and King of those who follow Him. The Christian's response to Christ as Savior is one of praise and faith. Response to our Lord and King, however, must be one of worship and obedience. If one acknowledges the authority of Christ, then he must be concerned about his response to that authority. Obedience, therefore, is vital to the Christian life. A Christian acknowledges Christ as his Lord both by his lips and by his obedience. To acknowledge Christ as Lord with my mouth and then deny His Lordship by my lifestyle is hypocritical. A Christian's obedience is the AMEN at the end of his testimony.

—Robert M. Miller

---

[2]Alan Redpath, *The Making of a Man of God: Studies in the Life of David,* Fleming H. Revell Company, 1982, pp. 149–150.

[3]Oswald Chambers, *My Utmost for His Highest,* Dodd, Mead & Company, New York, New York, 1961, p. 209.

OCCULT

HOW SHOULD CHRISTIANS DEAL WITH THE OCCULT?

The Issue: In His wisdom God provided us with all the information we need through His revealed Word and His natural world. Yet, the lure of having our future told or an answer given by a ouija board, draws us into a frightening spiritual world controlled by forces opposed to God. What begins as simple satisfaction of curiosity often grows into a dependence on messages contrary to God's desire for our life. The Bible warns us that seeking guidance from the occult is dangerous and off limits for believers.

Key Biblical References:

And when they say to you "Seek those who are mediums and wizards, who whisper and mutter," should not a people seek their God? Should they seek *the dead on behalf of the living?*

To the law and to the testimony! If they do not speak according to this word, it is *because* there is *no light in them.* Isaiah 8:19–20

". . . nor shall you practice divination or soothsaying. You shall not make any cuttings in your flesh for the dead, nor tattoo any marks on you: I am *the LORD."* Leviticus 19:26b, 28

Additional References: Leviticus 20:6, 27; Deuteronomy 18:9–14, 20; II Chronicles 33:6; Jeremiah 14:13–16; Ezekiel 13:6–9, 23; Acts 8:9–13, 13:6, 16:16; Galatians 1:8–9; Ephesians 6:10–18.

What Others Say: Dr. John MacArthur, Jr., pastor of Grace Community Church in Panorama City, California; and the late Dr. Walter Martin, pastor, teacher, author and radio broadcaster.

John MacArthur, Jr.

I really believe that what Satan has accomplished today by the current preoccupation with the occult is the redirecting of people's attention away from the real issue of God's revealed truth. There is a natural fascination with the supernatural realm. Satan probably capitalizes on that by manifesting his overt activity, so as to draw minimal attention to his covert activity—lying, which is where he spends the majority of his effort.[1]

---

[1] John MacArthur, Jr. *God, Satan and Angels,* Word of Grace Communications, Panorama City, California, 1983, p. 90.

Walter Martin

The world of the occult is built on one word, experience. It is not built upon Authority, Revealed Authority. We must test all experience by Divine Authority.[2]

Application: Whether astrological forecasts in the local newspaper, a ouija board at a party, a fortune teller's prophesies, stories of reincarnation and extra-sensory perception, or involvement in witchcraft, the Christian has God's sure Word for what to do. In the Old Testament the Jewish people were instructed never to seek counsel from mediums of any kind (Leviticus 19:31). Those seeking or practicing occultic experiences were to be put to death (Leviticus 20:6, 27).

Because we do not live in a Jewish theocracy and now live in an age of grace, Christians are no longer instructed to stone to death those involved in the occult nor to have witch trials. In the New Testament, however, Peter (Acts 8:9–13) and Paul (Acts 16:16–18) identified those involved in the occult as controlled by Satan and needing Christ's forgiveness of sin.

Christians are instructed in Ephesians 6 how to prepare for spiritual battle against Satan and his forces. When Christians are truthful, careful in obeying God, at peace, trusting God, sure of their salvation and knowledgeable of His Word, they are prepared for battle and victory over Satan is guaranteed. Those praying for and using this spiritual armor know to avoid counsel from the occult and may be prompted by God, as Peter and Paul were, to confront mediums with God's truth. Those confronted with the freedom from sin that comes with personal acceptance of Christ's shed blood for them may become fearful, bitter and belligerent, but others will be freed from slavery and enter into new life. In this way we enter Satan's stronghold and go on the offensive against his kingdom.

—Tim Stranske

---

[2]Walter Martin, *World of the Occult Vol. II,* One Way Library, Costa Mesa, California, 1973, Tape: The Occultic Revolution, Side one.

OUIJA BOARDS

SHOULD CHRISTIANS PLAY
WITH OUIJA BOARDS?

The Issue: The Ouija Board has been around for centuries. The name "ouija" is derived from the French "oui" (yes) and the German "ja" (yes). The modern Ouija Board or "Yes Yes" Board is a simple device that consists of a small planchette (heart-shaped pointer) used on a smooth board on which are printed the letters of the alphabet, the numbers 0 to 9, and words "yes," "no," and "good-bye."

This device is often used among the fundamental doctrines and practices of the religions of Spiritism (also known as Spiritualism).

Our children are being exposed to this "game" at parties and at the homes of their friends, and with the help from the laws of our land, it is found on the game shelves of our stores right beside Monopoly.

Key Bible References:

"There shall not be found among you anyone who makes his son or his daughter pass through the fire, or one who practices witchcraft, or a soothsayer, or one who interprets omens, or a sorcerer, or one who conjures spells, or a medium, or a spiritist, or one who calls up the dead.

"For all who do these things are an abomination to the LORD. . . ." Deuteronomy 18:10–12

"Give no regard to mediums and familiar spirits; do not seek after them, to be defiled by them. . . ." Leviticus 19:31

Additional References: Leviticus 20:6–7; II Kings 17:17; Isaiah 2:6, 8:19; Acts 16:16–18.

What Others Say: Johanna Michaelsen, author; and Manly P. Hall, occult historian.

Johanna Michaelsen

But the simple fact is that Ouija is NOT a neutral device. Nor is it a toy. It is a dangerous spiritistic tool designed to contact spirit beings and develop psychic abilities.[1]

---

[1]Johanna Michaelsen, *Like Lambs to the Slaughter,* Harvest House Publishers, Eugene, Oregon, 1989, p. 64.

Manly P. Hall

The Ouija board . . . driven from most of the civilized countries of the world, is a psychic toy that has contributed many tragedies to man's mortal state. Automatic writing (an advanced form of Ouija), a weird fascinating pastime, may end in a wide variety of disasters. . . . He who listens too often to the whisperings of the "spirits" may find his angels to be demons in disguise . . . man . . . should leave these forces which may only lead to madness.[2]

Application: From the early books of the Old Testament, God instructed His people to have no participation in mediums and divination. God says, ". . . It is an abomination to the Lord." How easy the noted term—"game" (Ouija Board) deceives not only our young people but parents as well. We, who grew up in the 50's and 60's saw this experience with the Ouija Board as fun and harmless. To entertain, the use of the Ouija Board is in direct opposition to God's Holy Word!

Should Christians play with Ouija Boards? God says, NO, for its involvement is an abomination unto Him!

—Paul. H. Kemp

PARENTS

AT WHAT AGE ARE CHILDREN RELEASED FROM THE COUNSEL OF THEIR PARENTS?

The Issue: The task of parenting is all the more complicated by the uncertainty about the proper role of parents in the lives of their "adult" children. The age of legal accountability is eighteen in most states for most privileges (such as voting and marriage). In biblical history God set age twenty as the age of accountability for the sin of Israel's rebellion at Kadesh Barnea (Numbers 14:29). In the ancient Near East it was common for teen-agers to assume adult responsibilities. So there is no simple precedent. The question is twofold: At what age do children assume adult status; and what is their responsibility to their parents at that age?

---

[2]Manly P. Hall, *Questions and Answers—Fundamentals of the Esoteric Sciences,* The Philosophical Research Society, Inc., Los Angeles, California, 1979, pp. 95–96.

Key Bible References:

Children, obey your parents in the Lord, for this is right.

"Honor your father and mother," *which is the first commandment with promise:* "that it may be well with you and you may live long on the earth." Ephesians 6:1

My son, give attention to my words; incline your ear to my sayings.

Do not let them depart from your eyes; keep them in the midst of your heart; for they are life to those who find them, and health to all their flesh. Proverbs 4:20–22

"Every one of you shall revere his mother and his father." Leviticus 19:3

My son, hear the instruction of your father, and do not forsake the law of your mother; for they will be *graceful ornaments on your head, and chains about your neck.* Proverbs 1:8–9

Additional References: Proverbs 6:20, 13:1, 15:5; Colossians 3:20.

What Others Say: Bill Gothard, president of Basic Youth Conflicts; and Dr. James Dobson, family advocate.

Bill Gothard
The parental "chain of command" ends when they delegate that authority to someone else—as in marriage or the ministry. However, even before this, a certain measure of independence should be earned by learning to discern and obey the wishes of parents. When [the parents] are confident that [the children] will do what they would do in a given situation, they will give more freedom to make decisions. . . . Whatever our age, however, we are instructed in Scripture to always be responsive to our parents' counsel: "Hearken unto the father that begat thee, and despise not thy mother when she is old" (Proverbs 23:22).[1]

James Dobson
A child begins his life in a state of complete and total dependency on those whose name he bears. About twenty years later, however, at the other end of childhood, we expect some radical changes to have occurred in that individual. . . . By the time a child is eighteen or twenty, the parent should begin to relate to his or her offspring more as a peer. This liberates the parent from the responsibility of leader-

---

[1]Bill Gothard, *Basic Seminar Notebook,* Institute in Basic Life Principles, Oak Grove, Illinois, 1979, p. 37.

ship and the child from the obligation of dependency.... I believe we should give conscious thought to the reasonable, orderly transfer of freedom and responsibility, so that we are preparing the child each year for that moment of full independence which must come.[2]

Application: On the one hand, wise parents recognize that their authority over their children is limited because their ultimate goal is to prepare their children for independence. On the other hand, a wise son or daughter will always value the counsel of his parents. The God-fearing man or woman has two good reasons to give the highest possible priority to his parents' counsel:

> (1) He knows that the Scripture instructs him to give life-long and profound respect to his parents.
>
> (2) He knows that his parents' experience and maturity make them aware of insights that he has yet to discover. A child may be released from his parents' <u>authority</u> early or late according to his own maturity and capacity for independence, but the wise son or daughter will never neglect his parents' <u>counsel</u>.

—Claude (Bud) Schindler, Jr.

PARENTS

WHAT IS THE ROLE OF CHRISTIAN PARENTS WITH THEIR CHILDREN?

The Issue: It is not unusual for the Christian family to come under attack. It began with Adam and Eve. It certainly is not a modern day phenomenon. God gave us much direction in His Word for harmony and mutual respect between parents and children. Unfortunately, the world gives us much bad advice. Too often we are influenced by those who know nothing of the Scripture and a Christian world-view. God is greatly honored by families where parents use biblical principles in nurturing their children.

Key Bible References:

Children, obey your parents in the Lord, for this is right.

---

[2]James Dobson, *Dr. Dobson Answers Your Questions,* Tyndale House Publishers, Wheaton, Illinois, 1982, pp. 204–205, 211.

"Honor your father and mother," *which is the first command-ment with promise:* "that it may be well with you and you may live long on the earth."

And you, fathers, do not provoke your children to wrath, but bring them up in the training and admonition of the Lord.
Ephesians 6:1–4

Additional References: Deuteronomy 6:6–7; Psalm 78:5–8; Proverbs 22:6, 29:15, 17.

What Others Say: Joel Nederhood, radio speaker, "Back to God Hour"; and Dr. Henry R. Brandt, Christian psychologist.

Joel Nederhood
No matter how a father chooses to abandon his children, the results are always the same. As long as he refuses to face his deepest responsibilities as a father, his children are orphans for all practical purposes. If a father only provides his children with physical necessities, he provides them with no more than children receive who have been institutionalized because they have no parents. If a father refuses to discharge the most important responsibilities of fatherhood, he can not expect his wife to be a real mother either. Without the assistance of her husband, a mother is bound to become discouraged.[1]

Henry R. Brandt
A child has the right to expect that his parents know better than he and that they lead the way. He should be able to expect them to possess a conviction strong enough to carry him along, at times against his resistance or inertia. The decision on how to best satisfy the fundamental needs of a child rest not on the inexperience and inclination of a child, but on the parents' knowledge of the child's needs.[2]

Application: Nowhere does the world's philosophy of relationships have more potential for serious damage than in the parent-child relationship. A rigid, ultra-strict "My way is the right way," is just as unscriptural as "I want my child to make his own decisions."

Neither position allows for treating each child as an individual and giving personal guidance and understanding to children. Good com-

---

[1]J. Allan Peterson, Editor, *For Men Only,* Tyndale House Publishers, Wheaton, Illinois, 1973, p. 92.
[2]Henry R. Brandt, and Homer E. Dowdy, *Building a Christian Home,* Scripture Press, Wheaton, Illinois, 1960, p. 109.

munication is built when parents are willing to listen to their children's expression of disagreement if it is done respectfully. Children gain respect for parents who discipline and nurture with love, patience, and understanding.

God's pattern found in Ephesians chapters five and six portrays submission and respect by children and love and patient nurturing by parents. Whereas, most parents pay close attention to the "Children obey your parents in the Lord" section of these verses, parents often do not let the command not to exasperate their children have a great influence on the way they deal with their children.

Parents should carefully examine standards they expect of their children. Are the standards scripturally based and reasonable or are they derived from artificial human tradition? Parents who became Christians after they reached adulthood are often the most unreasonable with their own children. They desire so much to prevent their children from going through the hard times they did when they were young and unchristian that they lack the patience and understanding the Bible teaches us to have.

—Wallace Bourgeois

PEER PRESSURE

HOW CAN CHRISTIANS WITHSTAND PEER PRESSURE?

The Issue: Christians have friends or acquaintances who exert great influence over their thinking. It is sometimes easy to be swayed by others' opinions, ideas, and suggestions. Peer pressure is that powerful influence that one's friends or acquaintances can have to sway someone to conform to a certain set of standards, whether good or bad.

Key Bible References:

I beseech you therefore, brethren, by the mercies of God, that you present your bodies a living sacrifice, holy, acceptable to God, which is your reasonable service.

And do not be conformed to this world, but be transformed by the renewing of your mind, that you may prove what is *that good and acceptable and perfect will of God.* Romans 12:1–2

Do not be deceived: "Evil company corrupts good habits."
I Corinthians 15:33

I say then: Walk in the Spirit, and you shall not fulfill the lust of the flesh. Galatians 5:16

Additional References: Joshua 24:15; Romans 13:4; Philippians 4:13; I Peter 2:12.

What Others Say: Josh McDowell, speaker and author; and Charles R. Swindoll, pastor of the Evangelical Free Church in Fullerton, California.

Josh McDowell

In order not to compromise, you must become a man or woman of convictions. A conviction is a standard that you have committed yourself to keeping, regardless of what it costs you.

Swimming against the current requires a lot of strength. It is always easier to just go with the flow. For this reason it is important that your closest friends flow the right direction. You must surround yourself with friends who challenge you to daily live your life for Christ.[1]

Charles R. Swindoll

One of the great American myths is that we are all a bunch of rugged individualists. The truth of the matter is that most of us would do anything to keep from being different. We would much rather blend into the woodwork. One of our greatest fears is being ostracized, rejected by the "group."

It takes courage to stand alone, to resist alone—especially when the crowd seems so safe, so right. But remember God.[2]

Application: Peer pressure generally exists in two forms. It can be either positive or negative. Christians must make the decision to live for Jesus Christ and His standards and not for the group around them and their standards. Then believers will be able to stand alone even when it is difficult. Christians need to decide to be a positive influence on others in order to draw them to Christ. The believers' close friends must be chosen very carefully. Finally, when a Christian lives with an "I can do all things through Christ" attitude, God

---

[1]Josh McDowell and Bill Jones, *The Teenage Q and A Book,* Word Books, Publishers, Dallas, Texas, 1990, pp. 93–94.

[2]Charles R. Swindoll, *Living Above the Level of Mediocrity,* Word Books, Publishers, Waco, Texas, 1987, pp. 213, 224.

will enable the Christian to withstand negative peer pressure, to influence others positively for Jesus Christ, and to glorify Him.

—**Larry K. Green**

POLITICS

WHY SHOULD CHRISTIANS RUN FOR POLITICAL OFFICE?

The Issue: The American evangelical Christian community needs to become "salt" and "light" in the areas of the media (radio, TV, newspapers, and magazines) and politics (political parties and the three branches of government). Christ called us to be "salt" to preserve what is valuable; and "light" to shine in spiritually dark places and reveal truth. Christians should seriously consider serving God through being involved in politics and government service.

Working for local, state or federal government agencies may not involve serving in a political position per se. Many government positions are under Civil Service, which is usually non-partisan. However, almost all positions of high-level decision makers in the various state governments and the United States federal government are either elected positions or appointed positions which are obtained because of involvement in a particular political party.

Key Bible References:

Let every soul be subject to the governing authorities. For there is no authority except from God, and the authorities that exist are appointed by God.

Therefore whoever resists the authority resists the ordinance of God, and those who resist will bring judgment on themselves.

For rulers are not a terror to good works, but to evil. Do you want to be unafraid of the authority? Do what is good, and you will have praise from the same.

For he is God's minister to you for good. But if you do evil, be afraid; for he does not bear the sword in vain; for he is God's minister, an avenger to execute wrath on him who practices evil. Romans 13:1–4

"Should one who hates justice govern? Will you condemn Him who is *most just?"* Job 34:17

. . . to the judges, "Take heed to what you are doing, for you do not judge for man but for the LORD, who is with you in the judgment.

"Now therefore, let the fear of the LORD be upon you; take care and do it, for there is no iniquity with the LORD our God, no partiality, nor taking of bribes." II Chronicles 19:6–7

"Obey those who rule over you, and be submissive, for they watch out for your souls, as those who must give account. Let them do so with joy and not with grief, for that would be unprofitable for you." Hebrews 13:17

Additional References: Proverbs 8:12–16; Daniel 1:19–20; Romans 16:23; Philippians 4:22; Titus 3:1–2.

What Others Say: Robert F. Dugan, Jr., director, National Association of Evangelicals, Office of Public Affairs in Washington, D.C.; and Mark O. Hatfield, United States Senator (Oregon).

Robert F. Dugan, Jr.

Political involvement demonstrates the relevance of the gospel to the society in which we live. Not only that, but such involvement is necessary to guarantee the religious liberty which permits the preaching of the gospel. . . . Even though others might not acknowledge God's rule over the whole of life or that ours is a nation "under God," we must as Christians assert this truth and not apologize for it.[1]

Mark O. Hatfield

For the Christian man to reason that God does not want him in politics because there are too many evil men in government is as insensitive as for a Christian doctor to turn his back on an epidemic because there are too many germs there. For the Christian to say that he will not enter politics because he might lose his faith is the same as for the physician to say that he will not heal men because he might catch their diseases.[2]

---

[1]Robert F. Dugan, Jr., "Why This Book," *The High Cost of Indifference*, Richard Cizik, Editor, Regal Books, Ventura, California, 1984, pp. 9–11.

[2]Mark Hatfield, "How Can a Christian Be in Politics?", *Protest and Politics: Christianity and Contemporary Affairs*, Robert G. Clouse, Robert D. Linder and Richard V. Pierard, Editors, Attic Press, Greenwood, South Carolina, 1968, pp. 13–14.

Application: Since God created government, wouldn't it be wise for us to consider that it might be His will for us to serve Him there? In the Old Testament, David served God in his own land and Daniel, Hananiah, Mishael and Azariah served God in a foreign land (Daniel 1:19–20). Paul's friend, Erastus, was the city director of public works (Romans 16:23).

Every time we hear people complain about corrupt government officials or uncaring, mindless bureaucrats, we should prayerfully consider being a part of the solution to the problem—part of the army of godly people Christ is calling to political involvement and government service. Our country needs Bible-centered political decision-makers to preserve the values that made America great.

—**John Holmes**

POOR

WHAT IS THE CHRISTIAN'S OBLIGATION TO THE POOR?

The Issue: God's Word has a great deal to say about the poor and the Christian's obligation to them. First, we will always have them with us (Matthew 26:11) and second, our treatment of the poor reflects our attitude and treatment to God.

Some Christians believe that the status of being poor is directly related to laziness, sloth, or sin and therefore, they have no obligation to them.

Key Bible References:

"Then the King will say to those on His right hand, 'Come you blessed of My Father, inherit the kingdom prepared for you from the foundation of the world: for I was hungry and you gave Me food; I was thirsty and you gave me drink; I was a stranger and you took Me in; I was naked and you clothed Me; I was sick and you visited Me; I was in prison and you came to Me.'

"And the King will answer and say to them, 'Assuredly, I say to you, inasmuch as you did it to one of the least of these My brethren, you did it to Me.'" Matthew 25:34–36, 40

As each one has received a gift, minister it to one another, as good stewards of the manifold grace of God. I Peter 4:10

"And whoever gives one of these little ones only a cup of cold water in the name of a disciple, assuredly, I say to you, he shall by no means lose his reward." Matthew 10:42

He who despises his neighbor sins; but he who has mercy on the poor, happy is he. Proverbs 14:21

Additional References: Psalm 41:1–3; Luke 6:38, 12:33, 14:13–14; I Timothy 6:17–19; Hebrews 13:16.

What Others Say: Richard J. Foster, professor of theology and author; and Dr. Tom Sine, author, *Futurist,* speaker and consultant.

Richard J. Foster

Service that is duty-motivated breathes death. Service that flows out of our inward person is life, and joy and peace. The risen Christ beckons us to the ministry of the towel. Perhaps you would like to begin by experimenting with a prayer that a number of us have used. Begin the day by praying, "Lord Jesus, I would so appreciate it if You would bring me someone today whom I can serve."[1]

Tom Sine

What would happen if the sixty-nine million who profess to be Christian or the forty-five million who profess to be "highly religious" made the vast resources of our collective time, talents, homes, churches, Christian organizations, and communication networks fully available for the advancement of the future of God in a world of exploding need? I am convinced God by his power would set this world on its ear again and bring major global change through the reignited church of Jesus Christ.

Remember the first time God turned the world upside down? He did it with a small band of disciples and almost no resources except the power of God. We dare not underestimate what God can do with our small loaves and fishes if we give ourselves without reservation to his world-changing conspiracy . . .

. . . We have absolutely no idea of the difference he could make if we all gave him our lives and talents and resources.[2]

---

[1]Richard J. Foster, *Celebration of Discipline,* Harper and Row, San Francisco, California, 1978, p. 122.

[2]Tom Sine, *The Mustard Seed Conspiracy,* Word Books, Publishers, Waco, Texas, 1981, pp. 236–237.

Application: The Christian is <u>not</u> called to determine the reason or cause that someone is poor. The Christian <u>is</u> called to experience the joy of serving others and helping the poor <u>regardless</u> of the reason. As Christians generously share their resources to serve and meet the needs of the poor not only does the world become a better place to live but new and wider channels are opened. Through these channels the gospel of Jesus Christ is offered meeting the spiritual needs of mankind by offering salvation and new hope and change for today with a bright new promise for eternity.

—Ken Smitherman

POPULATION CONTROL

DOES THE BIBLE SUPPORT THE PRACTICE OF POPULATION CONTROL?

The Issue: Population control, defined as the ideas and practices geared toward regulating the number of human beings in the world, finds great support among those individuals who believe the world is over-crowded, exploited, and polluted. The proponents of population control practices, certainly numbering in the multiplied millions, believe that only strict measures taken to limit population growth will make life tolerable for future generations. This view is diametrically opposed to the biblical view of population matters. Biblical teachings support a large population spread over all the earth. Scripture supports the concepts of fruitfulness, multiplication, and filling the earth. The resulting conclusion is that a large population can be a blessing and not a curse.

Key Bible References:

Then God blessed them, and God said to them "Be fruitful and multiply; fill the earth and subdue it; have dominion over the fish of the sea, over the birds of the air, and over every living thing that moves on the earth." Genesis 1:28

So God blessed Noah and his sons, and said to them: "Be fruitful and multiply, and fill the earth."

"And as for you, be fruitful and multiply; bring forth abundantly in the earth and multiply in it." Genesis 9:1, 7

239

Behold, children are *a heritage from the* LORD, *the fruit of the womb* is His *reward.*

Like arrows in the hand of a warrior, so are *the children of one's youth.*

Happy is *the man who has his quiver full of them; they shall not be ashamed, but shall speak with their enemies in the gate.* Psalm 127:3–5

Additional References: Isaiah 8:18; Matthew 18:6; Hebrews 11:11–12.

What Others Say: Dr. Henry M. Morris; Cal Thomas; and the Advanced Training Institute of America.

Henry M. Morris

In spite of all the alarming propaganda of the past few years, there is really no serious population problem for the world as a whole. However, the supposed population explosion has been appropriated as one of the weapons in the arsenal of those doctrinaire liberals who are working hard to establish universal governmental controls.[1]

Whatever the world's "optimum" population may be, the same God who created the marvelous process of human procreation will also modify it as necessary, when the earth is actually "filled" to that optimum.[2]

Cal Thomas

Sadly, throughout history, medical science and physicians, who have heroically saved lives during plagues and other horrors, have been at the forefront of political efforts to exterminate certain classes of life that an authoritarian elite, answerable to no one but itself, deemed unfit to life. The Third Reich is only the most obvious of these unholy alliances between medicine and government. At least with Hitler we could film the results and hear the testimonies of those who survived. Technology has now brought us to the brink of the ultimate weapon of extermination, and it will be carried out in secret with nothing at all to photograph.[3]

---

[1]Henry M. Morris, *The Bible Has The Answer,* Creation-Life Publishers, Inc., San Diego, California, 1976, p. 266.
[2]Ibid., p. 267.
[3]Cal Thomas, *Uncommon Sense,* Wolgemuth & Hyatt, Publishers, Inc., Brentwood, Tennessee, 1990, p. 11.

When God says something in Scripture, it is important. When He repeats it, we must understand that it is *very* important. When He confirms a truth a third time (e.g., Genesis 1:28, 9:1, 9:7), He establishes it as a vital, universal, non-optional teaching.[4]

Application: It should be clearly understood that God's commands to "be fruitful, multiply, and fill the earth" have never been rescinded or fulfilled. It is also critically important that Christians understand that the biblical view of a growing population is totally consistent with the empirical evidence. Demographic data easily refutes the anti-growth positions. If one falls into the trap of sounding the alarm of the overpopulationists, then the practices almost universally accompanying such beliefs become more plausible. Thus, abortion, infanticide, euthanasia, homosexual activity, and government-mandated fertility and population-limitation programs are all seen as essential components in the population-control movement. Christians, of course, while fully understanding that a responsible application of biblical mandates is the proper course of action, must be quick to condemn these components and accept only those supported in God's Word.

—Timothy J. Hillen

POSSESSIONS

HOW SHOULD CHRISTIANS VIEW POSSESSIONS?

The Issue: The society in which we live places great importance on our possessions. We are encouraged by the "American Dream" to own a new house, fully furnished with new furniture, several TVs with VCRs, a computer system and many innovative necessities in the kitchen. Our clothes are current designer fashions. We enjoy many recreational activities, from camping, to skiing, to traveling abroad. And, to help us along the status road is the ever present, ever ready, credit card.

---

[4]"Insights Through Investigation," Advanced Training Institute of America, Oakbrook, Illinois, 1989, p. 2287.

Key Bible References:

"But seek first the kingdom of God and His righteousness, and all these things shall be added to you." Matthew 6:33

Jesus said to him, "If you want to be perfect, go, sell what you have and give to the poor, and you will have treasure in heaven; and come, follow Me." Matthew 19:21

. . . and sold their possessions and goods, and divided them among all, as anyone had need. Acts 2:45

Additional References: Psalms 17:14, 44:3; Luke 15:13.

What Others Say: Dr. Tim LaHaye, Christian author.

Tim LaHaye
Everyone is vulnerable to the temptations of materialism in some form. . . . Your problem area may be food, cars, clothes, or a hundred other items, but be sure of this: You are vulnerable to some enticing area of materialism.

Obsessed as we are with the "good life," people of all ages seem bent on seeking their place in the sun, instead of in the kingdom of God. I have yet to find a person who was dominated by a quest for riches, who enjoyed contentment.[1]

Application: There is nothing inherently wrong with having this world's goods. But when the world's pressures come down on us and we focus on the good things we possess rather than on Jesus, our priorities become confused and out of biblical perspective.

When the rich young ruler asked Jesus what he must do to be saved, Jesus told him to forfeit his possessions by giving them to the poor and then to follow Him. He could not do it—he could not give up all he had for he had so much. We must be willing to give up everything for Jesus' sake, no matter what the cost. The principle is this: It is acceptable to have possessions provided they were gained honestly. It is unacceptable when possessions "have us" and they become the focus of our lives.

—Margery W. Schantz

---

[1] Tim LaHaye, *The Battle for the Family,* Fleming H. Revell Company, Old Tappan, New Jersey, 1982, pp. 148–150.

PRAYER

WHAT ARE SOME BIBLICAL PRINCIPLES OF PRAYER?

The Issue: Most of the world's religions include some form of "prayer." How is Christianity different?

True prayer is, in its simplest definition, "actually talking to God." It is based upon the sure knowledge that God is there and that He hears us and cares about what we say (Hebrews 11:6). Among believers both private (Matthew 6:6) and public (Matthew 18:20; Acts 4:20–31) prayers are encouraged and blessed.

True prayer can include any or all of the following: worship and praise, thanksgiving, confession of sin and acceptance of forgiveness, intercession, and petition. Prayer can be lifted to God at any time and place, but nearly all mature and effective Christians have a specific time for regular <u>daily</u> prayer and fellowship with God. The best way to start daily prayer time is by reading the Bible. This way we give God a chance to speak to us before we speak to Him.

Key Bible References:

Delight yourself also in the LORD, and He shall give you the desire of your heart. Psalm 37:4

Then He spoke a parable to them, that men always ought to pray and not lose heart, . . . Luke 18:1

Therefore I exhort first of all that supplications, prayers, intercessions, and *giving of thanks be made for all men, . . .* I Timothy 2:1

Additional References: I Kings 8:22–53; Isaiah 65:24; Matthew 6:7–15; Ephesians 3:14–19; I Thessalonians 5:17.

What Others Say: Horatius Bonar; Andrew Murray; and John Calvin.

Horatius Bonar
Let us maintain unblunted the edge of our relish for prayer and fellowship with God, as the great preservative against the seductions of the age; for only intimacy with God can keep us from intimacy with the world.[1]

---

[1]Horatius Bonar, *God's Way of Holiness,* Moody Press, Chicago, Illinois, n.d., p. 121.

Andrew Murray

The union between the Vine and the branch is in very deed a prayer-union. The highest conformity to Christ, the most blessed participation in the glory of His heavenly life, is that we take part in His work of intercession: He and we live ever to pray.[2]

John Calvin

Words fail to explain how necessary prayer is, and in how many ways the exercise of prayer is profitable. Surely, with good reason the Heavenly Father affirms that the only stronghold of safety is in calling upon His name. By so doing we invoke the presence both of His providence, through which He watches over and guards our affairs, and of His power through which He sustains us, and of His goodness, through which He receives us.[3]

Application: God, who is infinite in power and knowledge is also infinite in His capacity to love and to relate and communicate. He has created man in his own image and equipped him and—commanded him—to communicate with God.

The biggest hindrance to a good prayer life is not that we do not know how, but that we do not do it; this is disobedience. Every Christian should search the scriptures for principles of prayer, but, more importantly, should practice a regular prayer life.

—**Fred Donehoo**

PRIDE AND SELF-ESTEEM

WHEN DOES SELF-ESTEEM BECOME PRIDE?

The Issue: Our modern culture places tremendous emphasis on the building of individual self-esteem. Developing a positive self-image must be balanced with the reality of our sinful natures and the possible encroachment of pride in ourselves and in our accomplishments. It is God's plan that we Christians have no confidence in our natural gifts or abilities, but rather rely upon the power of God to use us as vessels for His glory and purposes.

---

[2]Andrew Murray, *With Christ in the School of Prayer,* Fleming H. Revell, Westwood, New Jersey, 1953, p. 177.

[3]John Calvin, *Institutes of the Christian Religion,* Westminster Press, Philadelphia, 1960, Vol. II, p. 851.

Key Bible References:

For if anyone thinks himself to be something, when he is nothing, he deceives himself.

But let each one examine his own work, and then he will have rejoicing in himself alone, and not in another. Galatians 6:3–4

For I say, through the grace given to me, to everyone who is among you, not to think of himself *more highly than he ought to think, but to think soberly, as God has dealt to each one a measure of faith.* Romans 12:3

When pride comes, then comes shame; but with the humble is *wisdom.* Proverbs 11:2

But we have this treasure in earthen vessels, that the excellence of the power may be of God and not of us. II Corinthians 4:7

Additional References: Proverbs 16:18; Isaiah 14:11–15; Daniel 4:28–37; I Corinthians 1:20–31; Philippians 2:5–11, 3:4–11.

What Others Say: Bill Gothard, director of the Institute in Basic Youth Conflicts, Inc., author and lecturer; C. S. Lewis, author; and Don Matzat, author, pastor at Messiah Lutheran Church, St. Louis, Missouri.

Bill Gothard
Pride is reserving for yourself the right to make final decisions.

Pride is believing that you achieved what God and others have done for you.[1]

C. S. Lewis
Look for yourself, and you will find in the long run only hatred, loneliness, despair, rage, ruin, and decay. But look for Christ and you will find Him, and with Him everything else thrown in.[2]

Don Matzat
Most Christians today do not realize how important weakness, failure, discouragement, disappointment, suffering, testing, and trials are in the development of their Christian life. Through these dealings of God our natural sinful pride is being dealt with. God calls us away from ourselves so that through burying, rejecting, and denying self we may turn in faith unto our Lord Jesus and experience his life, peace, joy, and power.[3]

---

[1]Bill Gothard, *Men's Manual, Vol. I,* Institute In Basic Youth Conflicts, Inc., Oak Brook, Illinois, 1979, p. 141.

[2]C. S. Lewis, *Mere Christianity,* Collins Clear-Type Press, London, 1952, p. 188.

[3]Don Matzat, *Christ Esteem,* Harvest House Books, Eugene, Oregon.

Application: For the Christian, real self-esteem comes through a confident relationship with Jesus Christ. As transformed believers we can say with the apostle Paul, "If God is for us, who can be against us?" Such self-esteem is really Christ-esteem and magnifies Christ who lives in us.

The key question is. . . . Do we want some of the credit for the achievements in our lives, or will we humbly acknowledge our total dependence upon His Spirit for such accomplishments? Our world is crying for genuine people whose goal in life is to glorify Christ rather than build a personal kingdom on human efforts.

—**John Bennett**

PRISON

WHAT IS THE CHRISTIAN'S RESPONSIBILITY TO THOSE IN PRISON?

The Issue: The U.S. Department of Justice reported that in June, 1990, there were 755,425 men and women in state and federal prisons. Cut off from their families, cut off from positive influences, offenders languish in an environment better suited to teach them how to lie, steal, hurt, and hate better than ever. If someone does not reach out to these men and women, we can only shudder to think of what kind of people will be returning to the streets once they have served their sentences. Christians can ignore prisoners now if they want. They won't be able to ignore them when they move in next door.

Key Bible References:

"And He will set the sheep on His right hand, but the goats on the left.

"Then the King will say to those on His right hand, 'Come, you blessed of My Father, inherit the kingdom prepared for you from the foundation of the world:

. . . '"I was in prison and you came to Me."' Matthew 25:33–34, 36b

Remember the prisoners as if chained with them, and *those who are mistreated, since you yourselves are in the body also.* Hebrews 13:3

"The Spirit of the Lord GOD is upon Me, because the LORD has anointed Me to preach good tidings to the poor; he has sent Me to heal the brokenhearted, to proclaim liberty to the captives, and the opening of the prison to those who are bound; . . ." Isaiah 61:1-2

Additional References: Psalms 69:33, 79:11, 142:6-7.

What Others Say: John Wesley Lord, former United Methodist bishop of Washington, D.C., and Daniel Benson.

John Wesley Lord

A Christian view of punishment must look beyond correction to redemption. It is our Christian faith that redemption by the grace of God is open to every repentant sinner, and that it is the duty of every Christian to bring to others by every available means the challenge and opportunity of a new and better life.[1]

Daniel Benson

Surely Matthew 25:35-40 imposes an affirmative duty on Christians to visit people in jails and prisons. That passage of scripture is not filled with conditions and qualifications about the people in jail being good people, or innocent but falsely accused, or possessing real potential for ultimate rehabilitation. It simply speaks in terms of visiting people who are in prison. . . . If Jesus really meant that we should actually visit all kinds of dirty, dangerous, foul-smelling, unpleasant people in equally dirty, dangerous, foul-smelling, and unpleasant prisons, that places a rather substantial burden on us.[2]

Application: Every Christian is called to be a witness of the love of Jesus Christ—and the Holy Spirit equips each of us to do so. During the years of Prison Fellowship's ministry, I've seen thousands of Christian volunteers—"ordinary" believers—make incredible, dramatic differences in the lives of thousands of men and women behind bars. Christ calls us to manifest His love to "the least of these"; and when we do, His love can penetrate even the hardest of hearts.

Because of this, prison ministry is one of the most effective ways that Christians can make a difference in our society, which has just about given up when it comes to prisons and our criminal justice system. People believe there's no human solution to our national crime crisis. And they're right. But when Christians penetrate the

---

[1]John Wesley Lord, as cited in "Fact & Quote," August 1988, a publication of Prison Fellowship.
[2]Daniel Benson, "Christian Concern About Prisons," *The Reformed Journal,* April 1977.

prison system, sharing the love of Christ with offenders, one by one by one, and those offenders' lives are changed through the power of the Holy Spirit, skeptical secular observers will see the power of God at work. That's not only acting in obedience to our biblical mandate to visit those in prison; it's contributing to a mighty witness for Christ to society at large.

—Charles W. Colson

PRISONERS

WHAT IS THE BIBLICAL ANSWER TO THE SECULAR WORLD'S ATTEMPT TO REHABILITATE CRIMINALS?

The Issue: Prisons simply do not rehabilitate criminals. The U.S. Department of Justice has found that two-thirds of all inmates are re-arrested within three years of their release from prison. The world cannot strip offenders of their dignity, expose them to violence, homosexual rape, and spirit-crushing monotony, and expect them to come out better people. What is the biblical response to crime, and what clues does the Bible give us about how offenders can become contributing members of society?

Key Bible References:

"If a man steals an ox or a sheep, and slaughters it or sells it, he shall restore five oxen for an ox and four sheep for a sheep." Exodus 22:1

Then Zacchaeus stood and said to the Lord, "Look, Lord, I give half of my goods to the poor; and if I have taken anything from anyone by false accusation, I restore fourfold."

And Jesus said to him, "Today salvation has come to this house. . . ." Luke 19:8–9

For I am not ashamed of the gospel of Christ, for it is the power of God to salvation for everyone who believes, . . . Romans 1:16

Additional References: Exodus 21–22; Psalm 119:9; Isaiah 32:16–18.

What Others Say: Billy Graham, evangelist; and Daniel W. Van Ness, author and president of Justice Fellowship.

Billy Graham

The moral dilemma in our country demands a spiritual solution. Only a change of heart will restore a prisoner's life.[1]

Daniel W. Van Ness

The Hebrew word for peace is *shalom*. This rich word connotes completeness, fulfillment, wholeness—whole relationships. It describes the relationship God wanted with his people, and wanted them to have with one another. . . . Crime breaks that peace. The biblical understanding of crime acknowledged that a relationship—albeit a destructive one—was created when an offender harmed a victim. The responsibility of the justice system, then, was to hold the offender responsible, make good the victim's losses, and through reconciliation restore *shalom* to the community.

In the last 25 years, criminologists and criminal justice professionals have grown increasingly skeptical of rehabilitation as the guiding principle of punishment. It has not worked. . . . What is beginning to emerge may be a new strategy against crime: Offenders must be held responsible for their criminal acts. Victims must have their losses restored. The community must be protected.[2]

Application: As Exodus 22:1 and Luke 19:8–9 clearly show, the biblical response to crime is punishment with a purpose: Offenders must repay their victims and their communities. Imprisonment today often impedes true justice by prohibiting offenders from making things right. Of course, community safety comes first: prisons protect the community from dangerous offenders. But nearly half of the inmates in the United States are nonviolent offenders who don't need to be in prison. Society can punish them by making them take responsibility for their actions: by paying back their victims, performing community service, and undergoing drug or alcohol abuse treatment when necessary.

Ultimately, though, purposeful punishment alone will not change criminals. The change must come from within. The offender must choose a new way of thinking and acting. The Gospel of Jesus Christ is the greatest catalyst for that kind of change. I've seen Christ enable men and women—even those behind bars whom soci-

---

[1]as cited by Donald Smarto, *Justice and Mercy,* Tyndale House, Wheaton, Illinois, 1987.
[2]Daniel W. Van Ness, "Healing the Victims of Crime," *Christianity Today,* November 21, 1986.

ety had labeled as hopeless—to live new lives and take on the responsibilities of productive citizenship.

—Charles W. Colson

PROTECTION

WHAT DO THE SCRIPTURES SAY ABOUT DIVINE PROTECTION?

The issue: Christians are quite familiar with the many examples of God's protection of His people given to us in the Old Testament as shown by such examples as the protection of Shadrach, Meshach, and Abed-Nego in the fiery furnace (Daniel 3:19–26), Daniel in the lions' den (Daniel 6:16–22), the Israelites in the parting of the Red Sea (Exodus 14:21–22), the horses and chariots of fire around about Elisha (II Kings 6:14–17), and the story of David and Goliath (I Samuel 17:48–50). However, Christians often fail to depend on or even recognize the continuing protection of God's people in today's world.

God's protection of His own is just as evident today as in the past. He shows His love toward His children by holding back the forces of evil in our world as He protects us from the many pitfalls that surround us in our individual lives as well as in the lives of those in the body of Christ. Above all we have the assurance that He has redeemed us from the judgment of sin and death.

Throughout life God's protection of those whom He loves is a reminder that we are creatures in need of His constant care. In addition God's protection is a reminder that we are all sinners in need of His unending viligance and protection from the wiles of Satan.

Key Bible References:

The LORD is my rock and my fortress and my deliverer; My God, my strength, in whom I will trust; my shield and the horn of my salvation, my stronghold. Psalm 18:2

My help comes from the LORD, who made heaven and earth.

He will not allow your foot to be moved; He who keeps you will not slumber.

Behold, He who keeps Israel shall neither slumber nor sleep.

The LORD is your keeper; the LORD is your shade at your right hand.

The sun shall not strike you by day, nor the moon by night.

The LORD shall preserve you from all evil; He shall preserve your soul.

The LORD shall preserve your going out and your coming in from this time forth, and even forevermore. Psalm 121:2–8

But the Lord is faithful, who will establish you and guard you from the evil one. II Thessalonians 3:3.

Additional References: Genesis 28:15a; Joshua 1:5; Psalm 91:11; Isaiah 41:10, 43:1–2; John 10:28–29; I Corinthians 10:13.

What Others Say: Charles H. Spurgeon (1834–1892), pastor of the Metropolitan Tabernacle in London from 1859 until his death in 1892; and Charles W. Colson, former special counsel to President Richard Nixon, presently president of Prison Fellowship Ministries.

Charles H. Spurgeon
Though the paths of life are dangerous and difficult, yet we shall stand fast, for Jehovah will not permit our feet to slide; and if he will not [permit] it we shall not suffer it. If our foot will be thus kept we may be sure that our head and heart will be preserved also. In the original the words express a wish or prayer—"May He not [permit] thy foot to be moved." Promised preservation should be the subject of perpetual prayer; and we pray believingly; for those who have God for their keeper shall be safe from all perils of the way.[1]

Charles W. Colson
I had always wondered, in secret fear, what it would be like to be told I had cancer. I thought I would be shattered. But I had prayed for the grace to withstand whatever the doctors found. And, as many have discovered before me, I saw in the confrontation with fear and suffering that there is nothing for which God does not pour out His grace abundantly. I felt total peace—and great thankfulness that a merciful God had brought me to that recovery room.[2]

---

[1]Charles H. Spurgeon, *The Treasury of David: An Expository and Devotional Commentary on the Psalms,* 7 vols., Guardian Press, Grand Rapids, Michigan (1870–1885), 1976, 6:415.
[2]Charles Colson, *The God of Stones and Spiders,* Crossway Books, Westchester, Illinois, 1990, p. 148.

Application: Through the Bible, we know that God is our Protector in both life and death, prosperity and adversity, in sickness and in health, in the good and bad times. There is no such comfort for the unbeliever. For him, circumstances are random events in a universe of chance. No protection is forthcoming. Hope for a solution is just as random as the events that brought about the adversity. The Christian knows ". . . that all things work together for good to those who love God, to those who are called according to His purpose" (Romans 8:28).

Even when death occurs, God is protecting the Christian from the judgment of sin. Death cannot have its final victory because the Lord is the Christian's Protector. The hope of glory far outweighs any earthly encumbrance. "What then shall we say to these things? If God is for us, who can *be* against us?" (Romans 8:31). The promise of protection does not guarantee an absence of pain and suffering. Sin has made these a reality that only glorification will ultimately remedy. But in those times when adversity has overwhelmed us like a flood, the Christian knows that our cries to God will be heard. Our limited abilities are a constant reminder that we cannot preserve ourselves. It is in weakness that we are strong, strong in the strength of His might. We glory in the fact that divine protection is given to those of us who love the Lord.

—Miriam Heiskell

RACIAL DISCRIMINATION

WHAT DOES THE SCRIPTURE SAY ABOUT RACIAL DISCRIMINATION?

The Issue: Racial discrimination, also known as racism or racial prejudice, is a social disease that has plagued mankind throughout history. It is the basic assumption or belief that certain races of men are by birth and nature superior to others. The root cause of racial discrimination is man's sinful nature. It is expressed in hatred and/or a false sense of pride esteeming oneself better than another.

Key Bible References:

I charge you before God and the Lord Jesus Christ and the elect angels that you observe these things without prejudice, doing nothing with partiality. I Timothy 5:21

There is neither Jew nor Greek, there is neither slave nor free, there is neither male nor female; for you are all one in Christ Jesus. Galatians 3:28

Beloved, if God so loved us, we also ought to love one another. I John 4:11

Additional References: Luke 9:51–61, 10:25–37; John 4:1–26; I Corinthians 12:13; Ephesians 2:11–22; Colossians 3:9–11.

What Others Say: Dr. John Warwick Montgomery, Bible scholar and teacher.

John Warwick Montgomery

. . . Racial integration is thoroughly Christian, for God created men and Christ died for all men. The consequence is that "there is neither Jew nor Greek: ye are all one in Christ Jesus." (Galatians 3:28) One of the greatest blots on the history of American churches is their toleration of the prejudicial treatment of minority races. No legitimate effort should be spared to help black Americans and other minorities to achieve full civil and social rights—and this requires direct opposition to unjust and immoral legislation.[1]

Application: American society in general has made some progress in overcoming this issue of racial discrimination in the past two decades. There are still, however, segments of both American society and people groups around the world who still struggle for social justice and equality. As long as sin is present in the world mankind will be faced with racism, what Thomas Jefferson called, "The disease of morbid minds."

The Samaritans were a people group in the Bible who were considered half-breeds and were discriminated against by the Jews. Jesus challenged this practice in John chapter 4 when He encouraged the Samaritan woman to ask a favor of Him, so He could have the opportunity to lead her to the truth. Later in this same passage, it reads, "Then they said to the woman, 'Now we believe, not because of what you said, for we ourselves have heard *Him* and we know that this is indeed the Christ, the Savior of the world'" (John 4:42).

"Many people tailor their religion to fit the pattern of their prejudice."[2]

---

[1]William J. Krutza and Philip P. DiCillo, *Facing The Issues 3*, Baker Book House, Grand Rapids, Michigan, 1973, p. 30.

[2]E. C. McKenzie, *14,000 Quips and Quotes*, Baker Book House, Grand Rapids, Michigan, 1990, p. 419.

"No Christian is strong enough to carry a cross and a prejudice at the same time."[3]

—Larry J. Moore

REBELLION

AT WHAT POINT ARE CHRISTIANS IN A STATE OF REBELLION?

The Issue: Rebellion is defined as open defiance or opposition to established authority. The word "rebellion" appears only in the Old Testament, but the concept it conjures carries into the New Testament and unfortunately into the church of today. Rebellion in the Old Testament most often is translated from the Hebrew root word "marah," which means bitterness. The word "disobey" also is derived from marah. There seems to be a direct relationship between rebellion and disobedience, and bitterness. It is almost as though rebellion and disobedience are each a product of bitterness. In order for Christians to be free from acts or thoughts of rebellion, they must rely upon the knowledge and power of the Word of God to extricate them from the entanglement of bitterness.

Key Bible References:

For rebellion is as *the sin of witchcraft, . . .* I Samuel 15:23

"For I see that you are poisoned by bitterness and bound by iniquity." Acts 8:23

Let all bitterness, wrath, anger, clamor, and evil speaking be put away from you, with all malice. Ephesians 4:31

Additional References: Proverbs 17:11; Isaiah 65:2.

What Others Say: Guy P. Duffield and Nathan M. Van Cleave; and Catherine Marshall, Bible scholars and authors.

---

[3]Ibid., p. 419.

Guy P. Duffield and Nathan M. Van Cleave

Five times Lucifer lifts up his will against the will of God. It can be thus seen that the first sin was that of rebellion against, and total independence of, God.[1]

Sin is willful rebellion against God. Such an attitude cannot but bring forth evil results.[2]

Catherine Marshall

If we hold resentments, grudges, bitterness—no matter how justified we think they are—these wrong emotions will cut us off from God.[3]

Application: We are living at a time when there seems to be an increase in the quantity and complexity of problems and pressures which confront us. This is not only true of the secular world, but, also of the world of Christendom. Problems and pressures can cause Christians to trust more completely in the Lord and look to Him for solutions, or they can render them victims of bitterness and rebellion. Oftentimes, difficulties confront Christians from other Christians, even from those in positions of leadership and authority. Great care must be taken to preclude the harboring of bitterness and ultimately entering into a state of rebellion. Christians are in rebellion at the point they allow bitterness to permeate their thoughts and actions.

When the children of Israel became thirsty as their wanderings were in the beginning stage, and water was found, but was bitter or undrinkable, they became rebellious against Moses. Moses was instructed by God to pierce the water with a specific tree. This solved the bitterness problem for the water, but marah continued in the lives of the Israelites. It takes the insertion of a specific tree—the Cross of Jesus, into the cause of bitterness and rebellion to bring about a satisfying solution.

—**Charles E. Monroe**

[1]Guy P. Duffield and Nathan M. Van Cleave, *Foundations of Pentecostal Theology*, L.I.F.E. Bible College, Los Angeles, California, n.d., p. 150.

[2]Ibid., p. 167.

[3]Catherine Marshall, *Beyond Our Selves*, McGraw-Hill Book Company, Inc., New York, New York, n.d., p. 172.

REFORM

WHAT IS GOD'S PATTERN FOR SPIRITUAL REFORM?

The Issue: True spiritual reform must begin internally in the heart of a believer. A believer first sees God's glory and then recognizes his or her own frailty and sin. Awed by the grace of God, the repentant believer responds out of love with a renewed obedience to God and His Word. True spiritual reformation will result in the believer externally influencing his or her society in a positive way.

Key Bible References:

". . . if my people who are called by My name will humble themselves, and pray and seek My face, and turn from their wicked ways, then I will hear from heaven, and will forgive their sin and heal their land." II Chronicles 7:14

"A new commandment I give to you, that you love one another; as I have loved you, that you also love one another.

"By this all will know that you are My disciples, if you have love for one another." John 13:34–35

Open your mouth for the speechless, in the cause of all who are appointed to die.

Open your mouth, judge righteously, and plead the cause of the poor and needy. Proverbs 31:8–9

Additional References: Psalm 51:10–13; Matthew 5:14–16, 28:18–20; James 1:22.

What Others Say: Francis A. Schaeffer, author and founder of L'Abri Fellowship.

Francis A. Schaeffer

In the midst of the world, in the midst of our present culture, Jesus is giving a right to the world. Upon His authority He gives the world the right to judge whether you and I are born-again Christians on the basis of our observable love toward all Christians.[1]

---

[1]Francis A. Schaeffer, *The Complete Works of Francis A. Schaeffer,* Crossway Books, Westchester, Illinois, vol. 4, p. 187.

Love—and the unity it attests to—is the mark Christ gave Christians to wear before the world. Only with this mark may the world know that Christians are indeed Christians and that Jesus was sent by the Father.[2]

Application: Motivated inwardly by the grace of God, believers outwardly demonstrate God's love to a needy world. Spiritual reform is marked by God's children actively bringing God's truth to bear on the issues of the day: cooking food and building shelters for the poor, opening their homes and hearts for unwed mothers, and helping to set free all those who are physically, emotionally, or spiritually oppressed.

Having yielded their lives to the Lordship of Christ, the body of Christ exhibits a love for the brethren, demonstrates a lifestyle of sacrificial giving, and acts out of compassion for those in need. They reflect the holiness of God; rely on the power of God's Spirit; and possess the fruit of the Spirit in increasing measure.

—John W. Whitehead

REPENTANCE

WHAT DOES THE BIBLE TEACH ABOUT REPENTANCE?

The Issue: There are two aspects of repentance. The type of repentance most often used is a godly repentance used to describe the condition of one who chooses to forsake his former way of life and follow Jesus as His Lord and Savior. This involves sorrow for sin which results in a complete change of heart.

The second use of the word repentance means regret or sorrow resulting in a change of mind. It can be the result of having been caught in the act of wrongdoing or it could be sorrow for the punishment inflicted. This, however, is not the godly sorrow that leads to the salvation experience. It can also be sorrow because of a conviction of sin which results in confession and the re-establishment of a right relationship with God and man.

---

[2]Ibid., p. 204.

Key Bible References:

For godly sorrow produces repentance to salvation, not to be regretted; but the sorrow of the world produces death. II Corinthians 7:10

"Repent therefore and be converted, that your sins may be blotted out, so that times of refreshing may come from the presence of the Lord, . . ." Acts 3:19

"If your brother sins against you, rebuke him; and if he repents, forgive him." Luke 17:3b

Additional References: I Kings 8:46–52; Luke 24:46–47; Acts 2:38, 20:21; II Peter 3:9.

What Others Say: Dr. Harold M. Freligh, former professor of English Bible and Theology at St. Paul Bible College and Nyack College.

Harold M. Freligh

Repentance is that act whereby one recognizes and turns from his sin, confessing it to God.

Repentance is not at the same time a professed sorrow for sin and a willing continuation in sin. It is possible to feel sorry for our sins and yet have no desire to quit sinning. Many a sinner is not ready to repent because he is not ready to give up his sins. John is caught cheating in his examination. He is penalized by receiving an F. He is sorry he has been caught, but the times he has not been caught bother him not a whit. He is remorseful, but not repentant, and is just as ready to cheat again if he can get by with it. Ed has cheated without being caught, but his conscience bothers him. Finally he goes to his professor, confesses the whole thing, and offers to take any penalty imposed upon him. He is repentant and ready to quit the cheating business![1]

Application: Repentance is one of the most important concepts in Scripture.

Repentance is a necessary part of the salvation experience—change of heart as emphasized in Ezekiel 14:6, 18:30; Acts 26:19–20. Repentance also is used to indicate a change of mind as an expression of sorrow as we note in Revelation 2:5 and 3:19.

Repentance must be present before salvation becomes reality. When a person repents, God forgives her or his sins (Acts 2:38, Luke

---

[1]Harold M. Freligh, *The Eight Pillars of Salvation*, Bethany Fellowship, Inc., Minneapolis, Minnesota, 1962, pp. 19, 20.

24:47). Repentance determines man's relationship with others. When conflict occurs between two people and one repents, the other is to forgive. Luke 17:3-4 says, "Take heed to yourselves. If your brother sins against you, rebuke him; and if he repents, forgive him. And if he sins against you seven times in a day, and seven times in a day returns to you, saying, 'I repent,' you shall forgive him."

Repentance restores man's fellowship with God and with fellow man.

—James R. Swanson and Arvil E. Holt

REPUTATION

SHOULD CHRISTIANS BE CONCERNED ABOUT HAVING A GOOD REPUTATION?

The Issue: Who doesn't desire a good reputation—to be well liked and considered a good person? In our own way to be known for making our mark on the world seems to be a very worthy goal. But is a good reputation something Christians should work toward? What is it that Christians should be known for?

Key Bible References:

For do I now persuade men, or God? Or do I seek to please men? For if I still pleased men, I would not be a servant of Christ. Galatians 1:10

"If the world hates you, you know that it hated Me before it hated you.

"If you were of the world, the world would love its own. Yet because you are not of the world, but I chose you out of the world, therefore the world hates you." John 15:18-19

Additional References: Daniel 6; I Corinthians 1:20-31; Hebrews 11.

What Others Say: Oswald Chambers, author, evangelist and teacher.

Oswald Chambers
Concentrate on God, let Him engineer circumstances as He will, and wherever He places you He is binding up the brokenhearted through you, setting at liberty the captives through you, doing His

mighty soul-saving work through you, as you keep rightly related to Him. Self-conscious service is killed, self-conscious devotion is gone, only one thing remains—"witnesses unto Me," Jesus Christ first, second and third.[1]

Goodness and purity ought never to attract attention to themselves, they ought simply to be magnets to draw to Jesus Christ. If my holiness is not drawing towards Him, it is not holiness of the right order, but an influence that will awaken inordinate affection and lead souls away into side-eddies. A beautiful saint may be a hindrance if he does not present Jesus Christ but only what Christ has done for him.[2]

Application: The question can be most easily answered by looking to a Christian's supreme example: Jesus Christ. Was Christ concerned about his reputation? To some He was one who ate with the tax collectors and sinners (see Matthew 9:11). To others He was one who healed the sick and mended the brokenhearted.

It is evident that Jesus certainly wasn't concerned about what the world thought of Him. Rather He committed His life to pleasing His Father. It is a matter of emphasis. A good reputation may (or may not) come as a result of a lifestyle that is obedient to Christ, but it is not a goal to be sought.

—**Cheryl K. Jackson**

WHAT ARE THE BIBLICAL PRINCIPLES FOR REST, RECREATION, AND RELAXATION?

The Issue: Rest is ordained of God. The example set at the beginning of the Bible when God created the world confirms that God wants us to include rest and relaxation in our lives. God created the world in six days, and He rested on the seventh day. In the New Testament, Jesus recognized the need for relaxation and invited His disciples to come away and rest for a time. The work ethic that is followed by

---

[1]Oswald Chambers, *Oswald Chambers: The Best From All His Books, Volume II*, Oliver-Nelson Books, Nashville, Tennessee, 1989, p. 344.

[2]Oswald Chambers, *My Utmost For His Highest*, Dodd, Mead & Company, Inc., New York, New York, 1935, p. 85.

many Christians eliminates rest and relaxation from their schedules. To take time to relax can be viewed as a character weakness. The Scriptures clearly indicate, however, that a Christian should take time to rest and relax.

Key Bible References:

Six days you shall labor and do all your work, but the seventh day is *the Sabbath of the LORD your God. In it you shall do no work: you, nor your son, nor your daughter, nor your manservant, nor your maidservant, nor your cattle, nor your stranger who* is *within your gates.*

For in *six days the LORD made the heavens and the earth, the sea, and all that* is *in them, and rested the seventh day. Therefore the LORD blessed the Sabbath day and hallowed it.* Exodus 20:9–11

And He said to them, "Come aside by yourselves to a deserted place and rest a while." For there were many coming and going, and they did not even have time to eat.

So they departed to a deserted place in the boat by themselves. Mark 6:31–32

Additional References: Exodus 23:12, 34:21; Leviticus 23:3.

What Others Say: Tim Hansel, founder of Summit Expedition.

Tim Hansel

We are called to be faithful, not frantic. If we are to meet the challenges of today, there must be integrity between our words and our lives, and more reliance on the source of our purpose.

Unless the LORD builds the house,
They *labor in vain who build it;*
Unless the LORD guards the city,
The watchman stays awake in vain.
It is *vain for you to rise up early,*
To sit up late,
To eat the bread of sorrows;
For *so He gives His beloved sleep.*

Psalm 127:1–2

I believe that the Enemy has done an effective job of convincing us that unless a person is worn to a frazzle, running here and there, he or she cannot possibly be a dedicated, sacrificing, spiritual Christian. Perhaps the Seven Deadly Sins have recruited another member—Overwork.

We need to remember that our strength lies not in hurried efforts and ceaseless long hours, but in our quietness and confidence.

Leisure—giving yourself permission to get involved in life—can become: the path of blessing, the hope of peace, the hinge of praise.[1]

Application: Life appears to be on "fast-forward." The pace that has been set in order to function in our society is demanding and continually changing. Daily schedules are characterized by busyness. Christians are not exempt from this way of living. The manifestation of this lifestyle can cause Christians to "almost" serve God but not take time to commit to a deep, spiritual relationship. On the other hand, Christians may become so immersed in Christian service that they become Christian workaholics and are imprisoned by their service.

The Bible teaches that Christians are to take time to rest. In Psalm 46:10, the psalmist says, "Be still, and know that I *am* God." As Christians make the choice to include rest and relaxation in their lives, it provides the avenue through which a deeper, more profound lifestyle can develop. Quietness before God allows Him to refresh our souls, our minds, and our bodies.

—**Barbara Nikkel**

RETALIATION

WHAT DOES THE BIBLE SAY ABOUT RETALIATION?

The Issue: Christians living in relationships with others often find themselves having been unfairly treated or injured by another person or persons. These experiences may manifest themselves from the hands of a stranger, an employer, a business associate, a friend, or even a family member. Our natural tendencies are to seek revenge or retribution to satisfy our pride or correct the wrong that we believe has occurred. Our reaction, if handled improperly as a Christian, can result in malice, resentment, and embitterment as the motivational force in our life.

---

[1]Tim Hansel, *When I Relax I Feel Guilty,* David C. Cook Publishing Co., Elgin, Illinois, 1979, pp. 55, 64.

Key Bible References:

"You shall not take vengeance, nor bear any grudge against the children of your people, but you shall love your neighbor as yourself. I am the Lord." Leviticus 19:18

"But I tell you not to resist an evil person.

"But whoever slaps you on your right cheek, turn the other to him also." Matthew 5:39

Repay no one evil for evil. Provide things honest in the sight of all men.

If it is possible, as much as depends on you, live peaceably with all men.

Beloved, do not avenge yourselves, but rather *give place to wrath; for it is written,* "Vengeance is Mine, I will repay," *says the Lord.* Romans 12:17–19

See that no one renders evil to anyone, but always pursue what is good both for yourselves and for all. I Thessalonians 5:15

Additional References: Proverbs 20:22, 24:29, 25:21–22; I Peter 3:9.

What Others Say: Matthew Henry, Welsh Bible scholar, pastor and author; and D. Martyn Lloyd-Jones, physician, theologian and pastor of Westminster Chapel, Buckingham Gate, London.

Matthew Henry
We must not be revengeful. We may avoid and may resist it, so far as is necessary to our own security; but we must not render evil for evil, must not bear a grudge, nor avenge ourselves, nor study to be even with those that have treated us unkindly, but we must go beyond them by forgiving them. The law of retaliation must be made consistent with the law of love. It will not justify us in hurting our brother to say that he began, for it is the second blow that makes the quarrel.[1]

D. Martyn Lloyd-Jones
This whole tendency to wrath and anger, to retribution and retaliation is there at the very depths of human nature. Not only is nature "red in tooth and claw," mankind is also. Look at children, for example. From our very earliest days we have this desire for revenge; it is

---

[1]Matthew Henry, *Commentary on the Whole Bible,* Zondervan Publishing House, Grand Rapids, Michigan, 1961, p. 1225.

one of the most hideous and ugly results of the fall of man, and of original sin.[2]

Application: Our personal relationship with Jesus and His scriptural requirement for holiness demands that vengeance and requite may only be placed in the hands of God. The injury or hurt we have received at the hands of another may seem unbearable, but revenge in a vindictive sense is strictly forbidden by God's word. Instead, a spirit of love and grace must permeate our very souls to respond in a Christ-like spirit that commands us to love our enemies, return good for evil and forgive for harm inflicted.

As Christians, the biblical direction is simple and plain, "You shall not. . . ."

—Gary J. Herring

REVERENCE

WHAT DOES THE BIBLE TEACH ABOUT REVERENCE?

The Issue: Christians continue to be bombarded by many influences vying for control of the mind. It is sad to say, but in many circles of Christendom, reverence takes a backseat. Scripture makes it very clear that if man is to be fulfilled in victorious Christian living, reverence must be recognized and practiced.

Key Bible References:

For who in the heavens can be compared to the LORD? Who among the sons of the mighty can be likened to the LORD?

God is greatly to be feared in the assembly of the saints, and to be held in reverence by all those who are around Him. Psalm 89:6–7

"A son honors his father, and a servant his master. If then I am the Father, where is My honor? And if I am a Master, where is My reverence? says the LORD of hosts. . . ." Malachi 1:6

---

[2]D. Martyn Lloyd-Jones, *Studies in the Sermon on the Mount,* William B. Eerdmans Publishing Company, Grand Rapids, Michigan, 1979, p. 271.

Therefore, since we are receiving a kingdom which cannot be shaken, let us have grace, by which we may serve God acceptably with reverence and godly fear. Hebrews 12:28

Additional References: Leviticus 19:30; Matthew 21:37.

What Others Say: R. C. Sproul, lecturer and author.

R. C. Sproul

The idea of holiness is so central to biblical teaching that it is said of God, "Holy is His name." His name is holy because He is holy. He is not always treated with holy reverence. His name is tramped through the dirt of this world. It functions as a curse word, a platform for the obscene. That the world has little respect for God is vividly seen by the way the world regards His name. No honor. No reverence. No awe before Him.[1]

Application: I remember the first time I was on a 747 Jumbo Jet. Awesome! Little ol' me and a couple hundred other people were actually lifting off the ground and going skyward. I was impressed . . . and somewhat frightened.

David experienced something like this as he wrote in the 29th Psalm, "The voice of the LORD *is* powerful; . . . full of majesty, . . . breaks the cedars, . . . shakes the Wilderness . . ." awesome!

What will it take for Christians to recognize God, who He is, and because of this reverence Him?

Not only should God be reverenced for who He is but what He is . . . Creator and Controller of the universe.

God deserves the same reverence and devotion from us that we show our own parents—because of who He is.

When reverence for God is acknowledged and enforced by the Christian, that person will know and claim the promises and provisions of God—who is worthy of our reverence.

—Royce F. McCarty

---

[1]R. C. Sproul, *The Holiness of God*, Tyndale House Publishers, Wheaton, Illinois, 1985, p. 24.

RUNAWAYS

WHAT IS THE CHRISTIAN RESPONSE TO YOUNG PEOPLE WHO ARE RUNAWAYS?

The Issue: Youthful rebellion is by no means a new phenomenon. It does, however, seem to characterize our society as never before. When young people run away and become involved in immorality, what is the Christian response? Do we condemn their sinful attitudes and lifestyles? Do we "write them off" and pretend they don't exist?

There are biblical principles, examples, and illustrations that can help us respond to runaways with God's love and patiently show them His way out of their rebellion and hurt.

Key Bible References:

Train up a child in the way he should go, and when he is old he will not depart from it. Proverbs 22:6

All we like sheep have gone astray; we have turned, every one, to his own way; and the LORD has laid on Him the iniquity of us all. Isaiah 53:6

"And not many days after, the younger son gathered all together, journeyed to a far country, and there wasted his possessions with prodigal living."

"And he arose and came to his father. But when he was still a great way off, his father saw him and had compassion, and ran and fell on his neck and kissed him." Luke 15:13, 20

Additional References: Deuteronomy 5:33, 6:4–9; Psalm 51; Proverbs 19:18; Ephesians 4:32, 6:4; Revelation 3:19.

What Others Say: Dr. James C. Dobson, founder and president of Focus on the Family; Jacob Aranza, minister and author; and Truman E. Dollar, pastor, and Dr. Grace H. Ketterman, child psychiatrist.

James C. Dobson
Obviously, teenagers possess a free will and I would not excuse those who engage in irresponsible behavior. But they are also

victims—victims of a peer-dominated society that often leaves them lost and confused. And my heart goes out to them.[1]

Jacob Aranza

As you continue to pray and respond correctly to your child, God will give him the opportunity to come in repentance and be broken before he is crushed by his rebellion.

No child wakes up one morning deciding to become a rebel. Many times it springs from longstanding, unresolved hurt.[2]

Truman E. Dollar and Grace H. Ketterman, M.D.

There comes a time in dealing with a rebellious child, when nothing more can be done. If you have reached this place, with all the help you can get, let your child know you love him and accept him as he is. Tell him that you will wait for him to return—either physically or emotionally to you.[3]

Application: Whether you are the parent, teacher, or friend of a runaway, you must respond—as Christ did to all hurting people—with compassion. The runaway you encounter may simply be asserting his independence and exercising his free will, or she may be running from an abusive family environment. In any case, the Christian response is one of love, which, by definition, includes patience and empathy.

Children need to be raised in an atmosphere of mutual respect, where relationships are more important than rules. They need consistent, loving, appropriate discipline administered jointly by parents who love God and love each other. They need role models at home, school, and church who live the principles they preach. When the adults they look to fail them, rebellion may be the result. Often our only answer is to seek forgiveness where we have failed, fervently pray, and patiently wait.

—Carol Sipus

---

[1]James C. Dobson, *Children At Risk,* Word Books, Publishers, Dallas, Texas, 1990, pp. 5–6.

[2]Jacob Aranza, *Lord! Why Is My Child a Rebel?,* Huntington House, Inc., Lafayette, Louisiana, 1990, pp. 38, 61.

[3]Truman E. Dollar and Grace H. Ketterman, M.D., *Teenage Rebellion,* Fleming H. Revell Company, Old Tappan, New Jersey, 1979, p. 192.

SALVATION

WHAT IS THE BASIC NEED
OF EVERY PERSON?

The Issue: When God created Adam and Eve He placed them in the Garden of Eden; a place of great beauty and peace. With only a few protective limitations placed upon them by God they were allowed to move and live freely in the garden. For some inexplicable reason Adam became careless with God's Word and disobeyed. That disobedience broke the relationship God had with Adam and subsequently all mankind. This separation from God brought both physical and spiritual death to Adam and all his descendants.

However, God provided a means whereby that relationship could be restored and the disobedience of all mankind remedied. His provision is salvation from the harmful consequences of sin through faith in the death, burial, and resurrection of His Son, Jesus Christ. It is through the blood that Christ shed on the cross on which He was crucified that we are cleansed from our sin in the sight of God.

Anyone who asks Christ to be their personal Lord and Savior is promised eternal life and freedom from bondage to sin and its corrupting results.

Key Bible References:

". . . for all have sinned and fall short of the glory of God, . . ."
Romans 3:23

But God demonstrates His own love toward us, in that while we were still sinners, Christ died for us.

Much more then, having now been justified by His blood, we shall be saved from wrath through Him.

For if when we were enemies we were reconciled to God through the death of His Son, much more, having been reconciled, we shall be saved by His life. Romans 5:8–10

For "whoever calls upon the name of the LORD shall be saved."
Romans 10:13

Additional References: Isaiah 12:2; Matthew 20:28; John 3:16–17; Ephesians 2:8–9; Hebrews 9:27; I John 1:1–2, 2:2.

What Others Say: Lewis Sperry Chafer, founder and first president of Dallas Theological Seminary, Bible teacher, author and editor; and Billy Graham, evangelist and author.

Lewis Sperry Chafer

According to its largest meaning as used in the Scriptures, the word salvation represents the whole work of God by which He rescues man from the eternal ruin and doom of sin and bestows on him the riches of His grace, even eternal life now and eternal glory in Heaven.[1]

Billy Graham

... the Bible teaches that God was [is] a God of love. He wanted to do something for man. He wanted to save man. He wanted to free man from the curse of sin.[2]

Application: All mankind is overwhelmed by the problems that confront us. Solving these problems is the challenge of every society. Worldly philosophers believe solutions are to be found in the efforts of mankind. Men of science, education, government, medicine, and others work to bring order and control to the human condition. Some rely solely on the scientific method while others seek help from sources like the "gods" of eastern mystical religions. They do not seek the help of the God of the Bible.

John Dewey, first president of the American Humanist Association, stated that religion is simply an invention of man to help him cope with the stresses of life. He and others like him do not believe there is a God to look to for help and no reason to be concerned about sin against a non-existent being.

The Scriptures make it clear that the fool says in his heart there is no God and the beginning of wisdom is the love, honor, and respect of God. When we admit that there is a God and that He has revealed Himself to us in His Word, the Bible, we must agree with Him that we have sinned against Him. We have nothing to give to God that can purchase or earn our release from the penalty of sin. It is only through belief in, and confession that Jesus Christ is His Son, that He became a human and died on Calvary's cross, was buried and came back from the dead and is now seated at God's right hand that we can be saved from that penalty. Without God's help we cannot be saved from the consequences of our sin.

—William J. Calderwood

---

[1]Lewis Sperry Chafer, *Major Bible Themes,* Dunham Publishing Company, Findlay, Ohio, 1953, p. 154.

[2]Billy Graham, *Peace With God,* Word Books, Publishers, Waco, Texas, 1984, p. 90.

SATANISTS

HOW SHOULD CHRISTIANS RESPOND TO THOSE WHO WORSHIP SATAN?

The Issue: Isaiah 14:14 recounts the day Satan declared: "I will be like the Most High." Satanists make the same pledge for personal prominence. Lured by Lucifer, they fall prey to immoral messages in heavy metal music, occult films, and literature like the *Satanic Bible* and the *Necronomicon*. Christians can respond to those who worship Satan through prayer and the use of appropriate Scripture.

Key Bible References:

Be sober, be vigilant; because your adversary the devil walks about like a roaring lion, seeking whom he may devour. Resist him, steadfast in the faith, . . . I Peter 5:8–9a

Put on the whole armor of God, that you may be able to stand against the wiles of the devil.

For we do not wrestle . . . against flesh and blood, and against the spiritual forces of evil in the heavenly realms. Ephesians 6:11–12

Therefore God also has highly exalted Him and given Him the name which is above every name, that at the name of Jesus every knee should bow, of those in heaven, and of those on earth, and of those under the earth. Philippians 2:9–10

You are of God, little children, and have overcome them, because He who is in you is greater than he who is in the world. I John 4:4

Additional References: Acts 1:8; Romans 8:31, 37; Ephesians 4:27; Philippians 4:13.

What Others Say: Mark I. Bubeck, author.

Mark I. Bubeck

We have essentially two offensive weapons to use against Satan. They are the Word of God and prayer. . . . As the believer uses it, the Word can penetrate, cleanse, and change the believer's life and in so doing, cut away Satan's grip on that life. . . . There is no substitute for persistent, steady, consistent application of God's word against Satan.[1]

Prayer directly affects how people hear the Word. That is why prayer support for revival crusades can help bring many souls to Christ. It helps to remove the spiritual blindness and deafness that Satan wants of man as effective and far-reaching as prayer. A person of God can literally change the world through his prayers without leaving the confines of his home.[2]

Application: Christians who respond to those who worship Satan fight a serious battle. Many Satanists view themselves as victims of a competitive world and an adversarial society. They turn to Satanism as a way to derive a swift sense of power and prestige. Satanists are determined to break all of the Bible's Ten Commandments and violate the seven deadly sins: pride, lying, murder, a wicked heart, quickness to do evil, a false witness, and causing discord. To Satanists, man's true enemy is guilt, instilled by Christianity.

Christians should arm themselves with the Word of God and prayer. As messengers of God, we must educate Satanists as to the spiritual consequences of not accepting the salvation of Christ on the cross. We must also recognize that most Satanists are non-affirmed people who live lives of rejection and emotional dysfunctionalism. They don't understand God's love, but readily relate to Satan's hate. Those who rebel against God should know that the price of dabbling with the devil will be eternal death.

—Bob Larson

SELF-ACTUALIZATION

WHAT DOES THE BIBLE SAY ABOUT SELF-ACTUALIZATION?

The Issue: Many psychologists who are known as self-theorists and a few liberal theologians promote the idea that people have a high level of motivation resulting from one's basic needs. This they

---

[1]Mark I. Bubeck, *Overcoming the Adversary,* Moody Press, Chicago, Illinois, 1984, pp. 114, 116.
[2]Ibid., p. 129.

271

called self-actualization and is considered to be the highest level of need. At this high level of actualization theorists claim there are peak experiences which are marked by rapturous feelings of excitement and tension, or peace, quietude, and a deep sense of relaxation. These experiences are being promoted as thinking skills. These peak experiences are considered to be a result of developing and realizing one's fullest potential and becoming everything one is capable of becoming.

Self-actualization advocates teach the concept of reaching deep within yourself to your inner goodness. The Bible, of course, does not teach self-actualization but teaches us to reach out to God for help, for strength and wisdom in order to be fulfilled as a Christian. Numerous scriptural passages indicate that help, power, peace, and wisdom come from God through prayer, obedience to the Word of God, and a dependence on the Holy Spirit for spiritual insight.

Key Bible References:

Until now you have asked nothing in my name. Ask, and you will receive, that your joy may be full. John 16:24

"And all things, whatever you ask in prayer, believing, you will receive." Matthew 21:22

Be anxious for nothing, but in everything by prayer and supplication, with thanksgiving, let your requests be made known to God; and the peace of God, which surpasses all understanding, will guard your hearts and minds through Christ Jesus. Philippians 4:6–7

. . . for the kingdom of God is not food and drink, but righteousness and peace and joy in the Holy Spirit. Romans 14:17

Additional References: John 15:4–11; II Corinthians 5:15; James 1:5; I Peter 5:7.

What Others Say: Dr. Tim LaHaye, educator, Bible scholar and author; and Bob Larson, Christian apologist and author.

Tim LaHaye
Once man thinks he is independent of God, he becomes self-centered; suddenly he and his wants become the measure of all things. Today's philosophy of education is obsessed with self-actualization, self-sufficiency, self-satisfaction.[1]

---

[1]Tim LaHaye, *The Battle For The Mind,* Fleming H. Revell Company, Old Tappan, New Jersey, 1980, p. 70.

Bob Larson

Self-actualization was "invented" by Abraham Maslow, a friend of Timothy Leary. He developed the theory of "self-actualization," living to one's full potential, as the means of achieving psychological health. Psycho-technologies have invaded the work force with the intent of "self-actualization" (otherwise known as "enlightenment" or "contacting one's inner divine nature"). Most New Age influence enters through the human resources development department of large companies. A representative of Digital Equipment recently warned, "I see the training industry being used to proselytize New Age religion under the deceptive marketing of increased productivity, self-actualization, and self-improvement.[2]

Application: Christian parents, teachers, school administrators, pastors and all Christians need to be aware of the influence of theories or practices that promote self-actualization through a special altered state of consciousness. Visualization and guided imagery are a part of these techniques in "higher order thinking skills." Parents with children in public schools should object to practices or techniques of contacting one's inner self or a type of self-hypnotic state that are considered a part of "higher order thinking skills."

It is clear that Christians are to look to God for help and not into one's self (see John 10:10b).

—Kenneth A. Stone

SELF-CONTROL

WHAT DOES THE BIBLE TEACH
ABOUT SELF-CONTROL?

The Issue: How important is self-control in a Christian's life? To help answer this question, think back to the last sporting event you attended or watched. The game was played by a set of rules which were strictly followed. Imagine the confusion that would have occurred had there been no rules or no referees. Each team and player would interpret his own boundaries, penalties and scoring system.

---

[2]Bob Larson, *Straight Answers On The New Age,* Thomas Nelson Publishers, Nashville, Tennessee, 1989, pp. 21, 240.

In the "game of life" however, we have not been left without a rule book. God Himself has clearly provided guidelines and standards by which we as Christians are to live. Most of us know these "rules," but occasionally have trouble following them. Self-control is the exercising of one's God-given strength in order to live the "game of life" in God's way. It goes beyond just knowing what is right. It involves the control or governing of our desires in order to please God.

Key Bible References:

But the fruit of the Spirit is love, joy, peace, longsuffering, kindness, goodness, faithfulness, gentleness, self-control. Galatians 5:22

But also for this very reason, giving all diligence, add to your faith virtue, to virtue knowledge, to knowledge self-control. . . . II Peter 1:5–6

. . . but hospitable, a lover of what is good, sober-minded, just, holy, self-controlled. . . . Titus 1:8

Additional References: Proverbs 25:28; I Corinthians 7:5; I Thessalonians 5:6, 8; II Timothy 3:3; I Peter 1:13, 4:7, 5:8.

What Others Say: D. G. Kehl and Jerry Bridges, Christian authors.

D. G. Kehl
Self-control is "the ability to avoid excesses, to stay within reasonable bounds."[1]

Jerry Bridges
Self-control is "the exercise of inner strength under the direction of sound judgment that enables us to do, think and say the things that are pleasing to God."[2]

Application: The walls which typically surrounded ancient cities were the primary means of defense against "unwanted guests" or unfriendly invaders. The Old Testament account of Nehemiah demonstrates the importance of this wall. When Nehemiah received the news that the Jerusalem wall was broken down, he quickly sought God and developed a plan for its repair. He knew that without this "wall of defense," Jerusalem would be left unprotected, easy prey to an enemy.

---

[1]D. G. Kehl, *Control Yourself!* Zondervan Publishing House, Grand Rapids, Michigan, 1982, p. 25.

[2]Jerry Bridges, *The Practice of Godliness,* NavPress, Colorado Springs, Colorado, 1983, p. 164.

In the same way, we need these "walls of defense" in our own lives. Satan is our enemy, the invader of our soul. Proverbs 25:28 says: "Like a city whose walls are broken down is a man who lacks self-control" (NIV). As Christians, we all face daily struggles and battles. These may be against Satan, the flesh, or even our own wrong attitudes. Self-control is our first "wall of defense." It is essential that we exercise it so that we do not become easy prey to the enemy. Self-control is essential for success in the pursuit of any worthy goal, including that of living a vibrant, growing Christian life.

—**Kent W. Vanderwood**

SELFISHNESS

WHAT DOES THE BIBLE SAY
ABOUT SELFISHNESS?

The Issue: Selfishness is often referred to in the Scriptures as withholding what is good from others. It is caring more for one's own need than for the needs of others. Selfishness is closely related to pride and jealousy. It manifests itself in several ways such as not giving out of our abundance, ignoring the needs of others, loving ourselves more than those around us, and refusing to lend a hand to those in need.

When Christians take their eyes off God and are primarily concerned with themselves, then they are allowing their natural sin nature to control them rather than the Holy Spirit which is in them.

Key Bible References:

Let each of you look out not only for his own interests, but also for the interests of others. Philippians 2:4

We then who are strong ought to bear with the scruples of the weak, and not to please ourselves.

Let each of us please his neighbor for his good, leading to edification.

For even Christ did not please Himself; but as it is written, "The reproaches of those who reproached You fell on Me." Romans 15:1–3

. . . And he died for all, that those who live should live no longer for themselves, but for Him who died for them and rose again. II Corinthians 5:15

For men will be lovers of themselves, lovers of money, boasters, proud, blasphemers, disobedient to parents, unthankful, unholy. . . . II Timothy 3:2

Additional References: Psalm 38:11; Proverbs 18:17; Zechariah 7:6; Matthew 19:21–22; James 2:15–16.

What Others Say: Lawrence O. Richards, author and teacher.

Lawrence O. Richards

Paul looked with awe at Jesus' willing surrender of the prerogatives of Deity to become a human being, and to die for us on a cross. But the self-sacrifice of Jesus is also a powerful call to the believer.

If you have this attitude toward our brothers and sisters in Jesus, there will be unity. And we will truly be one, in spirit and purpose. We, like Jesus, will live to serve. And in serving we, like Jesus, will find the way of exaltation.[1]

Application: In our world today it is the norm for people to be more concerned with their own needs than with the needs of others. It is our sinful nature to be selfish and protect our own interests. Many wrongs that we do are because of this basic problem that lies within us because of the fall of man. We lie, cheat, steal, and harm others out of an evil heart that is futilely attempting to protect its own life and all that sustains it.

As Christians, we must follow the example of Christ and lay aside our own lives for the interests of others. Christ said ". . . he who loses his life for My sake will find it. . . . And whoever gives one of these little ones only a cup of cold *water* in the name of a disciple, assuredly, I say to you, he shall by no means lose his reward" (Matthew 10:39, 42).

The Bible promises that we will be blessed as we sacrifically deny self-interests and become increasingly concerned with the needs and interests of others.

—**Steve Camp**

---

[1]Lawrence O. Richards, *The Teachers Commentary,* Scripture Press Publications, Wheaton, Illinois, 1987, p. 935.

SEX EDUCATION

WHAT IS THE CHRISTIAN'S PERSPECTIVE ON SEX EDUCATION?

The Issue: One of the primary teachings of the Bible and one of the time-honored rights of American parents is the teaching of moral values to their children. But many in government and in education consider it their responsibility to educate the children of America in the area of sex education. For several years advocacy organizations have provided the impetus for the teaching of sex education. In public schools, these courses are designed to be value-neutral or value-free.

The argument for this is that in today's diverse society it would be impossible to determine whose values to incorporate into the sex education curriculum, and the young should not be indoctrinated with someone else's beliefs. Undergirding most of these programs is the teaching that unmarried teen sexual activity is inevitable and good as long as it is "safe sex." The other primary belief being espoused is that the cause of most teen sexuality problems, including pregnancy and disease, is the lack of adequate sex education.

These beliefs are often diametrically opposed to what the Bible teaches about sex. Sex education cannot be value-neutral because sex is a quintessentially moral activity. In addition, these value-neutral sex education programs are not effective. A 1986 Lewis Harris poll found that students' likelihood of engaging in sexual activities increased if they had had a course in sex education. The likelihood for pregnancy and sexually transmitted disease increased for those who had sex education.[1]

Key Bible References:

Then God blessed them, and God said to them, "Be fruitful and multiply; fill the earth and subdue it; . . ." Genesis 1:28

And the LORD God said, "It is not good that man should be alone; I will make him a helper comparable to him."

Therefore a man shall leave his father and mother and be joined to his wife, and they shall become one flesh. Genesis 2:18, 24

---

[1]Dinah Richard, "The Wolf at the Door," *Citizen Magazine,* Focus on the Family, December, 1989, p. 15.

Behold, children are *a heritage from the* LORD, *the fruit of the womb* is *a reward.* Psalm 127:3

Train up a child in the way he should go, and when he is old he will not depart from it. Proverbs 22:6

Additional References: Exodus 20:14; Leviticus 18:22, 20:7, 10–21; Proverbs 5:1–6, 6:20–29; Matthew 5:27–28; Romans 12:1; I Corinthians 6:13–20, 7:2; Colossians 3:5–6; I Thessalonians 4:3–8; Hebrews 13:4.

What Others Say: William Bennett, former U.S. Secretary of Education; Dr. James C. Dobson, Christian psychologist and author; and Dr. Tim LaHaye, author and president of Family Life Seminars.

William Bennett
Sex education is . . . about character and the formation of character. A sex education course in which issues of right and wrong do not occupy center stage is an evasion and an irresponsibility.[2]

James C. Dobson
The assumption that physiologic information will inhibit sexual activity is about as foolish as thinking an overweight glutton can be helped by understanding the biologic process of eating.[3]

Tim LaHaye
I have particularly been concerned over the tragic increase in teenage suicides during the same period that explicit sex education has corrupted our children's morals at school.[4]

Teaching sex education in mixed classes to hot-blooded teenagers without benefit of moral values is like pouring gasoline on emotional fires. An explosion is inevitable.[5]

Application: There are two primary ways to view sex education: from a humanistic, amoral position and from a Christian perspective. The humanistic, amoral approach to sex education currently being used in our public schools is worse than not teaching it at all because it leads to experimentation.

---

[2]William Bennett, In an address to the National School Board Association meeting in Washington, D.C., January 22, 1987.

[3]James C. Dobson, *Hide or Seek,* Fleming H. Revell Company, Old Tappan, New Jersey, 1974, p. 141.

[4]Tim LaHaye, *The Battle for the Public Schools,* Fleming H. Revell Company, Old Tappan, New Jersey, n.d., p. 149.

[5]Tim LaHaye, *Sex Education is for the Family,* Zondervan Publishing, Grand Rapids, Michigan, 1985, p. 17.

It is hard to overstate the importance of teaching sex education from a Christian perspective. The Bible begins with the drama of a man-woman relationship, and other stories of encounters of the sexes dot its pages. God, early on, demonstrates His plan and purpose for sex (Genesis 1:28, 2:24).

Sex is sacred, and this is clearly portrayed when Jesus used it to illustrate His relationship with His church. Only as children and young people are taught to recognize themselves in mind, body, and sexuality as God's special creations, rather than animalistic beings with sexual urges, can sex education have its proper meaning. Children are a gift from God and should be protected (Psalm 127:3). Christians should examine any sex education materials being taught to their children in their schools or elsewhere. To allow children to be taught value-free or value-neutral sex education is to teach untruth and is in violation of biblical teaching.

—Levan G. Parker

SEX ROLES

WHAT DOES THE BIBLE SAY TO THOSE WHO ADVOCATE REVERSED SEX ROLES?

The Issue: Man is to be a hedge, or protector, to stand up and protect what God has put on this earth. In the marriage relationship with a woman, he is to have a wife, they are to live in peace and he is to love her and see that she is not abused. His goal should be to please his wife.

The Bible says that the head of every man is Christ and the head of the woman is the man. And this man is to be strong and to be a follower of Jesus Christ. This biblical perspective of a man's relationship to his wife is diametrically opposed to the view of many people in today's "enlightened" environment.

Key Bible References:

. . . male and female He created them. Genesis 1:27

The proverbs of Solomon. . . . My son, hear the instruction of your father, and do not forsake the law of your mother; . . . Proverbs 1:1, 8

279

"A woman shall not wear anything that pertains to a man, nor shall a man put on a woman's garment, for all who do so are an abomination to the LORD your God." Deuteronomy 22:5

Additional References: Proverbs 31:1–31; I Peter 3:7.

What Others Say: Dr. James C. Dobson, psychologist and president of Focus on the Family; and Dr. Jay Adams, psychologist and author.

James C. Dobson

I firmly believe in the value of teaching traditional male and female roles during the early days. To remove this prescribed behavior for a child is to further damage his sense of identity which needs all the help it can get.[1]

Female sex role identity has become a major target for change by those who wish to revolutionize the relationship between men and women. We can make no greater mistake as a nation than to continue this pervasive disrespect shown to women who have devoted their lives to the welfare of families.[2]

Jay Adams

A boy needs to be taught that people should be able to clearly tell that he is a man because he dresses like a man, combs his hair like a man and walks like a man.[3]

Application: The books of Ruth and Esther show women working hard and accomplishing great things. This does not conflict with men taking a responsibility for aggressive, strong leadership patterned after Christ's leadership. A woman is to be respected. She should be held in high regard for her care of the family, her wisdom, her kindness. The Bible says, "Her children rise up and call her blessed; her husband *also,* and he praises her; (Proverbs 31:28).

—William Hewlett

---

[1] James C. Dobson, *Hide or Seek: Self-Esteem for the Child,* Fleming H. Revell Company, Old Tappan, New Jersey, 1979, pp. 139–141.

[2] James C. Dobson, *Straight Talk to Men and Their Wives,* Word Books, Publishers, Waco, Texas, 1980, pp. 152–153.

[3] Jay Adams, *The Christian Community Manual,* Baker Publishing, Grand Rapids, Michigan, n.d., p. 403 ff.

SEXUALITY

WHAT DOES THE BIBLE'S CREATION ACCOUNT TEACH US ABOUT OUR SEXUALITY?

The Issue: Our culture increasingly accepts the notion that a woman cannot be respected by herself or others until she carries all the responsibilities of a man and receives all the rights of a man. This affects her role in the home and in the church, and many Christians are bending their convictions to accommodate this "modern" view. What does the Bible say?

In the Genesis account of the creation and fall we see that men and women are equally made in the image of God, that each is equally a member of the earth-management team, and that woman is a distinct, unique creation (1:26–27). Reading further we see that man was made from the earth (2:7) to work in the earth (2:15), that he is given supervision of other earth creatures (2:19), and that he is in need of a helper (2:18). Woman, on the other hand is made from a person (2:21–22) to help a person (2:20) and is sensitive to the desires of a person (3:16).

New Testament commands are consistent with the creation account. In the home, the husband is commanded to be loving (Colossians 3:19; Ephesians 5:25–23), understanding (I Peter 3:7), patient (Colossians 3:19), to give his wife honor (I Peter 3:7), and to control his children with confidence and dignity (I Timothy 32:4). The wife, on the other hand, is simply commanded to be under authority (Ephesians 5:22–24; Colossians 3:18; I Peter 3:1–6).

Outside the home there seem to be no biblical restrictions on the role of women in society including government (Judges 4) and business (Proverbs 31).

Key Bible References:

Nevertheless let each one of you in particular so love his own wife as himself, and let the wife see that she respects her husband. Ephesians 5:33

Wives, submit to your own husbands, as is fitting in the Lord.

Husbands, love your wives and do not be bitter toward them. Colossians 3:18–19

Likewise you *wives,* be *submissive to your own husbands, that even if some do not obey the word, they, without a word, may be won by the conduct of their wives, . . .*

Finally, all of you be of one mind, having compassion for one another; love as brothers, be tenderhearted, be courteous.
I Peter 3:1, 8

Additional References: Genesis 1:26–28, 2:7, 15–25; Proverbs 31:10–31; Ephesians 5:22–33; I Peter 2:21–3:9.

What Others Say: Polycarp of Smyrna; and Matthew Henry.

Polycarp of Smyrna
We must gird on the armor of integrity, and the first step must be to school our own selves into conformity with the divine commandments. After that we may go on to instruct our womenfolk in the traditions of the faith, and in love and purity; teaching them to show fondness and fidelity to their husbands, and a chaste and impartial affection for everyone else, and to bring up their children in the fear of God.[1]

Matthew Henry
He was not made of gold-dust, powder of pearl, or diamond dust, but common dust, dust of the ground. Hence he is said to be of earth.

Probably it was revealed to Adam in a vision while he was asleep, that this lovely creature, now presented to him, was a piece of himself, and was to be his companion and the wife of his covenant.[2]

Application: The Scriptures make it clear that men and women are absolutely equal in worth and value. It also indicates that they are quite different in nature and roles, especially in the home and church. It is evident that these differences are created by God in order that men and women may function in the home to love one another and meet each other's needs and working together will function effectively as stewards of the earth, parents of children, and worshipers of God.

—Fred Donehoo

---

[1]Maxwell Staniford, trans., *Early Christian Writings, The Apostolic Fathers,* Dorset Press, New York, New York, 1968, p. 145.

[2]Matthew Henry, *Matthew Henry's Commentary on the Whole Bible,* Fleming H. Revell, London and Edinburgh, Gen., Chap. II, vss. 7, 23.

SIN

WHAT DOES THE BIBLE TEACH ABOUT SIN?

The Issue: Any serious student of God's Word will readily acknowledge that sin is a dominant topic from Genesis through Revelation. Sin, or any voluntary act known to be contrary to the character and will of God, is first introduced shortly after the creation narrative. Adam's sin of commission forever changed the status of man. Man, made in the image of God, knowingly chose to do wrong. Thus, man became abnormal. How God chose to deal with man's abnormality occupies the thoughts and permeates the writings of all biblical writers. To be sure, God's Word plainly teaches that all have sinned. God's penalty for sin is physical, spiritual, and eternal death.

God, however, in His incomprehensible plan of love and grace, gave mankind another opportunity. He chose to send the Savior, the only begotten of the Father, Jesus Christ. Jesus Christ offers salvation from sin, freedom from the paralysis of the sin nature, and the assurance of an eternal relationship with our Lord to all who confess their sins, repent of their ways, and seek the enabling power and presence of God's Holy Spirit.

Key Bible References:

Therefore, just as through one man sin entered the world, and death through sin, and thus death spread to all men, because all sinned—Romans 5:12

... for all have sinned and fall short of the glory of God, ... Romans 3:23

For the wages of sin is death, but the gift of God is eternal life in Christ Jesus our Lord. Romans 6:23

For I delivered to you first of all that which I also received: that Christ died for our sins according to the Scriptures, ... I Corinthians 15:3

Additional References: Proverbs 14:9; Isaiah 1:16–18; Matthew 1:21; John 1:29; Romans 6:6–12; II Corinthians 5:21; I John 1:8–9, 2:1.

What Others Say: Francis A. Schaeffer; A. W. Tozer; and R. C. Sproul, outstanding Christians scholars.

Francis A. Schaeffer

. . . all men are separated from God because of their true moral guilt. God exists, God has character, God is a holy God, and when men sin (and we all must acknowledge we have sinned not only by mistake, but by intention) they have true moral guilt before the God who exists. That guilt is not just the modern concept of guilt-feelings, a psychological guilty feeling in man. It is a true moral guilt before the finite-personal, holy God. Only the finished, substitutionary work of Christ upon the cross as the Lamb of God—in history, space, and time—is enough to remove this.[1]

A. W. Tozer

Sin has done frightful things to us and its effect upon us is all the more deadly because we were born in it and are scarcely aware of what is happening to us.

One thing sin has done is to confuse our values so that we can only with difficulty distinguish a friend from a foe or tell for certain what is and what is not good for us. We walk in a world of shadows where real things appear unreal and things of no consequence are sought after as eagerly as if they were made of the very gold that paves the streets of the City of God.[2]

R. C. Sproul

The forgetting of God is a relational forgetting. That is, He remembers it no more against me. When God forgives me of my sin He doesn't hold it against me. He bears no grudges. He harbors no lingering hostility. My relationship with Him is totally and completely restored.[3]

Application: C. H. Spurgeon frequently referred to sin as a horrible evil, a deadly poison! Unfortunately, sin is not oftentimes regarded with such disdain in contemporary society. As a matter of fact, since many non-Christians deny the legitimacy of moral absolutes, they either reject the concept of sin totally or greatly diminish its importance. It is important that Christians reject any thinking that diminishes or minimizes sin and its eternal consequences for mankind. Christians must constantly stress that since all have sinned, all need a Savior. Fortunately, since God's plan to deal with

---

[1]Francis A. Schaeffer, *The Complete Works of Francis A. Schaeffer, A Christian Worldview, Volume Two, A Christian View of the Bible as Truth,* Crossway Books, Westchester, Illinois, 1982, pp. 199–200.

[2]A. W. Tozer, *That Incredible Christian,* Christian Publications, Inc., Harrisburg, Pennsylvania, 1964, p. 14.

[3]R. C. Sproul, *Pleasing God,* Tyndale House Publishers, Wheaton, Illinois, 1988, p. 136.

sin is so unique and so complete, Christians can live effective daily lives without being perpetually crushed under the weight of their own nature and acts of wrong doing.

Praise God for his love, mercy, grace, and the opportunity to experience total reconciliation!

—Timothy J. Hillen

SMOKING

SHOULD CHRISTIANS OR ANYONE SMOKE TOBACCO?

The Issue: Satan would like to destroy a Christian's spiritual influence by any means he can and if by use of tobacco, the physical body is slowly destroyed, the Christian loses potential spiritual impact. The use of tobacco brings on a slow suicide. Why would anyone, Christian or non-Christian want to commit physical suicide? There is a responsibility to yourself and your loved ones, to take proper care of your body.

Key Bible References:

You are not restricted by us, but you are restricted by your own *affections.* II Corinthians 6:12

Or do you not know that your body is the temple of the Holy Spirit who is *in you, whom you have from God, and you are not your own?*

For you were bought at a price; therefore glorify God in your body and in your spirit, which are God's. I Corinthians 6:19–20

And everyone who competes for the prize *is temperate in all things. Now they* do it *to obtain a perishable crown, but we* for *an imperishable* crown. I Corinthians 9:25

Additional References: Luke 21:34–36; Galatians 5:19–20; Philippians 1:20.

What Others Say: Dr. Henry M. Morris, scientist, Bible scholar, and author; and the American Cancer Society.

Henry M. Morris

The believer should be controlled by the Holy Spirit (Ephesians 5:18), not by alcohol or anything else which might gain inordinate control over his will. Christians must not use either alcohol or tobacco, recognizing that these substances have acquired control over the bodies and wills of multitudes.[1]

American Cancer Society

- Cigarette smoke contains about 4,000 chemicals. Many are poison. More than 40 of them cause cancer.
- Your chances of getting lung cancer are 10 times greater than a nonsmoker.
- You are twice as likely to have a heart attack as a nonsmoker.
- Cigarette smoking is strongly linked with emphysema and chronic bronchitis.
- Pregnant women who smoke are more likely to have low birth weight babies or stillborn babies.
- Cigarette smoke is harmful to all who inhale it, including nonsmokers.
- Your children are twice as likely to be smokers when they grow up.

The fact that cigarette smoking is the main cause of lung cancer in smokers is well known. In 1986 the Surgeon General of the United States reported that involuntary smoking can cause lung cancer in nonsmokers. What this could mean is that tobacco smoke and radiation may have this in common, there are just no safe levels of exposure.[2]

Application: The facts show there is no safe tobacco, either smokeless or regular. Common sense tells us not to commit slow suicide by using any kind of tobacco and besides, why would anyone want to purposely harm his or her own body, which in turn affects other family members.

For the Christian, there are spiritual values that are more important than the physical satisfaction of using tobacco. When we satisfy physical appetites to the harm of the body, we are sinning against God who created our body. We are spiritual beings, not physical animals. When we do something that hurts us physically, it becomes a spiritual sin.

---

[1]Henry M. Morris, *Education for the Real World,* Creation House Publishers, San Diego, California, 1977, p. 195.

[2]American Cancer Society, pamphlet No. 2515–LE, revised 8/89.

Your body is a temple of the Holy Spirit, you have been bought with a price, therefore glorify God in your body.

—Marlin D. Miller

SPIRITUAL GROWTH

WHAT DOES THE BIBLE SAY ABOUT THE SPIRITUAL GROWTH OF CHRISTIANS?

The Issue: Christian life is not easy! It makes a continuous demand upon the best resources we can command. There is no place where one can stop and say, "I have arrived!" when it comes to spiritual growth and maturity.

Key Bible References:

. . . that He would grant you, according to the riches of His glory, to be strengthened with might through His Spirit in the inner man, that Christ may dwell in your hearts through faith; that you, being rooted and grounded in love, may be able to comprehend with all the saints what is the width and length and depth and height—to know the love of Christ which passes knowledge; that you may be filled with all the fullness of God. Ephesians 3:16–19

Only let your conduct be worthy of the gospel of Christ, so that whether I come and see you or am absent, I may hear of your affairs, that you stand fast in one spirit, with one mind striving together for the faith of the gospel, . . . Philippians 1:27

Or do you not know that your body is the temple of the Holy Spirit who is in you, whom you have from God, and you are not your own?

For you were bought at a price; therefore glorify God in your body and in your spirit, which are God's. I Corinthians 6:19–20

Jesus said to him, "You shall love the LORD your God with all your heart, with all your soul, and with all your mind."

"This is the first and great commandment." Matthew 22:37–38

Additional References: Luke 14:27, 33; John 8:31, 15:8; Galatians 2:20.

What Others Say: Dr. Ilion T. Jones, author, professor, and pastor.

Ilion T. Jones

Life is not easy. Any person makes a grave mistake who supposes that life is a Fourth of July picnic, or a weekend party, or who, in the language of an old hymn expects "to go to heaven on flowery beds of ease." Life can be grand and glorious, romantic and thrilling—and should be—but it is never easy.

Life makes a continuous demand upon the best resources we can command. It subjects our inner man to constant strains and stresses, as a house is subjected to the ravages of the elements and time. One must prod himself; keep his human relations in good repair; struggle daily with his conscience and against discouragement, inertia, and self-satisfaction; develop his physical and moral energies; discipline his emotions; control his thoughts; generate faith, courage, morale and optimism; be vigilant against getting entangled in the trivialities and the details of the daily rounds. There is no place where he can stop and say to himself, "I have arrived; I've got it made; I'm fixed for life; I can take it easy."[1]

Application: The moral standards of our time are lower than ever. Anything goes. The media is filled with profanity and sex. The Ten Commandments are no longer the base for our moral code. Immorality is sweeping the land. Multitudes of church members are engulfed by the waves of sin and worldliness and neglect.

In Isaiah 1:1–18, God is speaking about the sins of Israel. They have rebelled against Him, they have forsaken Him, they have provoked Him to anger with their sin and idolatry. They went through the form, but their hearts were not in it and God knew it. Then, just like God, He says, "Come now, and let us reason together."

How can we keep from becoming like Israel in Isaiah's day? The answer is found in the word GROWTH. We must be a disciple of the Lord Jesus Christ. That word disciple means, "A learner—a follower of Christ." It is more than filling the church on Sunday morning when it is convenient. It is more than going through the forms of religion. It is selling out to Christ. It is constantly growing in Him. It is persevering for the prize!

—Glen D. Cole

---

[1] Ilion T. Jones, *God's Everlasting "Yes"*, Word Books, Publishers, Waco, Texas, 1969, pp. 59–60.

STEALING

WHAT DOES THE BIBLE TEACH
ABOUT STEALING?

The Issue: Stealing, the taking of something that does not belong to us, without the owner's consent, has very broad application, and is a widespread problem in our society. The importance of this issue is made clear by God as far back as the issuance of the Ten Commandments.

Few cultures in the world place any virtue in stealing, and some even exact such penalties as hands being removed, or, in the extreme, the death penalty. Broadly speaking, stealing encompasses not only common theft but such things as stealing another's purity, as in immorality, stealing another's words, ideas, or music, as in plagiarism, stealing from the government, as in tax evasion, and stealing from the truth of Scripture as in heresy.

Key Bible References:

"You shall not steal." Exodus 20:15

"You shall not steal, nor deal falsely, nor lie to one another.

"You shall not defraud your neighbor, nor rob him. The wages of him who is hired shall not remain with you all night until morning." Leviticus 19:11, 13

Let him who stole steal no longer, but rather let him labor, working with his *hands what is good, that he may have something to give him who has need.* Ephesians 4:28

Additional References: Deuteronomy 5:19, 23:24; Matthew 15:19; Mark 11:17; John 10:1; I Peter 4:15.

What Others Say: Dr. Henry M. Morris, Bible scholar, author, and scientist.

Henry M. Morris
Students must respect the property of others. Not only outright theft, but also failing to take care of borrowed property (Ephesians 4:28), carelessness which results in damage to someone else's property, unfair business practices, failure to provide adequate work for one's wages (I Thessalonians 4:11–12) and other such practices (e.g.

"goofing off" on jobs for which one is paid), are all forms of stealing and must be scrupulously avoided by Christians.

Perhaps the worst form of stealing is to steal from God by failing to bring Him tithes and offerings from the material blessings provided us by Him. (II Corinthians 9:6–15).[1]

Application: There is a distorted modern proverb that says, "Stealing is an abomination unto the Lord, but a very present help in the time of trouble." In other words "the ends justify the means." In today's world, such justifications for stealing are commonplace. In one instance, income tax forms exaggerate deductions since the government is already getting too much. In another instance, holding back on tithes and offerings is understandable since the cost of housing takes a much higher percentage of income.

Stealing someone else's virginity is justified, since even our public institutions condone it, as long as it is done "safely." The ultimate example, in our world today, is in stealing the life of an unborn baby. This, too, is justified particularly when it probably would have been handicapped, or too expensive to care for, or unwanted, or inconvenient.

In short, amorality says that stealing is wrong in many instances. Occasionally however, it is not wrong. The Bible is profoundly clear, "You shall not steal" (Exodus 20:15).

—**Jeff Woodcock**

STEWARDSHIP

WHAT DOES THE BIBLE TEACH ABOUT STEWARDSHIP?

The Issue: God has blessed us with the ability to choose—from the eternal choice of asking Jesus Christ to be our Savior to the temporal choices and decisions we make on a daily basis. Ownership of this responsibility demands accountability. We must exercise our freedom of choice by seeking and following God's direction. Wise

---

[1]Henry M. Morris, *Education for the Real World,* Master Books, San Diego, California, 1977, p. 192

decision making comes from seeking God's wisdom. Wise choices come from seeking God's will. They result in following His ways.

Key Bible References:

"The fathers shall not be put to death for their children, nor shall the children be put to death for their fathers; a person shall be put to death for his own sin." Deuteronomy 24:16

"But he who did not know, yet committed things worthy of stripes, shall be beaten with few. For everyone to whom much is given, from him much will be required; and to whom much has been committed, of him they will ask the more." Luke 12:48

Trust in the LORD with all your heart, and lean not on your own understanding; in all your ways acknowledge Him, and He shall direct your paths. Proverbs 3:5–6

Additional References: Matthew 25:14–15; I Peter 4:10.

What Others Say: Dr. Warren W. Wiersbe, Bible scholar and author; and The Navigators.

Warren W. Wiersbe

Our purpose is not to get lost in curious doctrinal details. Nor is our purpose to attach or defend some pet doctrine. As Christians we have the responsibility to hear God speak in Jesus Christ, and to heed that Word. We want to echo the prayer of the Greeks: "Sir, we wish to see Jesus" (John 12:21). Our responsibility is to know Christ better and exalt Him more![1]

The Navigators

Christians have been set free in Christ—not to do whatever they please but to serve. Believers have been set free from sin to serve righteousness (Romans 6:18–19), set free from Satan to serve God (I Peter 2:16), set free from self to serve others (Galatians 5:13)—Christians are no longer under obligation to serve the things of the old life, but free to serve voluntarily the things of the new life.[2]

Many people measure the fruitfulness of their lives by the quantity of their activities. This does not necessarily give a true picture of the quality of their lives. What you are is more important than what you do.

---

[1]Warren W. Wiersbe, *Be Confident,* Victor Books, Wheaton, Illinois, 1982, p. 19.
[2]The Navigators, *Walking with Christ—Design for Discipleship, Book 3,* NavPress, Colorado Springs, Colorado, 1973, p. 38.

Today, the emphasis is placed upon doing and production. The Bible emphasizes being and character.[3]

Application: God's Word directs us in the paths we should follow. He allows us the freedom of choice to respond correctly to His love and guidance or to do what we want to do pragmatically. The responsibility to know God and to be obedient to His commands should have us responding in love and not simply "jumping through some candy-coated hoops." Our heavenly Father wants each of us to become all that we can be for His magnification and eternal reward. We need to be growing in Him daily. We need to be making Him known through each word and deed. This process is an ongoing one.

It should be our goal to end this process with the words, "Well done, good and faithful servant . . . Enter into the joy of your Lord."

—Glen L. Schultz

SUCCESS

WHAT IS THE BIBLICAL PERSPECTIVE OF A SUCCESSFUL LIFE?

The Issue: For many, success is that "pot of gold" at the end of the rainbow. One is considered successful if he or she has many possessions or has amassed great wealth. Success is also equated with power, privilege, and prestige. For some, success is climbing the social ladder or climbing the organizational ladder. But success, as the world comprehends it, must not be the life-long goal of the believer. Jesus bids the child of God to follow Him (Luke 9:23–26), to be His disciple (Luke 14:26–27), to serve rather than be served (Matthew 20:26–28), and to find success in knowing and doing the will of God.

Key Bible References:

"This Book of the Law shall not depart from your mouth, but you shall meditate in it day and night, that you may observe to

---

[3]The Navigators, *The Character of the Christian—Design for Discipleship, Book 4,* NavPress, Colorado Springs, Colorado, 1973, p. 5.

*do according to all that is written in it. For then you will make
your way prosperous, and then you will have good success."*
Joshua 1:8

*He shall be like a tree planted by the rivers of water, that brings
forth its fruit in its season, whose leaf also shall not wither;
and whatever he does shall prosper.* Psalm 1:3

*If the ax is dull, and one does not sharpen the edge, then he
must use more strength; but wisdom brings success.* Ecclesiastes 10:10

*Not that I have already attained, or am already perfected; but I
press on, that I may lay hold on that for which Christ Jesus
has also laid hold of me.*

*Brethren, I do not count myself to have apprehended; but one
thing I do, forgetting those things which are behind and
reaching forward to those things which are ahead, I press
toward the goal for the prize of the upward call of God in
Christ Jesus.* Philippians 3:12–14

Additional References: II Chronicles 31:21; Job 9:4, 36:11; Psalm
25:12–13; Proverbs 14:12, 16:16, 28:25; Mark 8:36; II Corinthians
3:5–6.

What Others Say: Anthony Campolo, Jr., professor; and William H.
Cook, pastor, First Baptist Church, Bartlesville, Oklahoma.

Anthony Campolo, Jr.
I believe that the Christian lifestyle does deliver success to people,
but not the kind of success that is understood by society. Jesus never
promised wealth, power, and prestige to those who would follow
Him. He warned that while foxes had holes and birds had nests, the
disciples were following One who would not have a place to lay His
head (Matthew 8:20).

Jesus clearly teaches a life after death, and it is that doctrine which
forces us into a deeper understanding of success and failure . . .
when compared with eternity, success and failure cannot be understood within the context of space and time. The New Testament
makes it clear that it may be hard to perceive the rewards of a godly
life this side of heaven, but beyond the grave the "first will be last,
and the last first" (Matthew 19:30). . . . Those who forego the prestige that the world offers will be blessed in a manner that this world
cannot understand. Christians who empty themselves of the need

for power and become servants of others in the name of our Lord will experience a joy that knows no bounds.[1]

William H. Cook

Success involves the continued achievement of being the person God wants me to be, and the continued achievement of established goals which God helps me set. It is a daily process, an hourly process, a moment by moment process. It concerns my person—it is not something out there, it first concerns something within me. Success involves being right with God. Success involves achieving the maximum that can be achieved with what God has given you. It is always related to God . . . it is connected with what God wants . . . with that in mind neither my person nor my goals will miss the mark.[2]

Application: Success is defined as attaining a favorable or satisfactory outcome. Society, however, tends to link the words success or successful and prosperous or prosperity together, as though they were synonymous. Both words appear in Scripture but they are used rather sparingly. Success is often more literally interpreted as meaning to be wise or to do wisely, as in Joshua 1:8. It is usually linked to having a close relationship with God. Those who know and obey God will succeed. The child of God who knows the Word and who lives by biblical principles will thus apply this God-given wisdom to all aspects of life. He will be successful in ways that please God. Prosperity in Scripture often denotes the realization of goals (Genesis 24:21), success in labor (Genesis 39:3), and the enjoyment of familiar relationships (Ruth 4:11). The Scriptures also warn that temporal prosperity is for this life only and has no lasting value. Job said, "my prosperity has passed like a cloud" (Job 30:15). John reminds us that our labor should be invested in that which endures to everlasting life and not for things which perish (John 6:27). The apostle Paul speaks of the things which are "seen" as being only temporary but "the things which are not seen *are* eternal" (II Corinthians 4:18). Paul also cautions us that our "work" will be tried by "fire" (I Corinthians 3:12–13), that is, the believers judgment seat. Peter, in addressing believers, said of the Father, "who without partiality judges according to each one's work" (I Peter 1:17).

---

[1]Anthony Campolo, Jr., *The Success Fantasy,* Victor Books, Wheaton, Illinois, 1980, pp. 138–144.

[2]William H. Cook, *Success, Motivation and the Scriptures,* Broadman Press, Nashville, Tennessee, 1974, pp. 44–45.

The Bible clearly teaches that the biblical perspective of success is being all that God intended us to be; to know Him, love Him, worship Him, walk with Him, and serve Him with every ounce of energy we possess (Colossians 3:23). Timothy reminds us that when the Lord saved us, He also "called *us* with a holy calling, not according to our works, but according to His own purpose and grace which was given to us in Christ Jesus before time began" (II Timothy 1:9).

Every Christian must choose either to work for self or work for God. If we choose to serve God, whether within the Church or in "secular" work, our all-consuming goal must be to honor Him and bring glory to His name. Success is God-given and for His glory. The ultimate success is thus realized at the time of the believers coronation, when he stands in the very presence of God and hears, "Well *done,* good and faithful servant; . . . Enter into the joy of your lord" (Matthew 25:21).

—John Schimmer, Jr.

SUICIDE

WHAT IS GOD'S ANSWER TO SOMEONE WHO WOULD TAKE HIS OR HER OWN LIFE?

The Issue: In the past two decades there has been a dramatic change in the issue of teen suicides. The number of suicides has tripled. Over 400,000 young people attempt suicide each year which translates into an excess of 1,000 per day. 6,500 adolescents succeed each year. The increase has been attributed to numerous causes, such as: family breakups, teenage pressure to compete, hopelessness and substance abuse. Since Christians are immersed in the American culture they find themselves wrestling with the reality and implication of this serious problem.

Key Bible References:

You shall not murder. Deuteronomy 5:15

I have come that they may have life, and that they may have it more abundantly. John 10:10b

Finally, brethren, whatever things are true, whatever things are noble, whatever things are *just, whatever things* are *pure, whatever things* are *lovely, whatever things* are *of good report, if* there is *any virtue and if* there is *anything praiseworthy— meditate on these things.* Philippians 4:8

"Hold your peace with me, and let me speak, then let come on me what may!

"Why do I take my flesh in my teeth, and put my life in my hands?

"Though He slay me, yet will I trust Him. Even so, I will defend my own ways before Him." Job 13:13–15

Additional References: Psalms 42:9–10, 51; Jude 24-25

What Others Say: Thomas D. Kennedy; and Kirby Anderson.

Thomas D. Kennedy
Life is a gift from God. To take one's own life is to show insufficient gratitude. Our lives belong to God; we are but stewards. To end my own life is to usurp that perogative which is God's alone. Suicide, the church has taught, is ordinarily a rejection of the goodness of God and it can never be right to reject God's goodness.[1]

Kirby Anderson
Here is a valuable quote . . . "Christians should take note of the important relationship between suicide and secularism. Many of the factors in the rise in teen suicide are the result of society's turn from God to self. Broken families, loss of community, and alcohol and drug abuse are all results of this shift and are also key contributors to the epidemic of teen suicide. While we should focus due attention on suicide prevention, the ultimate solutions are not psychological, but spiritual. Teen suicide is but one of the many bitter fruits borne by a society that has turned its back on God."[2]

Application: We live in a broken, hurting world. Sin has always produced that which is destructive and painful. Suicide is a result of sin. All throughout history, suicide has played a significant role, notably in the lives of many famous historical figures. Even in the Bible, we have recorded seven suicides. Judas, Saul, and Samson are the most well-known. Of these, the death of Samson at his own hand is the most difficult to interpret.

---

[1]Thomas D. Kennedy, "Suicide," *Christianity Today,* March 20, 1987, p. 23.
[2]Kirby Anderson, "Teenage Suicide, An Epidemic of Despair," *Moody Monthly,* February, 1987, p. 21.

Scripture never condones or approves of suicide. Rather, the whole focus of Scripture is *LIFE directed*. Words like hope, joy, peace, and faith are the marks of the life in Christ. In spite of this, even Christians commit suicide. Since Scripture only identifies that suicide is as forgivable by God as any other of the Ten Commandments, it is significant that research clearly teaches that people with biblical faith are far less likely to attempt a suicide.

—**Kenneth H. Tanis**

TELEVISION

WHAT IS A CHRISTIAN PERSPECTIVE OF TELEVISION?

The Issue: Tim LaHaye says, "Television is the most powerful assault on the human mind ever invented."[1]

Television clearly impacts our thought lives. Our thought lives, of course, determine our character. Solomon wrote, "For as he thinks in his heart, so *is* he" (Proverbs 23:7). We are responsible to God for what our ears hear and what our eyes see. Because television simultaneously involves the two principal human senses, hearing and sight, it has double the impact over other media sources such as print materials or radio.

Christians do not become stronger Christians by being exposed to non-Christian thought. Regrettably, most television programming does not meet the biblical standard for Christian consumption. The issue is—What is a Christian to do about non-Christian television?

Key Bible References:

"The lamp of the body is the eye. If therefore your eye is good, your whole body will be full of light.

"But if your eye is bad, your whole body will be full of darkness. If therefore the light that is in you is darkness, how great is that darkness!" Matthew 6:22–23

Finally, brethren, whatever things are true, whatever things are noble, whatever things are just, whatever things are pure, whatever things are lovely, whatever things are of good report, if there is any virtue and if there is anything praiseworthy—meditate on these things. Philippians 4:8

297

And do not be conformed to this world, but be transformed by the renewing of your mind, that you may prove what is that good and acceptable and perfect will of God. Romans 12:2

Therefore be followers of God as dear children.

And walk in love, as Christ also has loved us and given Himself for us, an offering and a sacrifice to God for a sweet-smelling aroma.

But fornication and all uncleanness or covetousness, let it not even be named among you, as is fitting for saints; neither filthiness, nor foolish talking, nor coarse jesting, which are not fitting, but rather giving of thanks.

For this you know, that no fornicator, unclean person, nor covetous man, who is an idolater, has any inheritance in the kingdom of Christ and God.

Let no one deceive you with empty words, for because of these things the wrath of God comes upon the sons of disobedience.

Therefore do not be partakers with them. Ephesians 5:1–7

Additional References: Proverbs 1:1–10; Matthew 7:17; Colossians 2:23.

What Others Say: Dr. Tim LaHaye, author and president of Family Life Seminars; Franky Schaeffer, Christian film maker and artist; and Jerry Bridges, vice president of The Navigators in Colorado Springs, Colorado.

Tim LaHaye
(1) Establish TV viewing as a privilege, not a right; consequently, the owner of the set has the option to regulate and approve its use.
(2) Only approved programs may be watched . . . news, sports, religious programs, public affairs, appropriate specials, and clean family programs (if you can find any).
(3) Set time limits for viewing. One or two hours a night of even morally neutral programming can adversely affect children at certain grade levels. Television can be a great time waster.

---

[1]Tim LaHaye, *The Race for the 21st Century,* Thomas Nelson Publishers, Nashville, Tennessee, 1986, p. 173.

(4) Once a program has violated your moral values, scratch it off your list. That violation is an indication of the kinds of programs you can expect in the future.

(5) Create alternatives to TV. After dinner, devotions, a game or two, a project, perhaps the evening news, homework, and bed time can complete any day's agenda.

The key to success is planning. If you don't control the television set, it will control you and your family.[2]

Franky Schaeffer

No TV, at least any level that can be called regular watching. Genie and I read works we consider to be of pleasurable literary value to them out loud each evening (easy to find—the English language is rich in children's and other literature). We try to bring them up to higher standards instead of talking down to them (as television thrives upon doing). We try to present as wide a panorama of culture exposure as is possible, and express something of the diverse beauty of God's world and his creatures' creation.

We try to offer honest answers to their questions, including "I don't know" when we don't. In reading the Bible to them, we don't skip the awkward parts. By the time the child has had Genesis, Exodus, First and Second Samuel read to him, there is nothing he doesn't know about![3]

Jerry Bridges

Jesus taught us in the Sermon on the Mount that God's commandments are intended not only to regulate outward conduct, but inner disposition as well. It is not enough that we do not kill; we must also not hate. It is not enough that we do not commit adultery; we must not even entertain lustful looks and thoughts.

Just as we must learn to bring the appetites of our bodies under control, so we must also learn to bring our thought lives under obedience to Jesus Christ. In fact, Paul warns us against misguided and wrongly motivated attempts to control the body that leave our thought lives unrestrained (Colossians 2:23). It is possible to curb the natural appetites of the body outwardly and yet be filled with all manner of inner defilement.[4]

---

[2]Ibid., p. 174.

[3]Franky Schaeffer, *Addicted to Mediocrity: 20th Century Christians and The Arts,* Cornerstone Books, Westchester, Illinois, 1981, p. 112.

[4]Jerry Bridges, *The Pursuit of Holiness,* NavPress, Colorado Springs, Colorado, 1978, pp. 117–119.

The television programs we watch, the movies we may attend, the books and magazines we read, the music we listen to, and the conversations we have, all affect our minds. We need to evaluate the effects of these avenues honestly, using Philippians 4:8 as a standard. Are the thoughts stimulated by these various avenues true? Are they pure? Lovely? Admirable, excellent, or praiseworthy?[5]

Application: Immorality is learned and television is an effective teacher of immorality. One seldom becomes immoral all at once. It happens over time. The Bible speaks of the basic human learning process as ". . . precept upon precept, line upon line . . ." (Isaiah 28:10). This applies to learning evil things as well as good things. Solomon said, "Keep your heart with all diligence, for out of it spring the issues of life" (Proverbs 4:23). In other words, guard your mind from vile programming on television and other media sources because from your mind your character is taking shape.

—Paul A. Kienel

TEMPTATION

WHAT DOES THE BIBLE SAY ABOUT TEMPTATION?

The Issue: Temptation is often confused with trials. Trials, which come from God, include hardships and difficulties. When these trials are successfully endured by the Christian, they result in stronger faith. However, temptations, which never come from God, are Satan's master plan for destroying fellowship within God's kingdom and creating discord within the lives of individuals.

Key Bible References:

No temptation has overtaken you except such as is common to man; but God is faithful, who will not allow you to be tempted beyond what you are able, but with the temptation will also make the way of escape, that you may be able to bear it.
I Corinthians 10:13

---

[5]Ibid., p. 119.

My brethren, count it all joy when you fall into various trials, knowing that the testing of your faith produces patience. James 1:2–3

Blessed is *the man who endures temptation; for when he has been proved, he will receive the crown of life which the Lord has promised to those who love Him.*

Let no one say when he is tempted, "I am tempted by God"; for God cannot be tempted by evil, nor does He Himself tempt anyone.

But each one is tempted when he is drawn away by his own desires and enticed.

Then, when desire has conceived, it gives birth to sin; and sin, when it is full-grown, brings forth death. James 1:12–15

Additional References: Matthew 4:1–11, 6:13, 26:41; Mark 14:38; Luke 8:13; I Timothy 6:9; Hebrews 4:15; I Peter 1:6–7; II Peter 2:9; I John 2:16.

What Others Say: Dr. Charles Stanley; Dr. Henry M. Morris and Martin E. Clark; and Anne and Ray Ortlund.

Charles Stanley

First of all, a defeating habit in your life will rob you of your confidence in the power of God to give people victory over sin. . . . Another reason is that choosing not to deal with sin ultimately leads to what Scripture calls a hard heart. . . . A third reason is that one sin always leads to another. . . . A final reason is that sin always results in death of some kind. James gives us an equation: Temptation + Sin = Death.[1]

Henry M. Morris and Martin E. Clark

The first thing the Christian must learn is that God does not lead him to sin. The apostle James clearly condemns the attitude of blaming God for tempting circumstances (James 1:13–15). God may test His children, a process designed to purify and strengthen them, but He does not lead them into sin. Without exception, sin results when Satan's temptation strikes a sympathetic chord in the human heart, and man has no one to blame but himself.[2]

---

[1]Charles Stanley, *Temptation*, Oliver-Nelson Books, Nashville, Tennessee, 1988, pp. 12–15.

[2]Henry M. Morris and Martin E. Clark, *The Bible Has The Answer*, Creation Life Publishers, San Diego, California, 1976, p. 237.

Satan will come after you in the fiercest temptations. He'll attack you in your three areas of weakness:

    (1) The lust or the cravings of the flesh: sexual immorality, overeating, addictive habits, laziness. . . .

    (2) The lust or the cravings of your eyes: excessive desires for beauty of any kind—cars, interior decoration, clothes, other persons of the opposite sex. . . .

    (3) The pride of life: overgrown appetites for money, status, or power, which lead to jealousy, slander, cheating, and "every form of malice" (Ephesians 4:31).[3]

Application: It is important for the Christian to understand that Satan is at war with God and his master battle plan is temptation. Through temptation, Satan attempts to destroy fellowship within the kingdom of God and create defeat and destruction within the lives of individuals. Victory over temptation can only be achieved through the Christian remaining vigilant in his daily walk with Christ. As Paul states in Ephesians, chapter six, we must put on the whole armor of God that we may stand against the wiles of the devil.

In addition, the Christian should keep in mind that temptation, within itself, is not sin. Sin only results when we yield to temptation. Christ was tempted by Satan in all areas but was victorious. His victory was through applying God's Word and through renewing His fellowship with His Father through daily prayer.

—**Joel Farlow**

TITHING

SHOULD CHRISTIANS TITHE?

The Issue: Many people believe Christians should tithe, that is, give ten percent of their income to the Lord. Some churches go as far as to require that their members tithe to the local church. Tithing was required under the Old Testament law. Is it binding on New Testa-

---

[3]Anne and Ray Ortlund, *Staying Power,* Oliver-Nelson Books, Nashville, Tennessee, 1986, p. 101.

ment believers, or do we conclude that we needn't tithe because we are "not under law but under grace" (Romans 6:14)?

Key Bible References:

"And all the tithe of the land, whether of the seed of the land or of the fruit of the tree, is the LORD'S. It is holy to the LORD.

"And concerning the tithe of the herd or the flock, of whatever passes under the rod, the tenth one shall be holy to the LORD.

"He shall not inquire whether it is good or bad, nor shall he exchange it; . . ." Leviticus 27:30, 32–33

"You shall truly tithe all the increase of your grain that the field produces year by year.

"And you shall eat before the LORD your God, in the place where He chooses to make His name abide, the tithe of your grain and your new wine and your oil, of the firstlings of your herds and your flocks, that you may learn to fear the LORD your God always.

"But if the journey is too long for you, so that you are not able to carry the tithe, or if the place where the LORD your God chooses to put His name is too far from you, when the LORD your God has blessed you, then you shall exchange it for money, take the money in your hand, and go to the place which the LORD your God chooses." Deuteronomy 14:22–25

"Bring all the tithes into the storehouse, that there may be food in My house, and prove Me now in this," says the LORD of hosts, "if I will not open for you the windows of heaven and pour out for you such blessing that there will not be room enough to receive it." Malachi 3:10

Now Jesus sat opposite the treasury and saw how the people put money into the treasury. And many who were rich put in much.

Then one poor widow came and threw in two mites, which make a quadrans.

So He called His disciples to Him and said to them, "Assuredly, I say to you that this poor widow has put in more than all those who have given to the treasury; for they all put in out of their abundance, but she out of her poverty put in all that she had, her whole livelihood." Mark 12:41–44

Additional References: Genesis 14:20; Numbers 18:21; Deuteronomy 12:6, 16:17; II Samuel 24:24; I Chronicles 29:9, 16; Proverbs 3:9–10, 11:24–25; Matthew 6:2–4, 19–20; II Corinthians 8:15, 9:6–8, 10–11.

What Others Say: Gene A. Getz, pastor of Fellowship Bible Church North in Plano, Texas and director of the Center for Church Renewal; and Ron Blue, Certified Public Accountant, financial planning and money management consultant.

Gene A. Getz

In both the Old and New Testaments, God teaches that giving should be systematic and regular. . . . This focuses an important question. What percentage should a Christian set aside on a consistent basis from his regular income? The Holy Spirit did not lead New Testament writers to reiterate and perpetuate the Old Testament pattern involving specific amounts and percentages. But even though Christians are not obligated to follow the [Old Testament tithing] system . . . [it] provides believers with a strong pragmatic model for evaluating their own giving patterns. . . . One thing is crystal clear: If Christians gave the same amounts to the church as the Jews gave to maintain their religious system, there would never be unmet economic needs in the ministry.[1]

Ron Blue

How much to give in quantitative terms is not as important as our attitude toward giving. . . . Through a consideration of the three P's . . . we can come to a right answer of how much: we should give *proportionately* on a *planned* basis, and on a *precommitted* basis. Give an amount that is proportionate to the amount that God has prospered you. You should, by planning, give more than a proportionate amount, and you should precommit to give some of the amount God provides on a totally unexpected basis.[2]

Application: Leviticus 27:30–33 required every Israelite to pay a tenth of all his income annually to support the priesthood. Deuteronomy 12:6–17 and 14:22–27 were understood by rabbinical scholars as requiring a second tithe, given annually to fund the national holidays and feasts. Deuteronomy 14:28–29 speaks of a third tithe, given every third year, to support the nation's poor. So those who lived under Old Testament law were required to give *more* than a tenth—actually about 23.3 percent. The funds supported Israel's theocratic government and constituted a tax not unlike our income taxes.

---

[1]Gene A. Getz, *Real Prosperity: Biblical Principals of Material Possessions,* Moody Press, Chicago, Illinois, 1990, pp. 118–119.

[2]Ron Blue, *Master Your Money,* Thomas Nelson Publishers, Nashville, Tennessee, 1986, pp. 220–222.

In addition to required tithes, the Israelites gave *freewill* offerings to God. Personal gifts to God Himself were always voluntary. No percentage or amount was ever specified, but each person gave whatever was in his heart to give (Deuteronomy 16:7; Exodus 25:2; I Chronicles 29:9; Ezra 1:6, 2:68–69, 7:16; Proverbs 11:24–25). These freewill gifts were *in addition* to the required tithe. The Tabernacle was built through freewill giving (Exodus 25:1–2, 35:5, 21, 36:5–7).

Scripture never speaks of Christians' giving to the local church as a tithe. Nor is tithing ever commanded in the New Testament. What Christians give to the Lord is always a freewill offering, not a tax. The clearest New Testament guideline for giving is II Corinthians 9:6–7: "But this *I say:* He who sows sparingly will also reap sparingly, and he who sows bountifully will also reap bountifully. *So let* each one *give* as he purposes in his heart, not grudgingly or of necessity; for God loves a cheerful giver."

—John MacArthur

TRANSCENDENTAL MEDITATION

WHAT IS THE BIBLE'S ANSWER TO TRANSCENDENTAL MEDITATION?

The Issue: Transcendental Meditation (The Science of Creative Intelligence) was founded in India by Maharishi Mahesh Yogi in 1958 and came to the United States the following year. Promising a sense of inner peace and well being, the movement was very popular in the 1960s and 1970s.

While claiming to be "nonreligious," Transcendental Meditation (TM) involves several practices and ideas taken from Hinduism. Participants take part in a ceremony that includes burning incense, offering fruits and flowers on an altar and offering a handkerchief to Guru Dev. During this ceremony, new converts also receive their personal "mantra," a nonsense word to be repeated over and over again during the daily meditation times.

In a 1977 court decision, TM was ruled to be a religion and as a result lost government funding for use in public schools and the military. It has gradually declined in popularity since that time, but still has many followers today.

Key Bible References:

"This Book of the Law shall not depart from your mouth, but you shall meditate in it day and night, that you may observe to do according to all that is written in it. For then you will make your way prosperous, and then you will have good success.
Joshua 1:8

I will also meditate on all Your work, and talk of Your deeds.
Psalm 77:12

I will meditate on Your precepts and contemplate Your ways.
Psalm 119:15

Let the words of my mouth and the meditation of my heart be acceptable in Your sight, O LORD, my strength and my redeemer.
Psalm 19:14

Additional References: Psalm 5:1–3; Matthew 12:30; Romans 12:2; Colossians 3:2.

What Others Say: Josh McDowell, author and lecturer and professor at Simon Greenleaf School of Law and Don Stewart, pastor-at-large of Calvary Chapel, Costa Mesa, California and professor at Simon Greenleaf School of Law.

Josh McDowell and Don Stewart
Transcendental Meditation (The Science of Creative Intelligence), though claiming to be a method of relaxation and personal growth without harmful side effects, can be a danger to the individual both emotionally and spiritually. Although some degree of success in relaxation can be achieved by practicing TM, the dangers far outweigh the benefits. There is a Christian alternative to TM and that consists of meditation on God's Word, the only source of real peace.[1]

Application: The fast pace of today's society has many people looking for ways to reduce stress and achieve inner peace. The Bible speaks clearly to both of these areas. First, any individual can have inner peace through a relationship with Jesus Christ. While not promising to remove life's difficulties, the Bible guarantees that "the peace of God, which surpasses all understanding, will guard your hearts and minds through Christ Jesus" (Philippians 4:7) if we bring our concerns to Him in prayer.

---

[1]Josh McDowell and Don Stewart, *Understanding the Cults,* Here's Life Publishing Company, San Bernadino, California. 1982, p. 111.

Second, biblical meditation will help to deepen a believer's relationship with God and improve his or her understanding of God's Word. This is accomplished by selecting a passage of Scripture and quietly reflecting on its content and meaning. While repeating the verses or reading them aloud, the truth they contain speaks to the believer. This process allows the Holy Spirit to reprove, correct, and instruct in righteousness (see II Timothy 3:16). Only meditation focused on God's Word will bring true peace and inner harmony to a person's life.

—**Michael E. Marrapodi**

TRUSTWORTHINESS

WHY IS TRUSTWORTHINESS ESSENTIAL TO THE BELIEVER'S TESTIMONY?

The Issue: No longer can it be assumed that a man will keep his word. In fact, most people cannot be trusted to do what they say. Trustworthiness, a term closely related to reliability, is a characteristic of people that is no longer held in high esteem in our society.

The effectiveness of a Christian's testimony is directly related to his trustworthiness. Christ's life and work was the perfect example of biblical trustworthiness. As a Christian, we must always strive to manifest perfect trustworthiness. In our families, with our friends, and in the workplace, Christians must keep their commitments at all costs.

Key Bible References:

It is *better not to vow than to vow and not pay.* Ecclesiastes 5:5

"If a man vows a vow to the LORD, or swears an oath to bind himself by some agreement, he shall not break his word; he shall do according to all that proceeds out of his mouth." Numbers 30:2

So the governors and satraps sought to find some *charge against Daniel concerning the kingdom; but they could find no charge or fault, because he* was *faithful; nor was there any error or fault found in him.* Daniel 6:4

Additional References: Psalm 15:1–2; Ephesians 4:25; Colossians 3:17; II Timothy 4:2.

What Others Say: Charles R. Swindoll, pastor of the Evangelical Free Church in Fullerton, California; and Michael Youssef, executive director of the Haggai Institute For Advanced Leadership Training in Atlanta, Georgia.

Charles R. Swindoll

Whether an executive or an apprentice, a student or a teacher, a blue or white collar worker, a Christian or a pagan—rare indeed are those who keep their word. The prevalence of the problem has caused the coining of terms painfully familiar to us in our era: *credibility gap.* To say that something is "credible" is to say it is "capable of being believed, trustworthy." To refer to a "gap" in such suggests a "breach or a reason for doubt." This is a terrible dilemma! Precious few do what they *say* they will do without a reminder, a warning, or a threat. Unfortunately, this is true even among Christians.[1]

Michael Youssef

Originally the oath referred only to serious matters, such as those dealing with life and death. As time went on, people started using the oath frivolously.

Among Arabs of today in the Middle East, I have heard oaths sworn for the most meaningless purposes. Once while I bargained with a tradesman for a curio of less than two dollars' value, he declared, "This is my final price. On the honor of God, I can go no lower. Already I make no profit on this sale. I swear by my God."

We both knew he was lying. Eventually he came down a few more cents on his "final" price. His oath meant nothing.

In contrast, Jesus said in the Sermon on the Mount, "Do not swear at all. . . . But let your *Yes* be *Yes* and your *No, No.* For whatever is more than these is from the evil one" (Matthew 5:34, 37).[2]

Application: Individuals who manifest trustworthiness stand in sharp contrast to the world around them. Trustworthiness: A living model of patience, determination, strength—regardless of shifty, rootless times. Trustworthiness thrives on sacrifice and unselfishness. It is never held captive to the whim or to circumstances. It is an obvious mark of maturity.

---

[1]Charles R. Swindoll, *Growing Strong in the Seasons of Life,* Multnomah Press, Portland, Oregon, 1983, pp. 203–204.

[2]Michael Youssef, *The Leadership Style of Jesus,* Victor Books, Wheaton, Illinois, 1986, p. 78.

One of the most wonderful, magnetic characteristics of the Lord Jesus Christ is His trustworthiness. When you need Him, He is there. "Jesus Christ *is* the same yesterday, today, and forever" (Hebrews 13:8). He's there even when you don't think you need Him! You're never too early or late. He's always available because He says He will be. He's trustworthy.

—**Ollie E. Gibbs and Thomas (Mickey) Bowdon**

UNDISCIPLINE

WHAT IS THE OUTCOME OF AN UNDISCIPLINED PERSON?

The Issue: Many people live a very undisciplined lifestyle. An undisciplined person is one who lacks or has limited self-control. Such a person is quite self-centered. Present day society is influenced by Humanism—a religion, along with other ideas, that teaches that man is responsible only to himself, which then leads to a self-centered way of life. Many factors may be involved in shaping such a person. He may have had a very poor home life, with little or no discipline. He may have had poor role models, who allowed him to do whatever he wished. Also, there may be sin in his life that has not been forgiven. These things result in selfishness and lack of self-discipline.

Key Bible References:

The fear of the LORD is the beginning of knowledge, but fools despise wisdom and instruction. Proverbs 1:7

He shall die for lack of instruction, and in the greatness of his folly he shall go astray. Proverbs 5:23

Go to the ant, you sluggard! Consider her ways and be wise, . . . Proverbs 6:6

For God has not given us a spirit of fear, but of power and of love and of a sound mind. II Timothy 1:7

Additional References: Proverbs 1:32, 13:18, 19:15, 25:28; Matthew 25:1–13.

What Others Say: Charles R. Swindoll, pastor of the Evangelical Free Church in Fullerton, California; and Henry Hildebrand, founder and chancellor of Briercrest Bible College.

Charles R. Swindoll

The overindulgence and underachievement of our age have created a monster whose brain is lazy, vision is blurred, hands are greedy, skin is thin, middle is round, and seat is wide. Color him baby blue!

What has spawned this strange, pillowy product? The Greeks would say: "A serious lack of enkrateia." That isn't a vitamin; it's a virtue—self-control.[1]

Henry Hildebrand

Discipline is an important requirement of leadership. J. Oswald Sanders places discipline as leadership's first quality, for without it the other gifts, however great, will never realize their highest possibilities. Only the disciplined person will rise to the occasion. He is able to lead others because he has first learned to follow.[2]

Application: The undisciplined person frequently is not receptive to instruction. He has difficulty accepting responsibilities and often is not dependable. Such a person either lacks goals or fails to achieve them with a reasonable degree of success. The lack of preparation and commitment leads to indifference and laziness. He is often a "flat person"; he lacks initiative and allows things like television to control his life. He also has difficulties in his relationships with others.

Furthermore, an undisciplined person is likely to have chaos in his life (Proverbs 1:7), and that is contrary to the principles of victorious living as found in God's Word.

God desires that all have a ". . . spirit of power, of love and of self-discipline," II Timothy 1:7 (NIV)

—Ed Balzer

---

[1]Charles R. Swindoll, *Come before Winter and . . . ,* Tyndale House Publishers, Wheaton, Illinois, 1985, p. 328.

[2]Henry Hildebrand, *Contemporary Leadership Dynamics,* Briercrest Books, Caronport, Saskatchewan, Canada, 1987, p. 70.

UNEQUALLY YOKED

SHOULD CHRISTIANS MARRY NON-CHRISTIANS?

The Issue: Marriage is a lot of hard work even for couples who seem to agree or appear "compatible" in many areas. Couples need all the help they can get and marrying a non-Christian can bring more stress and difficulty into the relationship. Having a common faith, while no guarantee of marital success, certainly helps settle many battles that could arise, such as church attendance, baptism, raising and discipling children, tithing, and ministry. Being of the same faith and purpose often produces common life goals that are so vital to a couple working together to succeed in their marriage.

Surprisingly, according to 900 teenagers surveyed, 88% of girls and 89% of boys said they definitely or probably would date someone of another religion. And about 69% of them actually have.[1]

Key Bible References:

Can two walk together, unless they are agreed? Amos 3:3

Do not be unequally yoked together with unbelievers. For what fellowship has righteousness with lawlessness? And what communion has light with darkness? II Corinthians 6:14

Additional References: Genesis 24:3, 28:1; Deuteronomy 7:3; Joshua 23:12–13; Ezra 9:12; Nehemiah 13:25.

What Others Say: Dr. Clyde M. Narramore, psychologist, author, and president of Narramore Christian Foundation; and Greg Speck, author and youth specialist with Moody Bible Institute.

Clyde M. Narramore

Admittedly, life—and marriage—may not *always* be a bed of roses, but there is absolutely no need for a marriage to become a field of battle. If Christian partners know a lot about each other before their marriage and if their marriage rests firmly on Biblical precepts, they will be better able to deal with problems as they arise.

---

[1]Eugene C. Roehlkepartain, *The Youth Ministry Resource Book,* Group Books, Loveland, Colorado, 1988, p. 44.

They will be able to gain from their mutual gifts and become a blessing to each other and to their children.[2]

Greg Speck

Don't settle for anything less than a godly man or woman. You have trusted Jesus Christ with your eternity; so you can trust Him with your dating relationships. If you will be patient, God will supply![3]

Application: Marriage is a relationship that develops with the contributions of both and when only one spouse desires to center their living in Christ a resistance often occurs from the other partner.

When two Christians enter into a sacred vow and covenant to put God first in both of their lives it casts a different focus on the entire direction and purpose the couple takes.

We are beings with the capacity for three dimensions to our lives; the spirit, soul, and body. Without Christ, our lives are spiritually dead and we are incapable of dealing with spiritual matters. Marriage must deal with spiritual needs, as well as soul (emotions), and body (physical). Without Christ we cannot understand God and His work in our spiritual life. God is able to save the unbeliever in all circumstances but we are not guaranteed that the unsaved individual will respond positively to the need of salvation. Placing ourselves in a situation that could lead to marriage with a non-Christian is veering off the path of Christ-centered living.

—Connie Mena

UNWED MOTHERS

WHAT SHOULD THE CHRISTIAN'S ATTITUDE BE TOWARD UNWED MOTHERS?

The Issue: Pregnancy outside of marriage is rampant in our present-day society. It is a major national, moral, and social dilemma. While looking for an easy way out, hundreds of thousands of young women, along with their preborn babies, have become the victims of

---

[2]Clyde M. Narramore, *Parents At Their Best,* Thomas Nelson Publishers, Nashville, Tennessee, 1985, p. 50.
[3]Greg Speck, *Sex: It's Worth Waiting For,* Moody Press, Chicago, Illinois, 1989, p. 215.

legalized abortion in our beloved country. Legalized abortion has become the key issue in nearly every political arena of recent years.

The rise of "positive alternative to abortion" ministries all across the country have helped thousands of young women with a crisis pregnancy. The options of parenting or placing the child in a loving Christian family have become the primary choices for those who respect the dignity of human life. This leads us to four distinct categories of unwed mothers: (1) Those who are currently pregnant; (2) parenting the child; (3) have aborted; or (4) placed for adoption. A discussion of these categories follows.

Key Bible References:

Brethren, if a man is overtaken in any trespass, you who are spiritual restore such a one in a spirit of gentleness, considering yourself lest you also be tempted.

Bear one another's burdens, and so fulfill the law of Christ.

For if anyone thinks himself to be something, when he is nothing, he deceives himself.

But let each one examine his own work, and then he will have rejoicing in himself alone, and not in another.

For each one shall bear his own load.

Let him who is taught the word share in all good things with him who teaches.

Do not be deceived, God is not mocked; for whatever a man sows, that he will also reap.

For he who sows to his flesh will of the flesh reap corruption, but he who sows to the Spirit will of the Spirit reap everlasting life.

And let us not grow weary while doing good, for in due season we shall reap if we do not lose heart. Galatians 6:1–9

Additional References: John 8:1–11; Romans 12:1–3; I John 2:1.

What Others Say: George Grant, author and leader.

George Grant
Planned Parenthood has been able to prevail over the Church simply because believers have allowed themselves to become assimilated into a corrupt and promiscuous culture.

The notion that it is primarily "rank heathens" or "flaming liberals" who are aborting their future away simply doesn't hold up under the facts.[1]

Application:

(1) Those who are currently pregnant: We must lift up the love and forgiveness of God for those who have been taken in a fault (Galatians 6:1). They must be motivated to use this as a time of true commitment to Christ by the unconditional love of God and His people; that God is truly the God of the second chance. This is where the Christian maternity care ministry fits in as a positive alternative to abortion. Our attitude toward young women who are currently pregnant should be one of compassion and direction. We should direct them to one of the crisis pregnancy ministries where they can receive specialized help at this critical time in their lives.

(2) Those who parent: Single parenting is very difficult but it is a far better alternative than abortion. We must encourage and assist the young mother who is parenting. She has made the correct choice to allow the baby to live; we should praise her on that point. The focus of her life is now consumed with taking care of her child. Periodic help with child care and support to assist her in the attainment of her personal goals are major needs facing her at this time. Critical concerns are the completion of her educational goals coupled with employment for financial support. The church must be her center of support emotionally, spiritually, and physically. She should be included in the church family with the view that God will provide her the husband of His choice at the proper time.

(3) Those who have aborted: We should embrace the unwed mother who is the victim of legalized abortion with deep compassion. A great number of these mothers experience post-abortion syndrome. These women need specialized therapy to facilitate working through this traumatic experience. Experiencing the forgiveness of God followed by specialized individual and group therapy is the best course of action.

---

[1]George Grant, *Grand Illusions, The Legacy of Planned Parenthood,* Wolgemuth and Hyatt Publishers, Brentwood, Tennessee, 1988, p. 201.

(4) Those who place for adoption: A birth mother who places a child for adoption with a loving Christian family makes a mature, loving choice. This decision grows out of a deep commitment to God's divine will for both mother and child. This decision is very difficult, requiring professional counseling to support the birth mother.

The birth mother who places a child for adoption is usually characterized by a maturity which not only recognizes God's leading but is also desirous for the family relationship enhanced by a Christian mother *and* father which is not afforded through single parenting. Our attitude toward the unwed mother who has placed should be one of understanding support. This mother is typically future-oriented and needs support in achieving her ultimate goals in life.

—Norman Pratt

VALUES

HOW ARE CHRISTIAN VALUES SUCCESSFULLY TAUGHT TO CHILDREN?

The Issue: Developing Christian values begins at home. A Christian family must make an intentional commitment to develop its lifestyle around biblical principles rather than around worldly standards. Unless such a commitment is made, the children do not have much of a chance of growing up with Christian roots. Society, the media, and peer pressure is so strong and full of worldly values that without a solid Christian family base, success is minimal for a Christian child. The teaching of the lifestyle of Christ begins with the role modeling of the parent based on the values that Christ taught. A child isn't really interested in the results of value-teaching, but in seeing the daily practice of Christian values as modeled by those he loves and admires. The family-life model will teach Christian truth and values more effectively than any words or instruction given. In other words what parents say and what parents do must agree.

Also, parents need assistance in the teaching of the Judeo-Christian value-base for their children. Two great resources available are the church and the Christian school. Firsthand involvement in a solid Bible-teaching church and the daily biblical teaching that can be experienced in a Christian school are tremendous tools available for the Christian parent. The role of the church is to provide support and stability to the family as it grows in spiritual values and maturity. This is also true of the Christian school. With the role modeling of the parents, the support and influence of the church, and the daily teaching experienced in a Christian school, a solid biblical base for Christian values will be provided.

This threefold process experienced over a standard eighteen-year child-raising period can provide the teaching of those Christian values cherished by Christ and desired by the Christian parents. Both God and the parents will be pleased with the results.

Key Bible References:

Therefore be followers of God as dear children.

And walk in love, as Christ also has loved us and given Himself for us, an offering and a sacrifice to God for a sweet-smelling aroma. Ephesians 5:1–2

Train up a child in the way he should go, and when he is old he will not depart from it. Proverbs 22:6

. . . Give instruction to a wise man, and he will be still wiser; teach a just man, and he will increase in learning.

"The fear of the LORD is the beginning of wisdom, and the knowledge of the Holy One is understanding." Proverbs 9:9–10

Additional References: Ecclesiastes 12:13–14; II Corinthians 3:2; Ephesians 5:15–17, 6:7–8, 12.

What Others Say: Tim LaHaye, founder and president of Family Life Seminars, pastor, founder of San Diego Christian Unified School System and Christian Heritage College; and Cal Thomas, twenty-eight-year veteran of broadcast and print journalism.

Tim LaHaye

Those Christians who seriously use their churches, the Word of God, and the ministry of the Holy Spirit will still be able to raise their families to love and serve God. It won't be easy, but historically, it never has been. This world system has always been opposed to the will and ways of God. Consequently, raising Christian children has always taken prayer, love, training, and sacrifice. The most powerful ring of insulation against the attacks . . . is your spiritual resources, the church, the Christian family model, and the Christian school.[1]

Cal Thomas

The measure and value of a person do not consist of the sum total of the material and disposable things he accumulates during the course of his life. Rather it consists of the level of his integrity with God, with his family, and with those who know him.

The late philosopher-theologian, Dr. Francis Schaeffer, illustrated this when he spoke of a giant ash heap near his home when he lived in St. Louis. He said he would often think that the ash heap was a monument to the folly of fallen humanity, who work all their lives just to acquire things that ultimately will be burned and produce a smell so putrid that no one wants to go near it.

If we want to produce people who share the values of a Christian democratic culture, they must be taught those values and not be left to acquire them by chance.[2]

Application: Values are developed with doctrine and reproof. The effects of this style of child-raising can be life-changing. For example, a study that was done by a professor at the University of Nebraska showed very clearly that people today are what they are because of the experiences and what they were taught during those early years. In the process of the study, it was found that all the values and doctrines that are taught between the ages of one and ten, subconsciously lock-in at age ten. In other words, the subconscious looks around at age ten and says, "This is the way life is" and then it accepts it. The study said that at this point, the values and doctrinal beliefs will not change unless there is a strong outside emotional stimulus. For example, a strong outside emotional stimulus could be a broken arm, the death of a favorite pet, or a serious car accident. Unless a strong emotional stimulus happens, the values taught up to age ten are locked in. This principle is a good reminder of the verse, "Train up a child in the way he should go, and when he is old he will not depart from it" (Proverbs 22:6).

The study continued and this same subconscious experience happens again during the teenage years and locks in at around age twenty-one. During these periods of time, ownership of convictions are taking place. These convictions are only as good as the informa-

[1]Tim LaHaye, *The Battle for the Family,* Fleming H. Revell Company, Old Tappan, New Jersey, pp. 207, 219, 222.

[2]Cal Thomas, *The Death of Ethics in America,* Word Books, Publisher, Waco, Texas, 1988, pp. 62, 102.

tion that has been taught. Good solid biblical doctrines must be taught and then reinforced as the student goes through emotional experiences. Once the child claims ownership of a Bible doctrine, he is on his way to Christian maturity. (By the way, I asked the professor if the salvation experience would be considered an emotional stimulus. The instructor was not a Christian—in fact, I was the only Christian in the class. I already knew the answer but I was curious to hear his answer.) His answer was a strong and definite, yes. In fact, he said that a child who has had a "religious experience" usually makes major changes in his life's view and belief. Another verse came to mind: "... but with God all things are possible" (Matthew 19:26b).

Christian families must be God-centered in their teachings (Deuteronomy 6:4–9). The long-term effect of such teaching is sound convictions and this will, in turn, begin to alter family living and produce strong values in the lives of the children.

—Thomas A. Scott

WILL OF GOD

HOW DO CHRISTIANS DETERMINE THE WILL OF GOD?

The Issue: Among Christians one of the most challenging and frequently asked questions is "How can I know the will of God in individual decisions?" God's sovereign will is God's predetermined plan for everything that transpires in His universe. God's moral will is revealed through His moral commands in the Scriptures which teach believers how to believe and live. The difficult one is God's individual will, the life plan which God has uniquely planned for each believer.

The traditional view is expressed as "sign posts" for guiding the individual Christian: The Word of God, the inner witness of the Holy Spirit, mature counsel, personal inclination, circumstances and common sense. These "sign posts" must line up harmoniously for guidance.

Gary Friesen wrote an alternative view, the way of wisdom:
　　(1) In those areas specifically addressed by the Bible, the re-

vealed commands and principles of God (His moral will) are to be obeyed.

(2) In those areas where the Bible gives no command or principle (nonmoral decisions), the believer is free and responsible to choose his own course of action. Any decision made within the moral will of God is acceptable to God.

(3) In nonmoral decisions, the objective of the Christian is to make wise decisions on the basis of spiritual expediency.

(4) In all decisions, the believer should humbly submit, in advance, to the outworking of God's sovereign will as it touches each decision.[1]

Key Bible References:

Your ears shall hear a word behind you, saying, "This is *the way, walk in it," whenever you turn to the right hand or whenever you turn to the left.* Isaiah 30:21

Therefore do not be unwise, but understand what the will of the Lord is. Ephesians 5:17

And do not be conformed to this world, but be transformed by the renewing of your mind, that you may prove what is *that good and acceptable and perfect will of God.* Romans 12:2

. . .not with eyeservice, as men-pleasers, but as servants of Christ, doing the will of God from the heart, . . . Ephesians 6:6

Additional References: Psalm 32:8–9; Proverbs 3:6, 11:14; Philippians 4:8; Colossians 1:9–10, 4:12.

What Others Say: Dr. John Stott, British pastor and writer; and Dr. Gary Meadors, professor at Grace Seminary, Winona Lake, Indiana.

John Stott

Although God promises to guide us, we must not expect Him to do so in the way in which we guide horses and mules. He will not use a bit and bridle with us. We are not horses or mules; we are human beings. We have understanding, which horses and mules do not. It is then through the use of our own understanding, enlightened by Scripture and prayer and the counsel of friends, that God will lead us into a knowledge of His particular will for us.[2]

---

[1]Gary Friesen, *Decision Making and the Will of God,* Multnomah Press, 1980.
[2]John Stott, *Your Mind Matters,* Inter-Varsity Press, London, 1973, p. 45.

Christian decision making is not a game of hide-go-seek or some magical process of receiving information from God. Rather, it is a process of world-view and value system development (Romans 12:1–2). This development includes three key areas. First, we must cultivate a view of how the Bible is to be used in the decision making process. Second, we must engage in an evaluation of the "inner man" and determine the role of conscience, peace, and subjective feelings, in the process of decision making. And, third, we must ascertain the role of the Holy Spirit in relation to the church age saints and decision making. When these issues have been addressed, we will have identified the foundations upon which a decision making model can be constructed.[3]

Application: The Lord's guidance is not a neatly packaged formula to be followed rigidly. Neither does he expect us to go on "hunches" and feelings. The answer lies in a cohesion of the so-called traditional method with the biblical alternative which Gary Friesen has introduced in his book. We must search the Scriptures and find the balance.

Our flesh would seek a rigid pattern and lean towards that direction that represents human expediency. A safe test on individual decisions not expressly noted in Scripture is that as much as I know my heart, and its motives, illuminated by the Holy Spirit I want God's will to be done. Even then I may err, but an honest error God will use for good (see Romans 8:28).

—Anthony C. Fortosis

WITCHES

ARE THERE GOOD WITCHES AND BAD WITCHES?

The Issue: The Scriptures tell us that Satan is very subtle and that he often disguises himself as an angel of light. Satan is a master at deceit, and one of the greatest deceptions which he has perpetrated upon society is in the realm of witchcraft and magic.

---

[3]Gary Meadors, *Foundations for Christian Decision Making,* Unpublished.

Through popular toys, movies, plays, television and storybook portrayal of witches that are cute and impish, but seemingly harmless, many have come to believe that witchcraft is not necessarily evil in itself. The inference is that good (white) witches are endowed with the same supernatural power that evil (black) witches have, but they are "good" witches because they choose to use their power for the good of others rather than for harm. This creates a very dangerous situation, because people feel a degree of safety in experimenting with magic and witchcraft as long as they intend to use it for good and not for evil.

Key Bible References:

"Give no regard to mediums and familiar spirits; do not seek after them, to be defiled by them: I am *the Lord your God."* Leviticus 19:31

"And the person who turns after mediums and familiar spirits, to prostitute himself with them, I will set My face against that person and cut him off from his people. Leviticus 20:6

"There shall not be found among you anyone *who makes his son or his daughter pass through the fire,* or one *who practices witchcraft,* or *a soothsayer, or one who interprets omens, or a sorcerer, or one who conjures spells, or a medium, or a spiritist, or one who calls up the dead.*

"For all who do these things are *an abomination to the* LORD, . . ." Deuteronomy 18:10–12a

Additional References: I Samuel 15:23; II Kings 9:22, 17:17, 21:6; II Chronicles 33:6.

What Others Say: Kenneth Boa, scholar and authority on cults and world religions; David W. Hoover, researcher, author and speaker on occult phenomena; and Nicky Cruz, evangelist, former gang leader, and son of spiritist parents.

Kenneth Boa
Many people who are involved in witchcraft claim to practice "white magic" instead of "black magic." They do not believe that they are in league with demonic powers. To the extent that they do utilize genuine power, however, they are dabbling with forces which are more diabolic than they suspect. The difference between white and black magic is more in degree than in kind. There is great danger in all forms of witchcraft because sorcerers are involved with powers much stronger than they. In order to effectively use these

powers for their own desires and ends, they must to some extent yield to and serve them. Satan's gifts are never free. Those who willingly receive them often become his slaves, whether they like it or not.[1]

David W. Hoover

Most writers correctly define white magic as black magic under a religious disguise. While the same supernatural forces are at work, the white magician uses Christian terminology in his rites and in many cases claims to be Christian and have supernatural powers from God. This form of magic is far more widespread than black magic where the devil is invoked.[2]

Nicky Cruz

Early in his psychic career Papa had dealings in what is called "black magic." A man asked him to put a curse on his enemy. Papa killed a black chicken, sprinkled the blood over the enemy's picture, and then drove a knife through the face. We heard that the man who had been hexed became violently ill. But then Papa turned entirely to "white magic" and refused to hex anyone after that. "The good spirits must help us drive away the bad spirits," he used to say. "There is no need to deal in destruction. It is better to build up than to tear down." What a confused mixture of truth and lies! What a horrible deception, my friend! We cannot fight demons using demons![3]

Application: The idea that some witches are "good" while other witches are "bad" is a cunning deception of Satan. The same demonic forces that empower the worker of black magic also empower the worker of white magic. The most noble of motives on the part of the individual performing white witchcraft does not negate the true satanic source of the powers that are brought to play. The Scriptures are very clear in their warning that believers are to have absolutely no dealings with these supernatural powers, white or black.

The child of God should abstain from any form of involvement in these deadly activities.

—Alan Arment

[1]Kenneth Boa, *Cults, World Religions, and You,* Scripture Press Publications, Wheaton, Illinois, 1977, p. 117.

[2]David W. Hoover, *How To Respond To The Occult,* Concordia Publishing House, St. Louis, Missouri, 1977, p. 21.

[3]Nicky Cruz, *Devil On The Run,* Dove Christian Books, Melbourne, Florida, 1989, p. 29.

WITNESSING

SHOULD EVERY CHRISTIAN WITNESS FOR CHRIST?

The Issue: The auxiliary verb should, used to formulate the issue we are considering, expresses an obligation. Was Calvary an obligation? Is the sharing of our eternal salvation to be understood as an obligation or is it in reality a natural overflow of a full, believing heart?

Key Bible References:

For with the heart one believes to righteousness, and with the mouth confession is made to salvation.

For the Scripture says, "Whoever believes on Him will not be put to shame." Romans 10:10–11

. . . and always be *ready to* give *a defense to everyone who asks you a reason for the hope that is in you, with meekness and fear; . . .* I Peter 3:15

"You did not choose Me, but I chose you, and appointed you that you should go and bear fruit, and that *your fruit should remain, that whatever you ask the Father in My name He may give you."* John 15:16

Additional References: Matthew 28:19–20; Acts 1:8; II Corinthians 5:20.

What Others Say: Joseph C. Aldrich, president of Multnomah School of the Bible and former pastor of Mariners Church, Newport Beach, California.

Joseph C. Aldrich

There is a legend which recounts the return of Jesus to glory after His time on earth. Even in heaven He bore the marks of His earthly pilgrimage with its cruel cross and shameful death. The angel Gabriel approached Him and said, "Master, you must have suffered terribly for men down there."

"I did," He said.

"And," continued Gabriel, "do they know all about how you loved them and what you did for them?"

323

"Oh, no," said Jesus, "not yet. Right now only a handful of people in Palestine know."

Gabriel was perplexed. "Then what have you done," he asked, "to let everyone know about your love for them?"

Jesus said, "I've asked Peter, James, John, and a few more friends to tell other people about Me, and My story will be spread to the farthest reaches of the globe. Ultimately, all of mankind will have heard about My life and what I have done."

Gabriel frowned and looked rather skeptical. He knew well what poor stuff men were made of. "Yes," he said, "but what if Peter and James and John grow weary? What if the people who come after them forget? What if way down in the twentieth century, people just don't tell others about you? Haven't you made any other plans?"

And Jesus answered, "I haven't made any other plans. I'm counting on them."

Twenty centuries later. . . . He still has no other plan. He's counting on you and me.[1]

Application: Mankind—our Christian witness—is Christ's method of evangelism on this earth! We are the design of God's heart for the world's eternal salvation! What an assignment! What a calling! No exception is made in God's Word for this privilege and responsibility. In the light of His imminent return—Yes! Yes! every Christian should witness for Christ!

—**Donna A. Wilson**

WOMEN

WHAT IS THE BIBLICAL PERSPECTIVE ON THE ROLES AND CONTRIBUTIONS OF WOMEN?

The Issue: Within both secular and Christian circles, there exists a great deal of indecision as to what constitutes the contributions and capabilities of women. A popular image of the modern woman is one

---

[1]Joseph C. Aldrich, *Life-Style Evangelism,* Multnomah Press, Portland, Oregon, 1978, pp. 15–16.

characterized primarily by a successful career which demonstrates a high degree of self-sufficiency and excellence.

But a question seldom explained is the biblical portrayal of women. The Bible speaks directly to the role of women and includes within its pages the lives of many women who were used of God to affect positive changes on their societies.

Key Bible References:

So God created man in His own image; in the image of God He created him; male and female He created them. Genesis 1:27

And the LORD God said, "It is not good that man should be alone; I will make him a helper comparable to him." Genesis 2:18

Nevertheless, neither is man independent of woman, nor woman independent of man, in the Lord.

For as the woman was from the man, even so the man also is through the woman; but all things are from God. I Corinthians 11:11–12

Wives, submit to your own husbands, as to the Lord.

Husbands, love your wives, just as Christ also loved the church and gave Himself for it, . . . Ephesians 5:22, 25

Additional References: Ruth; Esther; and Proverbs 31.

What Others Say: Elisabeth Elliot, speaker and author.

Elisabeth Elliot

We are called to be women. . . . God has set no traps for us. He has summoned us to the only true and full freedom. The woman who defines her liberation as doing what she wants, or not doing what she doesn't want is, in the first place, evading responsibility. Evasion of responsibility is the mark of immaturity. The Women's Liberation Movement is characterized, it appears, by this very immaturity.[1]

Application: The current debate centering on women presents two competing and extreme models of the role of women. If one chooses to embrace one vision, the other by necessity is violently rejected. On one pole are the proponents of radical feminism. For the radical

---

[1]Elisabeth Elliot, *Let Me be a Woman*, Tyndale House Publishers, Wheaton, Illinois, 1983, pp. 52, 54.

feminist, the feminine ideal is a woman who is assertive, outspoken, and competitive with the opposite sex, often to the point of strife. Equally harmful is the extreme in which women are viewed simply as the bearers of children, incapable of fulfilling any social role outside of marriage.

The biblical model, however, successfully mediates between these two poles by offering a dual message of reciprocity and reconciliation. Most importantly, God created **both** male and female. At creation, God intended no superior purpose solely for the man. On the contrary, God created the woman to work with the man in her own unique capacity. The woman was created with abilities differing from the man's in order to complement, not compete.

Women are created to work in harmony with men and this often manifests itself within the context of marriage. This, however, is not the only role that a woman is permitted to assume. The Bible gives examples of women, such as Esther, Deborah and Miriam, who functioned as prophetesses and heads of state. The Egyptian midwives, because they feared God more than Pharaoh saved the lives of many Israelite children. The Samaritan woman evangelized her town concerning the Messiah she had met at the well. Among the followers of Christ were women to whom He first appeared after His resurrection.

We can find true peace only by accepting what God has made us and by using the unique gifts and talents that only come with being a woman.

—Beverly LaHaye

WORK

WHAT IS THE BIBLICAL ETHIC FOR WORK?

The Issue: One's attitude towards work is critical to his or her sense of fulfillment and well-being. Viewed as a curse (Genesis 3:23), Satan uses the frustrations it produces and the weariness it generates to discourage and defeat the spirit. Viewed not only as a requirement of life, but as a means whereby one can learn, get ahead, and make a contribution to society, it is a blessing that brings contentment and satisfaction.

God's Word teaches that a positive response to work can make it a productive and beneficial force in the Christian's life. It exalts work as a dignified method by which we not only support life but also produce the wherewithal to further the Lord's work and to be generous to others, thus assuring the rewards of faithful stewardship. The Bible portrays work as an accepted fact of life and stresses the value of developing wholesome attitudes about it.

Key Bible References:

For even when we were with you, we commanded you this: If anyone will not work, neither shall he eat. II Thessalonians 3:10

"The LORD will open to you His good treasure, the heavens, to give the rain to your land in its season, and to bless all the work of your hand." Deuteronomy 28:12a

. . . every man should eat and drink and enjoy the good of all his labor—it is *the gift of God.* Ecclesiastes 3:13

Let him who stole steal no longer, but rather let him labor, working with his *hands what is good, that he may have something to give him who has need.* Ephesians 4:28

Additional References: Genesis 2:15, 3:23; Deuteronomy 30:9; II Chronicles 31:20–21; Proverbs 14:23, 18:9; Ecclesiastes 2:10, 3:9–13; Ephesians 4:28; Colossians 3:23; II Timothy 2:15.

What Others Say: Edward R. Dayton, director of Mission Advanced Research and Communication Center of World Vision International; and Jerry Bridges, vice president of corporate affairs for The Navigators.

Edward R. Dayton

. . . the Christian has a tremendous advantage over those who stand outside the Body of Christ. Since there is a higher, over-arching purpose, and meaning to all he does, a new definition is given to the concepts of both "work" and "leisure." Of all people, the Christian should be freed to see life as a whole and to see his vocation as a calling that is no less a part of God's plan than any other part of his life.[1]

---

[1]Edward R. Dayton, *Tools for Time Management*, Zondervan Publishing House, Grand Rapids, Michigan, 1974, pp. 189–190.

We should . . . look at our job or our business not in terms of larger salaries, greater commissions, or increased sales, but in terms of how we may best please God. Vocational success should not be measured in terms of one's bank account or material possessions but in terms of service to others that is acceptable to God. Such an attitude, rather than fostering indifference to work, should promote greater diligence. Paul told the Colossians that slaves were more accountable to God for their work than they were to their earthly masters. This principle obviously applies to employment relationships of today.[2]

Application: Work is basic to life: "If anyone will not work, neither shall he eat" (II Thessalonians 3:10). From the beginning man has been expected to work. Even before the Fall, Adam and Eve were to "tend and keep" the garden (Genesis 2:15). It is how we respond to work and resolve to benefit by it that determines whether it is a burden to be borne or a blessing of opportunity to be enjoyed. Christians are admonished to be diligent and wholehearted in their approach to work (Nehemiah 4:6; Colossians 3:23; II Timothy 2:15). Good attitudes toward work help assure the achievement of personal satisfaction and fulfillment. They are also a reflection of spiritual maturity.

—Earl R. Schamehorn, Sr.

WORKAHOLICS

WHAT DOES THE BIBLE SAY ABOUT THOSE WHO PLACE WORK PRIORITIES AHEAD OF FAMILY OBLIGATIONS?

The Issue: Work is one of the most important aspects of life. Man is created in the image of God. The Bible clearly tells us that God is a Worker. Thus man, God's image bearer is also a worker. But God created man as more than simply a work creature to maintain His creation. God breathed into man a soul, thus giving man the ability to seek God and know His will for man's life. Sinful man, in his

---

[2]Jerry Bridges, *The Practice of Godliness,* NavPress, Colorado Springs, Colorado, 1983, pp. 110–111.

fallen state, is constantly subject to substituting his own sinful priorities for God's priorities in his life. Thus work, which is God ordained, may be used to replace the highest good; knowing God and passing this knowledge on to our children.

Key Bible References:

And on the seventh day God ended His work which He had done, and He rested on the seventh day from all His work which He had done. Genesis 2:2

Then the Lord God took the man and put him in the garden of Eden to tend and keep it. Genesis 2:15

"Work shall be done for six days, but the seventh day shall be a holy day for you, a Sabbath of rest to the Lord." Exodus 35:2

Now it happened as they went that He entered a certain village; and a certain woman named Martha welcomed Him into her house.

And she had a sister called Mary, who also sat at Jesus' feet and heard His word.

But Martha was distracted with much serving, and she approached Him and said, "Lord, do You not care that my sister has left me to serve alone? Therefore tell her to help me."

And Jesus answered and said to her, "Martha, Martha, you are worried and troubled about many things.

"But one thing is needed, and Mary has chosen that good part, which will not be taken away from her." Luke 10:38–42

Additional References: Proverbs 12:11; John 6:27–29; I Corinthians 3:13.

What Others Say: Drs. Frank Minirth and Paul Meier, et al., noted Christian counselors and partners in the Minirth-Meier Clinic, Dallas, Texas; and Don Hawkins, et al., director of radio communications for Rapha, Inc., host and executive producer of "The Rapha Hour" on the USA Radio Network.

Frank Minirth and Paul Meier

I have learned to trust God, instead of myself, to rescue the world. . . . I have also learned to accept living in an imperfect world. There are needs everywhere. There are millions dying of starvation, millions who don't know Christ, millions who are lonely, millions in emotional pain. But a need is not a call for personal involvement. If

I tried to meet every need I see around me, I would go crazy and end up becoming one more needy person. I have an obligation to prayerfully consider my god-given responsibilities to my family and myself, and then to spend what spare time is left in meeting a few of the many needs of people around me. I have learned to accept the anger of those whose needs I don't have time for. It's part of the price of being a professional person in a selfish, depraved world! Even Christians are depraved, you know. But they are forgiven![1]

Don Hawkins
As we follow the example for living Jesus provided us, we can better order our priorities and align our lives to those things that matter most. Jesus' life exhibited an eternal quality because He lived with eternal values in view. As we set our life's goals, we need to adopt His Perspective and thereby find skill in handling the unpredictable circumstances of life.[2]

Application: The development of the Workaholic personality is a complex process, the explanation of which is far beyond the scope of this brief article. We purpose here to give an overview by noting the behaviors involved and pointing to The Solution. A noted authority in the area identifies four signs of a Workaholic:

    (1) The Workaholic exhibits an excessive commitment of time to his work, on a regular and ongoing basis;

    (2) The Workaholic's accomplishments are a frequent topic of his conversation;

    (3) The Workaholic cannot say "No" to added tasks; and

    (4) The Workaholic cannot rest or relax.

The central focus of the life of the Workaholic is his job performance.[3]

The solution to this dilemma is found in Christ and a complete understanding and acceptance of His grace. Because of what God has done in Christ on Calvary, we are set free from trying to pay the price for our own sin. The yardstick of acceptance with God by which we are measured is no longer our own performance, but that of the Savior. We are unconditionally accepted by God. We are therefore free to love Him and obey His direction in our life.

---

[1]Frank Minirth, Paul Meier, Frank Wichern, Bill Brewer, and States Skipper, *The Workaholic and His Family,* Baker Book House, Grand Rapids, Michigan, 1981, p. 17.

[2]Don Hawkins, Frank Minirth, Paul Meier, and Chris Thurman, *Before Burnout,* Moody Press, Chicago, Illinois, 1990, p. 159.

[3]Minirth, et. al, pp. 29–31.

In summary, ". . . the dynamic of grace-living provides the Workaholic with a new motivation for living and working. He is free to forgive because he is forgiven. He is free to love unconditionally because he is loved unconditionally. He is free to enjoy life a day at a time—there is no longer the constant accusation of a guilty conscience for he has been declared not guilty by God (Romans 3:22–25; II Corinthians 5:21). He is free to work in order to please God—he no longer has the futile struggle of trying to gain acceptance."[4]

—S. W. Warren

WORLDLINESS

WHAT DOES THE BIBLE TEACH ABOUT WORLDLINESS?

The Issue: All Christians have been told not to be worldly at one time or another. Most Christians would agree that it is sinful to be worldly. However, very few people can define worldliness and therefore, few Christians really know when they are worldly or when they are not. God's Word gives us direction on how we can be protected from being influenced by the world.

Key Bible References:

We know that we are of God, and the whole world lies under the sway of *the wicked one.* I John 5:19

For we do not wrestle against flesh and blood, but against principalities, against powers, against the rulers of the darkness of this age, against spiritual hosts *of wickedness in the heavenly* places. Ephesians 6:12

Do not love the world or the things in the world. If anyone loves the world, the love of the Father is not in him.

For all that is *in the world—the lust of the flesh, the lust of the eyes, and the pride of life—is not of the Father but is of the world.*

---

[4]Minirth, et. al, p. 158.

And the world is passing away, and the lust of it; but he who does the will of God abides forever. I John 2:15–17

Additional References: Matthew 5:3–12; John 17:15, 18; II Corinthians 10:3–5; James 4:4.

What Others Say: Bill Stearns, youth pastor and author.

Bill Stearns

The world is manipulated by Satan through an invisible system that appeals to one's physical desires, ego or will. Therefore, a Christian is worldly when he or she allows Satan to manipulate the physical desires, ego or will through his invisible system. Worldliness is a pattern, a lifestyle of being worldly, of being manipulated by Satan's system. So it's always sin. Is the enemy consistently manipulating a person's physical desires, ego, or will? If so, that person has stepped out into a lifestyle of worldliness.[1]

Application: Unfortunately most Christians determine worldliness by categorizing people, places and things. If a person doesn't go to certain places, associate with certain people, have certain things or do certain things, he or she isn't worldly. However, a person can have only Christian friends, only go to Christian activities, and still be worldly. Worldliness involves one's attitudes, values and motives. If we allow Satan and his system to control and influence our values, our motives and our attitudes we, in fact, will be worldly.

God has given each of us fleshly desires or drives, an ego and a will. Satan will continually try to influence these three areas of our lives so that we will be ineffective in having a preserving influence on the world around us. If a Christian is worldly, God doesn't stop loving him but His love cannot have any effect in his everyday life. A Christian must bring every thought under the captivity of Christ (evaluate the thought according to the Bible). Then we must make sure that what we value is what God values, what our motivation is must be God's motivation and what our attitudes are must be the attitudes God approves of in Scripture. Only when this happens will a Christian avoid worldliness and live a dynamic life for Christ.

—Glen L. Schultz

---

[1]Bill Stearns, *If the World Fits, You're the Wrong Size,* Victor Books, Wheaton, Illinois, 1981, pp. 29, 31.

WORLD MISSIONS

WHAT DOES THE BIBLE SAY ABOUT REACHING THE NATIONS WITH THE GOSPEL?

The Issue: Most of the Bible was written during a time when each nation served its own god—a god of their culture. The Hebrews were the exception. The Queen of Sheba was impressed at Jerusalem. The Ninevites were responsive to Jonah. In other words, the Old Testament period witnessed a strong Jewish proselytizing movement. Through Israel and later the Church, by attraction and proclamation, in both testaments, God's people told other nations about God. Since God created all the world, as Genesis says, one would expect Him to be concerned about all nations in the world. It is also consistent for Him to forbid the worship of false gods. The Great Commission did not suddenly transform the Christian movement into a missionary movement; it merely clarified one of its goals. In Scripture, both the Church and God are partners together in world missions. Acts 13:3 says "they sent *them* away" and 13:4 "being sent out by the Holy Spirit."

Key Bible References:

And the LORD said, "Shall I hide from Abraham what I am doing, since Abraham shall surely become a great and mighty nation, and all the nations of the earth shall be blessed in him . . . ." Genesis 18:17–18

"Go therefore and make disciples of all the nations, baptizing them in the name of the Father and of the Son and of the Holy Spirit, . . ." Matthew 28:19

I am a debtor both to Greeks and to barbarians, both to wise and to unwise. Romans 1:14

Additional References: Psalms 86:9, 117:1; Isaiah 42:6; John 1:9–12; Acts 1:8; Romans 15:20, 23; I Timothy 2:16.

What Others Say: Donald A. McGavran, missiologist and founding dean of the School of World Missions, Fuller Theological Seminary in Pasadena, California; and Ralph D. Winter, missionary statesman and director of the United States Center for World Missions in Pasadena, California.

Donald A. McGavran

Among other characteristics of mission . . . a chief and irreplaceable one must be this: that mission is a divine finding, vast and continuous. A chief and irreplaceable purpose of mission is church growth. Service is good, but it must never be substituted for finding. Our Lord did not rest content with feeding the hungry and healing the sick. He pressed on to give His life a ransom for many and to send out His followers to disciple all nations. Nor must service be so disproportionately emphasized at the expense of evangelism that findable persons are continually lost.[1]

Ralph D. Winter

Most conversions must inevitably take place as the result of some Christian witnessing to a near neighbor, and that is evangelism. The awesome problem is the additional truth that most non-Christians in the world today are not culturally near neighbors of any Christians, and that it will take a special kind of "cross-cultural" evangelism to reach them.[2]

Application: The command to "Go into all the world and preach the gospel to every creature" (Mark 16:15) was given to the disciples and through them to every Christian in the world. The Western world is nothing more than a mission field which has also become a missionary sending base. The same thing is now taking place in the Third World which until recently was perceived only as mission fields rather than as a network of sending bases. Nigeria has an association of mission agencies, one of which has sent over six hundred missionaries to unreached language groups inside and outside of Nigeria. In India more than fifty local mission agencies have formed the India Missions Association. More than three hundred Korean churches in the United States have formed the Korean World Missions Council. Similar associations also exist in Korea and other Third World nations.

It is to the glory of God and the credit of a growing number of nations that the gospel has taken a more significant place in their list of exports.

—Ronald R. Meyers

---

[1]Donald A. McGavran, *Understanding Church Growth,* Wm. B. Eerdmans Publishing Company, Grand Rapids, Michigan, 1970, p. 32.

[2]Ralph D. Winter, *Crucial Dimensions in World Evangelization,* William Carey Library, South Pasadena, California, 1976, p. 105.

WORRY

HOW CAN CHRISTIANS OVERCOME WORRY?

The Issue: There is no question that there is an alarmingly high degree of stress in every corridor of life. More illnesses are surfacing as worry-related. If one were to dissect worry, he or she would see that it is made up of a combination of fears and doubts. Worry has an hypnotic effect. It causes one to transfix his or her attention on the negatives that in turn renders the person ineffective. The one who worries accomplishes very little because his or her mind, instead of being creative, vacillates between fear and doubt. God's Word has incredible power, if applied, to overcome this negative emotion.

Key Bible References:

Be anxious for nothing, but in everything by prayer and supplication, with thanksgiving, let your requests be made known to God; and the peace of God, which surpasses all understanding, will guard your hearts and minds through Christ Jesus. Philippians 4:6–7

"Let not your heart be troubled; you believe in God, believe also in Me.

"In My Father's house are many mansions; if it were not so, I would have told you. I go to prepare a place for you.

"And if I go and prepare a place for you, I will come again and receive you to Myself; that where I am, there you may be also." John 14:1–3

Additional References: Psalm 37:1; Proverbs 3:6; Matthew 5:25–28.

What Others Say: John Haggai, pastor and author.

John Haggai

For your own peace of mind excel in at least one thing. Concentrate all your focus upon work. Gather in your resources, rally all your faculties, marshal all your energies, focus all your capacities upon mastery in at least one field of endeavor. This is a "sure-fire" antidote to the divided mind. Stop scattering your fire. Cease any half-hearted interests to be superb in everything. Ascertain the will of the Lord for your life. Enlist His help and strength through whom you can do all things. Strive for the mastery—and experience worry-killing poise through skill.[1]

Application: God's desire for each of His children is that we achieve the optimum level of spiritual growth. The way this growth is attained is by total submission to God and His Word on a daily basis. As growth takes place, one's creativity, effectiveness, and productivity also increase. The world, flesh, and the devil are always at odds with man's attempts to please and serve God. The sparks of worry evolve from the flesh when one takes his eyes off the Lord and looks at circumstances. If these sparks are not quenched by the Holy Spirit, then Satan fans these sparks with doubts and the flames of worry take over the emotions. To overcome worry, the following steps will help greatly:

    (1) Meditate on how much God loves you.
    (2) Read and believe without question His Word.
    (3) Be active in God's work.
    (4) Identify worry and confess it when you pray.
    (5) Work at being a praising person.

—Art Nazigian

YOGA

SHOULD CHRISTIANS PRACTICE YOGA?

The Issue: Yoga is a Hindu religious practice by which the yogi attempts to achieve transcendental experience through meditation. Through meditation, the practitioner seeks to control bodily functions and also hopes to arrive at a spiritual condition where the soul achieves oneness with God (the Buddhist equivalent of Nirvana).

Some Christians are in doubt as to whether there is anything unchristian in yoga because of the meditative aspect of the practice. Some see yoga as a supplementary means to achieving spiritual power, enlightenment or liberation. However, Christians who believe in the Bible as the sole authoritative guide for conduct would have no problem discerning the fact that Jesus said, "I am the way,

---

[1]John Haggai, *How To Win Over Worry,* Zondervan Publishing House, Grand Rapids, Michigan, 1959, pp. 79–80.

the truth, and the life. No one comes to the Father except through me." Also, that "there is no other name under heaven given among men by which we must be saved" Acts 4:12.

The crux of this matter is whether Christians need any other medium of achieving spiritual power, togetherness with God, or enlightenment except as provided for in the Scriptures. As would be shown hereafter, the answer is unequivocally **no!** Christ is sufficient for all we need for salvation, spiritual growth, and oneness with God.

Key Bible References:

". . . Not by might nor by power, but by My Spirit, says the LORD of hosts." Zechariah 4:6

Jesus said to him, "I am the way, the truth, and the life. No one comes to the Father except through Me." John 14:6

I can do all things through Christ who strengthens me. Philippians 4:13.

Additional References: John 8:36, 17:17; Acts 4:12.

What Others Say: The late Dr. Walter Martin, Bible scholar and founder/president of Christian Research Institute; and Bob Larson, author.

Walter Martin

Transcendental Meditation (attained through Yoga), is pantheistic in nature and one's goal is to lose one's personality in the oneness of God. This takes away from the unique and separate personality of God. Being is the living presence of God. The reality of Life. It is eternal truth. It is absolute in its eternal freedom.

In all its forms, Hinduism (including the practice of Yoga) denies the biblical Trinity, the Deity of Christ, the doctrines of atonement, sin, and salvation by grace through the sacrifice of Jesus Christ. It replaces resurrection with reincarnation and both grace and faith with human works. Peace with God is not achieved by looking inside oneself, but by looking up to Him of whom Moses and the prophets did write "Jesus of Nazareth, the Son and Christ of God."[1]

---

[1]Maharisha Mahesh Yogi, *'The Science of Being and the Art of Living,'* The New American Library, New York, New York. (From Walter Martin, "Kingdom of the Cults," p. 363.)

Bob Larson

Techniques employed in yoga are "designed to separate their minds from their bodies, practices that can lead to occult, out-of-the-body experiences."[2]

Application: In the early 1960s, young people across America somehow agreed that there was a problem generally with the society. They banded their philosophies for strength and went about in search of solutions; social as well as spiritual. The question then was "What do we want out of life and how do we get it?" The question thirty years later is still the same, "What do we want out of life and how do we get it?"

Modern society seems to be in love with itself. There is an obsession with self identity, popularity, material acquisitions, and self-preservation. We want to perceive all things and then we want to achieve all things. The Bible does admonish: "Let this mind be in you which was also in Christ Jesus" (Philippians 2:5). But what does it mean to have the mind of Jesus and how do we acquire such?

Yoga claims that the soul by nature is a pure spirit but that it has become identified with matter through ignorance. It (Yoga) promises, therefore, to set the soul free.[3]

This union with the divine spirit, according to Yoga, is attained by successive steps of self-control, religious observance, long contained suppression of breath, meditation and profound contemplation.[4]

As Christians, the only assurance we have of being set free from the bondage of sin is the grace of our Lord Jesus Christ, commuted to us for righteousness when we accept His sacrifice for us. The claims of Yoga are lost to ample evidence that those who engage in the practice are still not freed from the confines of mortal life, nor from spiritual bondage. Christian discipleship however, has brought many to say "Therefore if the Son makes you free, you shall be free indeed" (John 8:36).

—Joseph Alexander

[2] Bob Larson, *Straight Answers on the New Age,* Thomas Nelson Publishers, Nashville, Tennessee, 1989, p. 29.

[3] Walter Martin, *Kingdom of the Cults,* Bethany House Publishers, Minneapolis, Minnesota, 1985, p. 363.

[4] *New Encyclopedia Britannica,* Encyclopedia Britannica, Inc., Chicago, Illinois (15th Edition), 1988, p. 846.